Dictionary of Russian Historical Terms
from the Eleventh Century to 1917

DICTIONARY OF RUSSIAN HISTORICAL TERMS FROM THE ELEVENTH CENTURY TO 1917

Compiled by Sergei G. Pushkarev

Edited by George Vernadsky and Ralph T. Fisher, Jr.

New Haven and London, Yale University Press, 1970

Library of Congress catalog card number: 73-81426
Standard book number: cloth 300-01136-9, paper 300-01137-7

Designed by John O. C. McCrillis,
set in Times Roman type,
and printed in the United States of America by
Vail-Ballou Press, Inc., Binghamton, N.Y.
Distributed in Great Britain, Europe, Asia, and
Africa by Yale University Press Ltd., London; in
Canada by McGill-Queen's University Press, Montreal; and
in Mexico by Centro Interamericano de Libros
Académicos, Mexico City.

PREFACE

This dictionary is designed to assist English-speaking readers to understand the specialized terms they encounter in Russian historical sources and in English-language works on Russia, terms explained only briefly if at all in an ordinary Russian-English dictionary. Included are civil, military, and ecclesiastical offices and ranks at various periods; terms used in the political and judicial system and in social relationships; and terms from the realms of economics and finance, such as weights, measures, and monetary units, as well as the most noteworthy of the many special taxes and customs duties invented by Muscovite and Petrine revenue raisers. The most important terms referring to social categories and political, military, educational, and other institutions are supplied with brief historical sketches.

The dictionary generally does not cover such abstract notions as *natsional'-nost'* or *sobornost'*, titles of books and periodicals (with the exception of a few of the most important collections), biographical data, or geographical names.

Compound entries are alphabetized according to their basic nouns. For example, *dannaia gramota* is under G, *dumnye liudi* under L. For more on this and other essential points, see the Instructions for Users immediately following this preface.

This dictionary is the outgrowth of several decades of study in Russian history. For the translation and explanation of the historical terms, works of the following Russian, Soviet, and American historians were consulted: O. P. Backus, Jerome Blum, M. M. Bogoslovskii, L. V. Cherepnin (especially his *Russkaia Metrologiia*), H. W. Dewey, M. A. D'iakonov, M. V. Dovnar-Zapol'skii, M. T. Florinsky, B. D. Grekov, V. L. Ianin, V. O. Kliuchevskii (especially his *Terminologiia russkoi istorii*), N. M. Korkunov, A. A. Kornilov, M. M. Kovalevsky, S. Kucherov, G. V. Lantzeff, I. I. Lappo, A. S. Lappo-Danilevskii, V. N. Latkin, F. I. Leontovich, M. K. Liubavskii, P. N. Miliukov, V. T. Picheta, S. F. Platonov, D. I. Prozorovskii, N. V. Riasanovsky, G. T. Robinson, V. I. Sergeevich, I. I. Smirnov, S. M. Solov'ev, I. G. Spasskii, S. G. Strumilin, G. Vernadsky, S. B. Veselovskii, M. F. Vladimirskii-Budanov, and A. A. Zimin.

Where the opinions of the experts conflict, I have usually qualified my definition to indicate that doubt is present. In many instances, when a clear and convincing explanation of a term could be found in the works of an English-language author, I have used a direct quotation. Many quotations were borrowed, especially from the basic works of George Vernadsky (with regard to pre-Petrine Russia) and from the excellent book of Jerome Blum, *Lord and Peasant in Russia* (with regard to the history of the Russian peasantry).

The historical sources from which the terms for this dictionary were excerpted include those quoted in our Source Book (forthcoming) and many more. For pre-Petrine Russia the basic publication used was *Pamiatniki russkogo prava,* 6 vols., 1952–59, with its extensive subject indexes. For Kievan Russia the chief sources were *Pravda Russkaia* ed. B. D. Grekov, vol. I, 1940, vol. II, 1947, and the *Lavrentievskaia* and *Ipatievskaia* Chronicles.

For Muscovy the chief sources were the *Sudebniki* of 1497 and 1550, ed. B. D. Grekov, 1952, the *Ulozhenie* of 1649, and many other documents included in *Pamiatniki russkogo prava; Akty feodal'nogo zemlevladeniia i khoziaistva XIV–XVI vekov,* vol. I, ed. L. V. Cherepnin, 1951, and vol. II, ed. A. A. Zimin, 1956; and also the work of G. Kotoshikhin, *O Rossii v tsarstvovanie Alekseia Mikhailovicha,* 3d ed. 1884. For collecting historical terms of ancient and medieval Russia, I have used extensively the fundamental work of I. I. Sreznevskii, *Materialy dlia slovaria drevne-russkogo iazyka* and also G. E. Kochin, *Materialy dlia terminologicheskogo slovaria drevnei Rossii,* ed. B. D. Grekov, 1937.

For the West Russian terms used in the Grand Duchy of Lithuania during the fourteenth through sixteenth centuries, the sources were as follows: *The First Lithuanian Statute* of 1529, ed. K. Jablonskis, Minsk, 1960; the Second Statute of 1566, in the *Vremennik* of the Moscow *Obshchestvo istorii i drevnostei,* book 23, 1855, and the documents of the *Litovskaia metrika,* in *Akty Litovskoi Metriki,* vol. I in two parts, ed. F. I. Leontovich, 1896–97; *Akty Litovsko-Russkogo gosudarstva,* ed. M. Dovnar-Zapol'skii, in *Chteniia* of the Moscow *Obshchestvo istorii i drevnostei,* book 4, 1899; *Litovskaia Metrika,* vol. 1, ed. P. A. Gildebrandt and S. A. Bershadskii, in *Russkaia istoricheskaia biblioteka,* vol. 20, 1903. In some cases I referred to N. Gorbachevskii, *Slovar' drevnego aktovogo iazyka Severo-Zapadnogo kraia i Tsarstva Pol'skogo,* 1874, and to I. I. Nosovich, *Slovar' belorusskogo narechiia,* 1870. In general I have labeled terms from the Grand Duchy as West Russian (W.R.), and I have omitted Latin and Polish terms except to the extent that they were russified. The territories involved included not only those provinces later called Ukrainian and Belorussian, but also extensive regions later classified as Great Russian. The language of the documents is as different from modern Russian as it is from modern Ukrainian and Belorussian; hence it seems well to designate it as West Russian, even though contemporaries called it simply "ruskii." *

For the terms of the imperial period the chief source was the huge collection of the *Polnoe Sobranie Zakonov Rossiiskoi Imperii.* Also extensively used were articles concerning the eighteenth and nineteenth centuries in the encyclopedia

* The Statute of 1566 ordered the chief secretary to compile all the documents in Russian—*po rusku, literami i slovy ruskimi;* the official title of the grand duke was *Velikii kniaz' Litovskii i Ruskii;* Orthodoxy was called "ruskaia vera," and the West Russian population was called collectively "Rus'."

of Brockhaus and Efron and, for politics after 1905, the programs and other documents of the various political parties. In some cases, I also consulted V. Dal', *Tolkovyi slovar' zhivogo velikorusskogo iazyka; Slovar' tserkovnoslavianskogo i russkogo iazyka,* ed. Academy of Sciences, 2d ed. 1867; the extensive *Slovar' sovremennogo russkogo literaturnogo iazyka,* recently published by the USSR Academy of Sciences, 1950–65; and Max Vasmer, *Russisches etymologisches Wörterbuch.*

In my work I received much encouragement and help from Professor George Vernadsky, who read the manuscript with great attention and offered thoughtful and substantive suggestions, additions, and corrections. My thanks go also to our managing editor, Professor Ralph T. Fisher, Jr.; to the administrators of the Sterling Memorial Library at Yale, who made a separate room in the library building available to us and thus made the library literally my second home; to Mr. Benjamin Uroff, who presented to me his collection of terminological cards; to my son Boris, who was my first reader and critic and a very effective assistant; to Mr. A. N. Malyshev, who made several valuable suggestions; to Miss Adelaide Johnston, who was also helpful in checking my English draft; to Mrs. Ruth D. Kaufman and Mr. John Gudmundsen of the editorial department of the Yale University Press; and to Mrs. Jean Savage, our copy editor, who painstakingly prepared the manuscript for the printer.

S. G. P.

New Haven, Connecticut
January 1969

INSTRUCTIONS FOR USERS

1. Main entries are in bold face.

2. Subentries are italicized and indented in alphabetical order following main entries.

3. Main entries and subentries are cross-referenced. This is indicated by their being printed in SMALL CAPITAL LETTERS at the first mention within each entry.

4. Russian words are italicized (or in small capital letters for cross-references) the first time they appear in each entry, but usually not thereafter.

5. Plural endings are given for main entries and repeat the last letter preceding the part of the word that changes in the plural.

6. As an aid to pronunciation, stress marks are shown for main entries and subentries. The stress is on the same syllable in the plural unless otherwise indicated. Readers should be aware that in many cases the stress of a word changed from one period to another and also from one region to another, and that often the lexicographers themselves are uncertain.

7. In capitalization, customs in Russia, as in England, have changed over the centuries. In this volume there have been some gestures toward consistency, but no wholesale conversion to modern rules.

8. Transliteration is on the basis of the modern spelling, except in those few cases where retention of an earlier form might aid the reader. (See note following these instructions.)

9. Terms of more than one word are alphabetized under their main nouns. Users who know no Russian should therefore learn to recognize the endings typical of adjectives, which are inflected regularly for person and number (masculine, -yi, -oi, and -ii; neuter, -oe and -ee; feminine, -aia and -iaia; plural, -ye and -ie). Persons who have not studied Russian should bear in mind that, while adjectives usually precede the noun, Russian usage is more flexible in this respect than English, and in the Russian language of an earlier day especially, the noun frequently preceded the adjective.

10. A special bibliography is appended for this volume; it includes all references cited within the entries.

11. Dates given are according to the Julian calendar, which was used in Russia until 1918.

TRANSLITERATION

The transliteration system used in this dictionary is a modified Library of Congress system, omitting diacritical marks.

А а	A a	Р р	R r
Б б	B b	С с	S s
В в	V v	Т т	T t
Г г	G g	У у	U u
Д д	D d	Ф ф	F f
Е е	E e	Х х	Kh kh
Ж ж	Zh zh	Ц ц	Ts ts
З з	Z z	Ч ч	Ch ch
И и	I i	Ш ш	Sh sh
I i	I i	Щ щ	Shch shch
Й й	I i	— ъ	— "
К к	K k	— ы	— y
Л л	L l	— ь	— '
М м	M m	Ѣ ѣ	E e
Н н	N n	Э э	E e
О о	O o	Ю ю	Iu iu
П п	P p	Я я	Ia ia

A

ad"iúnkt, -ty. A position and rank established by the Statutes of the Academy of Sciences (1724) and by the University Statutes of 1804 and 1835, corresponding approximately to assistant professor. After 1863 this rank no longer referred to university teachers but remained in use in some higher technical institutions.

akadémiia, -ii. 1. The leading institution for scientific and scholarly research (AKADEMIIA NAUK); 2. A special higher school corresponding to a university in the system of general education.

Dukhóvnye akadémii: Institutions of higher learning for the Orthodox clergy. In the 19th century there were four dukhovnye akademii, in St. Petersburg, Moscow, Kiev, and Kazan'.

Akadémiia khudózhestv (Academy of the Arts): Established in 1757 in St. Petersburg for the visual arts—painting, sculpture, and architecture.

Akadémiia Naúk: The Academy of Sciences was opened near the end of 1725, on the basis of Peter the Great's decree of January 28, 1724. For lack of Russian learned men the Academy in the 18th century was staffed largely by foreigners (mostly Germans) invited by the government, and it published its works in Latin, German, or French. The great scientist M. V. Lomonosov was the most outstanding Russian member of the Academy in the 18th century. During the 19th century the Academy was gradually "russified," but welcomed as members many scholars abroad. According to the regulations of 1841, the Academy was divided into three departments (*otdeleniia*): (1.) natural sciences and mathematics; (2.) Russian language and literature; (3.) historical and philological sciences. To the departments were attached many committees and special research organizations, led by senior or full members of the Academy (called *ordinarnye* or *deistvitel'nye chleny*) and staffed by numerous auxiliary personnel. The Academy possessed libraries, archives, a printing house, museums, laboratories, and observatories, and it issued several series of periodicals and other publications. The Academy preserved its prerevolutionary character until 1927. Data for 1925 indicate that it had 42 full members (*deistvitel'nye chleny*); 19 honorary members (*pochetnye chleny*), of whom four were Russian and fifteen were foreign; and 268 corresponding members, of whom 103 were Russian and 165 were foreign. In 1927 it was renamed the Akademiia Nauk SSSR and was reshaped to suit the needs of the Soviet state.

Voénnye akadémii: Military higher schools for various branches of the armed forces. In the 19th century these included the *akademiia general'nogo shtaba*, the *artilleriiskaia akademiia*, the *inzhenernaia akademiia*, the *morskaia* (naval) *akademiia*, the *voenno-iuridicheskaia akademiia*, and the *voenno-meditsinskaia* (or *mediko-khirurgicheskaia*) *akademiia*.

akadémik, -ki. The term for a member of the Academy of Sciences.

akt, -ty. Deed; document; statement; agreement.

akt, at the university. A ceremonial meeting of faculty members and students at the end of the academic year or on the anniversary day of the university's foundation.

aktsíz. Excise; excise duties.

altýn, -ny (from the Tatar *alty* = 6). From the 14th century on, a monetary counting unit equal to 6 DEN'GI or 3 copecks. In 1704–26 it was minted as a small silver coin; in the 19th century copper coins worth 3 copecks and silver coins worth 15 copecks were minted; the latter were called PIATIALTYNNYI in the vernacular.

amanát, -ty. Hostages taken by Russian local government authorities from the Tatars and the native Siberian and Caucasian tribes as guarantees of their loyalty.

arkhiepískop, -py. Archbishop.

arkhieréi, -eii. Church hierarch.

arkhimandrít, -ty. Archimandrite, the head of a prominent monastery.

armáta (W.R.). Armament in general, esp. artillery.

arshín, -ny. A measure of length used from the 16th century on; in the 18th and 19th centuries the normal arshin was equal to 28 English inches or 71.1 cm.; an arshin was divided into 4 CHETVERTI and 16 VERSHKI; 3 arshiny comprised one SAZHEN'.

artél', -li. A cooperative association of workers or craftsmen working together by agreement, under the guidance of an elected head (STAROSTA or [V]ATAMAN).

asséssor, -ry. Assessor, advisor, assistant. Each of the KOLLEGII established by Peter the Great in 1717–18 had to consist of a president, a vice-president, four councillors and four assessory. After the kollegii were abolished, not the position but the rank of the *kollezhskii assessor* persisted as the 8th class in the Peter's TABEL' O RANGAKH. In some subordinate offices assessory (corresponding to the Russian term ZASEDATELI) existed in the 19th century.

assignátsiia, -ii. Paper money introduced by Catherine II in 1768–69. The over-issuing of assignatsii led to their depreciation, so that by 1810 one ruble in assignatsii was worth not 100 but only 25 copecks in silver. In 1839 the official exchange rate of assignatsii was fixed at 3.6 rubles for one ruble in silver, and in 1841–43 the assignatsii were replaced in part by a new kind of paper money, the KREDITNYE BILETY.

atamán, -ny (Ukr: *otáman*). A title held by elected cossack military commanders. At the head of the Don Cossack Host stood a *voiskovoi ataman,* and each cossack military unit, settlement (STA-NITSA), or embassy was usually headed by its own ataman. The elected commander of the Zaporozhian (or Dnieper) Cossack Host, or KOSH, was called *koshevoi ataman;* each head of a military unit known as a KUREN' was called a *kurennoi ataman.* In the 16th and 17th centuries in the Ukraine and Belorussia, occasionally a village elder (or STAROSTA) was called ataman. The term ataman (= *vataman*) was also used as a name for the head of a workers' or craftsmen's cooperative association (ARTEL').

B

bármy. Humeral, a part of the REGALIIA of the Moscow grand princes and tsars; a broad strip of silk overlaid with jewels and sacred images that covered the sovereign's shoulders during solemn receptions and other ceremonies.

bárshchina (or **boiárshchina**). Corvée, or obligatory work performed by the peasants, esp. by the serfs, for the landowner (*barin* = BOIARIN). Under the barshchina system the arable land of the estate was divided into two parts. One was farmed by the peasants for themselves. The other was managed directly by the owner and was cultivated by the compulsory labor of the peasants, each of whom was obliged either to till a certain plot on the master's land or to work a certain number of days weekly for the master. According to Emperor Paul's decree of April 5, 1797, a barshchina of three days a week was considered normal and sufficient for the landowner's needs. There was, however, no government regulation of the actual extent of the barshchina.

baskák, -ki. Mongol-Tatar officials appointed by the khans in the 13th and first half of the 14th centuries for supervision of the Russian princely administration and for the collection of taxes from the Russian population. Later the khans entrusted the princes themselves with the tax collection and ceased to appoint baskaki in Russia.

bélka, -ki (or **béla**). 1. Squirrel. 2. A squirrel's pelt, used for money in the early period. 3. A small monetary unit in northern Russia; in some Novgorod and Perm' regions, in the 14th–16th centuries, a belka was equal to 2 DEN'-GAS. 4. A unit of taxation in some regions of northern Russia in the 16th and 17th centuries; in these cases belka meant a certain part of the taxable property belonging to the taxpaying community.

beloméstsy (pl.). In Muscovy the people in the cities who were not included in the TIAGLO and were thereby freed from paying the taxes and performing the work obligations borne by the POSAD community.

benkárt, -ty (W.R.). A person born out of wedlock.

Berg-Kollégiia. Department of Mines. In 1717–18 Peter the Great established the *Berg-i-Manufaktur Kollegiia* for the development and regulation of the mining and manufacturing industries. In 1722 the Berg-Kollegiia was made a separate office. It was abolished in 1731 and reestablished in 1743; abolished again in 1783 and reestablished in 1796. After the establishment of ministries in 1802, a special Mining Department (*Gornyi Departament*) was created in 1807 and subordinated first to the Ministry of Commerce and after 1810 to the Ministry of Finance. See also KOLLEGIIA.

bérkovets, -vtsy. A weight unit equal to 10 PUDS.

beschéstie, or **bezchéstie.** 1. Injury to honor; offense; insult. 2. Monetary recompense for injured honor designated by law (from the RUSSKAIA PRAVDA until the *Ulozhenie* of 1649) according to the social position or service rank of the person insulted.

besermén, -ny, or **beserménin, beserméne,** or **busurmán, -ny.** Moslem.

bes(-z-)popóvshchina. The priestless groups of the Old Believers, STAROVERY, who renounced priesthood (see RASKOL'NIKI).

bezátshchina, or **bezátchina,** or **bezzádnitsa.** Escheat, the reversion of property to the state for lack of heirs.

bírchii, -chie. Tax collectors in the Grand Duchy of Lithuania; *birchie povetovye* (see POVET) and *golovnye* (chief).

birích, -chí. Herald, crier, a police official whose duty was to announce to the people the orders and statements of the government authorities.

blagochínie. Basically, good order. In the charter to the cities (1785) blagochinie was used in the sense of police (*blagochinie ili politsiia*), and the police office in the cities was called UPRAVA BLAGOCHINIIA. This meaning of the word blagochinie was preserved in the legislation of the 19th century.

blagochínnyi, -nye. Senior priest serving as superintendent over the clergy of several parishes.
   Voénnye blagochínnye: senior chaplains, ecclesiastical supervisors of the chaplains of several regiments.

blagoródnyi, -nye. Nobleman. In the language of the 18th century and in the charter confirming the rights and privileges of the nobility (1785), a synonym for DVORIANIN.

bliustítel', -li. 1. Overseer, supervisor. 2. The title of the Rector of the Moscow Slavonic-Greek-Latin Academy established in 1682–85.

blízhik, -ki, or **blízkii, -kie.** Relative; kin.

bobýl', bobylí. A class of the population resembling the cotters (cottagers) in the West. The term was in use chiefly in the 16th and 17th centuries, when the class of bobyli was evidently numerous and when the expression *krest'iane i bobyli* was often used in official documents, including the *Ulozhenie* of 1649. Bobyli were the lower class of the peasant population, some without any property, others possessing only small households without arable land, and others holding small plots of arable land (*pashennye bobyli*). Bobyli dwelling in cities were either craftsmen or hired workers. Bobyli with some taxable property were included in the community TIAGLO; the majority of them paid only a light OBROK.

bóchka, -ki. Barrel, a liquid measure equal to 40 VEDRA or 492 liters.

Bogdakhán, or **Bogdykhán.** A Russian term for the title of the Chinese emperor.

bogokhúl'nik, -ki. Blasphemer.

bogomólets, bogomól'tsy gosudárevy. Those who pray to God for the sovereign, a term for bishops, abbots, and priests that they used to refer to themselves in addressing the Grand Prince or the Tsar of Muscovy.

boiárin, boiáre. Boyar, a category of nobleman, usually of high rank. During the Kievan period (10th–12th centuries), the boyar class did not constitute a definite order from the legal point of view but played an important role in political and social life, along with the princes. The boyars (also called KNIAZHIE MUZHI, or prince's men) were the senior members of the princely DRUZHINA and served as the prince's councillors (DUMTSY), military officers, and administrative assistants. Aside from this aristocracy of service there was another element consisting of the local aristocracy of power and wealth, called in the chronicles *startsy gradskie* (city elders) or *muzhi narochitye* (prominent men); the literary term for them is ZEMSKIE BOIARE. Soon both elements, united as the *zemskie boiare,* entered the princely service, and the kniazhie muzhi became big landowners. During the 13th–15th centuries the boyars in northeastern Russia played the same dual role as free servitors of the prince and as landowners trying to bring the peasant population of their estates into economic and legal dependence. In Galicia in the 12th–14th centuries the boyars were a dominant force in political and social life. In the Novgorodian republic in the 12th–15th centuries the wealthy boyar class was the leading power in political, economic, and social life, although the Novgorodian boyars had always to reckon with the desires and demands of the popular VECHE, which elected or dismissed at will all members of the administration.

In the Muscovy of the 16th and 17th centuries the boyars formed the highest rank of the service aristocracy. The rank of boiarin could be formally granted only by the tsar. There were several scores of the most aristocratic families (including descendants of the former grand and appanage princes) from whom the tsar usually selected his boyars, who then served as the members of the BOIARSKAIA DUMA (the boyar council) and occupied the highest positions in the army command and in the civil administration. Under Peter the Great the rank of boiarin, as well as the boiarskaia duma as a state institution, was abolished. In the language of the lower classes of the population, esp. the peasants, the word boiarin (or barin) was used to denote lord or master.

In the Grand Duchy of Lithuania in

4

the 15th and 16th centuries, the boiare were a class of military servitors, some of whom stood economically close to the peasants. In that region, those boyars who preserved the status of nobility were called *boiare-szlachta.*

boiárin koniúshii: equerry boyar. During the 16th century he was a high ranking and important officer in the Moscow administration. Under his authority were many villages with vast fields and pastures as well as the equerry servitors who took care of the tsar's numerous herds of horses (under Tsar Fedor Ivanovich the post of boiarin koniushii was held by Boris Godunov).

boiárin pútnyi, -re -nye: a boyar (14th and 15th centuries) who served as head of a PUT', one of the departments of princely administration.

boiáre vvedénnye: literally, boyars introduced or admitted to the palace of the Grand Prince of Moscow, the boyars who constituted the inner circle of the sovereign's aides and advisers and were entrusted with special commissions in the various branches of princely administration. This term was used in Moscow documents mostly in the 14th and 15th centuries.

boliárin. Variant of BOIARIN.

bol'shevikí (pl.). Literally, majority-ites, from the Russian word *bol'shinstvo,* majority. The name was adopted by the Leninist faction of the Russian Social Democratic Workers Party at the second Party congress (in Brussels and London, in 1903) when Lenin, heading the influential group centered around the Party organ *Iskra,* pressed for a strictly centralized party composed of professional revolutionaries. The minority (MEN'SHEVIKI, from *men'shinstvo*) advocated a broad, freer organization of workers on the pattern of the German Social Democratic Party. During and after the Revolution of 1905–06, many other differences concerning socialist tactics arose between the two factions, who formally belonged to the same party but in fact attacked and denounced each other bitterly. In 1912 Lenin's adherents organized themselves as a separate political party called by the old name: the Russian Social Democratic Workers Party, but with "of Bolsheviks" added in parentheses. After the Bolshevik Revolution of 1917, the 7th Party congress in March 1918 adopted a new name for the Party, the Russian [later All-Union] Communist Party (of Bolsheviks). The "of Bolsheviks" was officially deleted from the Party name at the 19th congress in 1952 (see ROSSIISKAIA SOTSIAL-DEMOKRATICHE-SKAIA RABOCHAIA PARTIIA).

bor (from *brati,* to take), **chërnyi bor.** Literally, black collection, a general extraordinary tax paid by the Novgorodians, in the 14th and 15th centuries, to the Grand Prince of Moscow.

bratánich, -ichi or **bratuchádo, -da.** Brother's son.

brátchina, brátshchina (from BRATSTVO). 1. Fraternity or society. 2. A communal banquet held during major church holidays, esp. one headed by an elected STAROSTA, and endowed with the right to judge and to settle quarrels and conflicts among participants.

brátstvo, -va. Religious fraternity or society. Such groups played a prominent role in the Ukraine and Belorussia during the second half of the 16th century and through the 17th. They were established in cities with a significant Orthodox population and were attached to a prominent Orthodox church or monastery. Their purpose was to care for the religious, charitable, educational, and legal needs of the Orthodox population: to establish schools, hospitals, and asylums; to organize holiday festivities; and to care for the needy. The bratstva received their charters from Polish kings (Lithuanian

5

Grand Dukes) and from the Eastern patriarchs; the latter willingly accepted the bratstva under their favor and protection. After the Union of Brest (1596), which was accepted by the majority of Orthodox prelates, the bratstva became the stronghold of Orthodoxy in its struggle against the pressures from the Roman Catholic and the Uniate hierarchies.

bulavá. Mace, emblem of power of the Polish and Ukrainian HETMANS.

bunchúk, -kí. A high ornamented staff with a horse's tail affixed to it, a part of the regalia of the Ukrainian hetmans in the 17th and 18th centuries. The bunchuk served as the hetman's banner on military expeditions, in his travels, and at public assemblies.

Bund. The General Jewish Workers Union (*Vseobshchii Evreiskii Rabochii Soiuz*), a Jewish workers Social Democratic party in Western Russia, Poland, and Lithuania. Founded illegally in 1897, it joined the Russian Social Democratic Workers Party as an autonomous faction in 1898. In the party struggle between the BOLSHEVIKS and the MENSHEVIKS, the Bund sided usually with the Mensheviks.

burgomístr, -ry (from the Ger. *Bürgermeister*). A city official, also called BURMISTR. According to the charter of the cities (1785), the burgomistry, elected by a qualified constituency, formed, under the chairmanship of the GORODSKOI GOLOVA, an executive board of the city administration.

burmístr, -ry. 1. In the Grand Duchy of Lithuania (which included Ukrainian and Belorussian regions) the cities that had received self-government charters according to the Magdeburg Law elected an executive board (RADA) for the city administration; this was headed by the burmistry (selected from the rada's members). In Russia the office of the city burmistry was introduced by Peter the Great, who in 1699 established the BURMISTERSKIE PALATY (or RATUSHI), consisting of several elected burmistry, to manage the city administration and to collect state taxes. 2. On some large private VOTCHINY during the 18th and 19th centuries, the burmistr was the manager of the estate, entrusted with the supervision of the serfs' working obligations or with the collection of the quitrent. He was appointed by the landowner, sometimes with the prior approval of the peasant MIR.

busurmán, -ny (= *besermen*). Moslem.

butýlka, -ki. Bottle, a liquid measure, one half of a STOF and 1/20 of a VEDRO.

C

chad' (collect.). Children; retinue or servants; people in general.

chádo, cháda. Child, children.

cháshnik, -ki. Cupbearer. A rank and position at the court of the grand dukes of Lithuania and of Moscow grand princes, later tsars; the chashnik's special duty was to serve drinks to the tsar and his guests during court feasts.

cheliadín, (collect. pl.) **chéliad'.** Either slaves or members of the lord's household, persons with a specific legal status living and serving at the court of a prince, BOIARIN, or any other master.

chelobítnaia, -nye. In Muscovy, a petition or request presented to the tsar or to any government office. (*Bit' chelom:* to petition.)

chelovék, pl. *liúdi.* In Muscovy, chelovek, without an adjectival definition and with indication of a master, usually meant a bondman.

chelovék guliáshchii or **vól'nyi.** A man who did not belong to any private person and was not included in the community TIAGLO. (For explanations of various categories of the population by legal status and socioeconomic position, see LIUDI.)

cherezpolósitsa. 1. Generally, the scattering of one person's landholding among several plots of land, intermingled with the plots of other landholders. 2. In the peasant economy of the 18th and 19th centuries, the prevailing "strip-system of allotment holding" (G. T. Robinson, Index, p. 341), in which the plowland allotment of a household was not in one piece but consisted of numerous widely scattered strips assigned on the basis of soil quality, distance from the village, etc. The system required a common crop cycle and a common pasture right and presented a serious obstacle to agricultural progress (see OBSHCHINA KREST'IAN-SKAIA PEREDEL'NAIA).

cherkásy (pl.). 1. A Muscovite name for the Ukrainians, used esp. in the 16th and 17th centuries. 2. If cap., a city in the southern Ukraine.

chern'. The common people, the lower class of the population. In documents of the 17th century concerning cossack assemblies in the Ukraine, chern' commonly designated the mass of the rank and file cossacks, as opposed to the STARSHINA, the commanding officers.

chernéts, chernetsý or **chernorízets, -ríz-tsy.** An old Russian name for a monk (derived from his dark garments).

chernítsa, -tsy. Nun (see CHERNETS).

chertá. 1. Line, boundary. 2. In the 16th and 17th centuries in Muscovy, a line of fortifications that were built for protection of the southern and southeastern frontiers of the state; it was called the *zasechnaia cherta* (see ZA-SEKA).

chertá evréiskoi osédlosti. The Jewish Pale of settlement. After the three partitions of the Polish-Lithuanian State in 1772–95 and the annexation of the Grand Duchy of Warsaw in 1815, a great many Jews found themselves within the borders of the Russian Empire. They did not receive the right of free settlement within the whole territory of the Empire, but had to remain in the 10 provinces of Poland and the 15 western provinces of the Russian Empire. An exception was made for merchants of the first guild, for persons with higher education, for dentists, pharmacists, *fel'dshery* (physician's assistants), midwives, mechanics, and craftsmen. According to the so-called temporary rules of May 3, 1882, the Jews, even inside the Pale, were forbidden to settle anew outside of cities, towns, and MESTECHKI (settlements predominantly inhabited by traders and craftsmen) and to buy or to have mortgages on real estate outside of cities and towns. The legal limitations were directed against "persons of Jewish faith," and became invalid when a Jew adopted Christianity of the Eastern Orthodox, Roman Catholic, or Protestant denomination.

chervónets, -ntsy, or **chervónnyi, -nye.** A golden coin minted in the first half of the 18th century, worth about 3 rubles. In the second half of the 18th century and in the 19th century, golden coins with the official name IMPERIAL, worth 10 rubles, were minted; they were also referred to in the vernacular as chervonets.

chet' or **chétvert', -ti.** 1. One quarter. 2. The basic dry measure for grain, being one quarter of an *okov,* KAD', or BOCHKA. In the 16th and 17th centuries one chetvert' of rye varied from 4 to 8 PUDS (one pud = 40 Russian or 36 American pounds). In the 17th century the normal or official chetvert' was equal to 8 puds of rye, but there were many deviations from this norm. 3. A land measure equal to one-half DESIA-TINA (a desiatina = 2.7 acres). Since in most documents of the 16th and the 17th centuries concerning size of landholdings, the indicated land dimensions were calculated as lying "in the three fields," one chetvert' there was equal to 1½ desiatinas, or about 4.1 acres. 4. One of the four (later five) financial departments in Moscow in the 16th and the 17th centuries that collected taxes

7

from certain regions of the state to pay salaries to military servicemen. The sixth, called *Novaia* (new) *chetvert'*, collected revenues from alcoholic beverage sales and from customs duties. 5. An administrative rural district, a subdivision of an UEZD in the Northern Dvina region. 6. *Zhivushchaia* (inhabited) *chetvert'*. A taxable unit introduced in the 1630s, consisting of several (about 10 on the average) inhabited peasant homesteads, which for purposes of tax collection were combined in groups according to the prosperity and solvency of their owners. 7. A linear measure, one quarter of an ARSHIN.

chétii-minéi (pl.). Monthly readings. *Velitkiie* (great) *chetii minei:* A collection compiled by Makarii, Metropolitan of Moscow in the 16th century, of 12 huge volumes containing the lives of saints; sermons; interpretations of the Holy Scriptures; excerpts from works of Eastern church fathers; etc. The materials were arranged in order of days for every month. The chetii minei of Dimitrii, Metropolitan of Rostov, were compiled at the end of the 17th and the beginning of the 18th centuries.

chetverík, -kí. A unit of grain measure, dating from the 16th century, equal to one-eighth CHETVERT'.

chétvert'. See CHET'.

chetverták, -kí. A silver coin worth 25 copecks (one quarter of a ruble), minted in the 18th and 19th centuries (POLU-POLTINA).

chetyrekhvóstka. Literally, something having four tails; in the political jargon of 1905–06, universal, equal, direct, and secret suffrage.

chin, -ný. 1. Order; regulations. 2. Dignity. 3. In Muscovite Russia, a group or class of men of the same legal status or profession, corresponding approximately to the later term SOSLOVIE (estate), but not usually applied to the lower classes (*voinskii chin:* military men; *iereiskii chin:* the priests, the clergy). 4. In the 18th and 19th centuries, a rank of military officers and civil government officials according to the TABEL' O RANGAKH, issued by Peter the Great in 1722, which divided military officers and civil servants into 14 ranks, or chiny (from which the word *chinovniki* was derived).

chin tsárskii. REGALII, insignia of royalty.

chinsh (from Pol. *czynsz*). In the Grand Duchy of Lithuania, a quitrent (corresponding to the East Russian OBROK), or fixed payments made by peasants to the landowner for use of his land.

chisló. Number, in Russian. In the 13th and 14th centuries, the Mongol-Tatar census of the Russian population made for the purposes of taxation and of determining the quota of recruits to be drafted.

D

dácha, -chi. 1. Grant or granted property in general. 2. In the 18th and 19th centuries dacha in official documents meant a rather large area, marked off by the general land survey for a certain village, without demarcation of separate landholdings.

dácha poméstnaia: military service men in the Muscovite state (DVORIANE and DETI BOIARSKIE) had a claim to a certain amount of POMEST'E land, according to their rank and service; this was called their POMESTNYI OKLAD. In fact, they usually received less than their full OKLAD; the land actually given them was called their dacha.

dan', -ni. Originally, a tribute paid by the conquered Slavic tribes to their conquerers, the Varangians or Khazars; then one paid by the Russians to their Mongol-Tatar lords. Later, it came to mean a regular direct tax paid by the population to the government. In Muscovite Russia dan' or DANNYE DEN'GI continued to be exacted but did not play an important role in the state revenue system.

dan' groshóvaia or **serébrianaia.** In the Grand Duchy of Lithuania, a direct monetary tax paid by the peasants who lived on the lands belonging to the grand duke.

dánina gospodárskaia, -ny -kie. In the Grand Duchy of Lithuania, a landed estate granted by the sovereign.

dánnaia (*grámota*), **-nye.** A deed given for real estate.

dánnik, -ki. In general, a payer of tribute or taxes. In the Grand Duchy of Lthuania, a peasant living on the grand duke's estates and paying a monetary tax (DAN') to him.

dánshchik, -ki. Tax collector.

dar, -ry. Usually, a voluntary gift presented by the population to a prince or other master on various occasions. In the Novgorodian state it acquired the character of a customary fixed tax paid to the prince.

dávnost'. Old custom or right.

dávnost' zémskaia: a law ruling that a landed estate, the possession of which was not contested in court within 10 years, became the legal property of the possessor.

dédich, -chi. A person who inherits title or property from his ancestors.

dédina, -ny. A patrimony, a private estate (or a principality) inherited from one's ancestors.

dédizna, -ny. In the Grand Duchy of Lithuania, an estate inherited from one's ancestors.

dekabríst, -ty. Decembrist, a participant in the uprising of December 14 (O.S.), 1825, in St. Petersburg. The regime of Alexander I after the Napoleonic wars caused disappointment and resentment among liberal-minded Russian officers,

esp. those well-educated aristocratic Guards officers who were acquainted with and impressed by the ideas of the Enlightenment and the French Revolution. Two early secret societies, The Union of Salvation (SOIUZ SPASENIIA, 1816–17) and The Union of Welfare (SOIUZ BLAGODENSTVIIA, 1818–20), in lacking a directly revolutionary character failed to satisfy their more radical members, and in January 1821, the Union of Welfare was formally dissolved. By 1823, three revolutionary secret societies had been formed. The Northern Society in St. Petersburg was headed by two Guards officers, Nikita Murav'ev and Prince Sergei Trubetskoi, and a romantic poet, Kondratii Ryleev. According to the plan compiled by Murav'ev on the model of the United States Constitution, the future Russian state was to be a federative constitutional monarchy with a bicameral legislature and an emperor whose powers would be similar to those of the President of the United States. The Southern Society, formed in Tul'chin in Podolia, where the headquarters of the southern (second) army was situated, was headed by Colonel Paul Pestel'; in his political program, which he called *Russkaia Pravda* (Russian justice), Pestel' favored a strongly centralized egalitarian republic of Jacobin style and a radical agrarian program in which every citizen would have the right to a land allotment. The third revolutionary organization, formed in 1823 by several officers of the southern army and called The Society of United Slavs, had the additional goal of a democratic federation of all Slavic peoples. With all their plans for the future of the Russian state, including of course the abolition of serfdom, the members of these revolutionary societies nevertheless did not have a definite plan of action.

The interregnum after the death of Alexander I (when nobody knew which of his two brothers, Constantine or Nicholas, would be the emperor) gave the members of the Northern Society an opportunity to attempt (on December 14) an armed rebellion. It was supported by about 3,000 soldiers and sailors, but was defeated because the majority of the St. Petersburg garrison took the oath to Nicholas. A revolutionary attempt of the Chernigov infantry regiment in the Ukraine was also easily suppressed. Although a special court condemned 36 of the conspirators to death, Nicholas reduced the sentences so that only 5 of the Decembrist leaders (including Pestel' and Ryleev) were executed; 88 were sent to Siberia for hard labor (KATORZHNYE RABOTY) for various terms, and 14 for settlement in Siberia. In 1856 Alexander II granted full amnesty to all Decembrists who had survived the Siberian exile.

dekán, -ny. Head or dean of a FAKUL'TET (department) in the universities and other institutions of higher learning (see UNIVERSITET).

délo, delá. 1. Business or affairs in general. *Prikaznye dela,* official matters. *Zemskoe delo,* public affairs (those concerning the whole country or a local community). 2. Legal case and official files concerning a former litigation. *Gubnye dela,* criminal cases. *Otecheskie dela,* lawsuits deciding controversies in MESTNICHESTVO and concerning the official positions of the contestants' ancestors. 3. Obligatory work for the state or for a private master. *Gorodovoe delo,* a duty of the population to help in the construction and maintenance of city fortifications. *Boiarskoe delo,* the same as BARSHCHINA or BOIARSHCHINA, obligatory work performed by dependent peasants for their master-landowner.

dénezhka, -ki. A mid-19th-century copper coin worth one-half copeck.

dénezhnik, -ki. Minter.

dengá or **den'gá, déngi, dén'gi.** A term

borrowed from the Mongols not later than the 14th century. In modern Russian den'gi means money in general. The denga was a basic Russian monetary unit from the second half of the 14th century until the beginning of the 18th century, a small silver coin of irregular form with a changing silver content. The Novgorodian denga in the 15th century and the beginning of the 16th century was worth 2 Moscow dengi. A RUBL' (at that time simply a counting unit) contained 100 Novgorodian or 200 Moscow dengi. In 1534–35 the Moscow government started minting new dengi, called *dengi kopeinye* because they had a picture of a rider armed with a spear (*kop'e*). The *dengi kopeinye* (later named KOPEIKI) were two times heavier than the old dengi; therefore in weight and value they were equal to the Novgorodian dengi (or *Novgorodki*). During the 17th century the Moscow government minted both dengi and kopeiki in silver (with a short unfortunate experiment of minting copper copecks in 1656–62). From the beginning of the 18th century, when Peter the Great started minting silver rubles of 100-copeck value, copecks were minted only in copper. Denga meant sometimes a lesser unit of taxation within a TIAGLO-bearing community or a peasant labor unit on a private estate. Denga or dengi combined with various adjectives designated many direct and indirect taxes:

dánnye déngi: direct taxes (DAN').

desiátaia dengá: one tenth of the income. This and the *piataia denga* or *piatinnye dengi* (one fifth of the income) were extraordinary income taxes introduced in Muscovy in the 17th century to cover war expenses.

iamskíe déngi: a post tax for payments to the IAMSHCHIKI who operated the Moscow communications system.

obróchnye déngi: quitrent (OBROK).

podúshnye déngi, or *podúshnaia*

pódat' (see DUSHA): a "soul," or poll, tax introduced by Peter the Great's UKAZ of January 11, 1722, and abolished under Alexander III in the 1880s. The tax was imposed on all male persons (without distinction as to age and economic condition) of the lower classes of both rural and urban population, at a rate of 80 copecks per year from each soul (this rate fluctuated during the 18th and the 19th centuries). Exempt from this tax were the nobility, clergy, officialdom, and higher strata of the urban population, in general about 10 percent of the whole population in the 19th century.

poloniánichnye déngi: a special tax for the ransom of prisoners of war, established in the middle of the 16th century, regulated by the *Ulozhenie* of 1649, and exacted until the end of the 17th century.

rúzhnye déngi or *rúga:* a tax for the maintenance of the clergy.

vyvodnýe déngi: removal money, a payment to the owner of an estate from which a girl was taken away for marriage.

denshchík, -kí. 1. In the military language of the 18th and 19th centuries, first an orderly; then a private serving an individual commissioned officer. 2. On some estates, in the 18th century, a supervisor over the peasants' work in the landowner's fields.

departáment, -ty. A division of the highest government institutions—the State Council, the Senate, or the Ministries —in the 19th and early 20th centuries.

derévnia, -ni. In Muscovy, a hamlet, a small rural settlement with adjoining lands. In modern Russian, a small village; also, in general, countryside as opposed to city.

derzháva. 1. The realm, the state. 2. A part of the tsar's REGALIIA, a small globe adorned by jewels with the cross above, carried only on special occasions.

derzhávtsa, -tsy (Pol. *dzierzawca*). In the Grand Duchy of Lithuania, a prefect, a holder of a benefice from the grand duke. From the end of the 15th century on, this Polish term replaced the earlier Russian word NAMESTNIK. The derzhavtsy managed large estates belonging to the grand duke (i.e. to the state) and exercised administrative and judicial power over the local population.

desiatíl'nik or **desiatínnik, -ki.** Collector of the church DESIATINA (tithe) and a special official of ecclesiastical courts.

desiatína. A church tithe or other tax consisting of 10 percent of the value of crops and other agricultural products.

desiatína, -ny. A land measure. A normal desiatina was equal to 2,400 square SAZHENI or 2.7 acres. Desiatina also designated larger plots of 3.6 and c. 4 acres (3,200 or 3,600 square sazheni).

desiátnik, -ki. Decurion, approximately "corporal," an officer in command of a unit of 10 soldiers in pre-Petrine Russia.

desiátok, -tki. 1. A military unit of 10 men. 2. In rural or urban settlements, an administrative unit consisting of 10 households.

desiátskii, -kie. A lesser police agent normally elected by the men of 10 households (chiefly in rural settlements) and responsible for the public order in his DESIATOK.

detënyshi monastýrskie (pl.). The laborers on monastic properties in the 15 to 17th centuries. They were either orphans and other poor boys who had found asylum in the monastery and grown up there, or hired laborers from outside.

déti boiárskie (pl.). Lesser gentry in the Muscovite state. Probably they were originally impoverished members or younger sons of boyar families who had not attained boyar rank and position. In the 16th and 17th centuries they formed a numerous special class and made up the bulk of the Moscow tsar's military servitors.

déti boiárskie dvoróvye: a particular military detachment, a kind of tsar's bodyguard.

déti boiárskie gorodovýe (or *iz gorodóv*): the mass of the provincial service men. High church hierarchs (such as the Archbishop of Novgorod, the Metropolitan and later Patriarch of Moscow, or the Metropolitan of Siberia) had their own deti boiarskie.

déti dukhóvnye. Spiritual children. For the parish priest they were his parishioners; for the bishop, the people of his diocese.

detínets. The inner fortress of a city, an early name for a kremlin.

détskii, -kie. Adolescent. In the Kievan period they were the younger members of a prince's retinue (DRUZHINA), who formed an important part of his troops and also served as his executive agents in the spheres of justice and civil administration. In the Grand Duchy of Lithuania, even in the 16th century, the court agents sent to arrest suspects and to execute various court decisions and decrees were called detskie.

dévter or **défter** or **devtér', -ri.** A khan's charter concerning taxes or exemption from them. The term is borrowed from Turkish. The basis of the Turkish term is the Greek *diphthera* (hide, book, document).

diachók, or **d'iachók, diachkí,** esp. *diachók tserkóvnyi.* The reader and singer in divine services; sexton; psalmist; called PSALOMSHCHIK in the 19th century. The diachok often acted as a rural clerk.

diachók zémskii: in Muscovy in the 16th and 17th centuries, a public clerk in those local communities that enjoyed some measure of self-government.

diachók zémskii sudétskii: a public clerk in local elective courts.

diak or **d'iak, -kí.** Secretary. These men were the mainspring of the Moscow bureaucratic apparatus in the 15th to 17th centuries. In the 17th century the diaki numbered about 100 (according to Kotoshikhin). They were assistants or associates to the BOIARE and other heads of central government departments (PRIKAZY), and sometimes were themselves department heads. The diaki were also the associates of the provincial NAMESTNIKI and VOEVODY. In general they played a very important role in Muscovite administrative, judicial, and financial institutions, as well as in diplomatic relations with other countries.

In the Grand Duchy of Lithuania in the 15th and 16th centuries the term diaki was applied to the clerks who assisted the secretaries.

dúmnyi diak: in the 16th and 17th centuries in Muscovy, senior DIAKI (usually three or four but more by the end of the 17th century) who acted as members of the boyar DUMA and made reports on matters demanding the Duma's attention. They had the special title dumnyi diak as they were considered a sort of state secretary.

véchnyi diak: see VECHE.

zémskii diak: a public clerk or secretary in local communities, appointed by the elected local authorities.

diáklo. In the Grand Duchy of Lithuania, the rent in kind (mainly in grain) paid by the peasants to the grand duke or to other landowners.

diákon or **d'iákon, -ny.** A deacon, an ordained cleric who assisted the priest at church services.

distríkt, -ty. A territorial-administrative subdivision of the PROVINTSIIA in the 18th century. With the GUBERNIIA reform of 1775, the distrikt once again assumed its Russian name, UEZD.

diúim, -my. Inch, 10 LINII, 2.54 centimeters, one twelfth of a FUT.

dobrosóvestnyi, -nye. Literally, an honest or conscientious man. According to the law of 1838, which regulated the administrative and judiciary organization of the state peasantry, the term dobrosovestnye was applied to the members of the village (*sel'skii*) and VOLOST' courts.

dobýtok (W.R.). Property, esp. movable property; cattle.

doklád. 1. In old Russian legal procedure, the transfer of a lawsuit, or of any legal question, from a lower to a higher instance for reexamination and final decision. 2. In modern usage, a report by a government official to his superior; or by an executive organ or special committee of a public organization to a general meeting or assembly.

dokládchik or **dokládshik, -ki.** In the court organization of the Novgorodian Republic, a juryman of the higher court or a member of the court of appeals.

dokonchánie. An agreement, a treaty, esp. a peace treaty.

dólia, -li. 1. Part; share. 2. A small unit of weight, $1/96$ of a ZOLOTNIK. 3. A territorial unit with a predominantly fiscal purpose, instituted by Peter the Great in 1710. Each dolia, a subdivision of a GUBERNIIA, was to include 5,536 homesteads (DVORY) and was to be administered by a LANDRAT. The doli were soon abolished; in 1720 the guberniias were divided into PROVINTSII, and the provintsii into DISTRIKTY.

dom, dómy. In the old church language, a dom or house of the Holy Saviour, of the Holy Virgin, or of a Saint meant a monastery or a church, esp. a cathedral: *sobornyi dom.*

pitéinyi dom: a tavern, a house where alcoholic beverages were sold and drunk.

Rossíiskii Imperátorskii dom: the ruling imperial house. See FAMILIIA IMPERATORSKAIA.

vospitátel'nyi dom: an asylum for foundlings and homeless children, like those founded in Moscow in 1764 and in St. Petersburg in 1770.

domokhoziáin, -ziáeva. The official term in imperial Russia for the head of a peasant household.

Domostrói. Literally, household manual. A collection of rules concerning religious observances and everyday behavior, attributed to the priest Sylvester, who in the years 1547–53 was a close advisor to Tsar Ivan IV. The concluding part, a message from a father to his son, was probably Sylvester's work; the rest was probably a compilation of the everyday homilies of 16th-century Muscovy, edited by Sylvester.

doróga or **darúga, -gi.** Tatar financial official in Russia.

dostóinosti (pl.). High offices in the Grand Duchy of Lithuania.

dotsént, -ty. From 1863 to 1884, the rank of university teacher below the PROFESSOR rank. The university statutes of 1884, abolishing the rank of dotsent, established the rank of PRIVAT-DOTSENT instead.

dovód. Proof, evidence; indictment; proved accusation.

dovódchik, -ki. Executive agent of NAMESTNIKI and VOLOSTELI; constable; bailiff; prosecutor.

dozór, -ry. 1. A military patrol. 2. In Muscovy in the 17th century, a government inventory of population and tax records, for the purpose of revising tax assessments and registering ownership of land and peasants. See KNIGA DOZORNAIA.

drab, dráby. Foot soldiers in the Grand Duchy of Lithuania.

druzhína (collect., from *drug,* friend). In medieval Russia, a prince's retinue or bodyguard, who originally lived with their prince in or around his household (DVOR), serving as the nucleus of the armed force of his principality, and, if necessary, as his civil servants. The druzhina was usually composed of two parts: the senior members, called BOIARE or KNIAZHI MUZHI, occupied

13

commanding positions in military and civil administration and formed a body of the prince's advisors (DUMTSY or *boiare dumaiushchie*); the junior members—DETSKIE, OTROKI, GRIDI (later DETI BOIARSKIE)—were his guards and filled lesser civil and judicial administrative positions.

In Imperial Russia, the word druzhina designated units of the Russian militia (OPOLCHENIE) and also Slavic military detachments formed occasionally by Russia during wars. The Bulgarian druzhiny were formed in 1877 and participated in the Russo-Turkish war of 1877–78. A Czech druzhina was formed in Kiev in 1914 to participate in the war against Austria-Hungary.

dukhovénstvo. Clergy.

dúma. The original meaning: thought or thinking. By extension: advice, counsel, and then a body of deliberative advisors, a council.

boiárskaia dúma: a literary rather than juridical term, this boyar council to the Russian princes, later to the tsars, was an important customary institution in Russian political life, although its rights and functions were not systematically defined in a written law. The sources simply report consultations of the sovereign with his BOIARE, sometimes referred to in the chronicles as BOIARE DUMAIUSHCHIE or DUMTSY of the prince. In Muscovy the commonly used words *boiare prigovorili* clearly indicate deliberations and decisions of the boyar council, which is sometimes termed the SINKLIT. The Moscow boyar duma was composed of four ranks of members: boiare proper, OKOL'-NICHIE, DUMNYE DVORIANE, and DUMNYE DIAKI. All these ranks, and therefore membership in the duma, were granted by the tsar, although duma members of the first two ranks were usually appointed from only the several scores of aristocratic families.

The boyar duma normally took part in the legislative, administrative, and judicial affairs of the state, as well as in diplomatic relations with other countries. The SUDEBNIK of 1550 (art. 98) considered *boiarskii prigovor* (decision) a normal way of making new laws, although this rule was not always observed in practice. About 1700, Peter the Great abolished the boyar duma as an institution and the rank of boiarin as well.

gorodskáia dúma: municipal council. According to the municipal statutes of June 16, 1870, and June 11, 1892, the gorodskaia duma, elected by qualified city inhabitants, was to take care of the city's economic, medical, and educational needs; the duma elected the mayor of the city (GORODSKOI GOLOVA) and the members of the municipal executive board (GORODSKAIA UPRAVA); duma meetings were presided over by the mayor.

gorodskáia óbshchaia dúma: according to the charter of the cities of April 21, 1785, a general municipal council composed of representatives of the six categories of city inhabitants that elected the city's six-member executive board, the *gorodskaia shestiglasnaia duma.*

Gosudárstvennaia Dúma: State Duma, a nationwide representative assembly. It was suggested by M. M. Speransky in his reform plan of 1809, but did not become a reality until 1905. The manifesto and the statutes of August 6, 1905, announced the establishment of a State Duma with consultative powers, based on an indirect and restricted electoral system. In the face of continued revolutionary activities the manifesto of October 17, 1905, granted the Duma legislative powers and the right to participate in the verification of the legality of government actions. Then the decree of December 11, 1905, enlarged the franchise substantially, without changing the system of curial elections (by the landowners, the peasants, and the urban population). After the government's bitter conflicts with the First Duma in 1906 and with the Second in 1907, the new electoral law of June 3, 1907, although it preserved the rights of the Duma as an institution, reduced greatly the representation of the borderlands of the empire and made the landowners' representatives dominant in most of the provincial electoral assemblies. The Third Duma (1907–12) served its full five-year term, and the Fourth Duma (1912–17) survived until the February Revolution, which the Duma formally headed in its first stages.

dúmets, dúmtsy, or **boiáre dúmaiushchie.** A term for the princes' advisors, used occasionally in the chronicles.

dushá, -shi. Soul; person.

revízskaia dushá: in 1722, Peter the Great introduced the "soul," or poll, tax, called *podushnyi sbor, podushnaia podat',* or DENGI PODUSHNYE. The tax was imposed after a repeated census or REVIZIIA. After that the term revizskaia dusha meant a registered male person obliged to pay the poll tax (female "souls" were not counted by the census). In the spoken language of the 18th and 19th centuries (before 1861) the word dusha was often used in designating the number of male peasants belonging to a landlord.

dushegúbets, -btsy. Murderer, killer.

dushegúbstvo. Murder, assassination.

duván. Division of spoils among victors.

dvor, -rý. Household; homestead; yard; court. In the chronicles dvor sometimes meant the prince's military service men collectively. In the older periods, as in Muscovy in the second half of the 17th century, the dvor was a taxable unit.

bélyi dvor: in Muscovy, a homestead that was not included in the *posad tiaglo,* and was therefore free from the

taxes and work obligations imposed on the POSAD community.

chërnyi dvor: a homestead included in the TIAGLO.

gospodárskii dvor: in the Grand Duchy of Lithuania, (1) the court of the grand duke, or (2) a manorial house or homestead that was an administrative center for the population of large estates or districts belonging to the sovereign and administered by his NAMESTNIKI and DERZHAVTSY.

gostínyi dvor: the market square with the merchants' rows; a large hall with numerous stores inside.

Neméetskii Dvor, in Novgorod the Great: an autonomous German settlement, the main trading center in the extensive commercial relations between Novgorod and Western Europe.

opríchnyi dvor: see OPRICHNINA.

Patriárshii Dvor: in the 17th century, the central court for church administration and for the management of landed estates belonging to the patriarchal see.

pechátnyi dvor: printing house, esp. the one established by the government in Moscow in the middle of the 16th century.

pitéinyi (krúzhechnyi) dvor: liquor warehouse and tavern.

pozhilói dvor, or *pozhilóe:* the payment for the use of his homestead, made to the landowner by a peasant when he left an estate.

tiáglyi dvor: rural or urban taxable homestead inhabited by TIAGLYE LIUDI.

zémskii dvor: a police headquarters in the city of Moscow in the 16th and 17th centuries.

dvoréts, -rtsý. 1. Palace. 2. In a broad sense the dvorets, also called *bol'shoi dvorets* or *dvor tsarskii,* was a vast complex of buildings and lands with a numerous population of peasants and various servitors who saw to the needs of the tsar's extensive household (*dvortsovye zemli, dvortsovye krest'iane, dvortsovye slugi*). The dvorets proper was therefore the central office for the management of palace lands and the administration of their population. Among many particular DVORY it included the *kazĕnnyi dvor* or treasury chamber where money, gold, silver, and precious furs were kept.

dvorétskii, -skie. Majordomo who managed the economy and headed the administration of the prince's court and estates. In Muscovy in the 16th and 17th centuries it was a very important position occupied by a person who had the rank of BOIARIN or OKOL'NICHII and took part in the state's administrative and judicial activities. In the 17th century he headed an important financial office called the PRIKAZ BOL'SHOGO DVORTSA. In the second half of the 17th century, besides the *boiarin-dvoretskii* in office, several persons held this rank as an honorary title.

dvorianín, dvoriáne. Courtier. The first mention of dvoriane is found in the Laurentian chronicle under the year 1175 where it was used to indicate the people living at the prince's court, his servitors and servants. In the Novgorodians' treaties with their princes, dvoriane meant the prince's agents dispatched with official errands or messages. In the language of the first Lithuanian statute of 1529, a dvorianin is a nobleman holding a landed estate and obliged to perform military service on demand. In Muscovy in the 16th and 17th centuries the dvoriane, together with the DETI BOIARSKIE, made up the bulk of the active armed forces, ranking in the hierarchy between BOIARE and DETI BOIARSKIE. They held landed estates (VOTCHINY and POMEST'IA) and were under obligation to perform military service until the end of their lives or until their permanent disability. They also occupied various posts in

civil administration. Under Peter the Great the service obligations of the dvoriane remained undiminished (the term deti boiarskie disappeared from the official language in the 18th century). Access into the DVORIANSTVO or nobility was opened by Peter to all military commissioned officers and to civil servants having attained the rank of the 8th class (*kollezhskii assessor;* see ASSESSOR). In the 19th century the requirements for the achievement of noble status through service were raised, and the dvorianstvo was divided into hereditary (*potomstvennoe*) and personal (*lichnoe*) categories. The first was transmitted to descendants, while the status of personal nobility, held by the lower ranks, was limited to the holder himself. By a decree of May 28, 1900, *potomstvennoe dvorianstvo* was granted to a civil servant when he attained the rank of *deistvitel'nyi statskii sovetnik* (see SOVETNIK and TABEL' O RANGAKH), and to a military officer when he attained the rank of colonel (POLKOVNIK). The service obligations of the dvoriane were lightened in the first half of the 18th century and abolished in 1762 by Peter III. Catherine II, in 1785, granted the nobility a charter that confirmed their rights, liberties, and privileges and established their corporate organization. The regular assemblies of the nobles in each UEZD and each GUBERNIIA—called *uezdnoe dvorianskoe sobranie* and *gubernskoe dvorianskoe sobranie,* respectively—convened every three years and elected marshals of the nobility called, respectively, *uezdnyi predvoditel' dvorianstva,* and *gubernskii predvoditel' dvorianstva.* They played an important role in the local administration. The *dvorianskie sobraniia* also elected officials for local courts and the head of the district police, the ISPRAVNIK. After that the dvoriane became in fact a privileged legal class (SOSLOVIE) with practically unlimited power over their serfs, the monopoly of possessing inhabited landed estates, and an important role in the local civil administration. Some remnants of the dvorianstvo's privileged position in local administration were preserved even after the liberation of the serfs in 1861. The electoral laws for the State Duma (esp. the law of June 3, 1907) were favorable to the landowners (ZEMLEVLADEL'TSY) as a socioeconomic group, but not as a privileged legal class or estate.

dvoriáne bol'shíe: the dvoriane of higher rank, either all the DVORIANE MOSKOVSKIE or the best (*luchshie*) of them.

Dvoriáne Bózhie: literally, God's noblemen. A Russian term for the Knights of the German Livonian Order.

dvoriáne dúmnye: in the 16th and 17th centuries several DVORIANE were appointed members of the boyar DUMA; they constituted the third rank in the duma membership, following the BOIARE and the OKOL'NICHIE.

dvoriáne gorodovýe, or *iz gorodóv:* provincial DVORIANE (as opposed to the DVORIANE MOSKOVSKIE), the most numerous group of dvoriane in the 16th and 17th centuries.

dvoriáne gospodárskie or *korolévskie:* in the Grand Duchy of Lithuania, a group of service men attached to the court of the grand duke as his bodyguards. During military expeditions they formed a separate detachment; they also performed various functions in civil administration and legal proceedings.

dvoriáne moskóvskie, as opposed to GORODOVYE DVORIANE: in the middle of the 16th century about 1,000 men were chosen from among the best provincial DVORIANE and granted POMEST'IA near Moscow. They formed a kind of guards detachment for the Moscow tsar in peacetime and in military expeditions.

dvoriáne výbornye or *iz gorodóv výbor:* the top group of provincial DVORIANE who served as commanding officers of the units of the Moscow army.

dvoriánstvo. Nobility or gentry; the term commonly used in the 18th and 19th centuries to indicate the legal status and social class of the DVORIANE.

dvoróvye (*liúdi*) (pl.). In Muscovy, attendants of the tsar's court (DVOR). In the language of the 18th and 19th centuries, landless serfs who lived in or around their master's homestead (dvor) and performed housework and other services. At the time of the abolition of serfdom in 1861, the number of dvorovye of both sexes was about one and one half million (over 7 percent of the serf population).

dvórskii, -skie. The early term for DVORETSKII (used mainly in the 14th and 15th centuries), a steward or major-domo, who managed a prince's household and landed estates and took part in administrative and judicial activities. SLUGI POD DVORSKIM formed a lower class of the prince's servitors and servants, mostly bondmen, as opposed to SLUGI VOL'NYE (free servitors).

dvugrívennyi, -ye. A silver coin, worth 20 copecks, first minted in the second half of the 18th century.

dym, -my. Smoke; therefore, hearth or household, an old unit of taxation (see PODYMSHCHINA).

E

edinovérie. The agreement concluded in 1788–1800 between the Orthodox church and a part of the STAROOBRIADTSY POPOVSHCHINA (see under two separate entries) according to which the latter retained the right to perform church services using the old rituals and the books printed before the Nikonian church reform, on condition that they accept priests ordained by the official church hierarchy.

ednánie (W.R.). Negotiation; agreement.

efímok, efímki. The Russian term for Joachimsthalers, large silver coins minted in Joachimsthal in Bohemia and frequently used in other European countries. In the absence of Russian silver coins of large denomination, efimki were used in Muscovy in the 16th and 17th centuries. In 1655 for a short time they became an official monetary unit called *efimki s prizna-kami* (meaning, with marks), as they bore the Russian state emblem. Efimki were received from foreign trade operations and then either altered into small Moscow DENGI or used intact. In the mid-17th century the tsar's treasury accepted one efimok as equal to 50 copecks; and issued efimki s prizna-kami with a value of 64 copecks.

ekspedítsiia, -tsii. 1. A separate branch in the state administration or a subdivision in a large government institution. 2. An expedition.

ekzekútor, -ry. A business official; an executive in a government institution.

émets, émtsy. An old term for an executive agent sent by the court or by an administrator to find and arrest a suspect.

epárkhiia, -khii. Diocese.

epískop, -py. Bishop.

epitemíia. A penance imposed by church authorities for violation of church or monastic rules.

esaúl or **iasaúl, -ly** (borrowed from the Tatar). In the Ukraine in the 16th to 18th centuries and among the Don Cossacks and other cossack hosts, lieutenants or assistants to the HETMANS and ATAMANS in their activities as military commanders and civil administrators. The highest among the Ukrainian esauls was called the *general'nyi* or *voiskovoi esaul*. There were also esauls in the cossack regiments (*polkovoi esaul*) and hundreds (*sotennyi esaul*). In the imperial Russian armed forces the rank of esaul was preserved in the cossack regiments as the rank of the 8th class corresponding to the ranks of KAPITAN in the infantry or artillery and of ROTMISTR in the cavalry.

esdék, -ki. Colloquial for a Social Democrat (see PARTIIA, ROSSIISKAIA SOTSIAL-DEMOKRATICHESKAIA . . .).

esér, -ry. Colloquial for a Socialist Revolutionary (see PARTIIA SOTSIALISTOV-REVOLIUTSIONEROV).

ezd, ézdy. A fixed riding-distance allowance or fee for official agents or their messengers sent outside the city.

ezdók, -kí. Literally, rider; a messenger performing official duties.

F

fakul'tét, -ty. See UNIVERSITET.

Famíliia Imperátorskaia. Ruling house. The statutes concerning the Imperial Family (*uchrezhdenie ob Imperatorskoi Familii*) were issued by Paul I on April 7, 1797, and revised under Alexander III (July 2, 1886). They prescribed the order of succession to the throne and contained detailed rules about the composition, rights, privi-

leges, and means of maintenance of the ruling house.

fel'dmárshal, -ly. Fieldmarshal, the highest military rank according to the TABEL' O RANGAKH.

féndrik, -ki. Ensign or warrant officer, the 14th, or lowest, rank of military officer according to Peter the Great's TABEL' O RANGAKH. In the 19th century the rank of fendrik was not in use.

fiskál, -ly. Government inspector, observer, investigator. The office of fiskal (and OBER-FISKAL) was established by Peter the Great in 1711–14 in an effort to combat corruption and misuse of power by government officials. Fiskaly were appointed to all central, provincial, and municipal offices and to military units. The network of fiskaly was hated by the official world and was apparently helpless in achieving its goal; it was abolished in 1730.

folvárok, -rki (Pol.). In the Grand Duchy of Lithuania, a farm, a consolidated landholding.

fundát, -ty (W.R.). Charter founding a church or a monastery and granting it certain properties and rights; endowment.

funt, -ty. Pound. As a measure of weight the funt came into use in Muscovy in the 16th century. In the following centuries it was generally accepted, having replaced the comparable earlier measures *ansyr'* and *bol'shaia grivenka* (or GRIVNA). The funt was divided into 96 ZOLOTNIKI; its weight in the 19th century was officially fixed as equal to 409 grams (almost .9 lb.).

G

generál, -ly. A high rank in military service, established by Peter the Great's Table of Ranks (1722). The *general-fel'dmarshal* was the first rank in the army hierarchy. The second was the *general-ot-infanterii, -ot-kavalerii,* or *-ot-artillerii,* termed otherwise *polnyi* (full) *general* (under Catherine II, *general-anshef*). The third rank was the *general-leitenant;* the fourth, the *general-maior.* (See TABEL' O RANGAKH.)

generál-admirál. The highest rank in the imperial navy, corresponding to the *general-fel'dmarshal* in the army.

generál-gubernátor, -ry. Governor-general. According to the statutes on provincial administration of 1775, the top official of each GUBERNIIA. In the 19th century the head of the guberniia was called GUBERNATOR or *nachal'nik gubernii.* The office and power of the general-gubernator in the 19th century was limited to the two capitals and to such border regions as Poland, Finland, Central Asia, and the Far East. In those cases the general-gubernator was given jurisdiction over several guberniias. In the early 20th century there were general-gubernatory in Moscow, Kiev, Warsaw, Vilna, and in Finland; in Asia there were four governor-generalships:

Irkutskoe, Turkestanskoe, Stepnoe, and *Priamurskoe.* Sometimes in troubled areas the government appointed a military governor-general (*voennyi general-gubernator*).

generál-politsméister. Head of the newly created Ministry of Police according to the reorganization of the ministries in 1811. This ministry was abolished in 1819, and the maintenance of state security and public order was transferred to the Ministry of Internal Affairs (established in 1802).

generál-prokurór. The highest office in the central administration established by Peter the Great in January 1722. By the decree of April 27, 1722, the general-prokuror had a seat in the Senate, acting there as the "tsar's eye," to supervise all activities. The general-prokuror had under his direction the corps of other PROKURORY and FISKALY. After the establishment of the ministries in 1802 the minister of justice was entrusted with the duties of the general-prokuror.

generalíssimus. The highest possible rank in the military hierarchy from the time of Peter the Great, standing outside the Table of Ranks as an entirely exceptional distinction. Only three persons held this rank during the 18th century: Menshikov, Suvorov, and Prince Anton Ulrich von Braunschweig, consort of Princess-Regent Anna Leopol'dovna (in 1740–41). No Russian military commander held the rank of generalissimus in the 19th century.

gétman. See HETMAN.

gil'diia, -dii. Merchant organization in imperial Russia. The statute for the supreme municipal administration (*Reglament ili Ustav Glavnogo Magistrata*) of January 16, 1721, divided the urban population (REGULIARNYE GRAZHDANE) into two gil'dii: (1) big merchants, bankers, physicians, druggists, jewelers, painters; (2) retail traders and craftsmen of all kinds. By a decree of 1742 and the charter of the cities of April 21, 1785, the division into gil'dii was maintained only for the merchants, who were divided into three gil'dii according to their declared capital assets. There were only two merchant gil'dii from 1863 until the Revolution of 1917. The merchants united in gil'dii formed a distinct legal class (SOSLOVIE).

gimnáziia, -zii. A secondary school. The first one, the *akademicheskaia gimnaziia,* was established in 1726, attached to the Academy of Sciences; the second, founded in 1755, was attached to Moscow University. The decree of 1803 and the statutes on school organization of 1804 provided for establishment of a gimnaziia with a large curriculum (including Latin, French, and German) in each GUBERNIIA capital. Subsequent statutes concerning secondary schools were issued in 1828, 1864, and 1871. The statute of 1864 divided secondary schools into *klassicheskie gimnazii* and *real'nye uchilishcha* (see UCHILISCHE), the latter stressing science, mathematics, and technology. The statute of 1871, promoted by Minister of Education Count D. A. Tolstoi, strengthened the study of Latin and Greek in the classic gimnazii by making them compulsory and limited the study of the natural sciences (suspected of implanting materialism). Early in the 20th century this exaggerated classicism was reduced and the natural sciences were restored to their place. The course of gimnaziia education continued seven or (later) eight years. Graduates could enter the universities. In 1915 there were 474 klassicheskie gimnazii (with an enrollment of over 150,000) and 297 real'nye uchilishcha (with over 80,000 students). There were also numerous special secondary schools for boys. After 1860 the number of girls' secondary schools (*zhenskie gimnazii,* without obligatory ancient languages) grew rapidly and in 1914 exceeded 800 (with an enrollment of over 350,000 girls).

glásnyi, glásnye gorodskói dúmy. According to the municipal statutes of 1870 and 1892, members of the municipal council, elected by the qualified city constituency, electors of the city's executive board (GORODSKAIA UPRAVA).

glásnye zémskie. Elected members of a ZEMSTVO assembly. According to the zemstvo statutes of 1864 and 1890, the qualified constituency elected the members of the district zemstvo assembly (*uezdnye zemskie glasnye*); they elected the district executive board (*uezdnaia zemskaia uprava*) and members for the provincial zemstvo assembly (*gubernskie zemskie glasnye*); the latter elected the provincial executive board (*gubernskaia zemskaia uprava*).

glavá. Head, chief.

reméslennyi glavá: a prefect of artisans elected each year, according to the charter of the cities of 1785, which included the statute of craftsmen (*remeslennoe polozhenie*), by all corporations of city craftsmen or artisans. See GOLOVA.

glavnonachál'stvuiushchii. A term of the official language in the late 19th and the beginning of the 20th century, approximately equivalent to GENERAL-GUBERNATOR.

glavnoupravliáiuschii. The chief administrator of a government department, either equivalent or subordinate to a ministry.

gmína, -ny (Pol., from the Ger. *Gemeinde*). A rural unit in the Polish provinces corresponding to the Russian VOLOST'. The decree of February 19, 1864, as applied to the Polish provinces of the Russian Empire on behalf of the peasants who had been freed from the patrimonial jurisdiction of the landlords, introduced the *gminnoe upravlenie* (administration) and *gminnyi sud* (court), to be elected by the rural population but subordinate to the Russian district official, the *uezdnyi nachal'nik*.

god, gódy. Year.

l'gótnyi god, l'gótnye gódy: a period free from tax payments and work obligations, a privilege usually given to new settlers.

uróchnye gódy (or URÓCHNYE LETÁ): in a general sense, any fixed period or time limit. In a special sense, the time limit for the recovery of fugitive serfs; at the end of the 16th and during the first half of the 17th centuries, it varied from 5 to 15 years, until the *Ulozhenie* of 1649 completely abolished the time limit for the recovery of fugitives.

vykhodnýe gódy: a term used in the late 16th and early 17th centuries to indicate those years when the peasants' departure from their landlords' estates was permissible, according to the provisions enacted in the *Sudebnik* of 1550.

zapovédnye gódy: a decree presumably issued in 1580 "forbade the departure of all peasants either by their own efforts or by 'exportation' from their present place of residence . . . until such time as the tsar ordered that free

departure was once more permissible. The period of interdiction was known as the zapovednye gody, the forbidden years. During its duration the provisions of the Code of 1550 guaranteeing peasants the right to move were suspended. The first nationwide 'forbidden year' seems to have started in 1581. . . . Years in which peasant departure was forbidden soon became the rule." (Jerome Blum, p. 254.)

gofgeríkht, -ty, or **nadvórnye sudý.** The courts established by Peter the Great in St. Petersburg, Moscow, and eight other major cities in 1719, and abolished in 1727 (see SUD, in imperial Russia).

gofméister. A high courtier rank at the imperial court.

golová, gólovy. Head; person; body; body of a slain man; the value of the head, that is, the value set on a man's life. *Za gólovu:* (payment) for the head. *Výdati golovóiu:* to deliver a culprit in person to a plaintiff (into bondage).

golová, in the Muscovite period. A civil administrative official or a military commander.

izliúblennyi golová: according to charters granted in the middle of the 16th century by the government to the population of many districts, mostly in the northern regions, the local population was to elect izliublennye golovy to direct the local administration and courts, and to collect taxes imposed by the government.

ob"ézzhii golová (literally, riding around): a police officer in the city of Moscow.

osádnyi golová: assistant to the VOEVODA; his duty was to prepare the fortress for a siege (*osada*) and to lead the defense in case of a siege.

písemnye or *pís'mennye gólovy:* military officers serving as assistants to the VOEVODA (mostly in Siberia in the 17th century), primarily as secretaries.

pushkárskii golová: commander over PUSHKARI (Muscovite artillery-men).

strelétskii golová: colonel in a *strel'-tsy* regiment (see STRELETS).

tamózhennyi golová: the head of a customshouse.

vérnye gólovy (tamózhennye and *kabátskie):* the heads of customshouses and of liquor warehouses; they were elected by the local population when the government ordered the collection of customs duties on goods in transit or excise taxes on the sale of alcoholic beverages; they worked under oath (*na vere;* from that the term, *vernye*), swearing to perform their duties honestly.

zastávnyi golová: head of a ZASTAVA, which was either a military lookout post guarded by a small detachment, or a frontier control point for checking and assessing transported goods.

golová, in the imperial period. An elected head of a rural or municipal administrative unit.

gorodskói golová: according to the charter of the cities of 1785, and to the municipal statutes of 1870 and of 1892, the gorodskoi golova was the elected head of the city administration.

volostnói golová: in the 18th and 19th centuries, the head of the VOLOST' administration, elected by the state peasants and confirmed by the government authorities. After the reform of 1861, the term for this office was VOLOSTNOI STARSHINA.

golovníchestvo. Amends payable to the relatives of a murdered person.

golovník, -kí. Murderer.

golovshchína, -ny. 1. Murder. 2. Fine imposed for murder, or penalty paid by the culprit to the relatives of the slain person or to the master of a slain bond-man.

gon, -ny. Hunt or chase.

góny bobróvye: beaver habitations.

gon'bá iamskáia. The system of communications in Muscovy and the obligation of the local population (often converted into money payments) to supply horses and vehicles for the IAMSHCHIKI who handled communications for the government.

górlo. Throat. In the Grand Duchy of Lithuania, *gorlom karati* meant to punish by hanging; *gorlo tratiti,* to be executed.

górod, -dá. Originally, a fortified settlement; later, an administrative center and market for the surrounding countryside, a place where trade and industry were concentrated. During the Kievan period a score of important cities became economic centers and political capitals for their regions, ZEMLI (lands), the seats of princes and the centers of VECHE (popular assembly) activities. They were regarded as *starshie goroda* (elder cities), while the others were considered their PRIGORODY (by-towns or dependent towns). In Muscovy a gorod was predominantly a military and administrative center, while the traders and craftsmen (the POSADSKIE LIUDI) inhabited the POSAD or settlement surrounding the fortress (the KREML'). The word gorod in official documents often also referred to the entire territory of which the town was the administrative center. Peter the Great established BURMISTERSKIE PALATY (later RATUSHI) as units of urban self-government with elected BURMISTRY. In 1718 *gorodovye magistraty* were established, headed by a GLAVNYI MAGISTRAT. Heavy tax burdens and requirements that the townspeople serve as the government's trading and financial agents hindered the free development of urban life, and after Peter's death bureaucratic administration of cities again predominated.

In 1775, under Catherine II, Russia was divided into 40 provinces or GUBERNIIAS; each of them was divided

22

into an average of 10 districts or UEZDS; thereafter the Russian towns were divided into two principal categories: *gubernskie goroda* and *uezdnye goroda,* administrative centers of provinces and districts respectively. The charter of the cities of 1785 formally reestablished urban self-government with elected MAGISTRATY and RATUSHI (administrative and judicial bodies) and abolished the obligatory services of the townspeople, but genuine self-government and successful economic and cultural development in the towns began only with the municipal statutes (*gorodovoe polozhenie*) of 1870. The subsequent growth continued despite several unhappy modifications brought by the statutes of 1892. At the beginning of the 20th century the number of settlements with the legal status of gorod was 931 in the whole of the Empire. There were also many settlements urban in character (called POSELOK, STANITSA, POSAD, MESTECHKO) but without the legal status of gorod. On the eve of World War I, the population of cities and other urban settlements comprised 18 percent of the total population of the Empire.

páshennye gorodá: a term from the 17th century meaning the Siberian towns to which peasants were assigned for the purpose of supplying the local garrison.

pripisnýe gorodá: small towns subordinated to the provincial centers; after the administrative reform of 1775, such subordinate towns were called *uezdnye goroda* (see GOROD).

gorodníchii, -chie. In the Grand Duchy of Lithuania, town chief, an official who supervised the maintenance of fortifications and collected taxes from the VOLOSTI. In the Russian Empire of the 18th and 19th centuries, police commissioner, the head of the police in UEZD centers (*uezdnye goroda*); the

office was established in 1775 and abolished in 1862.

gorodník, -kí. Builder of city fortifications (in the Kievan period).

gorodók, gorodkí. 1. A fortification. 2. A small town. 3. A settlement of the Don Cossacks in the 16th and 17th centuries (later called STANITSA).

gorodovói, -výe. A city constable, a lower-rank policeman maintaining order and security in the city streets in the 19th and early 20th centuries.

gospóda or **gospodá.** Literally, lords, in Novgorod and Pskov (during the period of their independence), the council of higher notables consisting chiefly of former high officials (POSADNIKI, TYSIATSKIE, STAROSTY). In Pskov it acted also as the supreme court.

gospodár'. The sovereign, a usual title of the grand duke of Lithuania.

gost', gósti. 1. In the Kievan period, wholesale merchants who were engaged in commercial operations with other countries or with other cities. In Muscovy, the richest group and the highest rank of merchants (according to Kotoshikhin, only about 30 men); they received the honorary title of gost' from the tsar and, while forming the top layer of the Moscow merchant community, acted also as the government's agents in collecting state revenues (customs duties and liquor excises) and in conducting state trading operations. 2. According to the charter of cities of 1785, a temporary city resident coming from another city or from a foreign country.

gost'bá. Trading, esp. with foreign countries.

gostín(n)oe. A tax on the storehouses used by foreign merchants at the marketplace.

gosudár', -ri. In a broad sense, lord or master. In Muscovy it was a usual form of address by peasants to landlords or to other persons of high standing. The title gosudar' was used in particular for the Muscovite sovereign, usually referred to in official documents as *velikii gosudar'* (the great sovereign) and *gosudar' vseia Rusi(i)* (sovereign of all Russia). The word was later preserved in the emperor's title: *Gosudar' Impe-rator.*

gotovízna (W.R.). Money in cash.

grabëzh, -zhí. 1. Robbery or plundering. 2. In the legal language of the Kievan period, also confiscation of the property of a convicted criminal.

gradonachál'nik, -ki. An official who administered a city and its adjacent ter-ritory with the authority of a governor (GUBERNATOR).

gradonachál'stvo, -va. An administrative unit consisting of a city and its adjacent territory under the authority of a GRA-DONACHAL'NIK. In 1914 there were eight gradonachal'stva, in St. Petersburg, Moscow, Odessa, Sebastopol, and four other cities.

grámota, -ty (from the Greek *gramma,* pl. *grammata,* meaning lines of a drawing, picture, figures, characters). 1. Alpha-bet. 2. Knowledge of reading and writing. 3. Writing, letter, deed, char-ter, and, in general, any written docu-ment, official or private. In Muscovy of the 15th to 17th centuries, a huge num-ber of gramoty of all kinds were in use, such as those treated below:

béglaia grámota: court document concerning return of a fugitive bond-man to his former master.

bérezhnaia, berezhónaia grámota: protective charter, safe conduct.

bessúdnaia or *bezsúdnaia grámota:* a court decision, without trial, in favor of one of the litigants after his opponent had failed to appear before the court on the prescribed date; a default judgment.

blagoslovénnaia grámota: written blessing from a hierarch, esp. a charter of a bishop appointing a priest for a cer-tain parish.

dánnaia grámota: grant charter, esp. a land grant.

dél'naia or *razdél'naia grámota:* an agreement concerning division of prop-erty.

dértnaia grámota: a document re-pealing some former document, or confirming ownership of a landholding.

dogovórnaia grámota: an agreement, a treaty.

dokládnaia grámota: a document presented by a lower official to a higher one for confirmation.

dokonchál'naia grámota: an agree-ment in general, esp. a peace treaty.

dukhóvnaia or *dushévnaia grámota:* last will, testament.

gubnáia grámota: criminal statute or charter originally issued by the govern-ment at the request of local communi-ties; it granted permission for elected officials to investigate and to punish crimes; the earliest known charter of this type was issued in 1539. In the 17th century the administration of justice in criminal affairs by elected GUBNYE STAROSTY (elders) and GUBNYE TSELO-VAL'NIKI (sworn assistants) became a general rule.

kabál'naia grámota or *kabalá:* either a promissory note acknowledging a debt or an engagement of oneself into bondage in return for a loan.

kréstnaia grámota or *khréstnaia grámota:* an agreement or treaty con-firmed by an oath (kissing the cross).

kúpchaia grámota: purchase deed.

l'gótnaia grámota: charter granting privileges, immunities, or tax exemp-tions to private persons, to church insti-tutions, or to local communities.

l'zhívaia grámota: a document either counterfeit or formally wrong.

menóvnaia grámota: exchange deed.

mezheváia grámota: document fixing and describing boundaries between landholdings.

24

mírnaia grámota: peace treaty.

mirováia grámota: An agreement between two litigant parties resolving their dispute.

nastól'naia grámota: charter granted to bishops or to heads of monasteries confirming their installation.

nesudímaia (zhálovannaia) grámota: a charter granting privileged jurisdiction to church institutions or secular landowners. The *Ulozhenie* of 1649 (chap. X, art. 153) abolished this type of charter and declared previously issued ones invalid.

obél'naia grámota: a charter granting immunities from taxes and work obligations.

obysknáia grámota: an investigation warrant.

okrúzhnaia grámota: a circular edict or letter.

opásnaia grámota: a protective charter, safe conduct, particularly for foreign ambassadors and merchants.

otpústnaia or *otpusknáia grámota:* document releasing a bondman; it had to be signed by the master and registered by the responsible office.

otvódnaia grámota: document determining and describing the boundaries of a landholding.

polétnaia grámota: court document granting a debtor permission to pay his debt in installments.

pólnaia grámota: document by which a man sold or gave himself into full bondage (POLNOE KHOLOPSTVO).

poméstnaia (zhálovannaia) grámota: document granting a POMEST'E to a service man.

poriádnaia grámota: in the 16th and the first half of the 17th century, a contract between a landlord and a newly arrived peasant by which, in return for a plot of land and a grant in aid, the peasant obligated himself to cultivate his plot and to pay dues (OBROK) or to perform work equal to that exacted from other peasants on the estate.

poslúshnaia grámota: literally, obedient. With this document, the government, in granting a VOTCHINA or a POMEST'E to a service man, ordered the peasants on this landholding to be obedient to their new landlord concerning payments and work demanded.

právaia grámota: written court decision handed over to a litigant who won a lawsuit; the document usually included the record of the court proceedings and the court's decision.

pristavnáia grámota: document granted by a court to a bailiff (PRISTAV) empowering him to summon defendants and witnesses, to perform searches, or to carry out the court's sentences.

proézzhaia grámota: a travel permit securing free passage; esp. a permit to go abroad, a foreign passport.

razdél'naia grámota: an agreement concerning division of property.

raz"ézzhaia or *razvódnaia grámota:* document fixing and describing the boundaries between neighboring landholdings.

razmëtnaia, rozmëtnaia, vzmëtnaia, or *skládnaia grámota:* declaration of war, usually with explanation of reasons.

riádnaia grámota: an agreement concerning property in general, or a special agreement governing the dowry and property relations of two parties contemplating marriage.

shértnaia grámota: a charter confirmed by Moslem oath (SHERT').

skládnaia grámota: see RAZMETNAIA GRAMOTA.

sobórnaia grámota: act of a SOBOR.

sróchnaia grámota: summons fixing the date for an appearance in court.

stávlen(n)aia grámota: charter from a bishop appointing a priest or a deacon for a certain parish.

súdnaia grámota, or *o sudé:* charter containing rules concerning legal procedure and the exercise of justice in general. The two important charters of this kind were those confirmed by the VECHE of Novgorod the Great and of Pskov.

tamózhennaia grámota: a charter specifying the rates and the regulations for exacting customs duties.

tarkhánnaia or *torkhánnaia grámota:* from the Tatar *tarkhan* or *torkhan* meaning a free man not obliged to pay tribute. A charter exempting the grantee from paying taxes or from other kinds of financial obligations. According to the *Sudebnik* of 1550 (art. 43) the granting of tarkhannye gramoty was prohibited, but in fact the government issued them after that date.

grámota tarkhánnaia i nesudímaia: a document combining fiscal immunities and a privileged jurisdiction.

ukáznaia grámota or *ukáz:* a decree, order, or instruction, esp. one issued in the name of the tsar.

ustávnaia grámota: in the 15th and 16th centuries, an administrative charter given by the central government to local administrators (NAMESTNIKI and VOLOSTELI), regulating the KORM (food allowance) they were to receive from the local population in kind or in money.

zémskaia ustávnaia grámota: beginning in the 1550s, a charter from the tsar granting to local communities (at their request) the right to be administered by elected *zemskie starosty, golovy,* or *sudii,* who also collected state taxes and delivered the money to the state treasury in Moscow (see STAROSTA, in Muscovite Russia).

zémskaia ustávnaia grámota: the Russian literary term for the charters in the Grand Duchy of Lithuania (called originally PRIVILEI) granted in the 15th and 16th centuries by the grand dukes to particular lands (such as *zemli*

Kievskaia, Volynskaia, Smolenskaia, Polotskaia, Vitebskaia) confirming the inviolability of their old customs, rights, and privileges.

ustávnaia grámota: during the time of Emancipation (1861–63), a statutory charter or inventory specifying the size and location of a peasant allotment and the corresponding compensation to the landlord.

utverzhdénnaia (sobórnaia) grámota: the long charter adopted by the ZEMSKII SOBOR in February, 1613. It recounted historical events from olden times until the Time of Troubles, confirmed the election of the young Mikhail Fedorovich Romanov as tsar, and explained the reasons for his election to the throne; the character was signed on the reverse side by all the members present at the sobor.

verítel'naia grámota: diplomatic credentials.

vkládnaia grámota: charter conferring property to a monastery or a church, usually with the stipulation that the church would pray for the soul (*po dushe*) of the donor (after his death) and those of his relatives.

vól'naia grámota, or OTPUSKNÁIA: document releasing a bondman.

vópchaia grámota: a general charter, as distinct from one to a named person.

vótchinnaia (zhálovannaia) grámota: document giving an estate into hereditary ownership.

vvóznaia grámota: entry charter, a document empowering the new holder of an estate to take possession of it and ordering the peasants to be obedient to their new master.

vzmétnaia grámota: see RAZMETNAIA GRAMOTA.

zakládnaia grámota: document of pledge or mortgage.

zazývnaia grámota: summons before a court.

zhálobnaia grámota: written complaint presented to a government office.

zhálovannaia or *zháloval'naia grámota:* a charter granting properties, rights, privileges, or immunities.

grazhdanín, grázhdane. In modern Russian, citizen in general. In the official language of the 18th and 19th centuries the term grazhdane meant certain categories of the urban population. According to Peter the Great's statute of 1721 for the department of municipal government (*Reglament ili Ustav Glavnogo Magistrata*) the urban upper and middle classes (divided into two GIL'DII) were called *reguliarnye grazhdane,* while unskilled workers, day laborers, domestic servants, and serfs did not belong to the community of regular citizens. The charter of cities issued in 1785 designated one of the six categories of the urban population *imenitye grazhdane* (distinguished citizens). These included the former and incumbent elected city magistrates; educated people with high school diplomas; architects, painters, sculptors, and composers (members of or holders of diplomas from the academy of arts); and the big capitalists, bankers, and wholesale merchants.

pochëtnye grázhdane, potómstvennye i líchnye: honorable citizens, [both] hereditary and personal, a particular legal class (SOSLOVIE) established by Nicholas I's manifesto of April 10, 1832. It included government officials and persons with higher education who did not belong to the nobility, the upper group of merchants and industrialists, and the legitimate children of personal nobles. The members of this class enjoyed freedom from the soul tax, military conscription, and corporal punishment.

grid', or **grídi** (collect.). The junior retainers of a prince, a word of Scandinavian origin.

grídnitsa, -tsy. The house, hall, or barracks in the prince's court where his GRID' lived.

grívenka, -ki. A unit of weight in the 13th to 17th centuries. Two kinds of grivenka were most widely used: the *grivenka skalovaia* (from *skalvy,* scales), which equaled c. 205 grams or 48 Russian ZOLOTNIKI and was also called the *malaia* (small) *grivenka;* and the *bol'shaia grivenka,* equal to 96 zolotniki, which was also referred to as GRIVNA. A *grivenka rublevaia* (later called RUBL') was a silver bar weighing about 205 grams or half a pound.

grívennik, -ki. A silver coin, minted first in the time of Peter the Great, equal in value to 10 copecks.

grívna, -ny. An old unit of weight usually equal to c. 410 grams (or 96 Russian ZOLOTNIKI); it was called also *bol'shaia grivenka.* In the 18th century the grivna as a unit of weight was replaced by the FUNT (pound).

grívna, -ny. An old monetary unit. The word grivna supposedly meant originally a necklace made either of small silver coins or of small pieces of silver. Then grivna came to mean a unit of weight and a monetary unit, either real or for counting purposes. Monetary systems and their components in the Middle Ages, in Russia as elsewhere, differed in various regions, cities, and principalities and were continuously changing, so that it is difficult or almost impossible to compare the real values of medieval and modern monetary units. Sources of the Kievan period mention the *grivna kun* and the *grivna serebra* (silver grivna). KUNA or KUNITSA means marten, and it is generally accepted that before the appearance of a metallic monetary system the pelts of martens and other fur-bearing animals served as money in Russia. The grivna serebra was a silver bar weighing either about one pound or half a pound. In the 12th

27

century the grivna serebra was considered equal to 4 grivny kun. Sources of the 12th and 13th centuries mention also a difference between old *kuny* (*kuny vetkhie* or *starye*) and new ones (*kuny novye*). The grivna kun at various times contained as little as 20 and as many as 50 kuny. In the 14th and 15th centuries the grivna as the basic monetary unit was replaced by the RUBL'. In Muscovy of the 15th to 17th centuries the grivna was considered equal to 20 DENGI, and ten grivny made one rubl'. In the 18th century the term grivna was replaced by GRIVENNIK (a silver coin equal to 10 copecks). For additional information on grivna, see I. G. Spasskii, *Russkaia monetnaia sistema,* pp. 27–67; L. V. Cherepnin, *Russkaia metrologiia,* pp. 29–40; V. L. Ianin, *Denezhno-vesovye sistemy Russkogo srednevekoviia. Domongol'skii period;* D. I. Prozorovskii, *Moneta i ves v Rossii do kontsa XVIII stoletiia;* G. Vernadsky, *Medieval Russian Laws,* Introduction, p. 24; and S. G. Strumilin, *Ocherki ekonomicheskoi istorii Rossii,* pp. 33–38.

gromáda. See HROMADA.

grosh, -shi or **-shí** (Pol. *grosz,* Ger. *Groschen,* Lat. *grossus*). Any of several coins. In Russia the grosh was minted in the 1720s; it was equal to 4 DENGI or 2 copecks. In the 19th century a copper coin worth 2 copecks was minted without using the old name. The word grosh survived only in the vernacular to designate a minimal quantity of money (*ni grosha* = not a penny).

grosh litóvskii: a small coin in the Grand Duchy of Lithuania; a KOPA GROSHEI contained 60 groshi and corresponded approximately to the Muscovite POLTINA or half a RUBL'; one grosh was equal to 10 PENEZI.

grosh shirókii: a larger Lithuanian silver coin equal to approximately 20 Muscovite copecks.

grunt. See KGRUNT.

gubá, -by. 1. A sea bay in northern Russia. 2. A rural administrative district in northern and northwestern Russia. 3. After the 1540s a criminal judicial district headed by the elected GUBNOI STAROSTA with his assistants (GUBNYE TSELOVAL'NIKI). The gubnye organs investigated, prosecuted, and punished criminal offences in their districts, which in the 17th century coincided usually with UEZDY.

gubernátor, -ry. The head of the administration of a GUBERNIIA in imperial Russia. His rights and duties were stated in detail in the *obshchii nakaz grazhdanskim gubernatoram* (the general instruction for civil governors) of June 3, 1837. According to this instruction the gubernator, as NACHAL'NIK GUBERNII, was the head of the province, the chairman of the administrative organ called the GUBERNSKOE PRAVLENIE, the guardian (BLIUSTITEL') of the "supreme rights of the autocracy," and the chief protector of public order and well-being. With the introduction of local self-government in the second half of the 19th century, the gubernator was also entrusted with supervision of the ZEMSTVOS and municipal organs.

gubérniia, -ii. A major administrative division of imperial Russia. By his decree of December 18, 1708, Peter the Great divided Russia into eight large provinces or gubernii, each headed by a GUBERNATOR. In 1719 the number of guberniias was increased to eleven. Each guberniia was divided into several PROVINTSII headed by a VOEVODA or *vitse-gubernator.* The statute on guberniia administration (*Uchrezhdeniia dlia upravleniia gubernii*) of November 7, 1775, divided Russia into 40 guberniias headed by NAMESTNIKI or GENERAL-GUBERNATORY (in the 19th century by gubernatory), and created an elaborate system of guberniia and UEZD administration. Each guberniia was divided into several (on the average about 10) districts or uezdy. At the beginning of the 20th century there were 50 guberniias in European Russia not including Finland, Poland, and the Caucasus. Most of the provinces in the Caucasus, in Central Asia, and in the Far East corresponding to the guberni-

ias were called OBLASTI (divided into OKRUGA). In 1914, there were in the whole of the Empire 78 guberniias, 20 oblasti, and 2 separate okruga.

gubnói. See GUBA; also GRAMOTA.

gvalt. See KGVALT.

H

hétman, -ny. (from the Ger. *Hauptmann*). Chief military commander in the Grand Duchy of Lithuania and in Poland.

dvórnyi or *pól'nyi hétman:* an associate of the NAIVYSSHII HETMAN.

velíkii or *naivýsshii hétman:* supreme military commander with almost unlimited power over the soldiers during military expeditions.

hétman, in the Ukraine. From the end of the 16th century the military commander of the Ukrainian Cossacks, subordinate to the Polish *hetman koronny*. After the Cossack-Ukrainian revolution under the leadership of Bogdan Khmel'nitskii and after the Pereiaslavl' agreement with the Moscow government (in 1654), the hetman was recognized as supreme commander of the cossack military forces and head of the civil government in the Ukraine. After the division of the Ukraine between Russia and Poland according to the treaty of Andrusovo (1667), each of the two parts of the Ukraine (divided by the Dnieper River)

usually had its own hetman. At first the hetman of the left bank Ukraine was elected by the cossack RADA (the general meeting), later by the STARSHINA (military officers). In 1722 Peter the Great established the MALOROSSIISKAIA KOLLEGIIA (headed by a Russian brigadier) in Glukhov for the administration of the Ukraine and, after Hetman Skoropadskii's death (1722) prohibited the election of a new hetman. The post of hetman was filled again in 1727–34 and in 1750–64, but the real autonomy of the Ukraine was not reestablished. The Malorossiiskaia Kollegiia was abolished in 1728; in 1734 it was replaced by the *Malorossiiskoe pravlenie* (administration), and in 1764 it was reestablished under its old name; it consisted of eight members, four Ukrainians and four Great Russians. The *general-gubernator Malorossiiskii*, appointed by the Empress, was then vested with supreme authority in the Ukraine.

hromáda, -dy. A rural community in the Ukrainian and Belorussian regions and the meeting of its members.

I

iábednichestvo. Deliberately false accusation.

iábednik or **iábetnik, -ki.** In the Kievan and Novgorodian period, a prince's or court's agent, a bailiff. In Muscovy, a slanderer or calumniator, who presented to the court or to any office a deliberately false accusation against an innocent person.

iam, iámy (a Tatar word). 1. Post-horse stations placed on public roads every 40-50 VERSTAS (25-30 miles), serving the communication needs of the government. 2. *Iam,* or *iamskaia povinnost'.* The duty of the local population (the communities of TIAGLYE LIUDI) to help the government in the organization and maintenance of the system of communication and transportation called IAMSKAIA GON'BA. The population was obliged to build the post stations on the public roads, to hire post-drivers (IAMSHCHIKI), and to deliver horses and vehicles for traveling government agents and for the transportation of goods belonging to the government. In the 16th century this service duty was replaced by the monetary tax called IAMSKIE DENGI.

iamshchík, -kí. 1. Iamshchiki or IAMSKIE OKHOTNIKI in Muscovy were post-drivers, a special category of peasants who had to carry the mail and government goods, and to provide transportation for official travelers gratis and for private persons by agreement. At first they were selected and hired by the local communities individually; later they themselves formed professional communities. They lived in suburban settlements (IAMSKAIA SLOBODA) and owned arable lands and pastures for themselves and for their horses. 2. Sometimes the word iamshchik was used in documents to designate an agent who organized and directed the postal service. The more proper term for those agents in Muscovite documents was *iamskie prikazchiki* (pl.).

iarlýk, -kí. A Tatar term meaning a charter of the khan, esp. a charter granting privileges and immunities.

iarýga, iarýzhka, pl. **iarýzhnye.** In Muscovy, lower police servants taken from the TIAGLYE communities to serve as messengers, watchmen, and the like.

iása (*Yasa*). Mongol word meaning order or decree. The Great Yasa was the Imperial Code of Chingis-Khan drawn up in the early 1200s (see G. Vernadsky, *The Mongols and Russia,* pp. 99–109).

iasáchnye (*liúdi*) or **iasáchniki.** Native tributary people, mainly in Siberia and in the Ural region, who paid the government a tax in furs (IASAK).

iasák. A Mongol-Tatar word meaning tribute. After the Russian conquest of Siberia the native tribes of Siberia and of the Ural region paid the government a tax in furs, called the iasak, which in the 17th century was an important source of state revenue, used for the export trade and for payments to the tsar's servitors.

iasaúl. See ESAUL.

iasýr'. Turko-Tatar word meaning war prisoner, captive; in Muscovy it designated Oriental captives, esp. native captives in Siberia (it was officially prohibited to enslave a iasyr').

iatróv', -vi. Sister-in-law (brother's wife).

iávka, -ki. 1. Statement or declaration, request or application, presented to the court or to any other office. If presented in writing, it was called a *iavka pis'mennaia.* 2. Fee for the registration of a declaration or other document presented to an office. 3. In the *Ulozhenie* of 1649 (chap. 25, art. 20) iavka means also permission to keep and to sell a certain quantity of alcoholic drinks. 4. Presentation of goods intended for sale for registration, assessment, or taxation. 5. Fee or duty paid for the registration of goods intended for sale.

iávka gostínaia or **z gostéi.** A duty paid on goods imported by foreign merchants.

iazýk, -kí. 1. Language, tongue. 2. Nation, group of tribes, people in general (*Slovenskii iazyk* [collect.] = Slavs). 3. Heathen or foreigner. 4. Interpreter or guide. 5. Prisoner taken for the purpose of getting information about enemy forces. 6. Witness (in general). 7. In Muscovy, witness accusing somebody of perpetrating a crime.

ieréi, -ii (from Greek *hiereus* = SVIA-SHCHENNIK). Priest.

ieromonákh, -khi. A monk ordained as a priest.

igúmen, -ny (from Greek *hegoumenos*). Abbot, a head of a monastery.

igúmeniia, -ii (fem.). Head of a women's convent.

iménie, -iia. Property in general and, esp., a landed estate. In the statutes of the Grand Duchy of Lithuania in the 16th century, imenie was the normal term for a landed estate, while in Muscovy it was called either VOTCHINA (hereditary estate) or POMEST'E (estate on service tenure). After Peter the Great this difference was formally abolished. The imperial decree of March 17, 1731, designated votchiny and pomest'ia equally as *nedvizhimoe imenie votchina* (immovable property with full ownership). In the Russian Empire (mostly in the western regions) a *maioratnoe imenie* (or *maiorat*) was a landed estate conferred in entail. The Lithuanian Statutes of 1529 and 1566 distinguished several kinds of imeniia:

lezháchoe iménie: immovable property in general.

otchíznoe iménie: patrimonial estate.

rukhómoe iménie: movable property.

siábrenoe (or *sébrenoe*) *iménie:* property belonging to a group of small proprietors called SIABRY.

supólnoe iménie: landed estate held jointly by several proprietors.

zémskoe iménie: landed estate the holder of which was obligated to perform military service when demanded.

imperátor, -ry. This title of the Russian monarch was accepted by Peter the Great in 1721. According to the decree of November 11, 1721, the tsar's new title ran as follows: *Bozhieiu pospeshestvuiushcheiu milostiiu* [by God's helping grace] *My Petr Pervyi, Imperator i Samoderzhets* [autocrat] *vserossiiskii, Moskovskii, Kievskii, Vladimirskii, Novgorodskii, Tsar' Kazanskii, Tsar' Astrakhanskii, Tsar' Sibirskii* . . . Then followed a long list enumerating other possessions of the Russian crown. In 1809, after the annexation of Finland, the title *velikii*

kniaz' Finliandskii, and in 1815 the title *Tsar' Pol'skii,* were added to the Emperor's title. Often a short form of the title was used: *Imperator i Samoderzhets Vserossiiskii, Tsar' Pol'skii, Velikii Kniaz' Finliandskii, i prochaia, i prochaia, i prochaia* (and others).

imperiál, -ly. A golden coin, equal to 10 rubles, minted from 1755 through the 19th century. After Witte's monetary reform of 1897, the imperial was equated to 15 rubles.

Impériia Vserossíiskaia. Designation of the Russian state from Peter's act of October 22, 1721, until the abdication manifestoes of Nicholas II and his brother, Grand Duke Mikhail Aleksandrovich, on March 2–3, 1917. Although vserossiiskii is usually translated as all-Russian in this or other usages, it really meant nationwide or empirewide, pertaining to the whole political community, including Russians and non-Russians.

indíkt, -ty. In the Byzantine system of chronology, adopted by the Russian church, a fifteen-year period, with the year beginning on September first.

ínok, -ki (=CHERNETS, CHERNORIZETS, *mnikh, monakh*). Monk.

inokíniia, -ni. Nun.

inoródtsy (pl.). Ethnic groups with a special legal status. According to the Code of Laws (*Svod Zakonov,* ed. 1899, vol. IX, art. 762) the inorodtsy included the native tribes of Siberia, Central Asia, and Trans-Caspia; the Kalmyks and Kirghizes leading a nomadic life in the European and Asian steppes; the Samoyeds of the Archangel region; and the Jews.

inovérets, inovértsy. A term used in Russian legislation meaning persons belonging to one of the non-Christian religious faiths, such as Jews, Moslems, Buddhists, or heathens. Sometimes the term inovertsy was applied also to the Christians of a non-Orthodox denomination.

31

inozémets, -mtsy. Foreigner.

sluzhílye inozémtsy: foreigners hired by the Muscovite government.

inventár', -rí. In a special sense of the word, regulations covering peasants' work obligations and payments to their landlords, such as those introduced in 1847–48 by the government of Nicholas I in the provinces of Kiev, Volhynia, and Podolia.

iosifliánin, iosifliáne. Josephite, or follower of Iosif Sanin, Abbot of the Volok Monastery (d. 1515); their guiding principles were a close alliance of the church with the secular power, an emphasis on ritualism in church life, defense of the monasteries' landownership, and severe suppression of all kinds of heresies.

ishchéia, -ii (= ISTETS). Plaintiff.

ispolóvnik, -ki. See POLOVNIK.

ispráva. Due process of law; investigation, trial, and decision of a case, and satisfaction of the right party.

isprávnik, -ki. Chief of police in the UEZD; called also *zemskii ispravnik* or KAPITAN-ISPRAVNIK. The office was established by the statutes on guberniia administration of 1775. From 1775 until 1862 the ispravnik was elected by the uezd nobility; after 1862 he was appointed by the governor of the GUBERNIIA.

istéts, istsý. The primary meaning is plaintiff, but sometimes the term was applied to both litigant parties.

ístina or **ístoe.** The principal of a loan, the amount on which interest accrues.

istór or **istóra, -ry.** 1. Expenses. 2. Damages, losses.

iurt, iúrty (a Turkic word meaning habitations). Settlement or camp of the native tribes in the Eastern regions and the lands belonging to it. The word iurty was applied also, in the 16th and 17th centuries, to the Don Cossack settlements including their lands and waters.

izbá, ízby. 1. House (in modern Russian, esp. a peasant house). 2. Hall in a palace. 3. In Muscovy, an office building and the office itself.

prikáznaia izbá: an administrative office, esp. the office of the provincial VOEVODA.

razbóinaia izbá: central office directing the prosecution of robbers and bandits; in the second half of the 16th and the 17th centuries it was called the RAZBOINYI PRIKAZ.

s"ézzhaia izbá: PRIKAZNAIA IZBA.

stolóvaia izbá: the banquet hall in the Moscow Kremlin in which the ZEMSKII SOBOR usually assembled.

tamózhennaia izbá: customs house.

uézdnaia izbá: the building and the office of the UEZD administration.

vsegoródnaia izbá: the municipal meeting house in Pskov.

zémskaia izbá: town hall; the place where the elected officials (ZEMSKIE STAROSTY and SUDII) administered justice for the local population and collected taxes.

izbirátel', -li. Constituent elector, the term applied in 1905–17 to persons qualified to take part in the State Duma elections.

izbylói, -lýe. Unregistered person, erroneously or wrongly omitted either from the lists of service men or from the tax lists.

izdél'e (see BARSHCHINA, corvée). Peasants' obligatory work for their landlords. *Izdél'nye krest'iane = bárshchinnye krest'iane,* peasants on corvée.

izgói, izgói. "The declassés of the Kievan civilization" (J. Blum, p. 55). "Various displaced social elements, such as freed slaves" (N. Riasanovsky, p. 54). The izgoi were either freemen or persons who had lost their legal status and economic position and put themselves under the protection of the church or of some secular lord; they were obliged to work for their protectors.

izliúb. Communal election in Muscovy; certificate of election.

izliúblennyi: elected person.

izórnik, -ki. Literally, plower, sharecropper; in the Pskov region, a tenant farmer who, by agreement with the landlord, leased a plot of arable land and usually received from his landlord some aid or loan (POKRUTA) in money, grain, or agricultural implements.

izvét, -ty. 1. Pretext, excuse. 2. Fraud, deception (*bez izveta* [in treaties]: without fraud). 3. Denunciation, accusation.

izvétnik, -ki. 1. A court agent. 2. Denunciator, informer, witness for the prosecution in court.

K

kabák, -kí. Tavern, a place for the sale and consumption of liquor, mainly vodka, which was a very important source of state revenue in Muscovy as well as in the Empire. The Moscow government either farmed out the sale of vodka in kabaki to OTKUPSHCHIKI, or managed the sale of vodka through *kabatskie golovy* and TSELOVAL'NIKI selected from the local population. The systems of farming and liquor excise changed during the 18th and 19th centuries. (See OTKUP.) The word kabak acquired a bad reputation in the eyes of officialdom, and the government changed the official name of the kabak in the second half of the 17th century to *piteinyi* or *kruzhechnyi dvor,* and then in the 18th century to *piteinoe zavedenie* (drinking establishment). But in the vernacular the word kabak retained its popularity, and the end of this highly popular "establishment" was brought about only by the state monopoly on spirits introduced in 1894–96 (vodka drinking inside state liquor stores was prohibited).

kabalá, -lý (an Arabic or Turkish word). In the legal language of the 15th-17th centuries it meant: (1) written acknowledgment of debt, a promissory note, called also *zaiëmnaia kabala;* (2) *sluzhilaia kabala* or obligation *za rost sluzhiti,* a contract of servitude, a pledge of individual lifelong service instead of payment of interest for a monetary loan; or (3) debt servitude itself, called also KABAL'NOE KHOLOPSTVO.

Kabinét Egó Imperátorskogo Velíchestva. In the 19th century, an office managing the properties belonging to the emperor. After 1826 it formed a part of the Imperial Court Ministry (MINISTERSTVO IMPERATORSKOGO DVORA).

Kabinét pri dvoré Eë Imperátorskogo Velíchestva (at the court of Her Majesty). Established by decree of Empress Anna, November 10, 1731, as the supreme government body consisting of three persons named *kabinetministry,* it was abolished by Empress Elizabeth's decree of December 12, 1741.

kad', -di. An old dry measure equal, approximately, to 14 poods (1 pood or PUD = 36 lbs.) (L. Cherepnin, p. 43); one quarter of it was a CHETVERT'.

kadét, -ty. 1. In imperial Russia: cadet, student of a military school (SEE KORPUS KADETSKII). 2. In the colloquial language after 1905, a member of the Constitutional Democratic Party (see PARTIIA KONSTITUTSIONNO-DEMOKRATICHESKAIA).

kagán. The old Turkic title for the head of the state. In the 8th to 10th centuries it was the title of the Khazar Khan. In the famous Eulogy of Metropolitan Hilarion (c. 1051–54) this title was applied to Grand Prince Vladimir of Kiev (d. 1015).

kamergér, -ry. An honorary court rank in the 18th and 19th centuries, granted to many higher civil officials.

kameńr: zémskie kameríry. A kind of provincial finance official instituted by Peter the Great to control tax collecting and bookkeeping. The order concerning his duties was issued on January 7, 1719. The office was abolished in 1727.

kameriúnker, -ry. A low rank at the imperial court, granted to young people from aristocratic families.

Kámer-kollégiia. An office established in 1718 to manage state revenues and to direct measures for improvement of the national economy. Abolished in 1785. (See KOLLEGIIA.)

kantoníst, -ty. In 1805–56, the term for the young sons of active soldiers; they were educated and trained in government schools and, after they had come of age, were obligated to enter the active army.

kantseliáriia, -rii. Office. In the 18th and 19th centuries each collegial government office had two divisions: (1) a PRISUTSTVIE (council), a policy-making body of the high officials, and (2) a kantseliariia, a bureau consisting of clerks and headed, normally, by a SEKRETAR'; it managed the correspondence and prepared reports for the prisutstvie. At the beginning of Peter the Great's reign, the council of boyars was called the *blizhniaia* (near) *kantseliariia*. In the 18th century the *tainaia* (secret) *kantseliariia* (or EKSPEDITSIIA) was the office of the political police (abolished in 1801). In the 19th century the kantselariia of the State Council was called the *gosudarstvennia kantseliariia,* and its head was the GOSUDARSTVENNYI SEKRETAR'.

kántsler, -ry. The highest rank in the civil service of the Russian Empire. In the 18th and 19th centuries the persons bearing this rank headed the foreign office (the last of them was Prince A. M. Gorchakov in 1867–82). In the Grand Duchy of Lithuania, the kantsler headed the state's KANTSELIARIIA and the state archives (METRIKA).

kapitán, -ny. Captain. In the army, an officer of the 8th class according to the TABEL' O RANGAKH. In the navy, *kapitan pervogo ranga* was the rank of the 6th class, corresponding to the POLKOVNIK in the army. *Kapitan vtorogo ranga* (the 7th class) corresponded to the PODPOLKOVNIK in the army. Kapitan also meant the commanding officer of a warship or of a merchant vessel.

Kapitán-isprávnik: the head of the district police according to the statutes on guberniia administration of 1775.

kaprál, -ly. Corporal; in the 19th century this rank was replaced by that of *mladshii* (younger) UNTER-OFITSER.

kápshchina or **kápshchizna.** In the Grand Duchy of Lithuania, excise from liquor paid by the tavern (KORCHMA) operators.

kashtelián, kashtelán, -ny (Pol. *kasztelan,* Lat. *castellanus*). The holder of an office (a *kashtelianiia*) established in the Grand Duchy of Lithuania on the Polish model (eleven of the thirteen kashtelianii were established in 1565–66). The kashtelian was the associate of the provincial VOEVODA as military commander; he was especially the commander of the castle (*castellum*) and its garrison, as well as of the mobilized SZLACHTA of the POVET.

kássa, -sy. 1. Treasury, office receiving and paying out money. 2. An insurance benefit fund. *Bol'nichnye kassy* were established by a law of June 23, 1912, as sick benefit funds for industrial workers, based on contributions from workers and management. The funds were managed jointly by the manufacturers and the workers' representatives.

kat, -ty. In the Grand Duchy of Lithuania, executioner, hangman.

kátorga. See RABOTY KATORZHNYE.

kazák, -ki, -kí (Ukrainian *kozak*). "The

34

word is supposed to derive from the Turkic word *kazak* which denotes a free frontiersman" (G. Vernadsky, *Kievan Russia,* p. 78). In the 16th and 17th centuries the most important cossack communities were the Ukrainian Cossacks and the three Russian hosts, the Don, Iaik (later known as the Ural), and Terek. The chief stronghold of the Ukrainian host was the ZAPOROZHSKAIA SECH' (*sich'*) below the rapids on the lower Dnieper River. All cossack communities were organized on democratic principles and governed by their elected ATAMANS. The ethnically mixed cossack communities were reinforced by a steady influx of peasants and slaves fleeing from oppressive burdens in Muscovy and in the Ukraine. They lived in almost incessant struggle with their Tatar and Turkish neighbors. In the 17th century (until 1671) the Don Cossacks were free allies of the Moscow government, which supported them regularly with grain, money, and military supplies. After the Razin rebellion they had to take a special loyalty oath to the tsar, and in the 18th century they gradually lost their freedom and became the tsar's subjects. Besides the free cossacks there were in the southern and eastern border regions of Muscovy, in the 16th and 17th centuries, *gorodovye* or *sluzhilye kazaki,* who formed part of the garrison in fortified cities and performed military service under the command of Muscovite VOEVODY. They usually lived in a suburban settlement called a *kazatskaia sloboda.*

The Ukrainian Cossacks, both Zaporozhians and registered cossacks (originally units in the Polish army), were the main activists in the anti-Polish uprisings in the Ukraine and in the revolution started by Bogdan Khmel'nitskii in 1648. After that the cossacks formed a dominant military class in the autonomous Ukraine (ruled by the elected HETMAN) under the protectorate of the Moscow tsars. In the 18th century the Russian government limited their autonomous status more and more until the Zaporozhian *Sech'* was abolished in 1775, and cossack regiments in the Ukraine were disbanded in 1783. The majority of the Zaporozhians were resettled in the Kuban' region and formed a new cossack host in the northern Caucasus; a minority emigrated to Turkey.

During the 19th century the Russian government furthered the establishment of new cossack forces in the southern and eastern borderlands of the vast empire in Asia. The cossacks formed regiments of irregular cavalry in the Russian army, and were defenders as well as colonizers of the borderlands. By the beginning of the 20th century there were eleven cossack hosts: Don, Kuban', Terek, Orenburg, Ural, Astrakhan', Siberia, Semirechensk, Transbaikal, Amur, and Ussuri. Each cossack VOISKO (host or force) included not only the combat personnel but all their dependents as well. The cossacks therefore formed a special social and legal class (SOSLOVIE) in imperial Russia, numbering over 3,000,000 people at the beginning of the 20th century. The cossacks drew their supplies largely from arable lands and pastures and were obligated to furnish their own horses when they entered army service.

kazák, kazakí. In the northern regions of Muscovy the term *kazak* was applied to hired workers.

kazánie, -niia (W.R.). Order, command, instruction.

kazn'. Punishment in general. (In the Grand Duchy of Lithuania, also, prison.)

smértnaia kazn': capital punishment, death penalty.

torgóvaia kazn' in Muscovy: flogging the culprit with the knout in the market square (*na torgu*).

kazná. A term used from the 14th century on. 1. Storehouse or depot for keeping all kinds of movable property; the property itself, including money, precious metals, furs, and so on. 2. Treasury, a financial office of the state; the state itself in its economic and financial aspects. The commonly used adjective *kazënnyi* meant belonging to the state. In Muscovy *kazna gosudareva* meant the state's financial apparatus in all its forms.

kaznachéi, -ii. Treasurer, a term used in Muscovy from the 14th century on. The statutes of 1775 on GUBERNIIA administration established the offices of the *uezdnyi, gubernskii* and *gosudarstvennyi kaznachei* (district, provincial, and state treasurer). The latter office was abolished with the establishment of the Ministry of Finance in 1802; the first and second existed until the Revolution of 1917.

kaznachéistvo, -va. Treasury office.

uézdnoe, gubérnskoe, and *gosudárstvennoe kaznachéistvo:* financial offices established in 1775 for receiving state revenues, keeping cash, and paying out money for all kinds of state expenses.

kelár', -ri. (Greek *kellarios*). Steward in a monastery. Before the state took over the monasteries' landed properties (in 1763) the *kelar'* was also the manager of the monasteries' landed possessions and their peasant population.

késar', -ri. The old Russian term for *Caesar*, monarch, emperor.

kgrunt, -ty. A landed estate in the Grand Duchy of Lithuania.

kgvalt, -ty (from the Ger. *Gewalt*) in the Grand Duchy of Lithuania. 1. Unexpected invasion by enemy forces. 2. Violence or attack in general. 3. Fine for perpetrated violence.

kgvaltóvnik, -ki. A criminal in the sense of perpetrator of acts of violence.

khártiia or **kháratiia, -tii** (from the Greek *chartia*). Parchment; charter; treaty.

khleb. 1. Bread. 2. Crops. 3. Grain. 4. Means of subsistence. 5. Duty in kind in Muscovy.

posópnyi khleb: the dues in grain that peasants in Siberia had to deliver for the support of Muscovite service men.

Sibírskii khleb: a duty in kind at the end of the 16th and during the 17th centuries. The peasants of northern and eastern regions in Muscovy were obliged to deliver grain for the sustenance of service men in Siberia. The exaction of the Sibirskii khleb was abolished in 1683–84, when Siberian agriculture became sufficiently developed to satisfy local needs.

strelétskii khleb: a duty in kind in Muscovy consisting of grain deliveries for the maintenance of the STREL'TSY units; during the 17th century it was gradually changed to monetary payments.

khlebopáshets, -tsy. Literally grain-plower.

svobódnye khlebopáshtsy: free cultivators. A law of February 20, 1803, authorized the liberation of serfs (with land allotments) by mutual agreement with their landlords. These peasants formed, within the state peasantry, a group called svobodnye khlebopashtsy. During the years 1803–55, 113,000 male peasants, about one percent of the serf population, entered the class of free cultivators.

khlop, khlópy (from the Pol. *chlop*). In the Grand Duchy of Lithuania, a peasant.

khodátai, -ii. Petitioner, solicitor.

khodátaistvo, -va. Request, petition.

khodók, -kí. Literally, walker or traveler. In general, a representative of peasant communities sent to solicit government offices in matters concerning communal interests. In a particular case, at the end of the 19th and in the beginning of the 20th century, the term khodoki was applied to the elected scouts who were sent into Siberia and Central Asia by peasants who wished to migrate there, with the purpose of exploring possible sites for settlement.

kholóp, -py. A male slave. (The corresponding term for a female slave was ROBA.) The slave in old Russia, as elsewhere, was considered not a person but, legally, movable property of his master. To emphasize the status of full bondage, the old documents used the terms *kholopy obel'nye* or *odernovatye;* later in Muscovy: *kholopy polnye, dokladnye* (whose bondage was confirmed by the DOKLADNAIA GRAMOTA), *kuplenye* (bought), or *starinnye* (inherited). A particular and important kind of slave in Muscovy in the 15th–17th centuries was the *kholop kabal'nyi.* He entered bondage status by means of the KABALA (KABAL'-NAIA GRAMOTA, *kabal'naia zapis'*), which was a pledge of lifelong service instead of payment of interest for a monetary loan. If the master of a kabal'nyi kholop died before him, the kholop, his wife, and children recovered their liberty (*Ulozhenie* of 1649, chap. XX, art. 15). The RUSSKAIA PRAVDA and still more the Muscovite legislation devoted much attention to regulating the legal status of bondage. In the *Ulozhenie* of 1649 the whole of Chap. XX, consisting of 119 articles, was devoted to legal regulations concerning KHOLOPSTVO. In the second half of the 17th century the class of slaves in Muscovy became too numerous for the masters' court services, and the masters settled their kholopy "behind the court" (*za dvorom*) for the cultivation of their arable lands. Such bondmen were named ZADVORNYE or DELOVYE LIUDI. When Peter the Great introduced the poll tax in 1719–23, he ordered the inclusion in the tax lists of all the landlords' subjects—the peasants and BOBYLI, the *polnye* and kabal'nye kholopy, the delovye liudi and the

domestic servants as well, without distinction as to their legal status—and all these classes were obliged to pay the poll tax at an equal rate. Thereafter slavery as a special legal institution, and the slaves as a particular legal class, disappeared in Russia, and the entire rural population living on privately owned landed estates formed the legally uniform mass of the KREPOSTNYE LIUDI (bondmen or serfs). In fact, with the virtually unlimited power of the landlords over their subjects, the legal status of the bondmen or serfs in the second half of the 18th century was not far away from the old slavery, and even the word RABY (slaves) was often applied to serfs.

kholóp gosudárev. The sovereign's slave, a designation the service men in Muscovy usually applied to themselves in addressing the tsar in writing or in speech.

kholópstvo. Status of servitude (slavery).

obél'noe, pólnoe, dokládnoe, starínnoe, or *kabál'noe kholópstvo:* see KHOLOP.

khorómy (pl.). A mansion.

khorúgov', -gvi. Banner, standard. In Russia, usually a church banner with sacred pictures. In the Grand Duchy of Lithuania, military standard, colors, and the military unit standing under the same banner.

povétovaia khorúgov': a banner and the military unit that included the SZLACHTA of the same POVET (district).

khorúnzhii, -zhie. An officer rank in Russian cossack regiments corresponding to the KORNET in the regular cavalry and the PODPORUCHIK (second lieutenant) in the infantry.

khorúzhii, -zhie. In the Grand Duchy of Lithuania, standard-bearer and military commander.

khorúzhii dvórnyi: associate of the KHORUZHII ZEMSKII.

khorúzhii povétovyi: standard-bearer and commander of the military unit formed by the SZLACHTA of the POVET (district).

khorúzhii zémskii: the chief standard-bearer and assistant to the HETMAN NAIVYSSHII.

khozhdénie po delám obshchéstvennym. 1. Walking (in sense of traveling) in matters concerning peasant communities. 2. The representation of a peasant community to government offices on behalf of its interests and needs. 3. The prosecution of community lawsuits.

khózhenoe. In Muscovy, the walking-distance fee or travel allowance for court messengers when they performed their duties inside a city.

khútor, -rá. A consolidated individual farmstead where a peasant, with his family, lived outside the village. The advancement of such farmsteads was one of the main goals of the Stolypin agrarian reform started in 1906.

kírka, -ki (Ger. *Kirche*). German Protestant churches. The *Ulozhenie* of 1649 (chap. XIX, art. 40) prohibited *nemetskie kirki* inside the city of Moscow, but permitted them in the Moscow suburbs "faraway from the [Orthodox] churches of God."

kizilbáshets, kizil'báshets, -shtsy. A Muscovite term for Persians. In the 17th century the Moscow merchants complained of commercial competition from Persian merchants coming to Russia.

kleinóty (pl., Pol. *klejnot*, from Ger. *Kleinod*). Literally, precious things. Insignia of power. Kleinoty of the Ukrainian hetman were the BUNCHUK, BULAVA (scepter), banner, and seal.

klet', -ti. A separate part of a house or an annex serving as a storeroom.

klir (Greek *kleros*, Lat. *clerus*). The clergy.

klírik, -ki. Clergyman.

kliroshánin, -áne, -áni. Clergyman or church servitor or singer.

kliúchnik, -ki, or **kliúshnik, -ki** (from *kliuch,* key). A housekeeper; a steward; a manager of a monastery's landed estate.

kmet', -ti (Pol. *kmiec*). In the Kievan period, warrior, military servitor. In Poland and in the Grand Duchy of Lithuania, peasant.

kniaz', kniaziiá, kniaz'iá, kniázi, kniazháta. Prince. Before the coming of the Varangian princes, in the 9th century, the eastern Slavic tribes of Poliane, Drevliane, Krivichi, and others had their own princes and princelings called kniaziia. Oleg—who became the ruler of Kiev in 882 and then united under his power the tribes of the eastern Slavs and the neighboring Finns—and his successor Igor' had the title *velikii kniaz' Ruskii* (they were so designated in the Russian versions of the treaties with Byzantium of 911 and 945). Later the Kievan prince bore the title *velikii kniaz' Kievskii.* After Yaroslav's death (1054) the great Kievan realm disintegrated into a group of separate principalities, and the process of disintegration continued during the 12th and 13th centuries. Each of the principalities (KNIAZHENIE) was headed by one of the descendants of Riurik who had been ruler, military commander, supreme judge, and legislator in his own domain. But during the Kievan period the prince's power was limited by the occasional intervention of the VECHE (people's assembly), which sometimes expelled an unpopular prince and invited a more acceptable one. The veche occasionally intervened also in decisions concerning war and peace with neighboring principalities or with foreign powers. In Novgorod the Great, the relations between the prince and the community and the limits of the prince's power were usually regulated by mutual treaties, and the prince here became in fact an elected official of the Novgorodian people.

During the 13th and 14th centuries the eastern Russian lands came under the power of the Tatar khans, and the western under the power of the Grand Dukes of Lithuania (of the Gedimin dynasty). At that time in eastern Russia the Grand Prince of Vladimir (*velikii kniaz' Vladimirskii*) was considered the senior Russian prince, but he himself was a subject of the Tatar khan and needed the khan's confirmation to keep his title and position. Under the supreme power of the Tatar khan the disintegration of large Russian principalities into many lesser ones continued as the descendants of Riurik multiplied and each received his own UDEL (appanage, a separate or apportioned possession) after his father's death. Several larger principalities were headed by princes who bore the title of grand prince, such as the *velikii kniaz' Vladimirskii* (later *Vladimirskii i Moskovskii*), and the princes of Tver', Riazan', Iaroslavl' and several others. The many small princes inside the larger regions were called *udel'nye kniaziia* (appanage princes). This process continued until the Grand Prince of Vladimir and Moscow started to consolidate the Russian territories in the 14th and 15th centuries, first with help of the Tatar khan, and after 1480 as an independent monarch. The numerous former udel'nye kniaziia formed then in Muscovy a group called *sluzhilye* or *sluzhebnye kniaziia,* who became the higher stratum of the service aristocracy in Moscow. This group increased as princes of foreign regions, such as Lithuania (*Riurikovichi* and *Gediminovichi,* descendants of Riurik and Gedimin), Georgia, and the Tatar countries, came into Moscow and entered Muscovite service.

During the imperial period the emperor granted the titles of *graf* (count) and kniaz' to his military or civil service men as a reward for outstanding service, whereas in Muscovy the title of kniaz' could only be inherited.

In the Grand Duchy of Lithuania the princes (KNIAZIIA, KNIAZOVE, KNIAZHATA), the descendants of Riurik and Gedimin, together with the Lithuanian PANY (lords), formed a powerful group of feudal aristocrats. In the late 15th and first half of the 16th centuries they even formally limited the power of the grand duke, who could not make any important decision without the advice and consent of the PANY-RADA (the aristocratic state council). *Velikii kniaz' Litovskii:* the usual title of the grand duke of Lithuania was as follows: *velikii kniaz' Litovskii, Ruskii, Pruskii, Zhomoitskii, Mazovetskii i inykh* (and others).

kniaz' kórmlenyi, in Novgorod the Great: in the 14th and 15th centuries, a prince whom the Novgorodians hired as a military commander, and to whom they gave certain towns or territories as KORMLENIE, the means of subsistence for him and his DRUZHINA.

kniázhata, kniazháta, or **kniázove.** In Muscovy, a collective name for the service princes. In the Grand Duchy of Lithuania, the group of feudal aristocracy consisting of descendants of the Lithuanian and West Russian *udel'nye* princes (*Gediminovichi* and *Riurikovichi*).

kniazhénie, -niia or **kniázhestvo, -va.** The power of the prince and the principality itself.

kníga, -gi. Book in general; the Holy Scripture; charter, letter; roll of paper or of parchment.

bárkhatnaia kníga: the velvet book, the register of the most aristocratic families, drawn up in Moscow after the abolition of MESTNICHESTVO in 1682.

dozórnaia kníga: government registers made in the 17th century as a result of updating previous population and

39

tax records (PISTSOVYE KNIGI) for the purpose of registering ownership of land and peasants and revising tax assessments.

gorodováia obyvátel'skaia kníga: a register of city dwellers as ordered by the charter of cities of 1785.

Kórmchaia kníga: the Russian (Church Slavic) version of the Byzantine NOMOKANON (digest of church canons and of some civil and penal laws). It was first printed in Moscow in 1650 under Patriarch Iosif, and then revised by Patriarch Nikon and printed in 1653. The Nikon Kormchaia was reissued in 1787 (in slightly revised form). The Iosif Kormchaia was (and still is) recognized by the Old Believers. It was reprinted in Moscow in 1912.

okládnaia or *okladnáia kníga:* book or register setting forth norms either for the payment of various taxes to the state or for various emoluments given by the state to its service men (in the form of POMEST'IA, money, grain, etc.)

pistsóvaia and *perepísnaia kníga:* pistsovye knigi (the oldest in existence dates from the end of the 15th century) contained a detailed description of all taxable objects, including population, homesteads, arable lands, pastures, and city businesses. The last such cadastre was completed in 1630. In the middle and later 17th century the censuses, called perepisnye knigi, registered only homesteads and their inhabitants belonging to the TIAGLYE (taxpaying) LIUDI.

rodoslóvnye knígi: registers of the noble (DVORIANSKIE) families.

rozmëtnaia or *razmëtnaia kníga:* communal book apportioning the total amount of tax imposed on a community among the various homesteads according to their economic strength.

rozriádnye or *razriádnye knígi:* lists containing the records of appointments of army officers and high civil officials

in Muscovy. They were compiled in the ROZRIADNYI PRIKAZ from the end of the 15th century.

knígi skazániia: in the Grand Duchy of Lithuania, books containing records of court decisions.

statéinye knígi, in Muscovy: (1) books including laws and decrees issued in the period between 1550 (when the Second *Sudebnik* was issued) and 1649 (when the *Ulozhenie* was published); (2) records of Moscow diplomats about their travels abroad and their negotiations with foreign governments.

ukáznye knígi prikázov: collections of boyar duma decisions (PRIGOVORY) and the tsar's decrees issued in the second half of the 16th and the first half of the 17th centuries in Muscovy, being laws added to, or interpretations of, the enactments contained in the *Sudebnik* of 1550.

ulózhennaia kníga: the Code of Laws issued in 1649, also called the ULOZHENIE or *Sobornoe Ulozhenie.*

kollégiia (or **kollégium**), **-gii.** Ministry or central government department in the 18th century. Nine were established by Peter the Great in 1717–18; several others came later. According to the decree of December 11, 1717, each kollegiia consisted of a president, a vice-president (Russian or foreigner in Russian service), four councillors (SOVET-NIKI), four assessors, and a chancellery; one councillor or assessor in each was to be a foreigner. The colleges replaced a cumbersome collection of Muscovite PRIKAZY. The nine colleges first established were:

Admiraltéiskaia Kollegiia: navy.

Berg-i-Manufaktúr-Kollegiia: mining and industry.

Kollegiia Inostránnykh Del: foreign affairs.

Iustíts-Kollegiia: justice.

Kám(m)er-Kollegiia: state revenues.

Kommérts-Kollegiia: commerce.

Revizión-Kollegiia: financial inspection and auditing.

Shtats-Kontóra (or *Shtats-Kontór-Kollegiia*): state expenses.

Vóinskaia Kollegiia: army.

The *Revizion-Kollegiia* was soon added to the Senate to check on all government institutions. The *Berg-i-Manufaktur-Kollegiia* was in 1719 divided into two separate offices. (See BERG-KOLLEGIIA and MANUFAKTUR-KOLLEGIIA.) The *Dukhovnaia Kollegiia* (ecclesiastical college) was established November 20, 1718, to replace the power and authority of the Patriarch of Moscow, and received its statutes (REGLAMENT) on January 25, 1721. It consisted of ten bishops and higher clerics appointed by the tsar and put under the supervision of the chief procurator (OBER-PROKUROR), who acted as the "tsar's eye." The later name for this highest church administration was SVIATEISHII PRAVITEL'STVUIUSCHII SINOD (Holy Governing Synod). In 1721 the *Votchinnaia Kollegiia* (replacing the Moscow POMESTNYI PRIKAZ) was established for matters concerning landed estates. In 1722 in Glukhov the *Malorossiiskaia Kollegiia* (headed by a Russian brigadier) was opened for the administration of the Ukrainian regions. It was abolished in 1728 and reestablished in 1764; at that time it consisted of four Ukrainians and four Russians, under the chairmanship of the *Malorossiiskii* GENERAL-GUBERNATOR, Count P. A. Rumiantsev. It was abolished in 1786. The *Kollegiia Ekonomii* was established in 1726 for the administration of landed properties belonging to the church institutions (chiefly monasteries). It was abolished in 1744 and reestablished in 1762–63 when the state took over the church's landed properties. In 1763 the *Meditsinskaia Kollegiia* was established for furthering medical education and medical care. It was absorbed into the Ministry of the Interior in 1802. In 1785–86 most of the colleges established by Peter the Great were abolished. Some of them were reestablished by Paul I. Only three of the old Petrine colleges —the army, navy, and foreign affairs —survived uninterruptedly until 1802, when they were transformed into the corresponding ministries.

kollégiia. Term used for some educational institutions.

kólo. 1. Wheel, circle. 2. Assembly of Zaporozhian Cossacks. 3. A chamber in the *seim* (parliament) of the Grand Duchy of Lithuania. After the reforms of 1565–66 the seim was composed of the two kolos: 1) The *kolo panov-rady* (see PANY-RADA) was an aristocratic chamber consisting of bishops, princes, and lords (PANY); some of them were present in the capacity of high state officials, others used their old hereditary or personal right to attend the RADA (state council). 2) The *kolo rytsarskoe* was composed of the representatives of the nobility (SZLACHTA), who elected two representatives from each POVET (district) to the seim; they were then called *posly povetovye.* The Polish group in the State Duma (1906–17) was called the *Pol'skoe Kolo.*

kolódnik, -ki. Prisoner of war or imprisoned criminal (from *kolodki,* stocks).

kománda, -dy. 1. Command. 2. Military detachment. 3. Ship's crew.

komissár, -ry. 1. *Zemskie komissary* were district administrators under Peter the Great. Their chief duty was to collect taxes in money and in kind for the sustenance of the army. They were subordinate to the KAMER-KOLLEGIIA. The order concerning their duties was issued on January 7, 1719. The office was abolished in 1727. 2. Komissary in the Grand Duchy of Lithuania were officials entrusted by the grand duke with the examination and decision of law suits.

komíssiia, -ii (and KOMITÉT). Commission. Term for numerous permanent or temporary government and quasi-governmental bodies established in Russia during the imperial period.

komíssiia dlia sochinéniia proékta nóvogo Ulozhéniia: the commission for drawing up a new Code of Laws; also called the Large Commission (*Bol'shaia Komissiia*) or the Legislative Commission (*Zakonodatel'naia Komissiia*); the latter term is incorrect, for the commission had only consultative powers. This commission, established by the decrees of December 14, 1766, and January 4, 1767, convened in Moscow in July 1767. It received from Empress Catherine a long instruction (NAKAZ) inspired by liberal ideas of the Enlightenment and based chiefly on the writings of Montesquieu and the Italian jurist Beccaria. The commission consisted of 564 deputies; 28 were representatives of the highest government institutions (the Senate, the Synod, and the colleges); all the others were elected representatives of various classes of the population: 161 deputies from the landed gentry, 208 from the townspeople (chiefly merchants), 79 from the state peasantry, 54 from the cossacks, and 34 from the INORODTSY (Samoyeds, Bashkirs, and others). The deputies brought with them written instructions from their constituencies expressing their desires and complaints. The discussions in the commission even touched upon the ticklish question of serfdom, but the deputies were unable to produce specific legislative proposals. With the outbreak of war against Turkey in 1768, the Large Commission was disbanded. It was not convoked again, and the work of legislation remained in the hands of the imperial bureaucracy.

redaktsiónnye komíssii: editing commissions, established in March 1859 to discuss the plans for peasant emancipation presented by the provincial committees, and to work out the general plans for peasant reform. They were three in number, but they worked jointly under the common chairmanship of General Ia. I. Rostovtsev, and, after his death, Count V. N. Panin. The commissions completed their work in October 1860.

verkhóvnaia rasporiadítel'naia komíssia: supreme administrative commission, established in February 1880 under the chairmanship of Count M. T. Loris-Melikov, with almost dictatorial power to suppress the revolutionary terrorist movement; the goal was seemingly attained and the commission was abolished in August 1880, when Loris-Melikov was appointed minister of internal affairs.

(uézdnye and *gubérnskie)zemleustroítel'nye komíssii:* district and provincial land-organization or land-settlement commissions, established by decree of March 4, 1906. During Stolypin's agrarian reform (started in November 1906) the zemleustroitel'nye komissii were entrusted with the important and complex task of apportioning and delimiting peasant plots for their transfer from communal to private ownership. The commissions consisted of local officials and of representatives from the ZEMSTVO and from the peasants.

komitét, -ty. Committee (see KOMISSIIA).

gubérnskie dvoriánskie komitéty po krest'iánskomu dély: committees of provincial landlords and officials, established in 1857–58. They were to consider suggested plans for peasant reform and to present them to the editing commissions (REDAKTSIONNYE KOMISSII) charged with working out the general plan for the reform, to be approved by the GLAVNYI KOMITET and by the State Council.

komitét minístrov: the Committee of Ministers. Before 1905 it was not a united government cabinet but only a meeting of the ministers for consultation, after which the appropriate minister had to report each question to the tsar for decision.

komitét po krest'iánskomu délu: committee for peasant affairs. The *osobyi* (special) komitet po krest'ianskomu delu established in January 1857 was at first secret like its predecessors, but by the decree of February 21, 1858, it was turned into the *glavnyi* (chief) komitet po krest'ianskomu delu and the secrecy was lifted. The committee, under the chairmanship of the tsar's brother Grand Duke Konstantin Nikolaevich, supervised and directed the preparation of the peasant reform preceding the liberation manifesto of February 19, 1861.

sekrétnye komitéty: committees set up by Nicholas I. Shocked and frightened by the Decembrist rebellion, Nicholas became aware of many shortcomings in the Russian social structure and state administration and he tried to improve the existing conditions from above. With this purpose in mind, he appointed, beginning in 1826, a series of sekretnye komitety to discuss measures for improvement in state administration and for gradual limitations of serfdom. The committees were composed of the highest state officials and were ordered to make their plans and proposals for reform in strict secrecy. The practical results of this eager bureaucratic endeavor were very modest.

voénno-promýshlennye komitéty: war-industries committees. Local committees, headed by the *Tsentral'nyi Voenno-Promyshlennyi Komitet,* were established in Russia in the summer of 1915 in order to alleviate the disastrous shortage of munitions at the front through a voluntary mobilization of private industry for defense work. The official regulations for the war-industries committees were issued on September 9, 1915.

komórnik, -ki. In the Grand Duchy of Lithuania, assistant to a PODKOMORYI; agent of other government or municipal officials.

kondítsii (pl.). Conditions, specifically those related to events in 1730. After the death of the boy-emperor Peter II, the VERKHOVNYI TAINYI SOVET (the Supreme Secret Council), consisting of eight aristocratic members, invited Anna, Duchess of Kurland (daughter of Ivan V and niece of Peter the Great), to ascend the Russian throne on condition that the real power should be in the hands of the Supreme Secret Council. The duchess accepted and signed the konditsii, but after arriving in Moscow and ascertaining that the gentry as a whole did not sympathize with the oligarchic plans of the Supreme Secret Council, she tore up the signed konditsii and proclaimed the reestablishment of the unlimited autocracy.

konéts, kontsý. Literally, end. The city of Novgorod the Great was composed of five districts or boroughs called kontsy. Each konets was a self-governing community, headed by an elected *konchanskii starosta* (elder).

kóniukh stáryi. Steward of grooms; master of stables.

koniúshii, -ie. Senior equerry; master of stables.

kontóra, -ry. Office or bureau, usually concerned with economic or technical matters.

kontr-admirál, -ly. Rear admiral, naval rank of the 4th class corresponding to the rank of *general-maior* in the army. See TABEL' O RANGAKH.

kontról', gosudárstvennyi kontról', and gosudárstvennyi kontrolër. An office established in 1811 for auditing state finances. In the 1860s the powers of the gosudarstvennyi kontrol' were enlarged. Provincial auditing bodies called KONTROL'NYE PALATY (chambers) were established in 1866.

kopá, in the Grand Duchy of Lithuania. Meeting of the rural community.

kopá or *kópnyi sud:* investigation and adjudication, on the spot, of a dispute concerning landed properties by an official of the grand duke (DERZHAVTSA) with the participation of representatives of the local population.

kopá, kópy. Three score.

kopá gróshei: a monetary counting unit equal to 60 groshi, in the Grand Duchy of Lithuania. It corresponded, approximately, to one Muscovite POLTINA or half a ruble.

kopéika, -ki. Copeck. Kopeiki or DENGI KOPEINYE were first minted in Muscovy in 1534–35. They were small silver coins equal to two *dengi.* The name kopeika derived, probably, from the picture of a rider with a *kopië* (*kop'ë,* spear) on the face of the coin. During the war crises in the middle of the 17th century the government started in 1655 to mint copper dengi and kopeiki with the nominal value of the silver coins. They rapidly depreciated, the whole financial and economic system of the state was shattered, and the experiment was soon abandoned. Under Peter the Great the whole monetary system was reformed; several kinds of silver coins were minted, and the kopeika in 1704 became a copper coin equal to $\frac{1}{100}$ of the silver ruble.

korchémnik, -ki or **korchmít, -ty.** 1. Keeper of a tavern. 2. He who keeps and sells liquor illegally.

korchémstvo. Illegal sale of liquor.

korchmá, -mý. Tavern. In the *Ulozhenie* of 1649 (chap. 25: *Ukaz o korchmakh*) korchma meant the illegal sale of alcoholic beverages. *Korchma pokutnaia,* in the Grand Duchy of Lithuania, was the illegal keeping and sale of liquor.

korm, -mý. A commemorative feast for monks and for poor people, held in a monastery on the anniversary of a person's death.

korm, kormý; kormlénie, -iia. Refers to the system of local administration in eastern Russia in the 14th–16th centuries. "For the administration and judiciary of local districts the grand duke relied upon his *namestniki* (lieutenants) and *volosteli* (agents in rural districts). These were paid no salary from the grand ducal treasury but had to 'feed themselves' off the country (the kormlenie system)—that is, they were entitled to receive maintenance from the local people as well as to keep for themselves a share of the court fees and taxes collected in each district." (G. Vernadsky, *Russia at the Dawn,* pp. 4–5). Originally the korm for the local officials was delivered in kind; the population brought bread, meat, and other foodstuffs for the official and his staff and hay and oats for their horses. Gradually the kormy were replaced by monetary payments. The amount of the payment in each district was regulated by a special government charter, and if the official, misusing his power, extorted more than he was legally entitled to, the damaged party had the right to sue him after he had left his office. The term of kormlenie in the same place was not long—usually one, two, or three years. The newly appointed NAMESTNIK or VOLOSTEL' received "entrance food" (*v"ezzhii korm*) when he first took office. During the average year the korm (in kind or in money) was paid two or three times; the normal ones were *Rozhdestvenskii* and *Petrovskii korm,* payments delivered at Christmas and on the Day of Saint Peter and Paul (June 29); in some districts a third korm at Easter (*Velikii den'*) was customary. The administration of the KORMLENSHCHIKI provoked many complaints on the part of the local population, and in the 1550s the central government, at the request of local communities, began

44

to abolish the kormlenie system and to replace it with the administration of elected local officials responsible for collecting taxes (OBROK) for the tsar's treasury instead of the kormy. In 1555–56 the government decided to abolish the kormlenie system entirely, but this decision was not carried out everywhere, and remnants of the system survived until the 17th century.

kórmchaia. See under KNIGA.

kormlénshchik, -ki. Local officials (NA-MESTNIKI and VOLOSTELI) in Muscovy in the 14th-16th centuries who were paid by KORMLENIE (receiving subsistence payments, in kind or in money, from the local population). See KORM.

kornét, -ty. An officer rank in the cavalry equal to the rank of PODPORUCHIK in the infantry (the rank of the 12th class in the TABEL' O RANGAKH).

kórob, -by or **korób'ia, -b'i.** A basket; a Novgorodian unit of dry measure in the 15th-16th centuries; according to L. Cherepnin, it was equal to 7 PUDY (1 pood or pud = 36 lbs.).

koromóla or **kramóla, -ly.** Conspiracy; treason; sedition.

koromól'nik or **kramól'nik, -ki.** Conspirator; traitor; rebel; seditionary.

kórpus, -sy or **-sá.** A large military unit, corps. At the end of the 19th century it included two infantry divisions, one cavalry division, and two artillery brigades, as well as special units. In wartime the full strength of the korpus was over 40,000 men.

kadétskii kórpus: military academy first established in 1731 for the sons of nobility. By the end of the 19th century there were twenty military schools with this name. The students were predominantly officers' sons. The korpus had a seven-year curriculum, including many subjects in general education. The youths graduated from the korpus had to go through the special two-year

VOENNOE UCHILISHCHE before they became commissioned officers.

pázheskii kórpus: see PAZH.

kórpus zhandármov: the military corps of political police established by Nicholas I in 1827. At first it was subordinated to the Third Department of His Majesty's Chancellery, and from 1880 on, to the minister of the interior. According to the regulations of 1867, each province was to have a *gubernskoe zhandarmskoe upravlenie,* a board consisting of several commissioned officers in command of several score lower-ranking personnel.

kórtoma or **kortomá.** Lease, rent.

kosh (Ukr.). 1. Camp. 2. Zaporozhian Cossack host.

koshevói, -výe (Ukr. *koshovy*), **koshevói atamán.** Elected commander of the Zaporozhian Cossack host.

kóstki (pl.). A medieval customs duty imposed on transported merchandise.

kotóra, -ry. Quarrel, conflict, internecine war.

kozák. See KAZAK.

kráichii, -chie. A court officer in Muscovy and in the Grand Duchy of Lithuania, whose duty was to serve the sovereign during gala dinners.

kramóla, kramól'nik. See KOROMOLA, KOROMOL'NIK.

kredít, kredítnyi bilét, -ye -ty. Paper money, introduced in 1841–43 to replace in part the older ASSIGNATSII: an essential part of the financial reforms carried out by the finance minister, Count Kankrin. (See RUBL'.)

kreml'. Kremlin, the inner fortress in old cities, including government buildings and the cathedral.

krépost', -ti. 1. In military language, a fortress. 2. In legal language, a title-deed, a written document certifying the ownership of landed property, or a contract of bondage.

krest'iánskaia krépost': "It became

customary in the second quarter of the 17th century for the tenants to give their landlord a written undertaking that they would continue to live on the allotments assigned to them until their death. . . . The dependence of the tenants on their lord, based in the past on the fact of their indebtedness, thus received a contractual character. The resulting relationship was known as *krest'ianskaia krepost'* from which serfdom—*krepostnoe pravo*—probably derived its name" (M. Florinsky, *I,* p. 281).

kúpchaia krépost': a deed of purchase (a term that survived until the Revolution of 1917).

krepostnýe (liúdi, or **krest'iáne)** (pl.). Initially a term for people who were bondmen by contract; later, a general term for serfs.

krest'iánin, krest'iáne, or **khrest'iánin, khrist'iánin, -iáne.** These words came into use in the 14th century. Their original meaning was Christians, and they were employed to distinguish the Orthodox Russian population in general from the dominant Tatars and from other non-Christian peoples. Later the word khrist'ianin retained the religious meaning—Christian—while krest'ianin became the term for a rural person, esp. a small farmer who possessed his own household and held a plot of arable land with appurtenances. The grand duke, later the tsar of Muscovy, was considered the supreme owner of all the lands in the country except the boyars' and monasteries' estates (VOTCHINY); but the peasants living on the sovereign's or state lands had possession (*vladenie*) of their plots, which was in fact very close to ownership, since they could buy and sell, mortgage, divide, and bequeath their plots. The situation gradually changed during the 15th-17th centuries when the government granted an enormous amount of state land as POMEST'IA

to servingmen. The peasants on those lands were obliged to obey their new landlords and to pay the OBROK or to perform the BARSHCHINA for them. Until the end of the 16th century the peasants had the right to move away from their master if they were oppressed by him; their right to move was recognized by the *Sudebniki* of 1497 and 1550; but that right was opposed by the service gentry (POME-SHCHIKI), who petitioned the government to stabilize the peasant labor force for them so that they could live and maintain service to the tsar. Beginning in the 1580s, the government gradually limited the peasants' right to move (see ZAPOVEDNYE GODY) until the *Ulozhenie* of 1649 completely prohibited peasant movement from one estate to another. For many peasants the right to move had already long been lost because of their indebtedness to the landlord, since they could not move without paying both their debts and the POZHILOE (payment for using the homestead). Peasants who had lived on the same votchina or pomest'e for generations (STAROZHIL'TSY) had gradually lost their right to move before the law of 1649. The poll tax introduced by Peter the Great in 1719–23 merged the whole mass of peasants and slaves living on private estates into one social group, the KREPOSTNYE LIUDI (bondmen), and the developments in the second half of the 18th century brought the KREPOST-NYE KREST'IANE or serfs into a situation not far removed from actual slavery. For the serfs, emancipation came only in 1861. At that time they numbered 21 million men, women, and children. A still more numerous group of peasants at that time were the state peasants (*gosudarstvennye krest'iane*), who did not know serfdom and whose economic and social conditions were somewhat better than those of the serfs. Even after the reforms of the 1860s the peasants were obliged to remain attached to their communities; after 1889 they were put under the supervision of land captains (ZEMSKIE NACHAL'NIKI). The decrees of 1906–10 under Prime Minister Stolypin granted the peasantry civil equality with other social groups and enabled them to transfer their allotment lands from the commune to private ownership. These changes effected remarkable economic and social progress for the peasantry during the period up to 1914. (See the following subentries for more details on specific categories of peasants.)

bárshchinnye krest'iáne: serfs who were obliged to work for their master in his fields (see BARSHCHINA).

béglye krest'iáne: fugitive peasants who had left their landlords in violation of legal provisions or a contract. The decree of 1597 limited to five years the time during which the landlord had the right to recover his fugitive peasant by court decision. Later the term was extended to ten years, and the *Ulozhenie* of 1649 abolished any time limit for the recovery of fugitives.

chernosóshnye krest'iáne: taxpaying state peasants, predominantly in northern provinces of Russia (the SOKHA was a taxable unit).

chërnye krest'iáne: state peasants, as opposed to those serving private landlords.

dvoróvye krest'iáne: in the 17th and 18th centuries, "the people who lived on the properties that belonged to the imperial court" (J. Blum, p. 493).

dvortsóvye krest'iáne: the peasants belonging to the tsar's DVORETS (palace) and attending to its various needs. After 1797 they were called UDEL'NYE KREST'IANE.

ekonomícheskie krest'iáne: the peasants who belonged to the church institutions (chiefly monasteries) before the landed properties of the church were taken over by the government in 1763–64. By a decree of February 26, 1764, the former church serfs were placed under the administration of a government office called the *Kollegiia Ekonomii,* and thereafter formed a state peasant category called ekonomicheskie krest'iane. They numbered about two million people of both sexes.

gosudárevy krest'iáne: the sovereign's peasants. In the 17th century (according to the *Ulozhenie* of 1649, chap. XI, art. 1) these were the peasants of *dvortsovye* villages (those belonging to the tsar's palace) and of the *chernye volosti,* the state peasants in general. "During the 18th century the tsars had taken over some of the court properties as their own personal possessions. The peasants on these properties were transferred from the court peasantry into a new category called the sovereign's peasants" (*gosudarevy krest'iane*). By 1762 there were 62,000 males in this class" (J. Blum, p. 494).

gosudárstvennye (or *kazënnye*) *krest'iáne:* state peasants in general, as distinguished from serfs; the term was used in the 19th century.

iasáchnye krest'iáne: peasants who paid taxes in furs (IASAK) in Siberia and in the Ural region.

izdél'nye krest'iáne: see BAR-SHCHINNYE KREST'IANE (*izdelie = barshchina*).

kazënnye krest'iáne: literally, treasury peasants, the same as GOSUDAR-STVENNYE. A general name for all the categories of state peasants before the reforms of 1861–66. In 1858 they numbered about 25 million people.

krepostnýe krest'iáne: initially bondmen by contract (KREPOST'); later, serfs in general.

obiázannye krest'iáne: literally, obligated peasants. "In 1842 there came a general *ukaz* authorizing contractual arrangements between masters and serfs which would leave all the land of the estates in the ownership of the former, but assign a portion to the use of the serfs in return for dues and services to be fixed by agreement" (G. T. Robinson, p. 62). Only about 25,000 male serfs were transferred into this status.

obróchnye krest'iáne: peasants, usually serfs, who worked for themselves but paid OBROK (quitrent) to their master-landlord.

páshennye krest'iáne: plowland peasants. In Siberia, peasants who had received from the government land allotments, livestock, and agricultural implements, and in return were obliged to till fixed plots of the tsar's arable lands to supply the local service men with foodstuffs.

poméshchikovy or *poméshchichii krest'iáne:* peasants who lived on the lands belonging to the POMESHCHIKI (service men) in Muscovy and to the nobility in general during the imperial period. On the eve of the emancipation of the serfs they numbered about 21 million people of both sexes (about 38 percent of the total population in the European provinces).

possessiónnye krest'iáne: serfs assigned to factories and iron foundries, chiefly in the Ural region. A decree of January 18, 1721, granted the proprietors of factories and plants (regardless of whether they were noblemen or merchants) the right to purchase villages with peasants; but the peasants were to be permanently assigned to those plants and the owners did not have the right to move them from their residences. The term possessionnye krest'iane came into usage around the end of the 18th century. In 1847 there were 178,000 male possessionnye serfs assigned to the 37 foundries in the Ural region.

pripisnýe krest'iáne: "In government-owned factories the needed workers were drawn from the state peasantry. The government attached these people to a specific enterprise, and so they were

known as 'assigned' (*pripisnye*) peasants." (J. Blum, p. 308.)

sóshnye krest'iáne: cadastral peasants, i.e., enrolled in the cadastral books called PISTSOVYE KNIGI or *knigi soshnogo pis'ma* (See SOKHA.)

starínnye krest'iáne or *starozhíl'tsy:* peasants in Muscovy who had lived on the estates of their landlords for generations and had lost the right to move from them.

tiáglye krest'iáne: see TIAGLO.

udél'nye krest'iáne: appanage peasants. After Paul I created the appanage in 1797, udel'nye krest'iane became the term for peasants inhabiting lands belonging to the imperial family. Before the reforms of 1861 there were about two million udel'nye peasants of both sexes. (See UDELY.)

vótchinnikovy krest'iáne: in Muscovy, peasants living on the lands of VOTCHINNIKI or hereditary owners of estates.

vrémenno-obiázannye krest'iáne: temporarily obligated peasants. According to the emancipation statutes of February 19, 1861, liberated serfs had to conclude agreements with their former master concerning payments for the land allotments received. Until then the peasants had to perform certain fixed obligations for their former master, and were called vremenno-obiazannye krest'iane. This status endured in some places for many years. It was completely eliminated by the government in 1881–82 when the redemption of the allotments was made obligatory for all former serfs.

zavódnye krest'iáne: in the general sense, well-to-do or well-equipped peasants. In a special sense, peasants brought to Siberia by the government in the 17th century, supplied with land and agricultural implements, and obliged to till a measure of plowland for the sovereign (to provide food for the service men).

krívda. Offense; injury; damage; injustice or crime in general.

króvnye or **krévnye.** Blood relatives (in the Grand Duchy of Lithuania).

krug, -gi. Literally, circle; assembly or meeting of the Don Cossack host and other cossack communities in southeastern and eastern Russia.

krug voiskovói. Assembly of the cossack host (VOISKO).

ktítor, -ry (from the Greek). 1. Founder of a church or monastery. 2. Patron of a church, churchwarden.

kukhmístr, -ry. A court office in the Grand Duchy of Lithuania.

kum and **kumá, kumov'iá.** Godfather and godmother of one's child; they were kum and kuma in relation to each other and also in relation to the child's parents.

kúna, kúny. 1. Marten. 2. Marten fur or pelt. 3. An old monetary unit. 4. Pl.: money in general. Before metallic currency came into use, cattle and furs had served as money in Russia as elsewhere; the words SKOT (cattle) and kuny were used in that sense. When the foreign small silver coins—the eastern *dirhems* and the western *denarii*—came into Kievan Russia, they were given the common local name, kuny. The kuna monetary system was, of course, different in various regions and changed with the times. The higher monetary unit, the GRIVNA KUN, contained in various periods and in various regions amounts of kuny ranging from 20 to 50. Sources of the 12th and 13th centuries mention differences between the old kuny (*kuny vetkhie* or *starye*) and the new ones (*kuny novye*). The term kuny in the general sense of money was dominant in Russia during the 10th-14th centuries, and only at the end of the 14th and in the first half of the 15th centuries was it gradually replaced by the terms DENGI and SEREBRO.

kúna chërnaia (in Novgorod the Great). See BOR (CHERNYI).

kunítsa, -tsy. Marten; money.

   novozhénnaia or *svádebnaia kunítsa:* a fee paid in the 14th-17th centuries by a newly married couple to the local administrator or to the secular or ecclesiastical landlord.

   vyvodnáia kunítsa: literally, marten for exit or for departing, a duty or fee paid to the local administrator or to the landlord when a girl was married and left her place of residence for another village or city.

kúpa. A term used in the RUSSKAIA PRAVDA. It is explained either as wages received by a ZAKUP from his landlord, or (more probably) as a loan received by a ZAKUP to be repaid by work for the landlord.

kúpchaia, -chie. Deed of purchase.

kupchína, -ny. Merchant, trader.

kupéchestvo. The status or the community of the merchant class (KUPETS).

kupéts, kuptsý. The term for members of the merchant class used during the whole course of Russian history. In Novgorod the Great, *kuptsy poshlye* (old or hereditary; also meant regular, of full value) were organized by the 12th century around the church of St. John. They formed a self-governing corporation headed by an elected elder (STAROSTA). In order to be recognized as a poshlyi kupets and admitted into membership in the St. John's Corporation (*kupechestvo Ivanskoe*), a merchant had to pay a big entrance fee amounting to 50 silver grivnas. Other terms for the upper merchant class in old Russia were *kuptsy dobrye, narochitye,* STAREISHII, VIACHSHIE and the like. In Muscovy the merchant class did not possess as much social influence and independence as in Novgorod the Great. The Moscow merchants (TORGOVYE LIUDI) did not have voluntary organizations but were organized by the government into three groups, the GOSTI, GOSTINAIA SOTNIA and SUKONNAIA SOTNIA. The members of these organizations were obliged to perform (without salaries) such government duties as financial agent, collector of direct and indirect taxes and other revenues, and agent in government trading operations. Peter the Great tried to enhance the status of the merchant class and give it a better organization; on the one hand, he impelled the merchants to organize commercial companies, and, on the other hand, he granted to the cities and towns a certain measure of self-government exercised by their elected MAGISTRATY. But the oppressive burden of government financial services and commercial operations remained the responsibility of the merchant class until the reign of Catherine II. In 1742 the merchant class was divided into three GIL'DII according to their declared capital assets, and this division was retained in the charter granted by Catherine to the cities in 1785. These gil'dii were headed by their elected elders (STARSHINY and STAROSTY). The laws of 1775 and 1785 granted the *gil'deiskoe kupechestvo* freedom from corporal punishment and from paying the poll tax. A law of 1863 ordered the division of merchants into only two gil'dii. The gil'deiskoe kupechestvo constituted a distinct legal class (SOSLOVIE) until the Revolution of 1917.

kuplenína, -ny (or **kúplia, -li**). A term for purchased landed estates in the Grand Duchy of Lithuania.

kúplia, -li. A purchase and the property so acquired, esp. a purchased landed estate. Also, a trading operation in general.

kurátor, -ry. With the founding of Moscow University (1755) the office of the university kurator was established; his duty was to protect and represent the

university. The later term for this office was *popechitel'*.

kurén', -ní. Barracks of a Zaporozhian Cossack company; that company as a military unit, commanded by a *kurennoi ataman*.

kuriltái or **kurultái.** "The assembly of clan leaders" in Mongolia (G. Vernadsky, *Mongols,* p. 6).

kursístka, -ki. Girl student of the VYSSHIE ZHENSKIE KURSY.

kúrsy (pl.): **výsshie zhénskie kúrsy.** Higher women's courses; university, or college, for women. The imperial, or government, universities were not coeducational, with short exceptions after 1905 and during World War I, but the desire for higher education was strong among Russian women, especially after 1860. To meet this demand, Professor V. I. Gerie in Moscow (in 1872) and Professor K. N. Bestuzhev-Riumin in St. Petersburg (in 1878) founded vysshie zhenskie kursy with a curriculum corresponding to that of the university and with university professors as teachers. Similar zhenskie kursy were organized in Kazan' and Kiev. In 1886 the minister of public education issued an order to stop further enrollment of women students and to close all zhenskie kursy by 1889. Only the Bestuzhev kursy survived. The Gerie Kursy opened again in 1900, after which vysshie zhenskie kursy were established in all the cities where imperial universities existed. Women's higher education made rapid progress after 1905; in 1915, according to official statistics, over 24,000 women were enrolled in institutions of higher education.

kustár', -rí. Peasant engaged in domestic or cottage industry. "The absence of restrictive guilds, the repeal by the government of the barriers to free entry into trade and industry, and the lagging of handicraft production in the cities, had much to do with the burgeoning of kustar production" (J. Blum, p. 302).

The kustari often worked in ARTELI, voluntary cooperative organizations headed by an elected STAROSTA.

kustárnye prómysly: cottage industries, an important branch of Russian economic life. They were developed especially in the central provinces, where the poor soil could not provide the peasants with sufficient subsistence. By the end of the 19th century the textile cottage industry was most highly developed in the provinces of Moscow, Vladimir, and Tver', the metalworking industry (production of knives, locks, nails, etc.) in the province of Nizhnii Novgorod, and the woodworking industry in the northern provinces.

L

lai or **láia.** Barking; abuse; insult.

lan, lány. A land measure in the Grand Duchy of Lithuania. In the 16th century the normal lan was a synonym for a VOLOKA or UVOLOKA and measured about twenty Russian DESIATINAS. Otherwise it was a land measure that varied considerably at different times and between various regions (see N. Gorbachevskii, *Slovar',* pp. 191 and 385).

landmilítsiia. From 1713 to 1775 a territorial army settled in the southern and southeastern border regions of the Empire. In 1775 part of it was converted into regular army regiments and the rest disbanded.

landrát, -ty. An office established by Peter the Great in 1713–16. Each landrat administered a district called a DOLIA; several landraty formed a board of councillors headed by the governor of the province.

landríkhter and **ober-landríkhter, -ry.** A short-lived office of magistrates serving in local courts (ZEMSKIE SUDY or *landgerikhty*) under Peter the Great.

lar'. 1. Coffer. 2. In Pskov at the time of its independence, the state archives, attached to the cathedral of the Holy Trinity.

láshman, -ny. Moslem peasants on the middle Volga who were obliged to prepare timber for the building of navy ships. "In 1718 Peter commanded the Muslims of Mordvinian and Tatar stock who lived along the middle Volga to cut and transport timber in the Admiralty forests of that region. . . . They were called *lashmany,* from the Low German *lashen,* to chop" (J. Blum, p. 500). By the end of the 18th century they numbered about 600,000 men. They were gradually freed from their special work obligation, and by the middle of the 19th century they were a part of the state peasantry.

láska gospodárskaia. In the Grand Duchy of Lithuania, favor, protection or grant of the grand duke.

láva. In the Grand Duchy of Lithuania, a collegial court in the cities governed according to the Magdeburg Law.

lávka, -ki. Shop or store.

lávnik, -ki. Court assessor, or juror, member of the court (headed by the VOIT) in the Lithuanian and West Russian cities that were governed according to the Magdeburg Law. In the Russian empire the law of February 19, 1864, on rural administration in the Polish provinces, established *gminnye sudy* (GMINA courts) consisting of elected lavniki who were peasant judges.

lávra, -ry (Greek *laura*). A highly venerated monastery; in the 18th and 19th centuries there were four *lavry* in Russia: *Troitse-Sergieva* near Moscow, *Kievo-Pecherskaia* in Kiev, *Aleksandro-Nevskaia* in St. Petersburg, and *Pochaevskaia* in Volhynia.

lechéts, -chtsý. Physician.

lëgkost' (W. R. legal language). Humiliation, insult, injury.

leitenánt, -ty. A rank in the navy corresponding to the rank of SHTABS-KAPITAN in the infantry (a rank of the 9th class according to the TABEL' O RANGAKH).

léktor, -ry. Lecturer. According to the university statutes of the 19th century the lektory were teachers of modern languages (French, German, English, and Italian) who did not possess the status and title of a PROFESSOR or DOTSENT (or PRIVAT-DOTSENT).

lentvóit, -ty. Deputy-mayor, serving under the VOIT (mayor) in the cities of the Grand Duchy of Lithuania governed according to the Magdeburg Law.

léta (pl.) (W.R. legal language). Literally, age.

doróslye léta or *zupólnye léta:* majority, full age or legal age.

detínye léta or *molodýe léta:* minority, legal infancy.

léta uróchnye. In Muscovy, "The time limit beyond which legal action could not be taken for the return of the runaway peasants" (M. Florinsky, p. 281). (See GODY UROCHNYE.)

léta vykhodnýe. See GODY VYKHODNYE.

léta zapovédnye. See GODY ZAPOVEDNYE.

létopis', -si. Chronicle, annals. The Primary Chronicle or POVEST' VREMEN-NYKH LET, in its Laurentian and Hypatian versions, is the basic source for the history of Kievan and Suzdalian Russia. The four Novgorodian and two Pskovian chronicles have similar importance for the early history of northwestern Russia. For Muscovy of the 14th–16th centuries the most important historical sources are the *Sofiiskaia, Voskresenskaia* and *Nikonovskaia* letopisi. All of the above named chronicles comprise the first fourteen volumes of the POLNOE SOBRANIE RUS-SKIKH LETOPISEI. Representing various styles and viewpoints, the letopisi provide valuable and often vivid information about not only religious but also political and military events.

l'góta, -ty. A temporary exemption from taxes or work obligations generally granted to new settlers by the state and by private landlords as well.

líbra, -ry. A weight unit in the Grand Duchy of Lithuania, equal, approximately, to 9/10 of the Russian FUNT.

líchba, -by (W.R.). Accounts.

likhodéi, -éii. Wrongdoer; political offender.

líkhva, -vy. Usury, interest for borrowed money exceeding the normal rate.

likhoímstvo. Extortion; usury.

líniia, -nii. Small linear measure, 1/10 DIUIM.

list, -ty, listý (legal language of the Grand Duchy of Lithuania). Letter, deed, charter, or any written document (the meaning of list corresponded to the Muscovite GRAMOTA).

dozvólenyi list: written permission.

gospodárskie listý: letters or orders of the Grand Duke.

sudóvye or *sudovýe listý:* court writs.

zapovédnye listý: orders to postpone a trial.

list pechátnyi. In modern Russia, sixteen printed pages in a book.

lítra, -ry. A Byzantine weight unit equal to approximately ¾ of the Russian FUNT; it served as the prototype for the Russian GRIVNA, later, funt.

litséi, -éii. An educational institution in Russia in the 19th century. The curricula varied: some were intermediate between secondary school and college, some corresponded to university faculties. The best-known was the *Aleksandrovskii litsei* founded in 1811 in Tsarskoe Selo (where Pushkin went to school) and transferred in 1844 to St. Petersburg. Also important were the historico-philological litsei of Prince Bezborodko, founded in 1805 in

Nezhin (in the Ukraine), and Demi-dov's *iuridicheskii litsei* in Iaroslavl' (also founded in 1805).

litsó = POLICHNOE. Corpus delicti in the sense of a stolen object.

litsóvannyi (ZLODÉI) (W.R.). A criminal caught red-handed.

liúdi (pl.). In the Kievan and Novgorodian period the term liudi was used to indicate the whole free population of any region, and was generally applied to the bulk of the free population in cities. In Muscovy the term liudi, with an adjective following, was used for many categories of people, domestic or foreign. In reference to nationality the sources use such terms as: *liudi litovskie, moskovskie, nemetskie, nogaiskie, pol'skie,* or *turskie.* In reference to residence: *liudi gorodskie, uezdnye, volostnye,* or *stanovye.* In reference to the masters of bondmen and peasants: *liudi boiarskie, dvorianskie, kniazhie, pomeshchikovy, votchinnikovy, monastyrskie, patriarshie,* or *mitropolichii.* In the later Moscow period and in the imperial period until 1861, the word liudi, followed by an indication of their master, usually meant bondmen, unfree domestic servants; in that sense the combination *liudi i krest'iane* was frequently used. In Muscovy and in the Grand Duchy of Lithuania liudi, with an adjective, was used to indicate various other legal, social, and economic groups of the population, as explained below.

béglye liúdi: fugitives.

bélye liúdi = *netiáglye:* residents of urban and suburban settlements not included in TIAGLO-bearing communities, and therefore free of tax-paying and work obligations.

bezpoméstnye liúdi: men who belonged to the gentry servitor class but did not hold any POMEST'E.

blízhnie gosudárevy liúdi: high-ranking servitors or closest advisers of the tsar.

bogadél'nye liúdi: poor people, permanent dependents of the church.

bol'shíe liúdi: big or important men. See DOBRYE LIUDI and LUCHSHIE LUIDI.

chërnye liúdi: black men. In Novgorod the term signified the lower classes of the city's free population in general. In Muscovy it meant the TIAGLO-bearing groups of the population; it was applied chiefly to the lower and middle groups of the urban and suburban population and to the state peasantry.

chinóvnye liúdi: military officers and civil officials possessing a service rank (CHIN).

chíslenye liúdi or *chisliakí:* counted men, thus those included in the census registers as a separate group. The term was a holdover from the Mongol period. Liudi chislenye were mentioned in the princely wills and inter-princely treaties of the Moscow royal house from the 14th to the early 16th centuries.

dánskie liúdi: registered taxpayers.

dátochnye liúdi: in Muscovy, recruits taken in time of war from the TIAGLO-bearing population of state lands and church landed estates, and from those VOTCHINY and POMEST'IA whose holders were unable, at the time, to perform military service.

delovýe (or *zadvórnye*) *liúdi:* a term from the 17th century meaning slaves who were settled outside their master's court on a homestead with a piece of land, and performed service (BARSHCHINA) in his fields.

dóbrye liúdi: literally, good men. Economically well-to-do and morally reliable people, whose presence was required, as jurors or assessors, in the courts of the NAMESTNIKI and VOLOSTELI in the 15th and 16th centuries.

dokládnye liúdi: slaves belonging to their master by virtue of a DOKLADNAIA GRAMOTA (see GRAMOTA).

domóvnye liúdi: people under the jurisdiction of church prelates.

dúmnye liúdi: on occasion, members of the boyar DUMA, but usually in the sources it referred only to the two lower ranks of Duma members, the DUMNYE DVORIANE and DUMNYE DIAKI, and not the BOIARE and OKOL'NICHIE.

dvoróvye liúdi: in Muscovy, servitors of the tsar's court; in the 18th and 19th centuries (before 1861) it meant domestic serfs of the POMESHCHIKI—"the household people, who lived in the household (*dvor*) of a serfowner, or in nearby huts, and spent their lives serving him and his family" (J. Blum, p. 455). On the eve of the Emancipation they numbered about 1,500,000 men, women, and children.

dvortsóvye gosudárevy liúdi: servitors at the tsar's court.

guliáshchie or *vól'nye guliáshchie liúdi:* literally, itinerant men (in Muscovy). "The people not attached to any *tiaglo,* and therefore free to move from place to place" (G. Lantzeff, p. 141). Itinerant craftsmen, hired workers, or even beggars. Some migrated to the free cossack hosts in the southern and eastern border regions. Peter the Great decreed that guliashchie liudi should enter some kind of military service, attach themselves to any TIAGLO-bearing urban or rural community, or become dependents of some private master. Sometimes the term guliashchie liudi was used in a broader sense to include not merely those legally free from any tiaglo but also fugitives (BEGLYE LIUDI) as well as landlords' peasants and POSAD men who had been temporarily released from their places of residence while retaining legal ties to their communities.

iasáchnye liúdi: tributary people, predominantly native tribes in Siberia, who paid tribute, or taxes, in furs (IASAK).

iúrievskie liúdi: in the 15th and 16th centuries, peasants who concluded contracts with their landlords for a one-year term, beginning November 26, *Iuriev den'* (St. George's Day) (B. Grekov, *Kratkii ocherk,* p. 181).

iúrtovskie liúdi: native tribes in Siberia and the Ural region whose temporary settlements and habitations were called IURTY (pl.).

izbylýe liúdi: those people erroneously omitted from the registers of taxpayers and serving men.

izvéchnye liúdi (W.R.): peasants who had lived for generations on the same estate and thereby lost the right to move elsewhere (corresponded to Muscovite term, STAROZHIL'TSY).

kabál'nye liúdi: bondsmen = KHOLOPY KABAL'NYE.

krepostnýe liúdi: in Muscovy, bondmen attached to their master by the power of a legal document (KREPOST'). In the imperial period before 1861, the term krepostnye liudi (*krepostnye krest'iane*) referred to the serfs in general.

kupécheskie liúdi = KUPTSY: merchants, tradesmen.

kúplenye liúdi: slaves acquired by a purchase deed.

likhíe liúdi: criminals, felons.

likhóvannye liúdi (W.R.): persons convicted by testimony of the neighborhood (see OBYSK POVAL'NYI).

lúchshie or *lútchie liúdi* (similar to BOL'SHIE, DOBRYE, or VIASHCHIE LIUDI): the worthiest or best men. Economically well-to-do and morally irreproachable men in urban and rural communities. The Sudebniks of 1497 and 1550 ordered that lutchie liudi, as representatives of the local population, should be present in the court of the NAMESTNIKI and VOLOSTELI in the capacity of sworn assessors (called in the Second Sudebnik *lutchie liudi tseloval'niki*).

malopoméstnye liúdi: service men who received POMEST'E lands of less than the normal and sufficient size.

masterovýe liúdi: craftsmen.

mésiachnye liúdi: in the 18th and 19th centuries until 1861, "A number of proprietors who used all or much of their land for their own production, converted their peasants into field hands who worked full-time for their master. The master furnished these people with food, clothing, and a small money wage. Because they received their payments once a month they were known as *mesiachnye liudi,* monthly people" (J. Blum, p. 532).

mirskíe liúdi: the members of an urban or rural MIR or community.

molódshie or *molódchie liúdi:* "younger" men. Members of the urban and the rural communities in Muscovy were usually divided into three groups: *lutchie, serednie,* and *molodchie* (best, middle, and younger). This division was made according to economic status and did not create legal distinctions between the groups, but it was important in practice since it was taken into consideration in the assessment of taxes and work obligations of the individual households.

nachál'nye liúdi: commanding officers or high civil officials; sometimes also church hierarchs.

naëmnye liúdi: hired people, either for work or for some special service.

narochítye liúdi: people of high standing, outstanding, important.

nepís'menye liúdi: persons not listed in the registry books. In the later rural vernacular, illiterates (= *negramotnye*).

nepokhózhie liúdi: immobile men, peasants in West Russia bound to the soil; they had lived for generations on the same estate and thereby had lost the right to move from it.

nevól'nye liúdi: bondmen in the Grand Duchy of Lithuania.

obróchnye liúdi: persons who paid quitrent. (See OBROK.)

obysknýe liúdi: those persons in a community who were subjected to a general investigation (POVAL'NYI OBYSK) and had to give testimony about the character and activities of a person suspected of a criminal deed.

ogovórnye liúdi: people accused of some crime by the testimony of accomplices, witnesses, or neighbors (LIKHOVANNYE LIUDI in West Russia).

okhóchie liúdi: volunteers, esp. for military service.

okól'nye liúdi: neighbors.

otchíznye liúdi (W.R.): patrimonial people, dependent peasants bound to their PAN (master), the hereditary owner of the estate on which they lived.

páshennye liúdi: plowmen, landplowing peasants.

pís'menye liúdi: registered taxpayers.

podorózhnye liúdi: travelers.

pogónnye liúdi: court agents, policemen, or even local people in pursuit of suspected criminals.

pokhózhie liúdi: mobile men, those not attached to the soil; in the Grand Duchy of Lithuania, peasants who retained their right to move from one landlord to another.

pólnye liúdi: people in full bondage, slaves.

polonënnye liúdi: prisoners of war.

posádskie liúdi: burghers or townspeople in Muscovy, "in the specific sense of the tiaglo-bound middle and lower classes of the urban population" (G. Vernadsky, *Mongols,* p. 373). These bourgeoisie lived in a POSAD (urban settlement), situated usually around a fortress or kremlin with its official and military establishment. The posady comprised chiefly traders and artisans but also other social elements, including some peasants. All these elements formed urban and suburban TIAGLO-bearing communities; they were obliged to pay taxes and to perform required services and work for the government. Their freedom of movement was gradually limited until the *Ulozhenie* of 1649 (chap. XIX) definitively bound the posadskie liudi to their communities. The highest-ranking posadskie liudi in Moscow were a small group of GOSTI (according to Kotoshikhin, p. 157, they numbered only about 30 persons); then followed its best (*lutchie*) elements organized in the GOSTINAIA SOTNIA and the SUKONNAIA SOTNIA. These groups were created by the government to serve its financial and commercial operations. The mass of the Moscow posadskie liudi formed the so-called CHËRNYE SOTNI; then there were the petty artisans (working partly for the tsar's court), hired workers, and other lower elements of the population who inhabited the SLOBODY (suburban settlements). The posadskie liudi in provincial cities and towns were usually divided according to their economic status into three groups: *liudi lutchie* (the best men), *serednie* (the middle men), and *molodshie* (the younger men). In the charter of cities of April 21, 1785, the posadskie liudi formed the sixth (and last) category of registered city dwellers, namely, the old inhabitants (STAROZHILY) of the city who made their living by retail trade, handicrafts, or as hired workers.

póshlinnye liúdi: agents of the NAMESTNIKI and VOLOSTELI who collected dues (POSHLINY) of all kinds from the local population.

póshlye liúdi = STARINNYE LIUDI: hereditary bondmen of a master.

liúdi pospólitye: the common people, in the Grand Duchy of Lithuania.

pribylýe or *príshlye liúdi:* newcomers.

prigovórnye liúdi: elected members of the temporary local councils formed in the provincial cities when the central government in Moscow was weak or was not recognized as a legal government (a term from the Time of Troubles, 1605–13).

prikáznye liúdi: civil officials of the Moscow government.

prostýe liúdi: in the Grand Duchy of Lithuania, common people as opposed to the dominant nobility. The grand duke promised not to elevate (*ne povyshati*) prostye liudi over SZLACHTA (the Statutes of 1529, sect. III, art. 10; and of 1566, sect. III, art. 15).

rátnye liúdi: military men.

riadovýe liúdi: peasants whose payments and work obligations in return for plots of land received were regulated by contract with a landowner.

síl'nye liúdi: (1) mighty and wealthy men; (2) oppressors, offenders.

sluzhílye liúdi: state servitors in Muscovy, from BOIARE and OKOL'NICHIE to STREL'TSY and PUSHKARI. The term referred mainly to military servitors, while civil officials were usually called PRIKAZNYE LIUDI. The top layer of the sluzhilye liudi (after boiare and okol'nichie) were DVORIANE and DETI BOIARSKIE, who formed the bulk of the Moscow armed forces. They were divided into *sluzhilye liudi moskovskie* or *moskovskikh chinov*—consisting of DUMNYE LIUDI, court servitors (STOL'NIKI, STRIAPCHIE and ZHIL'TSY), and DVORIANE MOSKOVSKIE—and *sluzhilye liudi gorodovye,* provincial dvoriane and deti boiarskie; the higher elements of them were DVORIANE VYBORNYE (or IZ GORODOV VYBOR). The next most important and numerous group were the *sluzhilye liudi po priboru* (servitors by contract); among them were the STREL'TSY (mainly infantrymen), PUSHKARI (cannoneers and cannon-makers), SLUZHILYE KAZAKI (as opposed to the *vol'nye* or free Cossacks in the southern and eastern border regions), IAMSHCHIKI (post drivers), *kazënnye plotniki* (government carpenters), *kuznetsy* (blacksmiths), and so on. In the 17th century invited foreigners entered Muscovite service and formed a group of SLUZHILYE INOZEMTSY. Foreign officers helped to organize trained regi-

56

ments of the Muscovite army according to the European models—*polki soldatskie, dragunskie,* and *reitarskie. Sluzhilye liudi iurtovskie* were auxiliary troops recruited from IURTY (settlements) inhabited by Tatars and various native tribes in Siberia and in the Ural region.

sóshnye liúdi: peasants registered in the cadastres called PISTSOVYE KNIGI in which the SOKHA was the basic taxable unit.

sótennye liúdi: members of the Moscow TIAGLO-bearing POSADSKIE LIUDI organized in SOTNI (hundreds).

srédnie or *serédnie liúdi:* middle people, the middle class of the urban and rural TIAGLO-bearing communities in Muscovy.

starínnye or *starodávnie liúdi* = STAROZHÍL'TSY: peasants in Muscovy and in the Grand Duchy of Lithuania who had lived for generations on the same landed estates and had thereby lost the right to move from their landlord.

tiáglye liúdi posádskie and *uézdnye:* "men of burden." In Muscovy, registered members of urban and rural settlements who were bound to their communities and obliged to pay taxes and to perform work for the government.

torgóvye liúdi: trading men; the term applied in Muscovy to all merchants and tradesmen except the highest group, the GOSTI.

tserkóvnye liúdi: clergymen and church servitors, and those laymen living on church properties and supported by the church.

ukraínnye or *vkraínnye liúdi:* inhabitants of the border regions.

velikoródnye liúdi: the high aristocracy.

viáshchie liúdi: important men. See DOBRYE LIUDI and LUCHSHIE LIUDI.

vladýchnye or *vlastelínskie liúdi:* people living on estates that belonged to the hierarchs' sees.

vóinskie liúdi: military men; the term was applied mostly to enemy military forces.

vól'nye liúdi: free men. In Muscovy, people who bore neither TIAGLO nor service obligations and were not enrolled in any urban or rural community. In the Grand Duchy of Lithuania, *liudi vol'nye* or SLUGI VOL'NYE were boyars and other free military servitors who lived on the estates of the sovereign or the high aristocracy.

vorovskíe liúdi (=VÓRY): outlaws, criminals, troublemakers; also rebels, political offenders.

výbornye liúdi: elected representatives in general. In Muscovy, members of the ZEMSKII SOBOR (called in documents: SOV'ET VSEIA ZEMLI) and elected officials in urban and rural communities; also community representatives entrusted with some special mission.

vyvolánye liúdi: in the Grand Duchy of Lithuania, outlawed criminals.

vyvoznýe liúdi: in Muscovy, peasants transferred from one master to another who had paid their debts to the old landlord.

zadúshnye liúdi: in the Kievan period, slaves freed by their masters and given to the church.

zadvórnye liúdi: ". . . those slaves who had homesteads and pieces of land that had been turned over to them by their masters. These bondsmen, who came to be known in the 17th century as *zadvornye liudi,* 'people who lived from [or behind] the master's *dvor,*' performed *barshchina* and other obligations for their owner" (J. Blum, p. 272).

zakúpnye liúdi: in the Grand Duchy of Lithuania, temporary bondmen who could achieve freedom after they had repaid their debt to the master through work for him (Statutes of 1566, sect. XII, art. 7).

zasedélye liúdi (W.R.): peasants who had lived on the same estate for a very long time and had thereby lost the right to leave their master (corresponds to Muscovite term STAROZHIL'TSY).

zémskie liúdi: in Muscovy, commoners, in general, as opposed to SLUZHILYE LIUDI and PRIKAZNYE LIUDI (military and civil servitors of the government).

zhilétskie liúdi: in Muscovy, commoners or civilians as opposed to SLUZHILYE LIUDI and PRIKAZNYE LIUDI (government servitors).

zhít'i liúdi: in Novgorod the Great, well-to-do men, "a sizable part of the Novgorodian middle class" (G. Vernadsky, *Kievan Russia,* p. 142). In the Novgorodian charters and treaties the zhit'i liudi occupied a place between BOIARE and KUPTSY (merchants); after kuptsy followed CHERNYE LIUDI.

lóbnoe mésto. An elevated area in Red Square in Moscow adjacent to the Kremlin wall. There the tsar made official appearances before the people, government statements and proclamations were read, and people gathered on special occasions.

lókot', lókti. A measure of length equal to ⅔ of an ARSHIN, c. 46 centimeters, or 18 inches.

lot, lóty. A measure of weight equal to $\frac{1}{32}$ of a FUNT, 3 ZOLOTNIKS, or 12.8 grams.

lóvchii, -ie. Hunting master or game warden, an official at the courts of old Russian princes, of the Grand Duke of Lithuania, and of the Moscow tsar. The lovchii managed all lands, people, and animals assigned to hunting, matters of great importance to the princes.

lozhníchii, -chie. Chamberlain (corresponding to the Moscow POSTEL'-NICHII). A court official in the Grand Duchy of Lithuania who managed the sovereign's bedroom and clothing.

lúpezh (W.R.). 1. Robbery. 2. Things robbed.

lupézhnik, -ki or **lupézhtsa, -tsy.** Robber, bandit.

M

magistrát, -ty. Office for municipal administration introduced in Russia by Peter the Great. The *glavnyi* (chief) *magistrat* was like a ministry of municipal affairs. According to the statutes (REGLAMENT) of January 16, 1721, the glavnyi magistrat was to establish municipal administration——the *gorodovye magistraty* (see GOROD)—in all the cities, and then to supervise and guide their activities. According to the *instruktsiia magistratam* issued in 1724, the city magistrat was to consist of one president, two burgomasters (BURMISTRY or *burgomistry*), and four councillors (RATMANY) elected by qualified constituencies. It was to take care of justice, public order, and the well-being of the city population, and to collect government taxes (the clergy, officialdom, and serfs were outside its competence). Peter's reform of the municipal administration failed to create viable and lasting self-government in the cities. In 1727 the glavnyi magistrat was abolished, and the gorodovye magistraty, called RATUSHI, were subordinated to the provincial administrators (VOEVODY). According to the statutes on provincial administration (*uchrezhdeniia dlia upravleniia gubernii*) issued in 1775, and to the charter of the cities of 1785, the magistraty (in more important cities) and the ratushi (in smaller towns) were municipal courts only for the local population, merchants, manufacturers, craftsmen, and hired workers. They were subordinate to the *gubernskii magistrat* in the capital of the province, which served as a court of appeal from the city courts. After the general judicial reform introduced in 1864–66, the municipal magistraty and ratushi were abolished.

maiétnost', -ti (W.R.). Property.

maiétnost rukhómaia: movable property.

maiór, -ry. An army officers' rank of the 8th class according to the TABEL' O RANGAKH of 1722. This rank was abolished in 1884.

malzhónka, -ki (W.R., from Pol.). Wife.

manakanún. Distortion of NOMOKANON.

Manufaktúr-Kollégiia. Department of Manufacturing. It was established in 1719 under a joint name, *Berg-i-Manufaktur-Kollegiia,* but was in the same year divided into two separate offices. The extensive *reglament manufaktur-kollegii* (of December 3, 1723) explained the goals and means of Peter's protectionist policy aimed at creating a large manufacturing industry in Russia. (See KOLLEGIIA.) The Manufaktur-Kollegiia was abolished under Catherine II by the decree of November 22, 1779, which proclaimed the principle of free economic activity by individuals without any supervision or regulation by the government. The Kollegiia was reestablished by Paul I, in 1796, and abolished definitively in 1804.

marshálok, -lki. Official. In the Grand Duchy of Lithuania, a term for certain officials of various functions.

marshálok dvórnyi: court marshal, assistant to the MARSHALOK ZEMSKII or his deputy; he headed the court servitors, and in wartime he was the commander of a military unit formed by the DVORIANE GOSPODARSKIE.

marshálki gospodárskie: officials of grand ducal administration in the Grand Duchy of Lithuania; they were also entrusted by the grand duke to make the decisions in certain types of legal suits.

marshálki povétovye: commanders of the mobilized SZLACHTA units in most of the POVETY after the reforms of the 1560s. The KASHTELIANY were commanding officers in those povety where

the capitals of the VOEVODSTVA were situated.

marshálok zémskii: marshal of the land. The highest official of the grand ducal court, the minister of the court. "This official was in charge of order and etiquette at the Grand Duke's court as well as at the meetings of the diet. In case of the Grand Duke's absence from the meetings of the council of lords, the marshal of the land represented there the person of the sovereign" (G. Vernadsky, *Russia at the Dawn,* p. 184).

mashtáler, -ry. Senior equerry in the household of the Grand Duke of Lithuania.

materízna, -ny (W.R.). A landed property that its present owner inherited from his mother.

méchnik, -ki or **mechenósha, -shy.** Sword bearer. A member of the old princely DRUZHINA, a prince's bodyguard who served also as an executive, similar to a sheriff, in the princely administration and court.

méchnyi, -ye. An office at the court of the Grand Duke of Lithuania.

men'shevík, -kí. Literally, the minorityites, the moderate faction of the Russian Social Democratic Party, headed by I. Martov, F. Dan, P. Axelrod, A. Potresov, and others. See PARTIIA, ROSSIISKAIA SOTSIAL-DEMOKRATICHESKAIA RABOCHAIA.

ménshie (liúdi). Smaller men (see LIUDI, MOLODSHIE).

mérnik, -ki. Land surveyor in the Grand Duchy of Lithuania.

meshchanín, mescháne (from West Slavic *mesto* = city or town). In the Grand Duchy of Lithuania, townspeople; in general, the burghers, who in most of the cities enjoyed self-government on the basis of the Magdeburg Law. The term meshchane came into eastern Russia in the 17th century, after several Ukrainian provinces had been united with Russia as a result of the Pereiaslavl' treaty of 1654 and the Russo-Polish War of 1654–67. In the 18th century the term meshchane in Russia was used in two senses: either it meant the entire commercial-artisan class in the towns and cities (like the Moscow term POSADSKIE LIUDI); or, in a limited sense, it designated only the lower groups of the city population, the petty tradesmen, craftsmen, and the like. In the 19th century it had only the latter meaning. According to imperial legislation the meshchane were a particular legal class (SOSLOVIE) which constituted in each city a *meshchanskoe obshchestvo,* headed by an elected *meshchanskii starosta,* with an executive board called a *meshchanskaia uprava.*

mésiachina (from *mésiats,* month). Monthly allowance, esp. a monthly allowance of food and other necessities for the maintenance of working slaves, or (rather seldom) for peasants deprived of land and forced to perform full-time work in the fields of the landlord.

mestéchko, -ki. In western provinces of the empire, settlements intermediate in size between towns and villages and inhabited by petty traders and craftsmen, often including many Jews.

méstnichestvo. In Muscovy, a system regulating the service positions of members of the high aristocracy. They formed a hierarchical ladder and their claim to service positions was based on their place (MESTO) on this ladder. "The respective positions of the princely and boyar families in the service . . . were regulated in the 1500s by a complicated system known as *mestnichestvo* (place order) which was based on the official Genealogical Directory prepared for the tsar (*Gosudarev rodoslovets*) and the lists of state and army officials (*razriadnye knigi*). On the basis of these two registers the tsar was expected to choose his councilors and to appoint high officials of his army and administration. Records of the previous service

of members of the boyar and princely families were consulted, together with genealogical seniority, to establish their respective positions in the service according to precedent" (G. Vernadsky, *Mongols,* p. 369). "A gradation of all the noble families was established. The descendants of the former Grand Dukes formed the top class; the original Moscow boyar families were considered the second group; next came the descendants of lesser princes and so on. Within each family distinctions between genealogically senior and junior members were strictly observed. In that way, filling the offices was an extremely complicated affair" (G. Vernadsky, *Political and Diplomatic History of Russia,* p. 169). Moreover, this system "led to endless and bitter conflicts among the leading boyar families" (M. Florinsky, *I,* p. 179). Sometimes, esp. during wars, the tsar ordered his haughty servitors to be *bez mest* (to serve without regard to their hereditary claims), but at the same time guaranteed that this would not set a precedent for future appointments. Eventually the system became intolerable for all participants, and in January 1682, the young Tsar Fedor Alekseevich confirmed the following decision of the Boyar Duma and the high clergy: "May this *mestnichestvo,* hateful to God, producing enmity, hateful to brotherhood, and destructive of love, perish in flames, and may it never be recalled in the future!" Then the numerous books containing lists of former appointments of high commanders were burned, to the joy of contemporaries and to the sorrow of future historians.

méstnik, -ki, or **-itsy.** In Muscovy, a person from the high aristocracy equal to another person in ancestral rank or standing.

mésto, -tá. 1. In West Russia, city or town. 2. In Muscovy, place, in general, esp. the hereditary position of a person on the hierarchical ladder of MESTNICHE-STVO. The word is used in various combinations, including those below.

mestá bélye (pl.): urban and suburban households or places exempt from taxes.

mésto lóbnoe: see LOBNOE MESTO.

sviatýe mestá: the Holy Land.

mestá prisútstvennye: a term from the imperial period meaning collegial government boards in provincial cities.

mestá ukraínnye: borderlands.

metél'nik or **metál'nik, -ki.** A court agent in the Kievan period.

métrika, -ki. A term used in the spoken language for *metrícheskaia kniga,* register of vital statistics. In the 18th and 19th centuries, parish priests registered births, marriages, and deaths among their parishioners; an extract from the metricheskaia kniga was called, informally, a metrika, or, in official language, *metricheskoe svidetel'stvo.*

Métrika Litóvskaia. The state archives of the Grand Duchy of Lithuania, consisting of 566 volumes in folio, containing documents of public and private nature from 1386 to 1794. General information about the *Litovskaia Metrika* and the fate of its documents in the 19th century is given in the *Entsiklopedicheskii Slovar'* of F. Brockhaus and I. Efron, vol. 19, pp. 199–200. See also: S. L. Ptashitskii, *Opisanie knig i aktov Litovskoi metriki;* N. G. Berezhkov, *Litovskaia metrika kak istoricheskii istochnik;* F. I. Leontovich, ed., *Akty Litovskoi metriki.* At the beginning of the 20th century four volumes of documents from the *Litovskaia Metrika* were published by the *Arkheograficheskaia Komissiia* in the collection *Russkaia Istoricheskaia Biblioteka,* vols. 20, 27, 30, and 33.

mezhá, mézhi. Boundary, a strip of land that served as a division between estates or single plots.

mezhevánie. Land surveying. The *gene-ral'noe mezhevanie,* according to the orders of 1754 and 1766, had for its goal the delimiting of boundaries between landed properties belonging to various villages.

mezhevshchík, -kí. Land surveyor; a term used from the middle of the 18th century, replaced by the term ZEMLEMER.

mézhnik, -ki. 1. A marker on field boundaries. 2. In the Pskov republic in the 14th and 15th centuries, a land surveyor.

mezléva. A tax in kind, in the Grand Duchy of Lithuania, imposed on peasant livestock and paid in small livestock or their products, frequently replaced by monetary payments.

miatézh, -zhí. Rebellion, riot, disturbance, disorder.

miatézhnik, -ki. Mutineer, violator of the peace. In this latter sense the *Ulozhenie* of 1649 speaks about *tserkovnye miatezhniki* as violators of order during church services.

míchman, -ny. A rank in the navy corresponding to the rank of PORUCHIK in the infantry (a rank of the 10th class according to the TABEL' O RANGAKH).

ministérstvo, -va. Ministry in the central government. The collegial system of central government established by Peter the Great had become completely disorganized by the end of the 18th century; most of Peter's KOLLEGII had been abolished under Catherine II, and, although Paul I had formally reestablished them, he had not brought order into the central administration. On September 8, 1802, a new system of central government was introduced by a law establishing eight new ministries: *Ministerstvo Voennykh Sukhoputnykh Sil* (war ministry, later called *Voennoe Ministerstvo); Ministerstvo Morskikh Sil* (navy ministry, later called *Morskoe Ministerstvo); Ministerstvo Inostrannykh Del* (foreign affairs); *Ministerstvo Vnutrennikh Del* (internal affairs);

Ministerstvo Iustitsii (justice); *Ministerstvo Finansov; Ministerstvo Kommertsii; Ministerstvo Narodnogo Prosveshcheniia* (public education). In 1810–11 (the period of Speranskii's influence) a new allocation of state duties among certain ministries was effected. According to the law of July 25, 1810, a special *Ministerstvo Politsii* was created for the maintenance of state security and public order; the Ministry of Internal Affairs was entrusted with "the supervision, extension, and encouragement of agriculture and industry," and the Ministry of Commerce was abolished. On June 25, 1811, the General Regulations for the Ministries (*Obshchee Uchrezhdenie Ministerstv*) and detailed instructions for the individual ministries were issued, whereby the ministries were organized as they would remain, essentially, until the Revolution of 1917. The ministerstva were divided into DEPARTAMENTY (each headed by the *direktor departamenta*); the departments, into OTDELENIIA (sections); the sections, into desks (STOLY). The minister had his assistant (*tovarishch ministra*) and a consultative body of high officials called the SOVET MINISTRA. In 1817, during Alexander's mystical phase, a peculiar ministry appeared, combining spiritual affairs and public education (*Ministerstvo Dukhovnykh Del i Narodnogo Prosveshcheniia*). In 1824 this combination was abolished. In 1819 the special Ministry of Police was abolished, and the functions of maintaining state security and public order were returned to the Ministry of Internal Affairs. Under Nicholas I two more ministries were established: in 1826, the Ministry of the Imperial Court and of Appanages (*Ministerstvo Imperatorskogo Dvora i Udelov),* and in 1837, the *Ministerstvo Gosudarstvennykh Imushchestv* (the Ministry of State Domains, or of state properties including the large class of state peasants).

In 1865 the *Glavnoe Upravlenie Putei Soobshcheniia* (Chief Administration of Transportation) was changed to the *Ministerstvo Putei Soobshcheniia.* In the same year the *Ministerstvo Pocht i Telegrafov* was established, but in 1868 it was included as a GLAVNOE UPRAVLENIE in the Ministry of Internal Affairs. In 1894 the *Ministerstvo Zemledeliia i Gosudarstvennykh Imushchestv* was formed; in 1905 it was renamed *Glavnoe Upravlenie Zemleustroistva i Zemledeliia* (Chief Administration of Land Organization and Agriculture). In the same year, 1905, the new Ministry of Commerce and Industry (*Ministerstvo Torgovli i Promyshlennosti*) was established.

mir, -rý. In the imperial period, peasant communities that had the function of regulating their own internal affairs (under supervision of the manorial administration—in serf villages before 1861—or of state officials). The mir preserved order in the village, regulated the use of communal arable lands and pastures, and until 1903 was collectively responsible for paying government taxes (see OBSHCHESTVO SEL'SKOE and OBSHCHINA). The Muscovite period knew not only peasant miry but also *posadskie miry* and *vseuezdnye miry* (communities formed by townspeople or by the whole population of a district, UEZD). The reforms of local administration in the 1550s granted the mir a rather broad field of self-government, but during the 17th century bureaucratic administration under the provincial VOEVODA subordinated the local miry, urban and rural, more and more to its command. During the Time of the Troubles (1605–13) the Muscovite miry, especially in the central and northern regions, were very energetic and successful in the struggle to reestablish order and national unity in the badly shattered Muscovite state.

mirováia (zápis'). A mutual agreement ending a legal conflict.

mitropolít, -ty. The title of the head of the Russian Orthodox church from its beginnings to 1589, when the *Patriarkh vseia Rusii* was created in Moscow. The Russian mitropolit resided in the 11th–13th centuries in Kiev, in the first quarter of the 14th century in Vladimir on the Kliaz'ma River, and after that in Moscow. For four and a half centuries the Russian church constituted canonically a diocese of the Greek Patriarchate of Constantinople. The Russian mitropolit was dependent on the patriarch for consecration. In 1448 the council of Russian bishops, because of their opposition to the Florentine church union of 1439, elected and consecrated Bishop Iona as metropolitan of Russia without the confirmation of the patriarch of Constantinople, thus making the East Russian church autocephalous. The West Russian Orthodox church, because of the policies of the grand dukes of Lithuania and the kings of Poland, remained under the authority of the patriarch of Constantinople and had its own metropolitan. In 1589 the Russian patriarchate was established in Moscow, and four archbishops (in Novgorod, Kazan', Rostov, and Krutitsy, a Moscow suburb) were elevated to the metropolitan dignity. In 1687 by agreement between the patriarch of Moscow and the patriarch of Constantinople (confirmed by the three Eastern patriarchs) the West Russian Orthodox church was transferred to the Moscow patriarchate and the Russian church was thus reunited. At the beginning of the 20th century there were three metropolitans in Russia, those of St. Petersburg, Moscow, and Kiev.

mólka, -ki; mólka iazýchnaia. Oral testimony concerning a crime.

monastýr', -rí. Monastery. Russian monasticism, which played such an important role in the religious, social, and cultural life of pre-Petrine Russia, began its development in the second half of the 11th century in Kiev, where St. Antonius (d. 1073) and St. Theodosius (or Feodosii, d. 1074) founded the famous Kievo-Pecherskii Monastyr' (the Monastery of the Caves). The most important monastery in Muscovy was the Troitse-Sergiev Monastyr', the monastery of the Holy Trinity, founded in the 14th century by St. Sergius (d. 1392). During the 14th-16th centuries, 104 urban and suburban monasteries and 150 monasteries in the forest wilderness (*pustynnye monastyri*) were founded in Muscovy.

mord, -dy (W.R.). Murder, assassination.

mórdka, -ki. A monetary unit of the KUNA system; according to D. Prozorovskii, the mordka in Novgorod the Great in the 15th century was equal to 20 VEKSHY, which were the smallest units of the kuna system.

morg, -gi (from the Ger. *Morgen*). A land measure in the Grand Duchy of Lithuania, equal to about ⅔ of a hectare or DESIATINA (the normal desiatina of 2.7 acres was slightly larger than a hectare).

moskóvka, -ki or **dengá moskóvskaia.** A small silver coin equal (in the 16th century) to ½ NOVGORODKA or KOPEIKA (see also DENGA).

mostovshchík, -kí. In Muscovy, a collector of the toll paid for crossing a bridge (*most*).

mostovshchína. A toll paid for crossing a bridge.

murzá, múrzy. A person of the Tatar gentry class.

muzh, múzhi. Man, a general term for the free population in old Russia. The people of Novgorod the Great and Pskov in the period of their independence, usually called themselves *muzhi vol'-nye* (free men). Terms to designate the higher strata of the muzhi were: *muzhi bol'shie, luchshie, narochitye, perednie, stareishie, viachshie;* for the lower: *muzhi men'shie, molodshie, prostye.*

kniázhie múzhi: in the 11th-13th centuries, the senior members of the prince's DRUZHINA (retinue), as opposed to its younger members—DETSKIE or OTROKI.

múzhi prigovórnye: in Muscovy, either (1) court assistants taken from the local population or (2) during the Time of Troubles (1605–13), men elected to the temporary councils in provincial cities.

múzhi súdnye: court assistants from the local population, like MUZHI PRIGOVORNYE.

muzhík, -kí (diminutive of MUZH). Literally, little man. "The name *muzhik* denoted a man (*muzh*) of a lower class (the term became familiar in Muscovy after the 16th century)" (G. Vernadsky, *Russia at the Dawn*, p. 203).

muzhikí tyiáglye: in the Grand Duchy of Lithuania, peasants performing obligatory tasks (BARSHCHINA) for the landlord.

muzhikí torgóvye: in Muscovy, trading peasants.

myt or **mýto.** At first, customs duties in general; later the customs duty from traded goods was called TAMGA, and the myto became a toll or transit duty paid (without regard to the value of the goods being transported) at the approaches to each city, on bridges for goods carried in wagons, and at river embarkments for goods transported in boats.

mýtchik or **mýtnik, -ki.** Collector of the MYT.

mzdoímstvo. Extortion (or taking) of bribes.

N

nachál'nik, -ki. Chief, superior, head of an office, institution, territory, or group of people. It is not possible to enumerate all the many kinds of nachal'niki in imperial Russia, but descriptions of certain well-known ones follow:

nachál'nik gubérnii: an official term for GUBERNATOR, the head of a province. A detailed description of his powers and duties was given in the *Nakaz* (instruction) *grazhdanskim gubernatoram* of June 9, 1837 (see GUBERNATOR).

krest'iánskii nachál'nik: peasants' superintendent, with powers comparable to those of the ZEMSKIE NACHAL'NIKI, established in Siberia by the *Polozhenie* (statutes) of June 2, 1898.

okruzhnói (or *okrúzhnyi*) *nachál'nik, -nýe -ki:* district superintendent. According to the regulations (*uchrezhdenie*) of April 30, 1838, for the administration of the state domains and the state peasantry, each GUBERNIIA or province was divided into several OKRUGA or districts, and each district

had an appointed okruzhnoi nachal'nik, who was the supervisor and guardian for the state peasants (until the general peasant reforms in 1861–66).

zémskii nachál'nik, -ie -ki: land captain or superintendent of the peasantry. According to the law of July 12, 1889, each UEZD or county was divided into several (usually four or five) UCHASTKI or sections headed by the zemskii uchastkovyi nachal'nik. He was appointed by the government, preferably from the local nobility, and granted extensive authority over peasant affairs; he held both administrative and judicial power in the village, and had to watch over and review all the decisions of the peasant MIR. This changed after the 1905 Revolution, when the decree of October 5, 1906, established the peasants' equality of civil rights with other social groups and limited the administrative and control powers of the zemskii nachal'nik. The law of June 15, 1912, was intended to deprive the zemskie nachal'niki of their judicial authority, while reestablishing the office of MIROVYE SUD'I, justices of the peace elected by the local ZEMSTVOS. The new court organization in the countryside was introduced in only 10 provinces before World War I.

nachál'stvo. Commanders; authorities; administration (colloquial).

sél'skoe nachál'stvo: village authorities.

volostnóe nachál'stvo: township administration, and so on.

nadély, nadél'nye zémli (pl.). Allotment lands, a specific kind of land tenure in imperial Russia. Under the general peasant reform of 1861–66, the former serfs and the state peasants received land allotments for which they had to pay (to the state) redemption dues in installments (VYKUPNYE PLATEZHI, which were abolished in 1905–06). In the great majority of provinces (except for several western ones) the lands were allotted not to individual peasants nor to peasant households but to peasant communities. These had the right to use their nadel'nye zemli by distributing and redistributing them among members, but did not have the right to sell or mortgage them. (The government of Alexander III issued a special law, of December 14, 1893, concerning "measures to prevent alienation of the peasant allotment lands.") According to the census of landholding in 1905, in 50 provinces of European Russia there were 12.3 million peasant (and cossack) households (DVORY) that held 138.8 million DESIATINAS of allotment lands; of them, 9.5 million households with 115.4 million desiatinas held their allotments in communal tenure. At that time there were only 101 million desiatinas of privately-owned lands that belonged to the owners of various classes (of them the nobility owned 53 million desiatinas). The legal status of peasant landholding changed during the Stolypin period, when the decree of November 9, 1906, and the law of June 14, 1910, granted individual peasants the right to turn their shares of communal allotment lands into private property.

nadzirátel', -li, okolótochnyi nadzirátel'. Ward overseer, police official in large cities.

naëm, naimý. 1. Hiring of a laborer or of a service man. 2. Wages paid for hired labor or service. 3. Lease of property.

nagánenie or **nahánenie** (W.R. from the Pol. *naganienie*). Insult, offense, false accusation.

naiézd, -dy. Invasion of or intrusion into another person's property.

naiézdom pakhát' páshniu. To plow arable land at a considerable distance from one's permanent residence.

naiézdshchik, -ki. A man who invaded or seized somebody else's property, a term used in the *Novgorodskaia Sudnaia Gramota* (see GRAMOTA SUDNAIA).

naimít, -ty. A free laborer hired by contract for temporary work. In the *Russkaia Pravda* the term was used as an equivalent for ZAKUP, a half-free indentured laborer who worked on the master's land to repay the principle or interest of a loan. In the *Pskovskaia Sudnaia Gramota* and in the Sudebniks of 1497 and 1550, the naimit is a person hired by one of the litigants to fight against the opposite party in a duel before the court.

dvórnyi naimít: hired worker in a master's household.

nakáz, -zy. Order, instructions, esp. those given by the central government to its subordinate officials. In Muscovy *nakazy voevodam* were detailed instructions to the provincial governors. A *gubnoi nakaz,* given to the GUBNYE STAROSTY, contained regulations concerning the investigation and punishment of criminal offenses. The imperial government also issued numerous nakazy, for example, the *nakaz gra-zhdanskim gubernatoram* (of June 3, 1837), a detailed description of the powers and duties of the GUBERNATOR. The State Duma established in 1905–06 also had a detailed nakaz regulating its procedures. Perhaps the best-known nakaz was the *Bol'shoi nakaz* (the Grand Instruction) compiled by Catherine II and given in 1767 to the Commission for compiling a new Code of Laws (KOMISSIIA DLIA SOCHINENIIA PROEKTA NOVOGO ULOZHENIIA), a document filled with the liberal ideas of the Enlightenment but devoid of practical results. The deputies of this Grand Commission also submitted nakazy from their constituencies listing their needs, grievances, and desires.

nakazánie, -niia. 1. Admonition, exhortation, advice. 2. Punishment.

naklád. 1. Expenses. 2. Usury, interest.

nalóga or **nalóg, -gi.** In Muscovy, burden; oppression; extortion. In the 19th century, taxes. (See also PODAT'.) They were divided into two categories: *nalogi priamye* and *nalogi kosvennye,* direct and indirect taxes. Direct taxes included the land tax (*pozemel'nyi nalog*), other taxes on immovable property, the tax on industrial enterprises (*promyslovyi nalog*), and the tax on revenues from monetary capital. In 1913 these brought the state treasury 272.5 million rubles or 8 percent of the total state revenues (3,417 million rubles). The indirect taxes (*kosvennye nalogi*) consisted of the customs revenue (*tamozhennyi dokhod*) and of excise taxes on alchoholic beverages (except vodka, which was a state monopoly or REGALIIA), tobacco, sugar, petroleum products, and matches; in 1913 they netted the state treasury 708 million rubles, or 20.7 percent of the total revenue; the most inportant of the indirect taxes were the customs duties, which in 1913 brought in 353 million

rubles or 10.3 percent of the total revenue.

naméstnichestvo. The office of the NAMESTNIK and the territory under his administration.

naméstnik, -ki. Lieutenant. In Muscovy in the 14th-16th centuries, the namestniki were local administrators and judges appointed by the grand prince (later by the tsar) for the major towns and adjacent territories (while the VOLOSTELI were appointed to rural districts). The most important of the namestniki was the *bol'shoi namestnik* (grand lieutenant) of the city of Moscow. After 1550 the namestniki and volosteli in many regions were replaced by elected judges and STAROSTY, and in the 17th century the VOEVODY became the chief provincial administrators, although some elements of local self-government were preserved (mostly in the northern regions), and criminal justice remained in the hands of elected GUBNYE STAROSTY and TSELOVAL'NIKI. Not only the grand prince but also the church hierarchs in Muscovy had namestniki for administrative and judicial functions: *namestnik mitropolichii* or *namestnik vladychin* (see VLADYKA). In the imperial period, a namestnik of the emperor was like a vicegerent or viceroy. The statutes concerning provincial administration (*Uchrezhdeniia dlia upravleniia gubernii*) of 1775 intended that each GUBERNIIA be headed by an imperial namestnik, the GENERAL-GUBERNATOR, who would have a GUBERNATOR as his assistant; but this duplication proved impractical, and soon the gubernator remained the only NACHAL'NIK GUBERNII. The namestnik or general-gubernator remained in some places with two or three provinces under his control, but in the 19th century the office of the namestnik with vast powers survived only in such borderlands as the Caucasus and Poland. In Poland the office of the namestnik was in 1874 replaced by the office of the general-gubernator, and in the Caucasus in 1883 by the office called *glavnonachal'-stvuiushchii grazhdanskoiu* (civil) *chast'iu*. In 1905 the office of the namestnik of the Caucasus was reestablished. In 1903 the ill-fated and short-lived NAMESTNICHESTVO of the Far East was established, to be abolished after the Russo-Japanese War.

naméstnik-derzhávtsa, -ki -tsy. In the Grand Duchy of Lithuania, a prefect, holder of vast domains. The crown domains were divided into a number of districts and each was headed by a grand duke's NAMESTNIK who had military, administrative, and judicial powers. Starting at the end of the 15th century, the old Russian term namestnik was gradually replaced by the Polish term DERZHAVTSA (*dzierzawca*); for a period both terms were used.

nariád. In old Russia, order. In Muscovite military language, the term had the special meaning of artillery.

naród. Nation.

Prostói naród: common people, lower classes of the population.

naródnichestvo. Populism, a current among the Russian intelligentsiia in the second half of the 19th century. The populists admired the common people, esp. the peasantry and the allegedly primordial Russian agrarian commune (OBSHCHINA), and hoped that Russia would pass over from the communal way of life to socialism, avoiding the bourgeois stage of European development. Narodnichestvo found its most active manifestation in the movement "to the people" in the 1870s, intended to show the peasantry a bright vision of socialism. After the failure of this enterprise the most active faction of the NARODNIKI formed a revolutionary terroristic organization called NARODNAIA VOLIA which in 1881 achieved the assassination of Alexander II. *Neo-narodnichestvo* emerged at the end of the 19th century in ideological battles against the thriving Marxists. The most active narodnik elements organized the radical (and terroristic) party of the *Sotsialisty-Revoliutsionery* (see PARTIIA) which demanded, as its chief socioeconomic goal, the socialization of the land, i.e., the abolition of private landholding and the distribution of land among the agrarian communes. The more moderate elements of the narodniki, mostly intellectuals, organized the party of the *Narodnye Sotsialisty*. In the First and Second State Dumas the numerous TRUDOVIKI accepted, in general, the populist program of resolving the agrarian question by the abolition of private ownership of land and the distribution of all arable lands among the toilers (*trudiashchiesia*). The intellectual leader of narodnichestvo was the publicist, N. K. Mikhailovskii (d. 1904); the political leader of the Party of Socialist Revolutionaries was V. M. Chernov.

naródnik, -ki. Populist (see NARODNICHE-STVO).

nasíl'stvo = nasílie. Violence.

naslédok, -ki (W. R.). Heir; descendant.

nasóp, náspy. An additional amount of grain due upon repayment of a grain loan; the nasop of grain loans corresponded to the ROST (interest) of money loans.

navézka or **naviázka, -ki.** In the Grand Duchy of Lithuania, a fine paid by the guilty to the offended for a personal offense, injury, or property damage.

nedél'shchik, -ki. Bailiff or constable in Muscovy, a court agent who arrested suspected criminals, summoned litigants to court, executed court decisions and so on. Nedel'shchiki worked in groups and alternated in shifts after a week of work, hence the term.

nedoímki (pl.). Arrears in peasant payments to the government.

nédorosl', -li. In Muscovy, a service man's

son who was under age and not yet ripe for the tsar's service. (See LIUDI SLUZHILYE.)

némchin or **némets, némtsy.** Foreigner from Western Europe in Muscovite terminology; hence there were *gollandskie nemtsy, gishpanskie* (Spanish) *nemtsy,* and so on. Only in recent times does it mean esp. German.

nestiazháteli (pl.). Non-acquirers. A group of monks in Muscovy who defended spiritual Christianity against exaggerated ritualism and who opposed monastery ownership of landed estates with dependent peasants. Represented by the *zavolzhskie startsy* (trans-Volga hermits) and headed by Nil Maikov (of the Sora Hermitage) and Vassian Patrikeev, the nestiazhateli proposed at the church council of 1503 that the monasteries be deprived of the right to own landed estates. Their motion was defeated by the majority, led by Iosif Sanin, Abbot of the Volok monastery.

net, néti, or **nétchiki** (*byl v nétekh*). In Muscovy, service men who failed to appear for military inspection or review ordered by government authorities.

nétets (W. R.) = NIATETS.

nevésta, -ty (W. R.). Woman.

nevéstka, -ki. In modern Russian, either daughter-in-law (wife of one's son) or sister-in-law (wife of one's brother).

nevólia (W. R.). Slavery.

nevól'nik, -ki (W. R.). Slave.

niátets, niátsy. Prisoner of war or imprisoned criminal.

niátstvo. Captivity; imprisonment.

nogáta, -ty. A monetary unit of the KUNA system; considered equal to 2½ REZANY or to ¹⁄₂₀ of the GRIVNA KUN.

Nomokanon. Byzantine digest of ecclesiastical canons and secular laws. For the Slavic version, see KORMCHAIA KNIGA. In some old Russian sources the term occasionally appears in the distorted form of MANAKANUN.

notárius, -sy. A state official, according to the judicial statutes (*sudebnye ustavy*) of 1864, who compiled or verified all kinds of legal documents, esp. those dealing with the transfer of immovable property, such as purchase-, donation-, or mortgage-deeds, or testaments. He made copies of these documents, which were bound and deposited in the circuit court (OKRUZHNYI SUD, see SUD) archives under direction of the *starshii notarius.*

novgoródka, -ki. Silver coin of Novgorod the Great, equal in Muscovy to 2 Muscovite DENGI (MOSKOVKI), or to one KOPEIKA.

novokréshchen, -énny and **-ény.** In Muscovy, a term for the Tatars and others of various eastern tribes newly baptized into the Orthodox faith.

novoporiádchik, -ki. In Muscovy, newly arrived peasant who received from his landlord a plot of land and concluded with him a PORIAD or PORIADNAIA GRAMOTA, an agreement concerning the conditions of tenure.

novoprikhódets, -dtsy. A peasant newcomer, as opposed to the STAROZHILETS or old inhabitant.

núzha. Necessity; hardship, oppression; compulsion, coercion, force; *vis maior.*

O

obáda, -dy. Slander, false accusation.

obél' = *obél'nyi* KHOLÓP. Full slave.

óber-fiskál, -ly. Chief inspector (see FISKAL). The decree prescribing the duties of the ober-fiskal was issued by Peter the Great on March 5, 1711.

óber-ofitsér, -ry. Company-grade officer in the Russian army; in this category four ranks of the commissioned officers were included: PODPORUCHIK, PORUCHIK, SHTABS-KAPITAN and KAPITAN (in the cavalry: KORNET, PORUCHIK, SHTABROTMISTR and ROTMISTR); the officers of higher ranks (MAIOR, PODPOLKOVNIK and POLKOVNIK) formed the category of SHTAB-OFITSERY.

óber-prezidént glávnogo magistráta. Minister of municipal affairs in 1721–27.

óber-prokurór, -ry, in the SENAT. Assistant to the GENERAL-PROKUROR, an office established by Peter the Great in a decree of January 12, 1722.

Óber-Prokurór Sviatéishego Sinóda. Minister of Church Affairs. Having established the DUKHOVNAIA KOLLEGIIA, soon renamed *Sviateishii Pravitel'stvuiushchii* SINOD (in 1718–21), Peter the Great appointed to the Synod a civil official called the Ober-Prokuror who, as the "tsar's eye," supervised activities of the Synod (the INSTRUKTSIIA to the Synod's Ober-Prokuror was issued on June 13, 1722).

ober-sekretár', -rí. Chief secretary in the SENAT.

obgovór, or **ogovór, -ry.** Accusation, esp. a false accusation.

obída, -dy. Insult, offense, injury, violation of property rights, other kinds of lawbreaking.

obílie. Abundance or wealth in general, esp. grain or other agricultural products.

obiránie gosudárskoe. The election of the tsar (in 1613).

óblast', -ti. 1. In Old Slavonic, power, domination. 2. A region and its population. In imperial Russia, a territorial administrative division corresponding to the GUBERNIIA (province). In the 19th century there were oblasti in the Caucasus, in Central Asia, in Eastern Siberia, and in the Far East. In European Russia there was only the *Oblast' Voiska Donskogo*—the land of the Don Cossacks. At the beginning of the 20th century there were in the entire Empire 78 guberniias and 21 oblasti.

obmóva, -vy (W.R.). 1. Excuse. 2. Blame, reproach, accusation.

oborónets testaméntu (W.R.). Literally, defender of a testament, executor of a last will.

obóznyi, -nye. Quartermaster in the Zaporozhian Cossack army.

óbraz ángel'skii. Literally, angel's image. In old Russia, monkhood, membership in a monastic order. *Velikii angel'skii obraz* meant the strictest monastic VOWS, or SKHIMA.

obrazhénie maiestátu gospodárskogo, in the Grand Duchy of Lithuania. Literally, *crimen laesae maiestatis*—insult or outrage of the grand duke; the real sense of the term, according to the Lithuanian Statutes of 1529 and 1566, was treason, desertion to the enemy.

obróchnik, -ki. Generally, persons who paid OBROK. Specifically in Muscovy, "men whose relations to the government were based on contract" (G. Lantzeff, p. 150). In Siberia, in the 17th century, obrochniki included clerks, interpreters, smiths, millers, jailkeepers, executioners, watchmen, and even gunners.

obrók, -ki. In general, a lump sum paid yearly. In old Russia obrok meant a fixed payment of various kinds, including taxes paid to the government, payments for services (see OBROCHNIKI), and payments for the use of state or private properties. In the 1550s, when Moscow granted self-government to the local communities, having abolished the power of the NAMESTNIKI and VOLOSTELI, it ordered the population of these communities to pay obrok, a tax in money to the treasury, instead of the abolished KORMY, which had been paid to the former namestniki and volosteli. In Muscovy and in the imperial period, obrok was payment to the government for the use of state lands, pastures, forests, fishing and hunting places, mills, shops and so on. Therefore obrok was rent for leased state properties; *otdat' na obrok* meant to lease lands and other properties; *obrochnye zemli* meant leased lands. In the 18th century, after the poll tax had been introduced (see under PODAT'), the state peasants had to pay, in addition to the regular amount of the poll tax, a payment called obrok or *obrochnaia podat'* as rent for the state lands they used. On the private landed estates in the 18th and 19th centuries (before 1861), obrok was the quitrent, in money or in kind, paid by the peasants to their masters. The *obrochnaia* system as opposed to the *barshchinnaia* system (see BARSHCHINA) predominated in the central provinces of European Russia where the soil was relatively poor. Here the landlords preferred to leave the arable lands to the use of peasants who had to pay a set amount of obrok. By the late 1850s the proportion of obrok peasants had risen to 68 percent in Moscow province, 70 percent in Vladimir, and 90 percent in Iaroslavl'.

óbshchestvo, -va. Society, association, corporation. It is not possible to enumerate here all the obshchestva organized in Russia in the 19th century. There were, aside from commercial corporations and joint stock companies (*aktsionernye obshchestva*), many societies for promoting natural and social sciences (the oldest was the *Vol'noe Ekonomicheskoe Obshchestvo* founded in 1765), literature and literary studies, the arts, education, technology, medicine, agriculture, and so on, as well as credit societies, societies for mutual aid and charity, and many others. A list of obshchestva existent in Russia at the end of the 19th century is found in the *Entsiklopedicheskii Slovar'* of F. Brockhaus and I. Efron, vol. 21, pp. 609–28. Some of the organizations called obshchestvo had an official character and require explanation, like those mentioned below.

dvoriánskoe óbshchestvo: a noble corporation. According to the charter of the nobility of 1785, the nobles (DVORIANE) were granted the right to form in each guberniia such a dvorianskoe obshchestvo with important public functions. The assembly of the corporation (*dvorianskoe sobranie*) elected (in each province and in each district) a marshal of the nobility (PREDVODITEL' DVORIANSTVA), assessors to the courts, and the police chief of the district (*zemskii ispravnik* or KAPITAN). Even after the reforms of 1861–64, the marshal of the nobility preserved some of his government functions, since he presided over the zemstvo assemblies and several government boards in the district administration. After the reform of the State Council in 1906, which was thereafter to consist of 98 elected members (along with not more than 98 appointed by the tsar), the provincial corporations of the nobility elected (by two-stage elections) 18 members of the State Council.

grádskoe óbshchestvo: city corporation. The charter of cities of 1785 granted the city dwellers (GORODOVYE OBYVATELI) the right to form a gradskoe obshchestvo; the assembly of the city corporation was empowered to elect the mayor (GORODSKOI GOLOVA) and other members of the municipal administration, as well as the members of the municipal court (MAGISTRAT), and was permitted to send representations to the governor concerning municipal needs and interests. Catherine's reforms, however, failed to create active and viable municipal self-government, which was achieved only by the municipal statutes (*gordovoe polozhenie*) of 1870 (see POLOZHENIE).

kupécheskoe óbshchestvo: the society or corporation of the merchants included in the merchant GIL'DII.

meshchánskoe óbshchestvo: see MESHCHANE.

sél'skoe óbshchestvo: organization of the village. The village community or MIR, as the self-governing organization of the peasantry, was recognized and regulated by imperial legislation. In the regulations (UCHREZHDENIE) for the administration of the state domains, compiled under the direction of Minister of State Domains Count P. D. Kiselev and issued on April 30, 1838, the more important responsibilities of the village assembly (SEL'SKII SKHOD) were: the election of village officers; the release of members of the community and the acceptance of new ones; the allotment and the redistribution of arable land among the peasants; the regulation of the use of the communal woodland and hayfields; the apportionment of "soul" tax obligations; the collection of state and local taxes; the fulfillment of the military conscription quota; and, in general, the meeting of the economic and legal needs of the community. Those powers of the sel'skoe obshchestvo among the state peasants were largely carried over into the POLOZHENIE of February 19, 1861. By its terms the liberated serfs were to form, in each village, a sel'skoe obshchestvo. Its organ, the village assembly (sel'skii skhod), according to art. 51 of the polozhenie, was granted the following powers: (1) to elect local village authorities and delegates to the township assembly (VOLOSTNOI SKHOD, the next higher administrative level in the countryside); (2) to sentence to banishment (by two-thirds vote) from the community any undesirable members; (3) to release members from the community and to accept new members; (4) to appoint guardians for minors; (5) to permit the division of household and property within large families; (6–7) to apportion the arable land and common land of the village among households; (8–9) to present complaints and appeals concerning communal affairs and to petition the authorities concerning communal needs; (10) to establish taxation to cover communal expenses; (11) to apportion state taxes and other obligations; (12) to establish the remuneration of village officials and to check their accounts; (13) to select the required

number of recruits for military service; (14) to apportion the OBROK and BAR-SHCHINA owed to the landlord in the case of temporarily obligated peasants; (15) to prevent or to recover arrears on various obligations; (16) to make loans and grants; and (17) to grant power of attorney on behalf of the community. In 1889 the peasant mir was put under the strict supervision and control of the ZEMSKII NACHAL'NIK, but the decree of October 5, 1906, which granted the peasants equality with other social groups in matters of civil rights, reduced the power of the zemskii nachal'nik over mir activities as well as the mir's power over the individual peasants.

óbshchina, krest'iánskaia pozemél'naia óbshchina. Peasant commune or community, predominantly in Great Russia. The distinctive characteristic of this organization was periodic redistribution and equalization of the arable lands among households, according to the number of male souls, or working hands, or eaters in each of them. After the distribution of plowlands each household managed its affairs on its own. This system of periodic redistribution of holdings became widespread in the 18th, and esp. in the 19th, centuries. In the Muscovite period the grand princes, later tsars, were considered the supreme owners of all the lands with the exception of monasteries' and boyars' VOTCHINY. But in fact the state peasants in the central and northern regions, in the 15th—17th centuries, disposed of their plots of arable lands and meadows like private property: they sold, mortgaged, exchanged, divided, donated, or bequeathed them. The usual formula of peasant landholding was: *zemlia velikogo kniazia a nashego vladeniia* (grand prince's land in our possession). Only the common UGOD'IA of each peasant VOLOST' (rural district), such as forests, lakes, rivers and fisheries, vacant lands, and the like, were disposed of by the MIR of the volost'. On the privately-owned landed estates the peasant newcomers concluded with the landlord an agreement (PORIADNAIA) which regulated the size and conditions of their holdings.

In the 17th and 18th centuries, when the peasants on the privately-owned landed estates became the serfs of their masters, the estate owners intervened more and more in the peasants' life and economic activities. The poll tax introduced by Peter the Great, equal in amount for all male souls, had to be collected by the landowner from his serfs. This collection task motivated the landlords to equalize the peasants' plots of land. On many estates, especially where BARSHCHINA was practiced, the landlords established a roughly uniform work and tax unit (TIAGLO), usually including one working peasant couple. From each unit equal obligations to the government and to the landlord were exacted. To equalize the ability of all such units to pay, an equal portion of land was to be allotted. The peasant MIR was charged with the distribution and the redistribution of the land allotments among the households. At the end of the 18th century the government endeavored to introduce equalization (*uravnenie*) among the peasants on the state lands as well. This goal was achieved in the first decades of the 19th century. In this way, "the peasant was converted into the temporary occupant of the strips allotted him by his commune" (J. Blum, p. 328). When the general peasant reform was carried out in 1861–66, the allotment lands (NADEL'NYE ZEMLI) were given—in the great majority of the provinces—not to the individual peasants nor to the peasant households but to the peasant communities, and the practice of communal land tenure with periodic redistribution of the arable lands became the legally established institution.

According to the land census of 1905, in 50 provinces of European Russia there were 12.3 million peasant and cossack households, which held 138.8 million DESIATINAS of allotment lands; of them 9.5 million households with 115.4 million desiatinas had their allotments in communal tenure. Communal landholding was favored by the populists as the transitional stage to a future agrarian socialism, and by the government as the old *ustoi* (basis) of the conservative rural way of life. The agrarian disturbances in 1905–06 forced the government to change its evaluation of communal conservatism and to start a new policy intended to give the peasants the right of personal property in their lands. The so-called Stolypin legislation of 1906 and 1910 granted the individual peasants the right to turn their shares of the communal allotment lands into private property. The response was considerable. During the years 1907–14 one third of all communal landholders either left their communes or declared an intention to leave them.

obvód. Boundary of a landed estate (in Muscovy).

obýshchik, -ki. In Muscovy, government investigator of criminal affairs.

óbysk, -ki. In modern Russian, a search in a house or any other place. In Muscovy, an investigation of any criminal affair.

likhóvan(n)yi óbysk: an investigation whose results were unfavorable for the person concerned, with adverse legal consequences for him.

povál'nyi óbysk: in Muscovy, a general investigation through interrogation of the neighborhood in order to get information about the character and activities of a suspect or to verify his testimony.

obyvátel', -li. Inhabitant.

gorodovýe obyváteli: according to the charter of cities of 1785, those city dwellers who were listed in the register of city dwellers and constituted the city corporation (GRADSKOE OBSHCHESTVO).

nastoiáshchie gorodovýe obyváteli: owners of real estate in the city.

svobódnye sél'skie obyváteli: according to the Code of Laws of 1832, state peasants or free rural inhabitants, in contrast to the serfs. The liberation manifesto and the statutes (POLOZHENIE) of February 19, 1861, granted the former serfs the legal status of svobodnye sel'skie obyvateli. In fact the peasants' civil rights and liberties (including freedom of movement out of the community) were restricted by the power of the MIR, and after 1889 by the strict supervision of the ZEMSKII NACHAL'NIK. Only the decree of October 5, 1906, granted the peasants equality with other social groups in matters of civil rights, thus completing the work of emancipation half done in 1861.

óbzha (or **obzhá**), **-zhi.** In the lands of Novgorod the Great, a property taxation unit that varied from region to region. After Novgorod's annexation by Moscow the obzha as a unit of tax assessment in northern regions was usually equated to 10 CHETVERTS in each of the customary three fields, or 15 DESIATINAS in all.

odnodvórets, -rtsy. One-homesteader, a term from the 18th and 19th centuries. Odnodvortsy were the descendants of Moscow service men settled on the southern and eastern frontiers, as were the STREL'TSY, PUSHKARI, (SLUZHILYE) KAZAKI, IAMSHCHIKI and the like, as well as the lowest and the poorest category of the DETI BOIARSKIE (who had not been admitted into the DVORIANSTVO). In the 18th century the odnodvortsy had the right to dispose of their lands (this right was gradually restricted) and even to own serfs. From 1713 to 1783 the regiments of the LANDMILITSIIA were recruited from the odnodvortsy of the southern provinces; later they had to furnish recruits for the regular army.

Like the peasants, the odnodvortsy were obliged to pay the poll tax (PODUSHNAIA PODAT'). "In the 1740's there were 453,000 male odnodvortsy. By the 1850's their number had grown to 1.9 million" (J. Blum, p. 479). Most of them lived in the provinces of Kursk, Tambov, Orel, and Voronezh. In 1868 the name and legal category of the odnodvortsy was abolished, and they were thereafter included legally in the common mass of the SEL'SKIE OBYVATELI.

ognishchánin, -áne. Household manager. A term from the *Russkaia Pravda,* it is derived from OGNISHCHE meaning hearth, and then household. In the prince's household the ognishchanin could have been a member of the prince's household, a senior member of the prince's retinue (like BOIARIN), or a manager of the household, a bailiff, a major-domo. The term ognishchanin has been explained and interpreted in historical literature in many different ways (see *Pravda Russkaia,* II, ed. B. D. Grekov, pp. 138–46).

ognishche, -shcha. Hearth, then house and household.

ogovór, -ry. 1. Charge, accusation, imputation of a crime, incrimination. 2. Slander, false accusation.

ogúrnik, -ki. Defaulter (in payment of taxes); in general, a disobedient or recalcitrant person.

okhmístr, -ry (from the Ger. *Hofmeister*). A court office in the Grand Duchy of Lithuania.

okhótniki iamskíe (pl.). Postriders in Muscovy. See IAMSHCHIK.

okhrána. Protection. *Usilennaia okhrana* (reinforced security) and *chrezvychainaia okhrana* (extraordinary security) were introduced by the "regulations (POLOZHENIE) on measures for the protection of state order and public security," issued on August 14, 1881. According to this polozhenie, the central government could declare a state of reinforced, or the higher degree of extraordinary, security for one year in places threatened by the activities of revolutionaries, and, if necessary, could prolong this state for a year more. In these places the governor-generals or governors could issue compulsory regulations (*obiazatel'nye postanovleniia*) for maintaining public order, forbid public gatherings, deport unreliable elements, give orders to carry out searches and arrests, and refer cases of attacks on officials and of other grave crimes to the military courts. The state of usilennaia okhrana was declared in 1881 in St. Petersburg, Moscow, and other cities and provinces and in many cases was maintained until 1917.

okhránka. The department of political police (slang). See OTDELENIE OKHRANNOE.

okhránnoe otdelénie. See OTDELENIE.

okhroménie (W.R.). Mutilation as a result of injury or beating.

oklád, -dy. 1. A fixed amount of tax imposed on a group of taxpayers.

Oklád dénezhnyi and *khlébnyi:* a rate of salary for service men, determined in money, and—for the Siberian serving men in the 17th century—also in grain.

Oklád poméstnyi: in Muscovy, the size of landed estates granted by the government to service men (DVORIANE and DETI BOIARSKIE) as POMEST'IA; it was a norm that changed for the various categories of service men; the actual grants (DACHI) were often less than the norms called for.

okládchik, -ki. In Muscovy, those service men who distributed among their companions the salary paid by the government. On private VOTCHINY in the 18th century, selected peasants who determined the norms of work and payment for individual peasant households.

okól'nichii, -ie. In several West Russian cities in the Grand Duchy of Lithuania (such as Smolensk and Polotsk), a member of the administrative and judicial councils. In central and eastern Russia, a court rank known from the beginning of the 14th century. The first meaning of the term was the people around (*okolo*) the (grand) duke or the tsar, "courtiers of the immediate entourage of the tsar" (G. Lantzeff, p. 6). In the 16th and 17th centuries the group of okol'nichie formed a high rank of the Moscow serving aristocracy (ranking immediately below the BOIARE). They were members of the Boyar DUMA and served as military commanders, ambassadors, judges, and administrators.

ókrug, -gá. Territorial administrative unit of various kinds in imperial Russia. In a province designated as an OBLAST', an okrug was a district corresponding to an UEZD in a GUBERNIIA. According to the *uchrezhdenie* (statutes) of 1838 on the state peasantry, the state domains in each guberniia were divided into several okruga (normally coincident with uezdy), and each okrug was headed by an OKRUZHNOI (or -NYI) NACHAL'NIK. After the peasant reforms in 1861–66, this special administration of the state domains was replaced by the general peasant administration. When the court reform of 1864 was introduced, each district under the jurisdiction of a justice of the peace (MIROVOI SUD'IA) was called a *mirovoi okrug* (normally there were four or five such okruga in every uezd). Entirely different were the UCHEBNYI OKRUG and VOENNYI OKRUG —large territorial units including several guberniias.

Uchébnyi ókrug: school district, established in 1803, headed by a POPECHITEL' UCHEBNOGO OKRUGA, or superintendent of the school district, who supervised all the school activities in his okrug and had a decisive voice in appointing (or confirming) school personnel. The extent of his powers changed in the course of the century. In 1803 six uchebnye okruga were established; by the end of the 19th century, there were ten uchebnye okruga in European Russia, one in the Caucasus, and one in Siberia.

Voénnyi ókrug: military district. Russian military organization and education were reformed in the 1860s and 1870s under the direction of War Minister D. A. Miliutin. In order to reduce the burdensome centralization of all military affairs in the War Ministry, several voennye okruga were established in 1862, each of them headed by a general called *komanduiushchii voiskami . . . voennogo okruga* (commander of troops of the such-and-such military district). The purpose of introducing the voennye okruga was mainly to facilitate the general or partial mobilization of the armed forces. By the end of the 19th century there were eight voennye okruga in European Russia, one in the Caucasus, and five in the Asian possessions.

oktiabrísty (pl.). Octobrists (see SOIUZ SEMNADTSATOGO OKTIABRIA).

ókup. Redemption; ransom, esp. ransom for prisoners of war (covered by the *Ulozhenie* of 1649, chap. 8).

opála, -ly. In Muscovy, the tsar's disgrace, disfavor, sometimes entailing banishment from Moscow or other punishment.

opéka. Guardianship, wardship.

opekún, -ný. Guardian. *Pochëtnyi opekun* (honorary guardian), a title established in 1798 and granted by the emperor to certain high officials connected with the charitable and educational activities of the "institutions of the Empress Maria" (Maria Fedorovna, 1759–1828, wife of Paul I).

opolchénie. Militia, host, auxiliary armed forces drafted from the civilian population in cases of urgent necessity. In the 19th century the opolchenie was called to arms during the Napoleonic wars (twice, in 1806 and 1812) and during the Crimean War (in 1853–54). According to the law of 1874 which introduced universal military service, the state militia (*gosudarstvennoe opolchenie*) was composed of all male inhabitants from conscription age (20–21 years) to the age of 40, who were not enrolled in the standing army but were capable of bearing arms. The law of 1891 prolonged the period of opolchenie duties until the age of 43 inclusive. The opolchenie therefore consisted of former soldiers who had finished their term of active service and reserve status (15 years altogether) and of others who had not served in the active army. The opolchenie was liable to be called to arms not only in case of a war, but in peacetime for short terms of military training. The last detailed regulations concerning the opolchenie were issued on March 1, 1911. Military units formed from the mobilized opolchenie were not called POLKI (regiments) but DRUZHINY.

opolchénets, -ntsy. A mobilized member of the OPOLCHENIE (in the vernacular), corresponding to the official term: RATNIK OPOLCHENIIA.

opráva (or UPRÁVA). Rendering of justice.

opríchnik, -ki. Member of the corps of bodyguards and political police created by Ivan IV early in 1565. Their number gradually increased from 1,000 to about 6,000 men. The commanding group of the oprichniki corps, carefully selected by the tsar for its loyalty to him, consisted of boyars (titled and not titled) and DVORIANE of old families. The rank and file were recruited from the petty gentry. Several foreign adventurers were also admitted, such as Heinrich von Staden, who left interesting memoirs describing vividly the criminal exploits of this gang. Their goal, as set by the tsar, was to eradicate supposed treason. The oprichniki swore absolute and blind obedience to the tsar in fulfilling this task. They had a somber black uniform and rode on black horses carrying a dog's head and a broom on the saddle as symbols of their task—to bite to death the tsar's enemies and to sweep treason out of the Russian land. Shielded by the tsar, they murdered and tortured suspected traitors (and their kin and servants) with full impunity and robbed and pillaged their victim's property at will. After 1572, when Ivan's senseless terror abated, this "satan-like host" (as a contemporary characterized them) was disbanded.

oprichnina (or **oprishnina**). Formerly, a possession or property set apart (*oprich, oprichnyi*—separate). During the difficult Livonian war, soon after Prince Andrew Kurbskii deserted to the enemy, Tsar Ivan IV, fearing the boyars' treason and having decided to exterminate all kinds of treason and traitors, established early in 1565 a special state institution called the oprichnina. Having established the corps of OPRICHNIKI, he introduced also an administrative reform, creating a state within the state. He first removed from the jurisdiction of the general state administration about forty towns and VOLOSTI, mostly in the central and northern provinces, and made these territories subject to the direct control of the tsar and the oprichnina administration. Later he extended his personal realm to about a third of the Muscovite state. In Moscow itself a special OPRICHNYI DVOR for the tsar was built, and several streets and suburbs (SLO-BODY) were taken into the oprichnina, but the main oprichnyi dvor of the tsar was established in *Aleksandrovskaia sloboda* (later the town of Aleksandrov, in Vladimir GUBERNIIA), about 60 miles northeast of Moscow. In the regions included in the oprichnina the tsar confiscated the landed estates of many boyars, princes, and other landowners and granted them to his oprichniki as POMEST'IA. The old owners, when not accused of treason and murdered, received land grants in other parts of the state. The parts of the Muscovite state not taken into the oprichnina were called the ZEMSHCHINA, and remained under the traditional administration headed by the Boyar Duma. The establishment of the oprichnina was followed by a severe and senseless terror, under which not only allegedly treacherous princes and boyars (with their families and servants) but masses of common people (many thousands of them in Novgorod in 1570) and clerics (including Metropolitan Philip) perished. After 1572 the terror abated, the corps of oprichniki was disbanded, and some of the confiscated landed estates were returned to their former owners or their descendants. Some historians interpret Ivan's oprichnina as a kind of class struggle aimed at eliminating the political influence of the princes and boyars and at strengthening the monarchical power with the support of the lesser nobility, but the facts hardly corroborate this theory. The power of the Muscovite tsar was never formally limited by the boyars; moreover, the boyars' preponderance in the administration remained intact after the oprichnina; even the MESTNICHESTVO which limited the tsar's freedom in choosing higher military commanders and civil administrators remained intact (until 1682). V. O. Kliuchevskii characterized the oprichnina as senseless and reckless slaughter devoid of sociopolitical meaning. And one can subscribe to N. Riasanovsky's statements (*A History of Russia,* p. 170): "The story of the *oprichnina* is that of civil massacre, not civil war. . . . Most important, the pathological element in the tsar's behavior cannot be denied." When Peter the Great wanted to abolish the influence of the boyar aristocracy in the government, he simply abolished the rank of BOIARIN and the Boyar Duma as a government institution. Not one person had to be murdered to achieve this goal. For a recent survey of historical literature concerning the oprichnina, see A. A. Zimin, *Oprichnina Ivana Groznogo,* Moscow, 1964. See also S. B. Veselovskii, *Issledovaniia po istorii oprichniny,* Moscow, 1963.

ordýnets, -ntsy. Horde-man, a member of one of the communities of men who performed various services, first, for the khans of the Tatar horde, then for Russian princes (a term from the 13th–15th centuries). According to V. Sergeevich (*Drevnosti . . .* I, p. 305), ordyntsy were service men of the grand dukes, who took care of the supply and escort of the Tatar envoys. According to M. Liubavskii (*Ocherk . . .* , 2nd ed., 1915, p. 113), ordyntsy in the Kievan lands were service men whose duty was to escort Lithuanian-Russian envoys to the Tatar horde. According to G. Vernadsky (*The Mongols and Russia,* pp. 225–26), in Galicia the term covered all the men liable for special services to the horde. "In a narrower sense, each village commune of this type was also called a horde. The services required from the *ordyntsy* in Muscovy must have been similar to those performed by the horde men and horde servitors in West Russia."

ordýnshchina. A special tax in the Grand Duchy of Lithuania collected for the so-called gifts sent to the Crimean Tatar khan.

orël dvoeglávyi or (mod. Rus.) **dvuglávyi.** The two-headed eagle, Russian state emblem (borrowed from Byzantium) from the end of the 15th century to 1917.

orúdie, -iia. 1. Instrument, implement, tool. 2. Work or business in general. 3. Lawsuit, litigation. 4. Legal document.

5. In modern military language: cannon, artillery piece.

orúzhnichii or **oruzhéinichii, -chie.** Arms bearer, an official in Muscovy who took care of producing and storing weapons.

osëdlost' usádebnaia. Peasant homestead, homestead plot.

oslúshnik (or **ogúrnik**), **-ki.** Defaulter; disobedient or recalcitrant person.

osmén(n)ik, -ki. Collector of customs duties (OSMNICHEE).

osmína, -ny. A dry measure; a measure of land equal to one half of a CHETVERT'.

osmníchee. Customs duty on transported goods, a tax of one eighth.

osochéne (W.R. from a Pol. verb, *osoczyc*). Accusation, denunciation.

osóchnik, -ki. In the Grand Duchy of Lithuania, warden of the grand duke's (the state's) forests and hunting places.

ospóda (coll.) = GOSPODA. Masters, lords.

ospodár', -ri. 1. Master, lord in general. 2. The sovereign, the grand duke of Lithuania or Muscovy.

ostróg, -gi. First, a fortification, fort, blockhouse (esp. in Siberia); then a settlement, a town erected on the spot. In modern Russian, prison.

ostrózhek, -zhki. A small OSTROG, fortification and settlement.

Osvobozhdénie Trudá. Emancipation of Labor, the first Russian Marxist group, founded in 1883 in Geneva by several Russian political emigrants, headed by G. Plekhanov (in collaboration with P. Aksel'rod, L. Deich and Vera Zasulich). In the same year Plekhanov published a booklet, *Socialism and the Political Struggle,* and in 1884 a book, *Our Differences (Nashi raznoglasiia),* a biting criticism of Populist ideology. Plekhanov's and his friends' works laid the foundation for the rather widespread Russian Marxist and Social Democratic movement in the 1890s and the early years of the 20th century.

otáritsa. In the *Russkaia Pravda,* property (a plot of land and agricultural equipment) given by the landlord, for temporary use, to a ZAKUP. For various interpretations of the term otaritsa, see *Pravda Russkaia,* II, KOMMENTARII, B. D. Grekov, ed., pp. 512–15.

otbói. Resistance of a litigant to the execution of the court's decision.

ótchestvo. In Muscovy, ancestral (hereditary) position on the aristocratic hierarchical ladder (see MESTNICHE-STVO). In modern Russian, patronymic.

ótchich, -chi. 1. One who owns or claims a hereditary landed estate, a province, or a realm. 2. In West Russia, hereditary serf, peasant who had lived for generations on the same landed estate and was denied the right to leave his landlord.

ótchina, -ny. 1. Fatherland. 2. Hereditary landed estate (VOTCHINA), also a landed estate granted by the sovereign into full and hereditary ownership. 3. Property in general. 4. Principality or realm held or claimed according to the right of patrimonial succession (the conference of the Russian princes at Liubech, in 1097, already accepted the principle that each of the princes had his otchina). 5. Old, paternal (ancestral) rules, ways, and customs.

ótchinnik, -ki. Owner of a hereditary landed estate (VOTCHINNIK).

otchízna. In the legal language of the Grand Duchy of Lithuania, a landed estate inherited from one's father. In modern Russian, fatherland (poetic).

otchuzhdénie prinudítel'noe. Compulsory expropriation, esp. as applied to the large landed estates in the leftist slogans of the early 1900s.

otdelénie or **otdelén'e, -niia.** A section in large governmental offices. The ill-famed *Tret'e Otdelenie Sobstvennoi Ego Imperatorskogo Velichestva Kantseliarii* (Third Section of His Imperial Majesty's Own Chancery) was established by Nicholas I in 1826 as the highest office of the political police. It headed the corps of the gendarmery to

keep watch on all suspicious and harmful people, if necessary sending them into exile and keeping them under police surveillance; it was to observe non-Orthodox religious sects, the schismatic Orthodox (Old Believers) and foreigners living in Russia. In 1880 the Third Section was abolished as an independent office, and a Department of State Police was established within the Ministry of Internal Affairs.

okhránnoe otdelénie or OKHRÁNKA (colloq.): security section. In St. Petersburg, Moscow, and other large cities, a special section for political police, established within the general police administration.

otéchestvo. 1. Fatherland. 2. Hereditary rights and claims; in Muscovy esp. hereditary position on the aristocratic hierarchical ladder (see MESTNICHE-STVO).

otéts dukhóvnyi. Spiritual father, or priest-confessor.

otkáz krest'iánskii (khristiánskii). The legal discharge of peasants by their landlords in Muscovy in the 15th and 16th centuries. "The peasant who planned to leave was required to give the landlord or his agent formal notice, or *otkaz* as it was called, of his intention to move. If he left without doing this he was considered a fugitive and could be made to return" (J. Blum, p. 249). According to the Sudebniks of 1497 (art. 57) and 1550 (art. 88), the legal peasant otkaz could take place only once a year, during one week before and one week after St. George's Day (November 26th O.S.). Before leaving, the peasant was obliged to repay his debts to the former master and the POZHILOE or compensation for using his homestead.

otkázchik, -ki. Special agent sent by landlords in Muscovy (mainly in the 16th century), who wanted to attract more working hands for their landed estates, in order to *otkazat'*, or to obtain the discharge of certain peasants from their landlord by paying up all the debts and dues those peasants owed their landlord (see OTKAZ). The new master of such peasants could also be called an otkazchik.

ótkup, -pá. Franchise. The Moscow government used two systems for collecting customs duties and selling liquor: either the franchise or farming-out system, otkup, under which OTKUPSHCHIKI paid the government a fixed amount of money in advance to buy a monopoly on liquor sales or customs-collecting in a given area; or the so-called VERNAIA SLUZHBA (service under oath), under which VERNYE GOLOVY and TSELOVAL'-NIKI, taken from the local population and bound by the appropriate oath (*vera*), performed these financial services for the government and turned over all receipts to the treasury. In 1681 otkupa were abolished, and vernaia sluzhba became predominant in the whole country. In 1753–54 internal customs duties were abolished, and in 1755 the vernaia sluzhba in the liquor trade was replaced by the franchise system. In 1765–67 this system was made obligatory for all the provinces of the empire except Siberia. The sale of liquor by government agencies was reestablished in 1817 and abolished again in 1827, when the government returned to the farming-out or franchise system. In 1863 otkupa were abolished once more and the excise system introduced. In 1894 and after, under Witte's financial administration, the treasury was given the monopoly for selling liquor (mainly vodka) throughout the empire.

In the *Ulozhenie* of 1649 (chap. 25, art. 18) the word otkup meant bribe, but otherwise (as in chap. 18) it referred to the franchise system as described above.

otkupshchík, -kí. A person who bought from the government a franchise for the monopoly on the sale of liquor or on collecting customs duties in a cer-

tain area. Therefore, in Muscovy there were *otkupshchiki kabatskie* and *otkupshchiki tamozhennye*. After internal customs duties had been abolished (in 1753–54) only kabatskie otkupshchiki remained, and therefore in the 19th century the word otkupshchik meant only the holder of a monopoly on liquor sales in a given area. This ill-famed profession disappeared after 1863, when the OTKUPA were abolished.

otmérsh(ch)ina or **otmórshina, -ny.** Landed estate or other property left intestate after the owner's death.

ótpis', -si and **otpíska, -ki.** A letter or legal document of various kinds.

ótpis' platébnaia: certificate of money received.

otpíska voevódskaia: a VOEVODA's report to the central government.

otpór. In the legal language of the Grand Duchy of Lithuania, defendant (OTVETCHIK); also, objection before the court against an accusation or against claims made by another party.

ótpuski iamskíe (pl.). Duty of the local population in Muscovy to provide horses, carriages, and guides for the IAMSKAIA GON'BA.

otpusknáia, -nýe (grámota, -ty). Document of manumission of a slave.

otród. Children, descendants.

ótrok, -ki. 1. Young man, adolescent. 2. In Kievan times, one of the younger members of the prince's retinue, often in charge of various administrative functions.

otrók. In the language of the *Pskovskaia Sudnaia Gramota* (see GRAMOTA SUDNAIA) of the 14th-15th centuries, the dissolution of the contract between landlord and peasant (IZORNIK) before the peasant moved away from the landlord's estate. Each of the two parties had the right of otrok, which was permitted by law only in a part of Novem-

79

ber. (See parallel Muscovite term, OTKAZ.)

ótrub, -bá. "A consolidated farm upon which the peasant actually lived was called a *khutor,* while a similar holding cultivated by a family who still lived elsewhere (usually in the old house beside the village street) was called an *otrub*" (G. T. Robinson, p. 236). The creation of consolidated plots on the peasant allotment lands (NADELY) was one of the goals of the Stolypin agrarian reform put into effect after the decree of November 9, 1906. The technical task of consolidating scattered strips of peasant communal land was very difficult and complicated. Nevertheless, by the end of 1914 about one million otruba had been laid out by the government land surveyors (while more than 2.8 million peasant householders had petitioned for such consolidation of their nadely).

otvétchik, -ki. Defendant (see OTPOR).

otvód, in old legal language. Successful defense against accusation. In modern legal language, challenge of witnesses or jurors.

otvód, in agriculture. The allotting of a plot of land or surveying of a landholding.

otvódchik, -ki. Land surveyor, or witness as to the boundaries of a landholding under litigation.

otvolochénie práva or **otvolóka.** In the legal language of the Grand Duchy of Lithuania, either discontinuance or delay of a lawsuit.

otzyvánie. In the legal language of the Grand Duchy of Lithuania, appeal to a higher court.

P

pádcheritsa or **pádshcheritsa, -tsy.** Stepdaughter.

páguba. Destruction, ruin. In the legal language of the 11th-13th centuries, damage.

pái, paí. Share.

pákholok, -lki (W. R., from the Pol. *pacholek*). Servant.

paláta, -ty. House; hall (esp. in the Moscow Kremlin); chamber; palace; tsar's court and courtiers. In Muscovy, also workshop (*masterskaia palata*). When used with an adjective the term usually meant office, board.

burmísterskaia paláta: an office created by a decree of January 30, 1699. "This institution, which soon received the name of Ratusha (from the German Rathaus), consisted of elected representatives of wealthy Moscow merchants and had under its jurisdiction the local *burgmester* [BURMISTR] offices" (M. Florinsky, p. 367). Later it became a local office for the city and GUBERNIIA of Moscow. In 1721 the GLAVNYI MAGISTRAT was established as the central state office for municipal affairs.

kazënnaia paláta: the financial board in each GUBERNIIA established by the statutes (*uchrezhdeniia dlia upravleniia gubernii*) of 1775. After the establishment of the ministries (1802), a provincial office of the Ministry of Finance. Before the establishment of the Ministry of State Domains (1837–38) the kazennaia palata also administered state lands and had jurisdiction over the state peasants.

kontról'naia paláta: a provincial auditing body established in 1866, subordinate to the GOSUDARSTVENNYI KONTROLËR. It checked and verified the financial accounts of provincial government institutions.

kupétskaia paláta or *prikáz kupétskikh del:* in Muscovy in the 17th century, an office for handling government merchandise, mainly furs that came from Siberia as tax in kind from the Siberian natives and then were traded by the government.

paláta poslóv (in Pol., *izba poselska*): the second chamber of the Polish parliament according to the constitutional charter of the Kingdom of Poland, of November 15, 1815. It was composed of 77 nuncios elected by the dietines (SEIMIKI) of nobles and 51 deputies from the GMINA assemblies; the latter were composed of non-noble landowners, manufacturers, merchants, and educated people.

potéshnaia paláta: an office in Muscovy in charge of staging amusements for the court.

rasprávnaia paláta: Chamber of Settlement, ". . . organized about the middle of the 17th century as a standing committee of the [Boyar] Duma . . . [the] *Raspravnaia palata* had a definite organization, held its meetings regularly, had its activity defined by the Ulozhenie and by decrees, and attended to the cases brought from different prikazes or to petitions of private individuals" (G. Lantzeff, p. 16).

sudébnaia paláta: any of various judicial bodies (see SUD). The statutes of 1775 (*uchrezhdeniia dlia upravleniia gubernii*) established in each GUBERNIIA a *palata ugolovnogo suda* (criminal court) and a *palata grazhdanskogo suda* (civil court). They were called also *palata ugolovnykh del* and *palata grazhdanskikh del.* Each of these *gubernskie sudebnye palaty* consisted of a president (PREDSEDATEL'), two councillors (SOVETNIKI), and two assessors, all appointed by the central government. By a manifesto of December 6, 1831, Nicholas I granted the provincial assemblies of the nobility the right to elect two candidates for the presidency of each palata. One of the candidates was then confirmed in office by the emperor.

sudébnaia paláta, according to the statutes of November 20, 1864 (*uchre-*
zhdenie sudebnykh ustanovelenii): a high court tribunal in each of several large cities, with jurisdiction over several provinces. It stood between the SENAT and the district courts (*okruzhnyi sud,* see SUD). It was divided into criminal (*ugolovnyi*) and civil (*grazhdanskii*) departments. The president (*starshii predsedatel'*) of the sudebnaia palata watched over the activities of the lower courts to check on their legality. The sudebnaia palata was the normal court for the trial of political crimes and of crimes perpetrated by government officials. It was also a court of appeals from district courts (in cases decided without a jury).

paláts (from the Pol. *palac*). Palace of the grand duke of Lithuania.

palómnik, -ki. 1. Pilgrim. 2. Description of a pilgrimage (esp. to the Holy Land).

pámiat', -ti. 1. Memory. 2. Day of a Saint (usually of his death). 3. Memorial service. 4. In Muscovy, various kinds of document, memorandum, note, notice, record, and so on.

doiézdnaia pámiat': a certificate given to a court agent sent to summon parties or witnesses to a trial.

kormováia pámiat': a voucher for a food allowance.

nakáznaia pámiat': memorandum of instructions given to an official.

pan, pány (W. R.). Master, lord, esp. master of serfs. In the Grand Duchy of Lithuania the group of pany (nontitled lords), together with the princes, constituted a powerful feudal aristocracy, possessing vast landed estates. Some of them had several hundreds of their own military men as well as many thousands of serfs; even many trading centers inhabited by merchants and artisans belonged to pany. The pany exercised decisive influence in the government through the Council of Lords (see PANY-RADA) and occupied the highest positions in the central and provincial administration. In legal proceedings they were exempt from the jurisdiction of the grand duke's lieutenants and STAROSTY, and subject only to that of the grand duke himself.

pány dukhóvnye: prelates.

pány khorugóvnye: literally, banner lords; upon mobilization of the army, those who had the privilege of providing their own detachments (several hundred men, mostly their own retainers) under their own command and their own banner.

pány-ráda, pány-rády or **pány rádnye.** The Council of Lords and its members in the Grand Duchy of Lithuania. It consisted, in plenary sessions, of the members of the high aristocracy, clerical and secular: the Roman Catholic bishops; the top provincial administrators (VOEVODY and KASHTELIANY); several officials of the central government, including the MARSHALKI (ZEMSKII, DVORNYI, and GOSPODARSKIE), the HETMANY (NAIVYSSHII and DVORNYI), and the PODSKARBI ZEMSKII (the secretary of the treasury); and several lords and princes on the basis of personal privilege. The pany-rada exercised legislative, administrative, and judicial powers and had a decisive voice in military and diplomatic matters; hence it limited—de facto and de jure—the power of the grand duke. "The Council of lords, and more specifically its inner circle, was the main driving power of the government. The constitutional authority of the council was formulated in the Charters of 1492 and 1506 and finally guaranteed by the First Lithuanian Statute of 1529. According to the latter, the sovereign (gospodar) pledged to keep intact all of the former laws and to make no new laws without the consent of the council (Rozdel III, article 6)" (G. Vernadsky, *Russia at the Dawn,* p. 185). The Second Statute of 1566 (sect. III, art. 12, and sect. II, art. 2) recognized the legislative powers, and

the power to declare a general mobilization of the armed forces and to impose a general tax for military expenses, as belonging to the general diet (see SEIM VALNYI).

panamár'. See PONAMÁR'.

panovánie (W.R.). Domination; reign.

pánstvo. The status of being PAN (lord); ownership of a landed estate; domination over a territorial unit or over a realm, and the territory itself; the state. The sovereigns of the Grand Duchy of Lithuania called it *panstvo nashe.*

pápa (from Latin). The old title of the patriarch of Alexandria (Greek *pappas*). The Russian word for the head of the Roman Catholic church, the pope.

pápezh. Pol. and W.R. word for the pope (Pol., *papiez*).

par, parenína, párina. Fallow.

párobok, -bki. 1. Boy. 2. Young servant in a master's household, esp. slave (*parobok nevol'nyi*).

pártiia, -tii politícheskaia, -kie. Political party, nonexistent openly in Russia before the Revolution of 1905–06. Two rather sizable and influential parties, the Social Democrats and the Socialist Revolutionaries, formed their organizations, underground and abroad, before the Revolution; but they were never legalized, although the Social Democrats had their deputies in all four State Dumas, and the Socialist Revolutionaries had their faction in the Second Duma. A moderate Socialist party of the NARODNYE SOTSIALISTY and a left-liberal KONSTITUTSIONNO-DEMOKRATICHESKAIA PARTIIA were also not legalized but were openly active in political life. The principal parties are identified individually below. Some of the political parties formed after the Revolution of 1905 were called not partiia but

SOIUZ, and are defined under this term.

Pártiia Demokratícheskikh Refórm: the Party of Democratic Reforms, a small group slightly to the right of the KADETS; its outstanding members were the editor and publisher of the *Vestnik Evropy,* M. Stasiulevich, and Professors M. Kovalevskii and V. Kuzmin-Karavaev.

Konstitutsiónno-Demokratícheskaia Pártiia, K.D. or *Kadéty:* the most important and largest nonsocialist party. Its other title was the Party of National Freedom (*Partiia Narodnoi Svobody*). The party was formed in October 1905 by the merger of the Union of Liberation (see SOIUZ OSVOBO-ZHDENIIA) and the Zemstvo Constitutionalist group. The political program of the party called for Russia as "a constitutional and parliamentary monarchy," with a parliament elected by a general, direct, equal, and secret ballot. The agrarian program of the party demanded an increase of peasant lands at the expense of large private estates, with a fair compensation being paid by the state to the former owners. The K.D. party was headed by P. N. Miliukov, historian and publicist, and included a host of notable intellectuals and zemstvo men, such as P. Struve, A. Kizevetter, F. Rodichev, I. Petrunkevich, F. Kokoshkin, A. Shingarev, M. Vinaver, V. Maklakov, and the two brothers Dolgorukov. In the first State Duma the K.D. faction with its 170 deputies played the leading role. There were about 100 K.D. deputies in the Second Duma, but the electoral law of June 3, 1907, greatly reduced the K.D. Duma representation.

Pártiia Mírnogo Obnovléniia: the Party of Peaceful Reconstruction was a short-lived group formed in 1907 when the Octobrists (see SOIUZ SEMNADTSA-TOGO OKTIABRIA) became a kind of government party, and some of the more liberal zemstvo men (like D. Shipov and M. Stakhovich) left the Octobrist soiuz to form their own party.

Pártiia Naródnoi Svobódy: see KON-STITUTSIONNO-DEMOKRATICHESKAIA PARTIIA, above.

Pártiia Naródnykh Sotsialístov: the People's Socialist Party, formed in 1906. It was to the right of the PARTIIA SOTSIALISTOV REVOLIUTSIONEROV. At the head of the P.N.S. stood a group of writers, publicists, and scholars connected with the Populist periodical *Russkoe Bogatstvo,* V. Miakotin, A. Peshekhonov, S. Mel'gunov, and others. The party held to the ideal of socialism, and its agrarian program demanded the nationalization of land and the use of land only by those who tilled it themselves. But taking into consideration the contemporary political changes in Russia, the party renounced the tactics of armed uprising and individual political terrorism.

Rossíiskaia Sotsial-Demokratíche-skaia Rabóchaia Pártiia, S.D.: the Russian Social Democratic Workers Party was an avowedly Marxist party formally organized in 1898 during a clandestine congress in Minsk. Its predecessors were the Emancipation of Labor (OSVOBOZHDENIE TRUDA) group founded in Geneva in 1883, and the Union for the Struggle for the Emancipation of the Working Class (SOIUZ BOR'BY ZA OSVOBOZHDENIE RABOCHEGO KLASSA) founded in St. Petersburg in 1895. The organ of the new party was *The Spark* (*Iskra*), published abroad and secretly distributed in Russia. The second congress of the Social Democratic party, which took place in 1903 (in Brussels and London), adopted the program and statutes of the party. In its program the new party declared itself "one of the detachments of the world army of the proletariat" and set itself the goal of social revolution by which the dictatorship of the proletariat would turn the means of production owned by the capitalist class into the common property of the society. Its immediate political task was the overthrow of the tsarist autocracy and its replacement by a democratic republic. During the congress the question of party organization gave rise to serious disagreement between two factions of delegates. The group headed by Lenin (majority-ites, BOL'SHEVIKI) wanted to establish the party as a small but strong clandestine organization of professional revolutionaries, while the minority-ites (MEN'SHEVIKI), headed by Martov, advocated a broad and free organization of workers on the pattern of the German Social Democratic party. During the years that followed, different views concerning socialist tactics in the revolution led to a bitter and continual struggle between the Leninists and the Mensheviks headed by Iu. Martov, F. Dan', P. Aksel'rod and others, while Plekhanov and Trotskii stood outside the factional struggle. The Russian Social Democratic Workers party entered the revolutionary period of 1905–06 in a state of fragmentation. In addition to the two main factions, the Bolsheviks and Mensheviks, there were several newly organized national Social Democratic parties, such as the BUND (Jewish Workers Union) and the Polish, Lithuanian, Latvian, Ukrainian, and Armenian Social Democratic parties. In the spring of 1906 the unity congress in Stockholm succeeded in achieving formal unification of the party and in obtaining the adherence to the Russian Social Democratic party of the Bund and the Polish and Latvian Social Democratic parties. The next party congress in London (1907) preserved the formal unity of the party, but the struggle between the two factions continued unabated, and at the beginning of 1912 the followers of Lenin were formally organized as a separate party, the Russian Social Democratic

Workers Party (Bolsheviks). Among the Mensheviks, after the Revolution of 1905–06, there emerged a faction of so-called liquidators, who doubted the necessity of an illegal revolutionary organization and wanted the Social Democrats to turn to work in trade unions and in cooperative, cultural, and educational societies.

Pártiia Sotsialístov Revoliutsionérov, S.R., or *eséry:* around 1900 the Populists, while struggling against Marxism, accepted some elements of Marxian theory. However they included in their idea of class struggle not only the proletariat but also the laboring peasantry (*trudovoe krest'ianstvo*) and the revolutionary intelligentsiia; they paid special attention to the peasantry, whom they wanted to attract to the revolutionary movement. At the end of the 19th century the Agrarian Socialist League was founded abroad, and a number of revolutionary-populist groups emerged in various regions of Russia. At the end of 1901 a congress of the representatives of these groups established the Party of Socialist Revolutionaries; its leader and theorist was V. Chernov. (Some other socialist revolutionary leaders were Catherine Breshko-Breshkovskaia, M. Natanson, N. Avksent'ev, and M. and A. Gots.) Its organ (published abroad) was *Revoliutsionnaia Rossiia.* The Party congress in 1905 approved the program which stated, as the main goal of the movement, a free and Socialist society. The Party's agrarian program demanded the "socialization" of land, the expropriation of private owners and the distribution of the land equally among the toiling members of the agrarian communes. The political program of the Party demanded the overthrow of the tsarist autocracy and its replacement by a democratic republic on "a federative basis for relations between the separate nationalities." As a tactical weapon in the struggle against "tsarism," the S.R. party accepted and widely practiced terror against all the defenders of the old order. It assassinated government officials from ministers of internal affairs down to police constables.

páshnia. Plowland, arable land.

páshnia desiatínnaia, gosudáreva: land cultivated as an obligation for the needs of the sovereign (GOSUDAR'), and of the state, in the border districts in the south of Muscovy and in Siberia in the 17th century. The purpose was to provide the service men with food. The amount of land to be cultivated was measured in DESIATINAS. In the south, the new settlers and peasants of each district under such obligation (Belgorod, Kursk, Oskol, Voronezh, and some others) had to plow a total of from 100 to 200 desiatinas per district. In Siberia a peasant had to plow one desiatina for the sovereign for each four desiatinas he plowed for himself.

páshnia dvoróvaia: manorial plowland, cultivated by serfs.

páshnia naézzhaia: arable land far distant from one's permanent residence.

pásynok, -nki. 1. Stepson. 2. In the Kievan period, younger members of the prince's retinue (like OTROKI, DETSKIE, GRID').

paterík. A collection of the Lives of the Saints.

patriárkh, -khi and **patriárshestvo.** Patriarch, the highest hierarch of the Orthodox church. Before 1589 the Russian church was headed by the *Mitropolit Moskovskii i vseia Rusi(i).* In January of that year the Moscow government, the council of Russian hierarchs, and the visiting Patriarch Jeremiah of Constantinople elevated the metropolitan of Moscow, Job, to the dignity of Patriarch of Moscow and of all the Russias. "Reluctantly the oriental patriarchs ratified Job's new title. The fifth, i.e.,

last, place was accorded to him in the rank of honor among the patriarchs. In spite of that, the creation of the patriarchal see in Moscow increased her prestige not only at home, but among all of the Greek Orthodox in the Near East as well" (G. Vernadsky, *Political and Diplomatic History of Russia,* p. 180). When Patriarch Adrian (1690–1700), a conservative hierarch who did not approve of Peter the Great's reforms, died, Peter did not summon the church council for the election of a new patriarch and appointed the metropolitan of Riazan', Stephen Iavorskii, to be a "guardian of the patriarch's throne." In 1718 Peter established, as the highest organ of church administration, the DUKHOVNAIA KOLLEGIIA (Spiritual College) which was soon renamed the Holy Synod (SVIATEISHII PRAVITEL'STVUIU-SHCHII SINOD). It consisted of several high hierarchs, but in fact was controlled by a secular official, appointed by the tsar, with the title OBER-PROKUROR SVIATEISHEGO SINODA. The Moscow patriarchate was not reestablished until the Church Council of 1917.

pazh, pazhí. Page, a boy from an aristocratic family who performed service at the court. Peter the Great introduced the ranks of the pazhi and *kamer-pazhi,* who, after several years of court service, were promoted to be commissioned officers. In 1802 a special military and general educational school called the *pazheskii korpus* was established for boys from aristocratic families.

pechál'nik, -ki. Defender, intercessor, solicitor.

pechálovanie. Intercession, solicitation; esp. the old custom of intercession by high clerics, before princes and tsars, in favor of an accused person.

pechátnik, -ki. Seal-keeper (a term known from sources as early as the 13th century), an official who kept the seal of a prince or tsar and affixed it to official documents issued from the prince's chancery. In 17th-century Muscovy the tsar's seal-keeper (*pechatnik gosudarev*) was usually a DUMNYI D'IAK.

pénia, -ni. A punishment, esp. a monetary fine.

péniaz', péniazi or **pénezi** (W.R.; in Polish, *pieniadz*, Ger. *Pfennig*). 1. A small silver coin in the Grand Duchy of Lithuania worth one tenth of the GROSH LITOVSKII. 2. Plural, money in general (the term was used from the end of the 12th century on).

peredél, -ly. Reallotment of peasant lands. In the 18th and 19th centuries communal peasant land (see OBSHCHINA PEREDEL'NAIA) was divided into several tracts according to the quality of the soil and the distance from the village. Each tract was divided into three fields for the purpose of crop rotation, and each peasant household received strips of land in each tract and each field according to its size. To equalize the economic conditions of its member households, the MIR periodically reallotted the strips of arable land among its members. The peredely were either *obshchie* (general redistribution of lands among all the members of the mir) or *chastnye* (partial), involving only some of the peasant families. The rules issued by the government on June 8, 1893, established a minimum term of 12 years for a general redistribution of communal lands; the mir decision (PRIGOVOR) on a general redistribution had to be approved by two thirds of the householders and confirmed by the district administrative authorities.

chërnyi peredél: literally, black (or general) redistribution of lands among the toiling people of the entire country. Chërnyi Peredel was the name of a small and short-lived group (1879–81) founded by G. Plekhanov and his friends. In 1879 the party called ZEMLIA I VOLIA (see also VOLIA) split into the NARODNAIA VOLIA, a terrorist organization aimed at an immediate political revolution, and the Chernyi Peredel, which opposed political terrorism and considered propaganda among the peasants the main weapon for the achievement of a social, agrarian, revolution.

pereëm. Reward for catching a fugitive slave.

pereëzshchik, -ki. A traitor who defects to the enemy with secret information (a term from the *Ulozhenie* of 1649, chap. VII, art. 20).

perelóg. Land which, after several harvests, was left to lie fallow for a number of years.

pérepis'. Census; *revizskaia perepis'*. See REVIZIIA.

perepíschik, -ki. In Muscovy, a registrar, one of those persons who, in the 17th century, compiled the PEREPISNYE KNIGI. In modern Russian, mainly copyists, but also persons taking a census (PEREPIS').

peresúd. 1. Review of a court decision by a court of appeals. 2. Payment for the review of a legal case.

peresúdchik, -ki. A judge reviewing a legal case.

perevedénets, -ntsy. Transferred person. The government in the 17th century needed agricultural colonists in Siberia and obtained them either by inviting VOL'NYE GULIASHCHIE LIUDI (free men, not enrolled in a TIAGLO) to the large Siberian areas, or by transferring to Siberia peasants from state villages in European Russia; the latter were then known as perevedentsy.

perevésishche, -shcha. A place where nets were hung to trap birds and wild animals.

perevét. Treason, secret communication with the enemy.

perevétnik, -ki. Traitor, a spy for the enemy.

perevóz, -zy. Crossing of a river and the toll for crossing a river in a ferry, which was collected by the *perevóz(sh)chiki* or ferrymen.

pervoprestól'nik. Primate, highest hierarch of the church.

pervoprisútstvuiushchii, -ie. The president of a Senate department, or of a general session of the Senate.

pervosovétnik. First councilor, the senior member of the Boyar Duma. In general, a leader of a group.

pervostatéinyi, -nye. 1. Prominent person in general. 2. In some large VOTCHINY in the 18th century, a leading peasant elected by the MIR to help the manorial administration.

pervosviatítel'. Primate, highest hierarch of the church.

peshekhódets, -dtsy. In Muscovy, a poor peasant who did not possess any work animals and did all his work for the landowner on foot.

peshéts, peshtsý. 1. Pedestrian. 2. Foot soldier (in Muscovy).

piad', -di. A measure of length, c. 23 centimeters (the distance between the ends of the extended thumb and forefinger).

piaták, -kí, or **piatikopéechnik, -ki.** A copper coin worth 5 copecks, minted first in 1723. In the second half of the 19th and the beginning of the 20th century, also a small silver coin equal to 5 copecks.

piátenshchik, -ki. A person who branded horses offered for sale and collected the duty called PIATNO.

piatialtýnnyi, -nye. A silver coin, minted beginning in 1760, equal to 15 copecks (or five old ALTYNY).

piatidesiátnik, -ki or **piatidesiátskii, -kie.** 1. Commander of a unit of 50 soldiers in Muscovy. 2. Elected local official who had the duty of preserving order in the community.

Piatidesiátnitsa. Pentecost.

piátina. 1. Every fifth sheaf of the peasants' grain, or a fifth part of all his agricultural produce paid to the landowner.

2. The fifth part of an income in general, paid as an extraordinary tax in Muscovy (= PIATINNYE DENGI).

piátina, -ny. The five Novgorodian provinces (*Votskaia, Obonezhskaia, Derevskaia, Bezhetskaia, Shelonskaia*) that comprised the old basic territory belonging to Lord Novgorod the Great.

piatnó. Branding of horses offered for sale, and the duty paid for this.

písar or **písar', -ri, -riá.** Scribe, clerk, secretary. In the Grand Duchy of Lithuania, *pisar* (secretary) *zemskogo povetovogo suda* (see SUD); *pisar zemskii,* chief secretary. In the Ukrainian Cossack army: *pisar sotennyi* (SOTNIA, one hundred); *pisar polkovoi* (POLK, a regiment); *pisar voiskovoi* (chief secretary of the army). In imperial Russia the *volostnoi pisar',* clerk of the peasant VOLOST' (rural district, township), played an important role in local peasant affairs. Each military unit—ROTA (company), battalion, and POLK (regiment)—as well as each staff and military institution, had one or more pisari.

písarstvo. Rank and office of the PISAR in the Grand Duchy of Lithuania.

píschee. A small duty paid for the registration of a document by a clerk (PISETS).

piséts, pistsý. In general, a clerk. *Pistsy tatarskie* or *ordynskie:* Tatar revenue agents who took a census of the Russian population for the purpose of taxation. In Muscovy, pistsy were service men who, aided by POD'IACHIE (clerks), compiled census books called PISTSOVYE KNIGI.

pishchál'nik, -ki (in Muscovy). 1. Musician. 2. Musketeer, soldier armed with fire arms (from *pishchal',* which could mean either a kind of flute or a musket).

pískup, -py (W.R.). Bishop.

pis'mó, pís'ma. Letter or document of various kinds.

pis'mó sóshnoe (in Muscovy): compilation of census books called PI-

87

STSOVYE KNIGI, when the basic taxable unit was the SOKHA.

zarúchnoe pis'mó: signed letter.

plákha, -khi. Scaffold; executioner's block.

platëzh, -zhí. Payment.

Vykupnýe platezhí: redemption payments. When in 1861 the serfs were liberated with land allotments, the government compensated the former masters for the lands allotted to the peasants by means of interest-bearing treasury bonds. The peasant communities were then obligated to pay the government, over a period of forty-nine years, for the lands received. The valuation of the lands allotted to the peasants was in itself not high (an average of 27 rubles for one DESIATINA, with yearly payments of about 1.6 rubles), but the extremely low productivity of peasant farming and the relative frequency of crop failures made the redemption payments a heavy burden and caused peasant payments to the treasury to fall steadily in arrears. In 1881 the government reduced the redemption payments by 20 percent on the average. The state peasants, according to the law of 1866, received their land allotments in larger sizes and on more favorable terms than did the former serfs. They had to pay an OBROCHNAIA PODAT' (annual rent) for their lands; in 1886 this was converted into redemption payments, which were to expire in 44 years. During the Revolution of 1905, under pressure of agrarian disturbances, the manifesto of November 3, 1905, abolished redemption payments for peasant allotment lands.

platézhnitsa, -tsy. In Muscovy, a book or register of taxes due to be collected in the next year.

plémia, plemená. Family; kin; relatives; tribe; people of the same origin.

plemiánnik, -ki. 1. Relative in general, kinsman. 2. Nephew.

plug, -gi (or RÁLO). Plow; in the Kievan and pre-Kievan period, a taxable unit in some places.

poberézhnoe. A duty or tax paid for the disembarkation of merchandise.

pobór, -ry. An obligatory payment (tax, dues, etc.), esp. a payment for official activities of court agents.

pobórets, pobórtsy povétovye. Tax collector in the Grand Duchy of Lithuania.

pobórshchik, -ki. In Muscovy, tax collector in rural communities in the northern regions.

póchet, póchty. Detachment of military men, formed, armed, and commanded by one of the PANY KHORUGOVNYE or princes in the Grand Duchy of Lithuania.

pochínok, -nki. A recently built hamlet and a new clearing of land for cultivation.

pódat', pódati. Tax, general term in imperial Russia.

gosudárstvennaia obróchnaia pódat': state OBROK tax, established in 1866 to be paid by the state peasants for the use of land considered legally to belong to the state. In 1886 this tax was raised and converted into VYKUPNYE PLATEZHI.

kazënnye pódati: taxes paid to the state treasury.

podúshnaia pódat': soul tax or poll tax, established by Peter the Great's decree of January 11, 1722, at a rate of 80 copecks per male person of the lower social classes, without distinction as to age or economic condition. The nobility, officialdom, and clergy were exempt from this tax. The tax was soon lowered to 74 and 70 copecks, but at the end of the 18th century it was raised to one ruble and in 1810–12 to 2 and then to 3 rubles. It was abolished in 1883–86.

podátok, podátki. Levy in money and in kind from the TIAGLYE LIUDI in the Grand Duchy of Lithuania.

podcháshi(i) (Pol. *podczaszy*). A court official in charge of beverages, in the Grand Duchy of Lithuania.

pod(d)iáchii or **pod'iáchii, -chie.** Clerk in Muscovy. According to Kotoshikhin, there were about 1,000 podiachie working in the central and local government institutions. Aside from the podiachie, who were officials, there were in the larger cities of Muscovy the so-called *ploshchadnye podiachie,* acting in the market square (*ploshchad'*), who compiled various kinds of documents for private persons; normally, they formed an association (ARTEL') with mutual responsibility.

póddánnye (pl.). In the Grand Duchy of Lithuania, a general term for dependent peasants; there were *poddannye gospodarskie, panskie,* and *klashternye,* i.e., subject to the sovereign, to the private landlords, and to the monasteries. In modern Russian, póddannye are citizens (subjects) of a country.

poddánshchina. A tax in the Grand Duchy of Lithuania, another term for SEREBSHCHIZNA.

pod"esaúl, -ly. A rank in the cossack troops corresponding to the rank of SHTABS-KAPITAN in the infantry (a rank of the 9th class according to the TABEL' O RANGAKH).

pod"ézd. A visit to a locality by a bishop or his representative and the payment received by him from the local clergy.

pod"ezdnói, -nýe. Messenger or adjutant of a prince.

podkomóryi, or **pidkomórii, -rie.** Office in the Grand Duchy of Lithuania, established on the Polish model. 1. A court office (*podkomorii gospodarskii*). 2. A judge in the POVET who handled litigation concerning landed estates of the SZLACHTA. (The office of the podkomoryi was defined in the Second Lithuanian Statute of 1566, sect. IV, art. 70.)

pódlinnik, -ki. Original document.

podmët. "Leaving things at another's house in order subsequently to accuse him of theft" (G. Vernadsky, *Mongols,* p. 356); this meaning of the term is clearly evident in the *Ulozhenie* of 1649, chap. XXI, art. 56.

podmétchik, -ki. A person who perpetrates PODMËT; in less plausible interpretations, traitor or spy.

podmóga. In Muscovy, an advance in money, grain, or animals given by a landlord to a newly arrived peasant to help him start the cultivation of a newly occupied plot.

podpíschik, -ki. In Muscovy, one who forges a document or the signature of another person. In modern Russian, subscriber.

podpolkóvnik, -ki. Lieutenant-colonel, a rank of the 7th class in the Table of Ranks. (See TABEL'.)

podporúchik, -ki. Second lieutenant, a rank of the 12th class in the TABEL' O RANGAKH.

podriád, -dy. Contract.

podriádchik, -ki. Contractor.

podrúchnik, -ki. A subject of a prince or other magnate.

podséka. An old tillage system in forested areas, in which trees were cut and patches of woodland burned out in order to make them fit for agriculture.

podskárbii. Treasurer (from Pol. *skarb,* treasury). In the Grand Duchy of Lithuania the *podskarbii zemskii* was the minister of finance and of state domains; the *podskarbii dvornyi* was his assistant.

podstóli(i). A court office in the Grand Duchy of Lithuania.

podsúdok, -dki. An assistant judge in the ZEMSKII SUD in the Grand Duchy of Lithuania.

podsusédnik, -ki. (W.R. pl., *podsusédki.*) Dependent, a member of the household not enrolled in the lists of the TIAGLYE LIUDI; apparently the same as ZAKHREBETNIK.

podúshnaia. Poll tax; see PODAT' PO-DUSHNAIA.

podvérnik, -ki. Court guard (in Pskov).

podvóda, -dy. Obligation of the local populace to furnish transportation for government agencies, carts or saddle horses with guides, or boats with rowers.

podvóiskii, -skie. Court agent and police officer in the Grand Duchy of Lithuania and in Novgorod and Pskov (in the period of their independence); his chief duty was to summon litigants before a court.

podvórie, -riia. A DVOR (household) in general, esp. a city household that belonged to an outside owner (like a monastery or a rich landowner).

podvórnik, -ki. A person who lived and worked in another's household.

podýmshchina. A tax exacted in Kiev and Volyn' provinces (in the 14th–16th centuries) from each DYM (smoke), therefore from each inhabited peasant house.

pogánin, pogányi, -nye; pogánstvo (collect.). Heathen, non-Christian; a foreign enemy.

pogolóvshchina. 1. Murder. 2. Penalty for murder. 3. In the Grand Duchy of Lithuania, a general extraordinary tax for military needs.

pogón, -ny. An old term for PROGON, a payment for travel expenses of official travelers.

pogóst, -ty. A settlement in northern regions with a church, cemetery, and marketplace; then, a rural administrative and fiscal district centered around this settlement, a part of the UEZD, like a VOLOST' (township). In modern vernacular Russian, cemetery.

pógreb. 1. Cellar. 2. Prison. 3. End, settlement of damages, liquidation of claims.

poklázha. 1. Load, freight. 2. Things given to someone for safekeeping, and the agreement about this transaction.

poklëp, -py. False accusation.

pokón. Custom, rule.

Pokróv, Pokróv Bogoróditsy. The Intercession of the Holy Virgin, a great Orthodox church holy day on October 1st (O.S.).

pokrúchenik, -ki. In Siberia in the 17th century, "the agents of the *voevodas* who carried on undercover business transactions of the *voevodas*" (G. Lantzeff, p. 120). In the 19th century, in the northern regions, members of fishermen's and craftsmen's companies (ARTELI), who received loans in money or equipment.

pokrúta. A term used in the Pskov charter for a loan or subsidy, in money or grain, granted by an owner of land to a tenant farmer (IZORNIK).

polávochnoe. Tax from the LAVKI, stores or shops.

póle, poliá. 1. Field; steppe. *Dikoe pole*, the wild or untamed steppe, the vast open plain on the southern frontier of the Moscow state. 2. Judicial duel.

polétnoe. Yearly payment.

políchnoe. Material evidence of theft or robbery.

polítsiia. Police in the 18th and 19th centuries. In Muscovy the local administrators, either appointed by the central government (as NAMESTNIKI, VOLOSTELI and VOEVODY) or elected by the local population (as STAROSTY and SOTSKIE), combined in their hands both judicial and police functions. The imperial government tried to organize the police as a separate branch of the administration. Peter the Great appointed in 1718 a *general-politseimeister* for St. Petersburg, and in 1721 an *ober-politseimeister* in Moscow. The statutes of GUBERNIIA administration of 1775 created the office of the GORODNICHII (appointed by the government) as the police head in cities and towns, while in the rural areas of each UEZD the police was headed by the ZEMSKII ISPRAVNIK or KAPITAN, elected by the assembly of the local nobility. The rural police was then called the *zemskaia politsiia;* its police office, called the *nizhnii zemskii sud,* was headed by the ispravnik, assisted by three ZASEDATELI. In 1782 the government issued a police statute (*ustav blagochiniia*) that established a police body called the UPRAVA BLAGO-CHINIIA in the cities and towns. The heads of police in St. Petersburg and Moscow were then called ober-POLI-TSIIMEISTER; in the capitals of the provinces (*gubernskie goroda*), politsiimeister; and in the district towns or county seats (*uezdnye goroda*), gorodnichii (see GOROD). In 1862 the office of the gorodnichii was abolished; the ispravnik was now appointed by the government, and his authority was extended to the whole territory of the uezd, including the uezdnyi gorod. The head of the police in the gubernskie goroda was the politsiimeister until 1917. The lower police organs, PRI-STAV and GORODOVOI, are explained under the corresponding terms. The highest organ of police administration was the Ministry of Internal affairs (from 1810 to 1819, the Ministry of Police).

politsiiméister or **politseiméister** or **politsméister, -ry.** Head of the city police.

poliúdie. In Kievan Russia, the prince's winter expeditions for collecting tribute and administering justice around the country; also the term for tribute itself. In the Grand Duchy of Lithuania, even in the 15th and 16th centuries, the term poliudie was used for the KORMY that the local population had to provide for visiting government officials or for landlords.

polk, -kí. In old Russia, a military host, troops in general; a large military unit; military expedition; war in general; a battle. In Muscovy, a large detachment or division of the army. "The standard division of the Muscovite army of the late 15th and the 16th centuries into five large units certainly followed the Mongol setup. Those units were known in Russian as *polki.* They were as follows: the center (*bol[']shoi polk,* literally the big division); the right arm division (*pravaia ruka*); the left arm division (*levaia ruka*); the advance guard (*peredovoi polk*); and the rearguard (*storozhevoi polk*)" (G. Vernadsky, *The Mongols and Russia,* p. 363). In the 17th century in Muscovy appeared the so-called *polki inozemnogo stroia* (*soldatskie, reitarskie,* and *dragunskie*), all regiments formed and trained on West European models. In the regular army created by Peter the Great, the polk or regiment became the basic military unit. At the turn of the 19th century, the infantry regiment consisted of 4 battalions or of 16 companies, altogether about 2,000 men (doubled in war time). The cavalry regiment consisted of 6 squadrons (about 900 men).

polkóvnik, -ki. Colonel, a rank of the 6th class according to the Table of Ranks. (See TABEL'.)

pólnaia (grámota). See GRAMOTA POLNAIA.

pólnitsa. 1. Full property right. 2. Full slavery.

polón. Captivity; captives; military booty in general.

poloniánik, -ki. Prisoner of war. The *Ulozhenie* of 1649 (chap. VIII, art. 1–7) established a special tax, paid by all the classes of the population, for the ransom of polonianiki.

polóvnik, -ki (from *polovina,* one half). Sharecropper. The polovniki were free but impoverished peasants, without land of their own, working as tenants on the lands of private landowners or of monasteries. "The share-cropper (*polovnik*) agreed to remain with the lord for an agreed upon number of years and to pay a fixed proportion of his crop to the lord as rental. The size of this share varied, ranging from one-fifth to as much as one-half. On his arrival the *polovnik* received a loan of cash or of grain from the landlord in order to get started on his farming, and to carry him over until he brought in his first crop" (J. Blum, pp. 100–01). The number of polovniki was great in the northern regions of Muscovy, and still considerable in the 18th century.

polozhénie, -niia. In imperial Russia, a statute that defined the legal status and activities of an administrative branch, a category of the population, or a self-governing institution (other terms with a similar meaning were UCHREZHDENIE and USTAV). The charter of cities of 1785 included the *remeslennoe polozhenie*, the statute pertaining to craftsmen's organizations. In 1861 the government issued the *obshchee polozhenie o krest'ianakh vyshedshikh iz krepostnoi zavisimosti*, the general statutes concerning emancipation of former serfs, and several additional statutes concerning this new class of free citizens. In 1870 (and in 1892) there was issued a *gorodovoe polozhenie* for the municipalities. There were also many other statutes called polozhenie.

poltína, -ny or **poltínnik, -ki.** Half a ruble, 50 copecks, minted as a silver coin from the beginning of the 18th century.

poludénga, -gi or **polúshka, -ki.** One half of a DENGA.

polugolová. Literally, a half of a head, an expression used sometimes to refer to a lieutenant-colonel in Muscovy, an assistant of the GOLOVA STRELETSKII who commanded a half regiment of the STREL'TSY.

poluimperiál, -ly. A gold coin minted first in 1755; until 1897 it was equal to 5 rubles, and after the monetary reform of 1896–97, 7½ rubles.

polupoltína, -ny. A silver coin worth a quarter of a ruble, or 25 copecks; in the vernacular, called CHETVERTAK.

polúshka, -ki. A copper coin introduced early in the 18th century; equal to one half of a DENGA.

pól'zovanie zemlëiu. A legal term denoting land tenure and use. The law of February 19, 1861, on peasant land tenure (*polozhenie o pozemel'nom ustroistve krest'ian*, art. 115) distinguished between *obshchinnoe pol'zovanie zemlëiu*, communal land tenure (see OBSHCHINA POZEMEL'NAIA), and *podvornoe nasledstvennoe* or *potomstvennoe pol'zovanie*, hereditary household tenure.

pomázanie or **miropomázanie.** Chrismation, anointing, a part of the coronation procedure of the tsar or of the emperor by which he became, in religious language, *pomazannik Bozhii* (one anointed by God).

poméra vólochnaia. A general land survey of the state domains in the Grand Duchy of Lithuania in the 1550s, designed to delimit the state lands (*zemli gospodarskie*) from private landed estates and to make the payments and work obligations of the state peasants more equitable and regular. All the state lands were divided into consolidated tracts called VOLOKA, each measuring about 33 MORGI or 21½ DESIATINAS. The voloka then became a basic tax unit (see M. Liubavskii, pp. 242–46).

pomérchii, -chie. Senior land surveyor in the Grand Duchy of Lithuania.

pomérnoe. Charge for the official measuring of declared goods, paid at the local customshouses.

pomérshchik, -ki. Collector of the customs duty called POMERNOE.

poméshchik, -ki. In Muscovy, "holders of military fiefs" (G. Vernadsky, *Mongols*, pp. 376, 451). "Until the early 18th century the holder of land on service tenure; later, the general name for noble landowners" (J. Blum, Glossary, p. 622). In 1731 the POMEST'IA were recognized as the private property of their holders; then by Peter III's manifesto of February 18, 1762, and by Catherine II's charter of 1785, the nobility was granted freedom from obligatory service. In this way the nobility —former pomeshchiki—became a privileged estate (with practically unlimited power over their serfs until the emancipation of 1861), and the former military servitors with conditional land tenure became privileged private landowners with the right to dispose of their landed estates and the peasants on them.

pomést'e, -t'ia (also **poméstie, -tiia**). A fief, inhabited land granted on the condition of military service. The first known case of such a grant (without using the word pomest'e) is to be found in the testament of Ivan Kalita of 1327. In Muscovy all lands (except boyar and monastery VOTCHINY) were considered the property of the grand prince, later the tsar; under prevailing economic conditions, however, the Moscow government had no other means of forming and maintaining an army than by granting inhabited landed estates to those obligated to perform military service. "In the latter part of the 15th century land held on condition of service began to be called a *pomest'e*, and its holder a *pomeshchik*" (J. Blum, p. 85). The POMESHCHIKI were obliged to serve until their death or disability, and to go to war or frontier guard duty with their own arms, horses, and dependent men (the regulations concerning military service of the pomeshchiki and VOTCHINNIKI were issued in the 1550s). The pomest'e system was further developed in the 16th century, and the pomest'e holders—DVORIANE and DETI BOIARSKIE—became the bulk of the Muscovite armed forces. The legal status of the pomest'e holding as a temporary and conditional one changed gradually during and after the second half of the

17th century. The *Ulozhenie* of 1649 (chap. XVI) allowed the pomeshchiki to exchange their pomest'ia among themselves, but only with the government's special permission and the registration of the transaction in the POMESTNYI PRIKAZ. By the end of the 17th century the pomest'ia tended more and more to become hereditary holdings. Peter the Great's decree of March 23, 1714, ordered that landed estates could be bequeathed to any of a testator's sons, at his discretion, but could not be divided; the decree, while limiting the right of disposal of landed estates in general, did not distinguish between votchiny (hereditary property) and pomest'ia. Empress Anna's decree of March 17, 1731, again permitted the division of landed estates among a testator's heirs, and, furthermore, explicitly recognized former pomest'ia and votchiny as the same kind of hereditary immovable property (*nedvizhimoe imenie* or *votchina,* see IMENIE), Obligatory service on the part of holders of landed estates was preserved until 1762, when the nobility was liberated from it by Peter III's manifesto of February 18, 1762. In such a way the former pomest'ia, originally granted as a reward for service as a necessity for one rendering such service, were turned into the full private property of private persons.

pomést'e prozhítochnoe: in Muscovy, that part of a POMEST'E left, after the holder's death, for the sustenance of his widow and children.

pomést'e výmorochnoe: escheated POMEST'E, left by a holder who died without legal heirs. Such pomest'ia reverted to the government.

pomínok, pomínki. 1. Church memorial service and feast for the memory of the dead. 2. "Gifts, whereby the donors expected to be remembered by a person in whose honor they were given" (G. Lantzeff, p. 131). 3. A gift to the Crimean Tatar khan, a euphemism for tribute. 4.

A payment of various kinds. 5. Bribe given to an official.

pómoch' (-shch'). Help; protection; auxiliary or allied troops.

pomóry (pl.). The Russian population of the extreme northern regions adjoining the White Sea and the Arctic.

poniatói, -týe. Witness taken from the local population to observe and, if needed, to testify that official acts (such as search or investigation) were performed by government agents in accordance with the law and pertinent regulations.

ponomár', -rí. Church servitor, sexton, reader and singer at church services.

ponoshénie. Offense, insult.

pop, popý. Priest.

    pop miriánin or *bélyi:* priest of the secular clergy.

    chërnyi pop (or CHERNETS): priest of the regular clergy, or IEROMONAKH, priest-monk.

popad'iá, -d'í. Wife of a priest.

popechénie. Looking after, caring for; management.

popechítel', -li. Superintendent. See KURATOR.

popechítel' uchébnogo ókruga. Superintendent of a school district. See OKRUG UCHEBNYI.

pópis, -sy (W.R.). List, register, inventory; register of military service men; inventory of a landed estate and a list of its inhabitants.

popláty, pl. (W.R.). Taxes and payments of various kinds.

poplúzhnoe (from PLUG, plough). A direct tax on tilled land.

popóvich, -chi. Son of a priest.

popóvna, -ny. Daughter of a priest.

popóvshchina. The movement and communities of those Old Believers (or Old Ritualists) who retained priests, as distinct from the BESPOPOVSHCHINA or priestless.

popóvstvo. The office and the dignity of a priest; the priesthood; the clergy.

popráva, -vy statútovaia, -vye. In the Grand Duchy of Lithuania, an amendment to the Code of Laws (STATUT).

póprishche, -shcha. An old measure of distance, equal to one VERSTA (according to L. Cherepnin, *Russkaia Metrologiia,* pp. 20, 23).

poráda, -dy (W.R.). Advice, counsel; consultation; consent.

porálie or **porál'skoe.** A direct tax on tilled land (like POPLUZHNOE).

porfíra. Royal purple mantle.

poriád, -dy. Order; agreement, contract, treaty; conference or congress for concluding a treaty.

poriádnaia (grámota, zápis'). See GRAMOTA PORIADNAIA.

poróchnye (pl.) **(chlény óbshchestva).** Harmful and pernicious members of a community. The general statutes of peasant emancipation issued on February 19, 1861 (arts. 51 and 54) granted the village assembly the right to expel (by a vote of two thirds of the householders) porochnye members from the community. Those expelled were then sent to Siberia as involuntary colonists. In 1885 there were in Siberia 3,751 such exiles from peasant communities (G. Kennan, I, p. 79).

porók, -ki. Vice, defect. In the old language, also a wall-battering ram.

pórub, -by. Prison.

porubézhie. Border and borderland.

porúchik, -ki. Lieutenant, a military rank of the 10th class in the (revised) Table of Ranks. (See TABEL'.)

porúchnaia or **porúshnaia, -nye (zápis').** In Muscovy, a written assurance (given usually by a group) of the reliability of a person as a loyal subject of the tsar, an elected official, a taxpayer, or, in general, as a person who could and would honestly fulfill his duty and obligations.

porúchnik, -ki (in modern Russian *poruchitel'* and OPEKUN). Guarantee, surety, pledger; also guardian, tutor, trustee.

porúka. Surety, guaranty; bail.

krugováia porúka: joint responsibility of a group, such as a workers association (ARTEL') or a peasant community (MIR). According to the law of February 19, 1861, the peasant communities liberated from the authority of the pomeshchiki were bound to fulfill their obligations toward the government *za krugovoiu porukoiu,* i.e., under the joint responsibility of the peasant mir. The krugovaia poruka of the mir was abolished in 1903.

posád, -dy. Urban settlement in Muscovy. Posady were situated around the city's kremlin or fortress, which included the government offices and the main churches. The posady were inhabited by trading men, craftsmen, hired workers, and the like (see LIUDI POSADSKIE).

posádnichestvo. Office and power of the POSADNIK.

posádnik, -ki. In the Kievan period, a prince's lieutenant appointed to govern a city and its surrounding province; either the junior members of the Riurik house or boyars served as the prince's posadniki (the later term for this office WAS NAMESTNIK). The office of the posadnik in Novgorod the Great and Pskov in the period of their independence was something else. In the 10th and 11th centuries the grand prince of Kiev appointed his posadnik in Novgorod as in other cities, but the Novgorodian VECHE began to play a more and more important role in political life, and in the first decades of the 12th century the Novgorodians assumed the right to invite a prince of their own choice and to elect—or dismiss— their posadnik. The Novgorodian posadnik was in fact the chief official of the Novgorodian administration, with vast authority not only in the city of Novgorod (as city mayor) but also as the governor of the vast Novgorodian territories. The chief duty of the elected Novgorodian prince was military command; in the civilian administration he was treaty-bound not to act without the posadnik's cooperation and consent. The posadnik's duties comprised administrative, judicial, and military powers (in the absence of a prince in Novgorod he commanded the Novgorodian army), as well as the conduct of diplomatic negotiations with Russian princes and foreign governments. His associate was the TYSIATSKII, also elected (and dismissed) by the veche. In Pskov, two posadniki were usually elected with executive power in both city and countryside. *Stepennyi posadnik* in Novgorod was the term for the incumbent posadnik. The *starye* (former) posadniki, together with the *starye tysiatskie,* and with the STAROSTY and SOTSKIE formed the Novgorodian SOVET GOSPOD (council of lords) which, in Kliuchevskii's words, was the "hidden but very active mainspring of the Novgorodian administration." (*Kurs, II,* pp. 87–88.)

posádskie (pl.). In Muscovy, POSAD inhabitants; see LIUDI POSADSKIE. According to the charter of cities of 1785, the posadskie were one of the six categories of townspeople; they made their living by retail trade, handicraft, or hired labor, and were not included in the merchants' GIL'DII and trade corporations (TSEKHI).

poság. Wedding; (W. R.) dowry.

poselénets, -ntsy. Settler. *Voennyi poselenets,* military settler; see POSELENIE.

poselénie, -iia. Settlement.

voénnoe poselénie: military settlement, of type established by Alexander I. Their forerunner in Russia was the LANDMILITSIIA of the 18th century, a territorial army settled in the southern border regions of the Empire and disbanded in 1775. Alexander's idea of settling regiments on state-owned land was as follows: "The soldiers would support themselves by farm work on holdings turned over to them, and would continue their military training so that they would always be ready for action . . . this scheme would allow Russia to have a large and well-trained army at comparatively low cost. The system would benefit the soldiers, too, for they would live with their families, [and] continue in the agricultural life to which they were accustomed . . ." (J. Blum, p. 501). The first military colony was established in the province of Mogilëv in 1810; beginning with 1816–17 the program was expanded rapidly. Besides settling regular army units in certain designated areas, the government converted all the state peasants in these zones into military colonists. Their sons, like regular soldiers' sons (who were called KANTONISTY), received military training from an early age and became regulars when they reached 18. By the end of Alexander's reign the military colonies included one third of the Russian army. At the end of 1825 the Special Corps of Military Settlements, under the command of the cruel disciplinarian General Arakcheev, consisted of 90 battalions of Novgorod settlements, and 36 battalions and 249 squadrons of Khar'kov, Ekaterinoslav, and Kherson settlements. Six infantry regiments were settled in Mogilëv province; there were also two artillery brigades. The government took care of the economic well-being of the settlers, but the continual toil and drill, the severe military discipline, and the minute regulation of the entire life of the colonists made their life unbearable. In the summer of 1831, during a severe cholera epidemic, a mass rioting of colonists occurred in Novgorod province. The riot was followed by cruel punishments, and the government was forced, in the fall of 1831, to change the military colonists of Novgorod province into a new class called farming soldiers (PAKHATNYE SOLDATY); in fact they were no longer part of the regular army, and their administration was made similar to that of the state peasants. Not until 1857–58 were the military settlers and the farming soldiers transferred to the state peasantry, and the separate corps of military settlements abolished.

poselénie, -iia (settlement) in Siberia, *ssýlka na poselenie* (exile; see SSYLKA). A type of punishment entailing limitations in civil rights but no imprisonment; it could be ordered by a court as a punishment in itself, or it could follow automatically a completed term of KATORZHNYE RABOTY, penal forced labor.

poseliánin, -áne (from SELO, village). Village inhabitant, a term sometimes used for peasant.

posëlok, -ki. In general, a small settlement, but by the turn of the 19th century several settlements still classed as posëlki in the industrial and coal mining regions of southern Russia, esp. in the Donets region, had grown to the dimensions of fairly large cities.

posél'skii, -kie. A steward of a large inhabited landed estate belonging to a prince, boyar, or monastery; also a steward for a small rural district.

póshev, -shvy. An old measure for salt, weighing about 15 PUDS (L. Cherepnin, *Metrologiia*, p. 67).

póshlina, -ny. An old tradition or custom; a traditional right or obligation; tax, customs duty, fee, or other kind of payment, esp. payment for various official acts. In 1913 the revenues from poshliny netted the state treasury 231 million rubles, or 6.8 percent of the state revenues.

póshliny pechátnye: in Muscovy, fees for the official sealing of documents.

póshlina poleváia: in the middle ages, a duty paid by the participants in a judicial duel (POLE).

póshliny súdnye or *sudébnye:* duties and fees for various court actions.

póshliny torgóvye: duties on trade.

póshliny tserkóvnye: Church duties and fees.

póshliny naslédstvennye: taxes on inherited property.

póshlinnik, -ki. Collector of fees or duties.

poslánnik, -ki. In its original meaning, an official sent by the sovereign on some special mission. In the diplomatic language of imperial Russia, envoy, minister, a diplomatic agent of the second rank, heading a diplomatic mission in less important countries, while a more important mission (POSOL'STVO) was headed by a POSOL (ambassador).

poslóvitsa, -tsy. In modern language, proverb, saying; in old Russian, also verbal agreement, accord, peace, harmony.

póslukh, -khi. In old Russia's courts, "witness claiming to have full knowledge of the case" (G. Vernadsky, *Kievan Russia,* p. 208); material witness; witness of a will or testament.

poslúshnik, -ki. Novice; lay brother in a monastery preparing himself to take monastic vows.

poslúshnitsa, -tsy. Novice; lay sister in a convent.

posluzhílets, -íl'tsy. Servitor, retainer.

posóbnik, -ki. Assistant or attorney, according to the charter of Pskov (art. 58), which permitted a posobnik to appear only if the litigant were a woman, a child, a monk, a nun, a very old man, or a deaf man.

posókha. 1. A tax on tilled land exacted from a taxable unit called the SOKHA. 2. People recruited from the sokha for auxiliary military service or for public works.

posól, -slý. In modern Russian, an ambassador, a head of a diplomatic mission (POSOL'STVO, embassy) in important countries. By the end of the 19th century Russian posly represented the imperial government in Austria-Hungary, France, Great Britain, Germany, Italy, Spain, Turkey, and the United States. In 1908 the Russian mission in Tokyo was made an embassy.

In the Grand Duchy of Lithuania the officials sent by the grand duke on a mission were called *posly gospodarskie.* In the 16th century there appeared *posly povetovye* or *posly z povetov,* deputies (two from each POVET) sent by the SZLACHTA of the povet to the general diet of the land (SOIM or SEIM VELIKII VAL'NYI).

When considerable Polish territory was acquired by Russia in 1815, and Alexander I granted the Kingdom of Poland a new constitution (November 15, 1815), the second chamber of the Polish parliament was called, in Russian, PALATA POSLOV (Pol. *izba poselska*), and the 77 deputies, elected by the szlachta of 77 povety, were called *posly zemskie povetovye.*

posól'stvo. Diplomatic mission, either permanent (embassy) or temporary.

posóshchina (W.R.). A tax on the tilled land unit, the SOKHA.

pospól'stvo (W.R.). Common people in towns and the countryside; the mass of the population except the nobility, the officialdom, and the clergy. Later the term pospol'stvo was usually applied only to the peasants.

posrédnik, -ki. Literally, mediator; often used in the sense of arbitrator.

mirovói posrédnik: arbitrator or mediator of the peace, an office created by the emancipation law of February 19, 1861 and essential to putting the reform into effect. The arbitrators were appointed for a three-year term by the provincial governor from the local nobility, subject to the confirmation of the Senate. Once appointed, they could be removed only by court order. In each province there were between 35 and 50 arbitrators, each carrying important responsibilities. They investigated disputes between peasants and landlords; they approved statutory charters (USTAVNYE GRAMOTY) that determined the size and the boundaries of peasant allotments and the compensation for the landlord; they supervised the activities of the organs of peasant self-government; and they also supervised the exercise of police and judicial authority in the countryside. Collectively the arbitrators of a district (UEZD) formed a conference (S"EZD) chaired by the marshal of the nobility. The people who assumed the difficult task of arbitrator were often the flower of the nobility-intelligentsia (including Leo Tolstoi). The office of mirovoi posrednik was abolished in 1874.

postél'nichii, -chie or **postél'nik, -ki.** Chamberlain, a court officer who supervised the sovereign's bedroom, clothes, and jewelry (another term for SPAL'NIK).

postói. The obligation of the local population to furnish lodging and food to military men or official travelers.

póstrig, -gi or **postrizhénie.** Haircutting; in old Russia, the custom of haircutting in the princely house that marked the transition of a boy from childhood into adolescence. In monasteries and convents, the ritual connected with taking monastic vows, or—for nuns—with taking the veil.

posúl, -ly. A promise of a gift or payment to a judge or other official in order to obtain a favorable decision of one's case; graft, bribe.

posúl'nik, -ki. Bribe-taker, grafter.

potéshnye (pl.). Playmates of the young Peter I—"A large group of young men, chiefly of lowly descent, with whom he indulged in his favorite pastime, military drilling" (M. Florinsky, *I*, p. 313). Peter started his military

games with the *poteshnye voiska* (play troops) in 1683. In 1691 his playmates became a regular military organization and formed two infantry regiments, the Preobrazhenskii and the Semenovskii (named after two Moscow suburban villages); these regiments came to be the elite of the imperial guards.

potiág (W.R.). See TIAGLO.

potók. In old Russian, banishment, exile.

potúg, -gi. In the Novgorodian lands in the 15th century, a synonym for POGOST. In the Grand Duchy of Lithuania, a household of TIAGLO-bearing peasants; also tiaglo, taxes, levies.

potúzhnik, -ki (W.R.). A group of peasants holding property in common who till their land, pay taxes, and fulfill work obligations jointly.

povédanie (W.R.). Report; testimony in court; accusation.

povelénie, -niia. Order, command, decision.

Vysocháishee (highest) *povelénie:* in imperial Russia, an emperor's order.

povérennyi, -nye. Attorney, lawyer, advocate.

prisiázhnye povérennye (pl.): sworn attorneys. An institution created by the statutes of November 20, 1864, reforming the judicial system. They constituted in each judicial district an autonomous group of lawyers electing their representative body (SOVET) and its chairman. Only persons with a law degree and with a sufficient knowledge of legal practice could enter the SO-SLOVIE of the prisiazhnye poverennye. Prospective lawyers, after graduation from the law department of a university, had to have five years of experience in judicial practice under the guidance of a qualified lawyer; such a young jurist was called a *pomoshchnik* (assistant) *prisiazhnogo poverennogo*. In order to meet the need for legal service, the law also permitted practice by *chastnye* (private) *poverennye* who did

98

not have higher legal education but who proved, on examination by the court, that they had a sufficient knowledge of laws and judicial procedures (the law regulating the status of the chastnye poverennye was issued in 1874).

povérstka, -ki (in modern Russian, *razverstka*). Assessment of the capability of various economic units to pay taxes and to fulfill other obligations.

Póvest' vrémennykh let. The *Book of Annals,* or *Tale of Bygone Years,* called also the *Primary Chronicle.* The principal source for the early Kievan period of Russian history. It was compiled by several authors in the Monastery of the Caves, near Kiev, around 1110 and before, and was revised by Sylvester, abbot of the St. Michael Vydubetskii monastery. (For modern publication, see bibliography.)

povéstka, -ki. Notice; summons to court; writ.

povét, -ty (Pol. *powiat*). District or township in the Grand Duchy of Lithuania. These districts in the 14th and 15th centuries varied greatly in size and administrative organization. In the *Akty Litovskoi Metriki,* edited by F. Leontovich (in 1896–97), containing documents from the 15th century, 96 povety were mentioned (Index, p. XVIII). In the 1560s the government of the Grand Duchy of Lithuania introduced administrative organization on the Polish model. The Grand Duchy was divided into 13 VOEVODSTVA with 1–5 povety in each voevodstvo. Each povet became a regular administrative and judicial unit with an established military and court organization (*sudovye povety*), and with regular representation of the nobility (*szlachta povetova*) in the VELIKII VAL'NYI SEIM (general diet, or parliament). In 1569, before the Liublin union of Poland and Lithuania was concluded, Poland had annexed 4 of the voevodstva, which included 10 povety.

povétniki (pl., W.R.). Inhabitants of the same POVET.

povínnost', -ti. Obligatory service or work for the state or for local needs; these obligatory labors were also called *natural'nye povinnosti.*

  izdél'naia povínnost': obligatory work of peasants (esp. serfs) for a landowner (see BARSHCHINA).

  podvódnaia povínnost': obligatory supplying of carts, horses, and guides to the military, to official travelers, or for the transport of government goods.

  rekrútskaia povínnost': the obligation of the population to provide recruits for the army. During the 18th and 19th centuries until 1874 only the lower classes of the rural and urban population were obligated to provide recruits for active military service. Until 1859 the term of service was 25 years.

  vseóbshchaia vóinskaia povínnost': universal military service. The tsar's manifesto and statutes of January 1, 1874, proclaimed that "All male inhabitants, irrespective of class, are subject to military service." Accordingly, all 21-year-old-men had to present themselves (in October of each year) at the district military office (*upravlenie voinskogo nachal'nika*). After medical examination, those who were able to serve had to draw lots, because the active army demanded yearly only about one third of the young men who reached conscription age. This third was enlisted in the active regular army, while the majority of young men was assigned to the OPOLCHENIE. The normal term of service in the army, by the law of 1874, was 6 years of active duty and 9 years in the reserve (ZAPAS); in the navy it was 7 and 3 years respectively. The statutes of 1874 granted extensive privileges and exemptions on the basis of education and family circumstances.

The statutes of 1874 were revised by laws of April 26, 1906, and June 23, 1912, which shortened the term of active duty in the army to 3 years but prolonged the term in the reserve to 15 years; in the navy the new terms were 5 and 5 years respectively.

póvod (W.R.). Plaintiff, prosecutor, accuser.

povóz. Transport obligations (also PODVODY, PODVODNAIA POVINNOST').

povóznik, -ki. Person obligated to fulfill transportation duties.

povóznoe. Monetary payment instead of fulfillment of transport obligations.

povýtchik, -ki. A clerk in a government office who managed the business correspondence of a POVYT'E.

povýt'e, -t'ia. Section, part. A subsubdivision of government offices; the PRIKAZY (pl.) in the 17th century and the KANTSELIARII in the imperial period were divided into several STOLY, and each stol was divided into several povyt'ia.

pozém. Payment for using another's land, quitrent.

pozémshchik, -ki. Tenant of another's land, payer of the POZEM.

pozhálovanie, -niia. Favor, reward, grant; esp. grant of a landed estate by the sovereign, and then the landed estate itself.

pozheléznoe. One of the court fees, apparently paid by a person put into fetters (ZHELEZO, iron).

pozhilóe. A term from the 15th and 16th centuries, the payment made by a peasant (who wanted to move) to his landlord for use of the house and farm buildings that he and his family had occupied during his tenancy.

pozhítok, -ki. Belongings, movable property; W.R., also advantage, profit, benefit.

pózhnia, -ni. Meadow, hayfield; also plowland.

pozóv, -vy. Summons to court.

pozóvnik, -ki. A court agent who summoned litigants to court.

pozóvnitsa or **pozývnitsa, -tsy.** Written summons; writ; subpoena.

pozýchka, -ki (W.R.). Loan.

prápor, -ry (W.R.). Banner, flag, colors, standard.

práporets, -rtsy (W.R.). A small flag fixed on a staff to designate a military unit.

práporshchik, -ki. Ensign or sublieutenant, a military officer rank of the 13th class in the Table of Ranks; in 1884 this rank was abolished in the active army and preserved only in wartime. In peacetime there were only the *praporshchiki zapasa* (reserve). (See TABEL'.)

právda. In modern Russian, truth. In old Russian this term had many meanings: justice; right; law; court; trial; legal procedures; testimony in court; oath; satisfaction for the victim of an injury.

Právda Rússkaia. Russian Law, the legal codes of the Kievan period. "In the reign of Iaroslav the Wise (1015–1054), the first Russian code of laws was compiled. Known as *Pravda Russkaia, . . .* this brief document is based upon the customary law and contains chiefly norms of penal law. . . . Some twenty years after Iaroslav's death his sons brought about a number of additional ordinances tending chiefly to reinforce the princely authority. That collection is known as the *Pravda* of Iaroslav's sons. . . . Taken together, Iaroslav's *Pravda* and the *Pravda* of his sons are known as the short version of the *Pravda*. In the course of the twelfth century the whole code was considerably enlarged and revised. Thus, the so-called Expanded Version of the *Pravda* came into being" (G. Vernadsky, *Medieval Laws*, pp. 4–5). Concerning the character and contents of the *Pravda Russkaia*, see G. Vernadsky, *Medieval Russian Laws*, pp. 4–17; *Kievan Russia*, pp. 207–09; also *Pravda Russkaia*, ed. B. D.

Grekov, I, Texts (1940); II, Commentaries (1947).

pravédchik, pravédshik, pravétchik, -ki. Bailiff or sheriff's assistant, the agent of central or local government offices in old Russia who executed court orders and sentences.

pravézh. In Muscovy, the exaction by force of a debt or damages from a defendant who had been found guilty by a court decision but had not satisfied the plaintiff's claims. According to the Ulozhenie of 1649, the recalcitrant debtor was to be flogged by rods (*batogi*) for a certain number of times based on the amount owed and then, if he did not pay the debt, his property was to be confiscated (partly or entirely) for the satisfaction of the creditor; if he was indigent he was given up in person (*golovoiu,* with his head) to the creditor and had to work off his debt.

pravítel', -li. Ruler or administrator.

pravítel' kantseliárii: chief secretary in a government office.

pravítel'stvo. Government. In documents of the 18th century (as in the statutes on guberniia administration of 1775) pravitel'stvo meant also a government organ, office, or institution, and the plural *pravítel'stvy* was used.

výsshee pravítel'stvo: the central government.

pravlénie, -niia. An executive board in the administrative system. Pravlenie was also the usual term for the boards that administered banks and various commercial and industrial companies.

gubérnskoe pravlénie: provincial board established by the statutes on GUBERNIIA administration of 1775. It consisted of the governor (as chairman), the vice-governor, several councillors (SOVETNIKI) and several high officials of the guberniia administration.

pravlénie universitéta: the executive board of a university administration.

Under the chairmanship of the REKTOR, it was composed of the deans (DEKANY) of each faculty and included also the *sindik,* or PROREKTOR, or *inspektor* (according to the university statutes of 1835, 1863, and 1884).

volostnóe pravlénie: the elected peasant township administration. According to the decree of August 7, 1797, governing the division of the state peasantry into VOLOSTI, the volostnoe pravlenie, headed by the VOLOSTNOI GOLOVA, consisted of several village elders and the clerk (PISAR'). According to the statutes on the state peasantry administration issued on April 30, 1838, the volostnoe pravlenie was composed of the volostnoi golova, as its head, and several assistants (ZASEDATELI). After the emancipation laws of February 19, 1861, the volostnoe pravlenie was headed by the *volostnoi starshina* (township elder, see STARSHINA); its members were village elders, tax collectors, and the clerk, who played an important role in township affairs. In general, the volostnoe pravlenie was more an executive organ of the UEZD (district) government administration than an organ of peasant self-government; the agency of peasant self-government was the MIR, in the form of the village assembly (SEL'SKII SKHOD).

právo. Right; law; code of laws; norm; regulations; judicial power; court; court procedures; witnesses and testimonies; power over persons or properties (*dominium*).

administratívnoe právo: administrative law.

dukhóvnoe právo (W.R.): church court.

estéstvennoe právo: natural law.

finánsovoe právo: principles and regulations concerning state finance.

gosudárstvennoe právo: state law, principles of state organization and functions.

grazhdánskoe právo: civil law.

mezhdunaródnoe právo: international law.

naslédstvennoe právo: rules and regulations concerning inheritance of property, and the right of inheritance.

obýchnoe právo: common law, customary (unwritten) law.

seméistvennoe právo: regulations concerning marriage and family relations.

torgóvoe právo: commercial law.

tserkóvnoe právo: church law, canon law.

ugolóvnoe právo: criminal law, penal law.

právy písanye (pl.). In the Grand Duchy of Lithuania, the written codes of law, the statutes issued in 1529, 1566, and 1588; the term was used in order to distinguish between the written state laws and the local customary law.

prázga. Quitrent (OBROK).

predsedátel', -li. President or chairman of a board, conference, congress, or assembly.

predstavítel', -li. Representative.

soslóvnye predstavíteli: a commission in the court system after the statutes of 1864 and the amendments of 1878 and 1889, consisting of a PREDVODITEL' DVORIANSTVA (marshal of the nobility), a GORODSKOI GOLOVA (city mayor), and a *volostnoi* STARSHINA (township elder), who were brought into the court procedures in the SENAT or in the SUDEBNAIA PALATA in cases of political crimes or of crimes perpetrated by government officials while on duty (such crimes were exempt from jury trial).

predvodítel', -li dvoriánstva. Marshal of the nobility. According to the statutes on GUBERNIIA administration of 1775 and the charter of the nobility of 1785, the nobility of each province formed the DVORIANSKOE OBSHCHESTVO (cor-

poration), which elected the provincial marshal of the nobility (*gubernskii predvoditel' dvorianstva*), while the assemblies of the nobility in each district elected their *uezdnyi predvoditel' dvorianstva.* The predvoditeli were elected for a term of three years and had to be confirmed by the government. The marshals of the nobility played an important role in the general administration of the province and the district, and after the establishment of the zemstvos in 1864 they chaired the zemstvo assemblies (*zemskoe sobranie,* see ZEMSTVO). The district marshal of the nobility was also ex-officio chairman of several administrative boards of the district (see UEZD).

preosviashchénnyi. His Grace or His Eminence, a title of the Orthodox hierarchs.

presvíter, -ry. Priest.

pribór. In Muscovy, recruiting by contract. People who served on this basis were called *pribornye sluzhilye liudi* or *sluzhilye liudi po priboru.* They included the STREL'TSY, KAZAKI, PUSHKARI, IAMSHCHIKI, etc., who were recruited for government service by contract and occupied an intermediate position between the higher class of service men (DVORIANE and DETI BOIARSKIE) and the mass of the TIAGLYE LIUDI. They were settled around the fortified cities and towns in border regions of the country and formed garrisons there. Their settlements were called SLOBODY (*sloboda streletskaia, pushkarskaia, iamskaia, kazatskaia*), and the government granted their slobody rather large areas of state lands. Gradually the contract service of these service men acquired the character of hereditary service, since their sons usually entered the father's profession. In the 18th century some of the descendants of the pribornye sluzhilye liudi were the ODNODVORTSY, who stood between the nobility and the state peasantry. In the second half of the 19th century they were merged legally with the peasantry. (See also under LIUDI.)

príbyl'shchik, -ki. Literally, profitmaker. Under Peter the Great, a person who devised new sources of revenue and was usually entrusted to administer the taxes he had invented.

pribýtok, -ki. Gain, profit in general; court fee(s) that went to the judges.

príchet or **pricht.** In a church, the priest, the deacon, and the other church servitors—D'IACHOK, later called PSALOM-SHCHIK (sexton), PONOMAR', and the like.

prichétnik, -ki. Church servitors (*tserkov-nosluzhíteli*), usually not including the ordained clerics.

pridánoe. Dowry.

prígorod, -dy or **prígorodok, -dki.** Literally, by-town or side town (in modern language, suburb). In old Russia, a junior town administratively dependent on a senior city such as Kiev, Novgorod the Great, Polotsk, Rostov, or Suzdal'. The cities sent their POSADNIKI into prigorody, and their court served as the court of appeal for the court of a prigorod. When a prigorod grew in strength and importance it could attain independence, as happened in 1347 to Pskov which had been considered a prigorod of Novgorod the Great; as a senior city Pskov itself had several prigorody in its region.

prígovor or **prigovór, -ry.** In modern Russian, usually a court sentence. Earlier it meant also a decision in general. In Muscovy *boiarskii prigovor* or *prigovor boiar* (gen. pl.) meant a decision, sentence, or resolution of the boyar DUMA. A decision of the POSAD or peasant MIR was also called a prigovor. After the peasant emancipation in the 1860s a written decision of the village assembly was called a *prigovor sel'skogo skhoda.*

prikáz, -zy. Order, command. In Muscovy *prikaz imiannoi gosudarev* meant tsar's order, and in imperial Russia *vyso-chaishii prikaz* was an emperor's order. In the early period of Muscovite history prikaz meant also a temporary responsibility given by the grand prince to one of his boyars. It was *prikazano* that the boyar administer some branch of the large palace household, some group of the palace servitors, or some territory attached to the palace. From the beginning of the 16th century, with the growth of the state territory and its administrative apparatus, those personal and temporary commissions developed gradually into permanent government departments—offices, bureaus, or agencies—with a fixed organization. The old term for the prikaz as a temporary commission or committee established ad hoc was used even in 1648–49, when a prikaz headed by Prince Nikita Odoevskii (with his four associates) was established for the special purpose of drawing up a draft of the new Code of Laws (the Ulozhenie of 1649). "The Muscovite *prikazy* were of three-fold origin. Some of them developed from the old court departments of the appanage period; others of them owed their inception to new administrative problems due to the formation of the Muscovite Empire; while yet others were born of a desire to centralize the more important administrative affairs. . . . The *prikazy* did not arise suddenly or on a single plan, but made their appearance gradually, and accordingly as the increased complexity of administrative problems demanded" (V. Kliuchevskii, *Kurs, II,* p. 341). Because of this the competence of the prikazy was often unclear and overlapping. Some prikazy handled a certain type of task throughout the whole of the country (such as the *Posol'skii, Pomestnyi,* or *Razboinyi* prikazy, or the *Bol'shoi Prikhod*); others had under their jurisdiction certain categories of the people (like the *Kholopii Prikaz* and the prikazy for various categories of military service men—*Streletskii, Pushkarskii, Kazachii, Reitarskii, Inozemskii*); still other prikazy had under their administration certain territories (like the *Sibirskii Prikaz,* the *Prikaz Kazanskogo Dvortsa,* the *Prikaz Malye Rossii*). Many prikazy were holdovers from the appanage period, and had under their management various branches of the palace household, like the *Koniushennyi* (department of the tsar's stables and horse-breeding), LOVCHII, and SOKOL'NICHII (in charge of the tsar's hunting). According to Kotoshikhin, in the 1660s there were 42 prikazy in Moscow. The list in the *Entsiklopedicheskii Slovar'* of Brockhaus and Efron, vol. 25, pp. 191–95, contains the names of 63 prikazy. The prikazy were headed, normally, by members of the boyar duma (BOIARE, OKOL'NICHIE, DUMNYE DVORIANE, or DUMNYE D'IAKI), but the real mainspring in the bureaucratic machine was the work of the secretaries (D'IAKI) with their clerks (POD'IACHIE). The famous Moscow *volokita* (red tape) was facilitated by this cumbersome and overlapping structure of the Muscovite central government. The more important prikazy are identified here.

Prikáz Bol'shógo Dvortsá or *Bol'shói Dvoréts:* the office that managed the vast complex of buildings and lands with a numerous population of servants and peasants who served the needs of the tsar's extensive household.

Prikáz Bol'shógo Prikhóda or *Bol'shói Prikhód* (the big revenue): the central financial organ, a kind of a state treasury or finance ministry.

Chelobítnyi or *Chelobítennyi Prikáz:* an office that received petitions (CHELOBITNYE) presented to the tsar and then distributed them among the relevant prikazy.

Iamskói Prikáz: the department that managed the communications and transportation system (see IAMSHCHIKI and GON'BA IAMSKAIA).

Prikáz Kazánskogo Dvortsá or *Kazánskii Doréts:* central office for administration of the territory of the former khanates of Kazan' and Astrakhan', the regions of the middle and lower Volga.

Kholópii Prikáz or *Prikáz Kholóp'ego Sudá:* the department in charge of registration and administration of affairs concerning slaves (KHOLOPY) and *kabal'nye kholopy.*

Prikáz Málye Rossii or *Malorossíiskii Prikáz:* this office, in the second half of the 17th century, was charged with affairs concerning the Ukrainian provinces united with Russia after the Pereiaslavl' treaty of union (1654) and the Russo-Polish war of 1654–67.

Monastýrskii Prikáz: established by the *Ulozhenie* of 1649 (chap. XIII), in accordance with the petitions of secular members of the ZEMSKII SOBOR of 1648–49, this department administered justice and settled litigations and claims concerning persons and properties belonging to the church, except for the estates belonging to the patriarch's see (EPARKHIIA). The creation of a secular office for such purposes met with resentment on the part of the church prelates (including Patriarch Nikon), and in 1677 the Monastyrskii Prikaz was abolished. Peter the Great reestablished it in 1701 and gave it authority also over financial management of the church and monastery estates. In 1720 the Monastyrskii Prikaz was abolished again, and in 1721 the church properties were transferred to the jurisdiction of the newly created Holy Synod. In 1726 a special office (KOLLEGIIA EKONOMII) was charged with the management of church properties. In 1762–64 the government took over the landed estates of the church along with their peasant population and put them under secular administration.

Poméstnyi Prikáz: the office that registered, granted, and, when necessary, redistributed the POME-ST'IA among the military servitors of the Muscovite state; it issued all documents concerning the holding of pomest'ia and VOTCHINY and decided claims and litigation concerning landed properties.

Posól'skii Prikáz (ambassadorial office): the central office for foreign affairs.

Preobrazhénskii Prikáz: a short-lived office for the investigation and punishment of political crimes established by Peter the Great in the Moscow suburb of Preobrazhenskoe. In 1718 the Preobrazhenskii Prikaz was replaced by the *tainaia* (secret) *kantseliariia* in St. Petersburg; it was abolished in 1729.

Razbóinyi Prikáz: the highest court for criminal affairs, the police office and criminal court.

Razriádnyi (Rozriádnyi) Prikáz or *Razriád (Rozriád):* a kind of war ministry. It administered appointments of army officers and supervised the condition of the fortresses, their armaments and equipment, and their garrisons.

Sibírskii Prikáz: the department in charge of the administration of Siberia.

Súdnye Prikázy Moskóvskii and *Vladímerskii:* high courts.

Prikáz Táinykh Del (under Tsar Aleksei Mikhailovich): Bureau of Secret Affairs, the tsar's chancery for dealing with those matters of state that he wanted to have under his personal supervision. This included the management of his vast landed estates and of his falconry and hunting establishments.

Zémskii Prikáz: the chief police and judicial office for the city of Moscow; it also collected taxes from the inhabitants of the Moscow POSAD.

prikáz, -zy. In Muscovy, also the term for the units—regiments or battalions—of the STREL'TSY commanded by GOLOVY or POLKOVNIKI. According to Kotoshikhin, in the city of Moscow in the 1660s there were more than 20 *streletskie prikazy,* each numbering between 800 and 1,000 men.

prikázy obshchéstvennogo prizréniia. Distinct from the Muscovite PRIKAZY, these departments were established in each GUBERNIIA capital by the statutes on guberniia administration of 1775. They dealt with health, welfare, and primary education. After the introduction of the ZEMSTVOS in 1864, these functions were transferred to the zemstvo institutions, and the prikazy obshchestvennogo prizreniia remained only in those guberniias that did not have the zemstvo organization.

prikázy patriárshie (pl.). In the 17th century, offices of higher administration and justice in the area directly subject to the patriarch's see (EPARKHIIA).

prikázchik or **prikáshchik, -ki.** 1. Government, monastery, or private official; steward or manager of an estate; administrator of a village or of a rural district. 2. Executor of a testament. 3. In modern Russian, also a sales clerk.

prikázchik, gorodovói prikázchik, -ýe -ki: In Muscovy, "town commissioners who administered their respective towns according to the instructions received from Moscow" (G. Lantzeff, p. 27). According to the *Sudebnik* of 1550 (art. 70) the gorodovoi prikazchik also verified the legality of arrests made by local officials (NAMESTNIKI and VOLOSTELI).

prikáznik, -ki. Executor of a testament.

prikhód, -dy. 1. Parish (in the northern regions of Muscovy often coincided with the VOLOST'). 2. Revenue.

príkup, -py. Purchase and property acquired by purchase; bargain, profit.

prímysl, -ly. Newly acquired property (a term used in princely testaments of the 14th and 15th centuries).

prípis', -si. Signature on documents (Muscovite term).

prirók. Suspicion, accusation, conviction by testimony in Muscovite legal language.

prisiága, -gi. Oath.

prisiázhnye (pl.). The commonly used term for the jury of twelve men, introduced by the statutes of judicial institutions of November 20, 1864. The jury decided questions of guilt in criminal affairs that were tried by the circuit court (*okruzhnyi sud,* see SUD). The official term for the jury was PRISIAZHNYE ZASEDATELI, sworn assessors. (See also POVERENNYI.)

prístav, -vy. A judicial or police official with various functions: bailiff; constable; warden; sheriff's deputy.

    stanovói prístav (introduced in the countryside in 1837): each UEZD (district) was divided into several STANY, and each of them was supervised by a stanovoi pristav who was subordinate to the *uezdnyi* ISPRAVNIK.

    sudébnyi prístav: court bailiff, an office established by the judicial statutes of 1864 for summoning litigants to court and for carrying out court decisions (esp. in civil lawsuits).

    uchástkovyi prístav: an officer in the police organization of imperial Russia who had under his supervision a part of the city called a POLITSEISKII UCHASTOK (a police precinct).

    zémskii prístav: a constable or bailiff of local self-government in the northern regions of Muscovy.

prístavstvo. Office and duties of a PRISTAV.

prisúd. 1. Jurisdiction and judicial district. 2. Court fee paid to a judge.

prisútstvie. In the official language of imperial Russia, a permanent bureau administering a certain category of affairs, or a special session for a special case. The decree of June 7, 1872, established a special session of the Senate (*osoboe prisutstvie pravitel'stvuiushchego senata*) as a judicial tribunal for political crimes against the state.

The Senate had to decide these cases together with the SOSLOVNYE PREDSTAVITELI (the marshal of the nobility, the city mayor, and the peasant volost' elder). In the second half of the 19th century the government established several bodies on the GUBERNIIA level called the *gubernskoe prisutstvie*. The provincial governor was ex officio chairman of all such bodies. In 1861 a special agency for peasant affairs—*gubernskoe po krest'ianskim delam prisutstvie*—was established as a higher echelon for the UEZD conference of peace arbitrators (*uezdnyi s"ezd mirovykh posrednikov*). This prisutstvie was composed of several high officials of the guberniia administration and four members of the local nobility. The municipal statutes of June 16, 1870, established a provincial bureau for municipal affairs—*gubernskoe po gorodskim delam prisutstvie*. Besides high officials of the guberniia administration, this prisutstvie included the chairman of the provincial ZEMSTVO executive board (*predsedatel' gubernskoi zemskoi upravy*), and the mayor (GORODSKOI GOLOVA) of the capital city of the guberniia. According to the zemstvo statutes of June 12, 1890, the provincial bureau for zemstvo affairs—*osoboe prisutstvie po zemskim delam*—was formed to watch over the expediency and legality of zemstvo activities. This prisutstvie, under the chairmanship of the governor, was composed of the guberniia marshal of the nobility, the vice-governor, the director of the fiscal chamber (*upravliaiushchii kazënnoi palatoi*), the prosecutor of the circuit court (*prokuror okruzhnogo suda*), and the chairman of the guberniia zemstvo executive board, or their legal deputies, plus one representative from the guberniia zemstvo assembly. In 1892 the two above named prisutstviia were united under the name *gubernskoe po zemskim i gorodskim delam prisutstvie*. In 1886 a special prisutstvie for factory affairs (*po fabrichnym delam*) was formed in several industrialized provinces to supervise the implementation of the factory work regulations issued in the 1880s. This prisutstvie included, besides the above-mentioned officials, the head of the guberniia department of gendarmes (*nachal'nik gubernskogo zhandarmskogo upravleniia*) and the factory inspector of the district (OKRUG).

privát-dotsént, -ty. A rank of university teacher corresponding to that of assistant professor. See also DOTSENT.

priviléi, -éii (from the Latin *privilegium*). A charter by which the grand duke of Lithuania and western Russia granted or confirmed rights and privileges of the SZLACHTA in general, or of the separate lands (*privilei* [*i*] *zemskie*) or cities belonging to the Grand Duchy. The first general privileii of Grand Duke Iagailo (Jagiello, who in 1385 became King of Poland as well), issued in 1387 and in 1413, granted or confirmed essential rights and privileges to the szlachta in the Grand Duchy but only to those who accepted Roman Catholicism. The very important general privilei of Grand Duke Kazimir, issued in 1447, confirmed and expanded the social privileges of the szlachta: the inviolability of their persons and properties; the right of manorial justice and administration without interference of the grand duke's officials; and the exemption of the population of the szlachta's landed estates from taxes and work obligations for the grand duke, who also promised not to accept the szlachta's subjects into the state domains. The privileii of grand dukes Alexander, of 1492, and Sigismund, of 1506, formally limited grand ducal power in favor of the PANY-RADA. The Russian lands belonging to the Grand Duchy—the provinces of Kiev, Volynia, Smolensk, Polotsk, and Vitebsk—received special privileii in which the grand duke obligated himself to preserve their old customs, rights, and institutions. "Each province enjoyed far-reaching autonomy secured by the grand duke's special *privilei* (charter). In the *privilei* issued to the Vitebsk land in 1561, the grand duke pledged . . . not to send the soldiers native to the land to garrison duty in any other land; and not to summon a viteblianin (inhabitant of the Vitebsk land) to Lithuania for trial" (G. Vernadsky, *Russia at the Dawn*, p. 179). Moreover, the grand duke promised that the person he appointed as governor (VOEVODA) in Vitebsk would be selected in accordance with the wishes (*po vole*) of the people of Vitebsk, and that he would render justice according to the local laws and customs with the participation of the local szlachta and city people (MESHCHANE). The cities in the Grand Duchy received from the grand dukes privileii that granted them self-government on the basis of the Magdeburg Law. The special charters of the grand dukes that granted landed estates, offices, or exemptions to individuals were also called privilei.

prizvolénie (W.R.). Consent, permission, approval. In the Second Lithuanian Statute (of 1566, sect. III, art. 12) the grand duke pledged not to enact new laws without the knowledge and advice of the PANY-RADA (the council of lords) and without prizvolenie of all the lands of the Grand Duchy, i.e. without the consent and approval of the general diet (SEIM VAL'NYI).

prodázha, -zhi. 1. In the Kievan period, a monetary fine paid to the prince by a convicted defendant for personal injuries or material damage inflicted by him (aside from the compensation paid to the victim). 2. Damage; illegal exaction, extortion. 3. Sale; trade in general.

próest', -ti (i volokíta). In Muscovy, expenses for sustenance incurred by a litigant owing to delays in judicial procedures.

proféssor (pl. in the official language, **proféssory;** in the vernacular: **professorá).** Professor. According to the university statutes of 1804, 1835, 1863, and 1884, there were two categories, *ordinarnye* and *ekstra-ordinarnye professory*, comparable to full professors and associate professors respectively. Assembled under the chairmanship of the REKTOR, they constituted the university council (SOVET UNIVERSITETA), the highest organ in the university administration. Its degree of autonomy varied with changes in the political climate (see UNIVERSITET).

progimnáziia, -zii. Secondary school established on the basis of the statutes on gymnasiums and progymnasiums issued in 1864. The progimnazii were established in those towns (mostly in district towns, *uezdnye goroda*) which did not have full GIMNAZII. The progimnazii at first had only four grades (*klassy*), but later many were expanded to six. Their curriculum was the same as that of the corresponding grades in the normal gimnazii. In the 1890s there were in Russia about 200 progimnazii for boys and more than 200 for girls, but in the early years of the 20th century, especially in the Duma period, most of the former progimnazii were expanded into full gimnazii. In 1914 there remained only 29 progimnazii for boys and 92 for girls under the direction of the Ministry of Public Education.

progón, -ny. 1. Passage, way, road. 2. Allowance for travel expenses paid to an official while traveling on duty.

prokurátor, -ry (W.R.). The representative of a litigant in court; advocate.

prokurór, -ry. State attorney, public prosecutor. The office was established by decree of Peter the Great, January 12, 1722. The GENERAL PROKUROR was to be "the tsar's eye" in the Senate, with the OBER-PROKUROR as his assistant (the decree on the duties of the general prokuror was issued on April 27, 1722). The statute on guberniia administration of 1775 established the office of the *gubernskii prokuror*, who oversaw legality and order in the procedures of the guberniia's judicial and administrative institutions. The judicial statutes of November 20, 1864, established the institution of the *prokuratura* as a separate branch of the judicial system, parallel with the *magistratura* (the judges) and the *advokatura*—the estate (SOSLOVIE) of the lawyers (PRISIAZHNYE POVERENNYE). An ober-prokuror (with assistants) was appointed for each of the Senate departments. A *prokuror sudebnoi palaty* (see SUDEBNAIA PALATA) was appointed in each high judicial tribunal in the provinces, and a *prokuror okruzhnogo suda* in each circuit court; both had several assistants, who were called *tovarishch prokurora.* The system of military justice included the *voennye prokurory*, headed by the *glavnyi* (chief) *voennyi prokuror.*

prómysel, prómysly. Industry, trade, craft; gainful economic activity in general.

kustárnye prómysly: domestic craft industry, cottage industry (see KUSTARI).

otkhózhie prómysly: seasonal work by peasants away from home. Millions of peasants (no available statistics) in areas where agriculture did not afford subsistence left their villages for months and worked in nearby or distant provinces, not only in agriculture but also in the timber industry, in mining (esp. in the coal mining of the Donets region), in the building industry in the cities (as carpenters, bricklayers, roofers, plasterers, housepainters), in river transport, and so on.

promýshlennik, -ki. In modern Russian, manufacturer. Also, in general, a man who worked for himself exploiting natural resources of various kinds. In Siberia in the 17th century the term *promyshlenniki* referred to Russian private traders and hunters who, working in groups, obtained valuable Siberian furs by trade with natives and by hunting, explored new lands, and often aided the regular service men in their military expeditions against restive natives.

promýt, promýta or **promýto.** The fine for an attempt to smuggle goods without paying the established customs duties (MYT or MYTO).

propiaténie. The fine for the sale or purchase of a horse without branding him and without paying a duty called the PIATNO.

propinátsiia or **právo propinátsii** (W.R.). The grand duke's prerogative to sell alcoholic beverages, a right that was one of his REGALII. "The grand duke could and often did transfer his rights of keeping taverns (*korchmy*) to private persons for a suitable fee, or grant it to the persons he wanted to favor. Thus many noblemen were able to acquire the right" (G. Vernadsky, *Russia at the Dawn,* p. 183).

proréktor, -ry. Associate to the REKTOR of Russian universities, according to the university statutes of 1863 and 1884.

proskúrnitsa, -tsy. A woman, preferably a middle-aged widow, who baked the wafers (communion bread) for the Orthodox divine liturgy; she was one of the so-called church people (LIUDI TSERKOVNYE).

prostéts, -tsý. In old Russia, a man of the common people; a layman.

prosvírnia. See PROSKURNITSA.

protamózhie. The fine for an attempt to smuggle goods without paying the established customs duty, the TAMGA.

protestátsiia, -tsii. In the legal language of the Grand Duchy of Lithuania, a declaration made in a document issued by or presented to a government office.

protíven', -ni. 1. A copy or a duplicate of a legal document, esp. of the minutes of court proceedings. 2. A court fee.

protodiákon, -ny. An elder deacon who usually participated in church services celebrated by a bishop.

protoieréi, -éii. Archpriest.

protokolíst, -ty. Clerk in charge of minutes.

protopóp, -py. Archpriest.

protopresvíter ármii i flóta. The head chaplain of the chaplains' corps in the imperial army and navy.

protór (usually in pl., **protóry**). Expenses, esp. costs caused by court procedures; damage, losses; extortion.

províntsiia, -ii. A territorial administrative unit introduced by Peter the Great early in the 18th century and abolished in 1775. In 1719 the number of GUBERNIIAS in Russia was 10; each was divided into a different number of provintsii; the number of all the provintsii was 47. Each provintsiia was divided into several DISTRIKTY (which previously and subsequently were called UEZDY). The chief administrator of each provintsiia was the VOEVODA.

prozhitók (*na prozhitók*). Means of subsistence or property in general. Esp. in Muscovy, that part of a POMEST'E granted to the widow and children of a dead service man—to the widow until her death or remarriage, to the children until their maturity; also the part of a pomest'e left for subsistence to a permanently disabled former holder.

psalómshchik, -ki. Sexton; reader and singer at church services.

psar', psarí (W.R. *psartsy*). Keeper of hunting dogs in the household of princes and boyars.

pud, pudý. 1. Measure of weight used in Novgorod the Great from the 12th century on. In Muscovy and in imperial Russia it was a basic unit of weight. The normal pud was equal to 40 FUNTY, 16.38 kilograms, or to 36.113 English pounds. 2. Scales. 3. Payment or fee for weighing of goods.

pul or **púlo, -ly.** In medieval Russia, a small copper coin of low value.

púshchenik, -ki. Freedman; they are mentioned among the TSERKOVNYE LIUDI or church people.

púshchenitsa, -tsy. A divorcee (from *pustiti,* to let go).

pushkár', -rí. 1. Artillery man, cannoneer in Muscovy. At first they were recruited by contract (*po priboru*), but later their service became hereditary. They lived mostly in suburban settlements (called *pushkarskie* SLOBODY) close to fortified cities and towns in border regions of the state. They served under the command of PUSHKARSKIE GOLOVY and SOTNIKI. Their slobody had land allotments from the government, and in peacetime the pushkari engaged also in trade and handicrafts. 2. Makers of cannons.

pushnína (collect.). Furs, fur skins; peltry.

pústosh, -shi. In W.R.: **pustovshchína, -ny.** Abandoned lands that had formerly been cultivated.

put', putí. Way, road, passage. 2. Travel, expedition. 3. Custom, rule. 4. Area of jurisdiction; department of administration. 5. In Muscovy, one of the various special branches of a prince's administration. "With the rapid expansion of the grand ducal economy, a number of special departments of administration of the domains were created, known as *puti* . . . , each headed by a special official (*putnik*) subordinate not to the *dvorski* but directly to the grand duke. These departments were those of falconry, the stables, the hunt, and food and drink" (G. Vernadsky, *Mongols,* p. 361). The Russian terms were respectively: *sokol'nichii put', koniushii put', lovchii put', stol'nichii put', chashnichii put'.* They were often headed by a boyar who was then called a *putnyi boiarin.*

put' chist. Free passage.

pútnik, -ki. 1. In modern Russian, traveler. 2. In Muscovy, *boiare putnye* were princely officials heading special branches of the prince's affairs (see PUT'). 3. In the Grand Duchy of Lithuania, SLUGI PUTNYE or *liudi putnye* were men who performed messenger service for the grand duke and for officials.

pýtka, -ki. Torture; as a method of investigation in criminal affairs torture is not mentioned in Russian legislation of the Kievan period. The first mention of it in legal sources is found in the *Sudebnik* of 1497. It was outlawed by a decree of Alexander I, September 27, 1801.

R

rab, rabý. Slave. In the 18th century serfs belonging to the nobility were also frequently called raby.

rabá, -bý, or more frequently used form, **robá.** Female slave.

rabóta, -ty. Work; in old Russian, also forced labor; slavery.

chërnaia rabóta: literally, black labor; unskilled, rough, arduous labor.

kátorzhnye rabóty (pl.): compulsory hard labor, a form of punishment introduced in Russia under Peter the Great by a decree of 1699. *Katorga* or *galera* were Russian terms for galley, and the sentence, *soslat' v galernuiu rabotu,* meant to condemn to the galleys (which were propelled by rowers). Later the convicts worked in mines, etc., or instead of hard labor, they served their sentences in strict imprisonment, but the term remained. After the period of katorzhnye raboty imposed by the court had expired, former convicts were sent to Siberia (or left in Siberia) as SSYL'NO-POSELENTSY, compulsory settlers. They remained limited in their civil rights and were forbidden to return to European Russia.

rábstvo. Slavery; enslavement; compulsory hard work; oppression in general.

ráda, rády (W.R.). Advice, counsel; a council and the members of a council, councillors.

ráda gospodárskaia, or *ráda velíkogo kniázstva litóvskogo:* the council of lords in the Grand Duchy of Lithuania, consisting of spiritual and secular dignitaries—*rady dukhovnye i svetskie.* For its composition and competence, see PANY-RADA. The plenary session, including all its members, was called *rada zupolnaia.* It was summoned when important questions had to be decided, and usually when the general diet (SEIM VELIKII VAL'NYI) was in session. In the intervals between the plenary sessions of the rada, its inner circle, known as the supreme or privy council (*rada naivysshaia* or *tainaia),* functioned on a permanent basis. This inner circle of the grand duke's councillors consisted of Roman Catholic bishops (who were present at the place of the meeting of the council), some VOEVODY and KASHTELIANY, the STAROSTY of Zhomoit and Lutsk, the two MARSHALKI *(zemskii* and *dvornyi),* and the secretary of the treasury (*podskarbii zemskii*).

ráda méstskaia: the council, consisting usually of 6 or 12 elected RADTSY, that was an organ of city administration in the cities that were self-governed on the basis of the Magdeburg Law. In some of these cities the rada (headed by the VOIT) was the only instrument for justice and administration; in others the city council was divided into the rada and the LAVA; in such cases the lava was the court for criminal affairs, and the rada handled administrative, economic, and financial affairs.

ráda vóiska Zaporózhskogo: the general assembly of the Ukrainian Cossacks (in the 17th century) summoned to elect the commanders of the cossack host or to decide important questions of current politics, like the rada in Pereia-slavl' (January 1654) that had to decide which of the neighboring sovereigns the cossacks should elect as their protector.

rádtsa or **ráitsa,** usually plural: **rádtsy** or **ráitsy** (W.R.). Councillors; elected members of the city administrative organ, RADA, in cities administered on the basis of the Magdeburg Law.

rálo. Plow; in some southern regions the ralo was a unit of taxation in the Kievan period.

raskhód, -dy. Expense(s).

raskhódchik, -ki. The bursar in some MIR communities in the 18th century.

raskól. Rupture, split, dissension; esp. in the church, schism.

raskól and **raskól'nik, -ki.** The official term for the church dissenters who left the Orthodox church organization in the second half of the 17th century. The dissenters called themselves STAROVERY (Old Believers) or STAROOBRIADTSY (Old Ritualists). The dissension arose when the church, headed by the imperious Patriarch Nikon, began, in 1654, to correct the religious service books in accordance with the Greek originals. The revised manual of church services (SLUZHEBNIK), issued in 1655, was not accepted by those conservative and nationalistic elements of the clergy and laymen who considered church reform an apostasy from old Russian piety. A bitter struggle ensued as the opposition found its leader in the person of the strong and fanatic archpriest Avvakum. The church council of 1666–67 approved the reform, anathematized all who refused to use the corrected books, and expelled the dissenters, as heretics, from the church. Although the reform in fact changed only slightly the old church rituals and some prayers, it produced bitter opposition against the dominant element in the church; there were energetic but futile attempts by the church hierarchy and the secular government to exterminate the so-called heresy. Archpriest Avvakum was burned at the stake in 1681. The Old Ritualists were forced to go underground. They founded secret communities mostly in the northern forest regions. Some emigrated abroad. Soon the Old Believers themselves were split into several groups. Those communities which retained the priestly order were called the POPOVSHCHINA (priest-possessing); those that renounced priesthood were the BEZPOPOVSHCHINA (priestless); the latter group split again and again into small sects (called *tolki* from *tolkovat'*, to interpret) with various teachings and rituals under various spiritual leaders. The attitude of the government toward the raskol changed with the general political climate. After the period of severe persecution a period of relative tolerance followed under Catherine II and Alexander I; under Nicholas I persecution was resumed, but was relaxed again under Alexander II. Only the year 1905 brought a virtual end to religious persecution. The decree of April 17, 1905, proclaimed full religious tolerance (excluding the most fanatical sects) and prescribed the use of the term staroobriadtsy instead of the old term raskol'niki in the official language. The anathema that had been pronounced in 1666–67 was rescinded by the church council of 1917–18.

raspráva. 1. In official language, rendering of justice. *Sud i rasprava* meant the trial and the execution of a court sentence (see SUD). 2. Peasant court in the 18th–19th centuries. According to the statutes of 1775 on GUBERNIIA administration, the lower rural district court for the state peasantry was called *nizhniaia rasprava,* and the higher (provincial) court was *verkhniaia rasprava.* The court presidents were appointed by the government; the members (ZASEDATELI) were elected by the state peasants. The statutes on the administra-

tion of the state peasantry of April 30, 1838, created the *sel'skaia rasprava* as a village court under the chairmanship of the village elder (*sel'skii* STARSHINA); it consisted of two village arbiters (called DOBROSOVESTNYE, literally honest or conscientious men) elected by the village assembly for three-year terms. The village court issued final judgments in disputes concerning property valued at not more than five silver rubles; it could sentence offenders to fines up to one silver ruble, to arrest and public labor up to 6 days, or to flogging with rods up to 20 strokes. The *volostnaia rasprava* was the township court under the chairmanship of the VOLOST' chief (*volostnoi golova*). It consisted of two volost' arbiters (dobrosovestnye) and served as the appeal instance from the sel'skaia rasprava.

Naródnaia raspráva. The People's Retribution (or vengeance), the name of an underground revolutionary organization founded in the late 1860s by Nechaev, and of a small revolutionary journal published by him in Geneva in 1869–71.

rasstríga, -gi. Defrocked priest or monk.

rat'. Troops; war; battle.

ratái, -ii. Plowman, a term from the Kievan period, also used in the Grand Duchy of Lithuania.

rátman, -ny. City councillor, an office introduced by Peter the Great. According to the statutes of January 16, 1721, on the Supreme Municipal Administration (GLAVNYI MAGISTRAT), ratmany in the cities were to be chosen from "the outstanding, good, well-to-do, and sensible people." According to statutes of 1724 the city MAGISTRAT was to consist of one president, two BURGOMISTRY, and four ratmany. These city aldermen or councillors were called *gorodovye ratmany.*

rátnik, -ki. Warrior, soldier.

rátniki opolchéniia: according to the 1874 law on universal military service, those registered in the *gosudarstvennoe opolchenie;* they were either soldiers who had completed their terms on active duty and in the reserves, or men who were able to bear arms but had not served in the active army; the ratniki were carried in the registers of the OPOLCHENIE until the age of 43.

rátusha, -shi (Ger. *Rathaus*). An organ of municipal administration established in 1699 by Peter the Great in Moscow. It was called at first the BURMISTERSKAIA PALATA and then the ratusha. Composed of elected RATMANY, it was to be a central organ for municipal administration in Russia, but with the establishment of guberniias in 1708 its jurisdiction was limited to Moscow. In 1721–27 the municipal governments were supervised by the GLAVNYI MAGISTRAT. In 1727 it was abolished, and the *gorodovye magistraty* or ratushi were subordinated to the provincial administrators (VOEVODY). According to the statutes on provincial administration of 1775 and the charter of cities of 1785, the MAGISTRATY (in the more important cities) and the ratushi (in smaller towns) were to function only as municipal courts for the local population; they were subordinated to the *gubernskii magistrat* in the capital city of the province. The ratusha consisted of one BURGOMISTR and two ratmany. After the introduction of the general court reform of 1864, the municipal magistraty and ratushi were abolished (in 1866).

rátusha méstskaia: in the Grand Duchy of Lithuania, (1) the city hall, the municipal building; (2) the city organ of municipal self-government in cities administered on the basis of the Magdeburg Law (see RADA MESTSKAIA).

razbór or **rozbór.** In Muscovy, a review of the service men to ascertain their military fitness and to decide, accordingly, on their appointments.

razdél imúshchestva. Division of property.

seméinye razdély (pl.) among the peasants: according to the statutes of February 19, 1861, and the law of March 18, 1886, the division of a large peasant household into two separate households, with a corresponding settlement concerning the division of family property, was to be approved by the village assembly (SEL'SKII SKHOD) in cases where it saw sufficient reason for the division and believed each of the two parts could function independently.

raz"ézd or **roz"ézd.** In Muscovy, demarcation between neighboring landed estates.

raz"ézzhaia, -zhie (grámota, -ty). A document fixing boundaries between landed estates.

razmët or **rozmët, -ty** (usually in pl.). In Muscovy, (1) apportionment of taxes and various levies among households according to their ability to pay; it was made by officials elected by the MIR; (2) assessment lists; (3) taxes and levies themselves.

razmír'e or **rozmír'e.** Rupture of the peace; armed conflict; declaration of war.

raznochínets, -ntsy. A term from the 18th and 19th centuries meaning people of various classes or—more often—people who had left the class or estate (SOSLOVIE; in the old language, CHIN) of their parents but had not formally entered another legal class. In the middle of the 19th century the raznochintsy were an important category of the professional intelligentsia. By the end of the 19th century the term had practically lost its meaning, as virtually nobody was interested in knowing to what soslovie the ancestors of a teacher, physician, engineer, lawyer, or journalist had belonged.

razrát'e. Rupture of peace; armed conflict.

razriád, or **rozriád, -dy.** Category, rank, sort, class.

dvortsóvye razriády: registers of court officials.

razriády (pl.) or RAZRIÁDNYE KNÍGI: official service registers, or lists of appointments of army officers and higher civil officials in Muscovy.

Razriád or RAZRÍADNYI PRIKÁZ: the central office of military affairs in Muscovy.

razriády in Siberia. In the 17th century, the four large territorial administrative units of Tobol'sk, Tomsk, Eniseisk and Irkutsk (at the end of the 17th century Verkhotur'e also for a short time). The towns in these four regions were *pripisany* (assigned) to the principal city, which was the administrative and military center for the whole region. "The *razriads* organized in Siberia were regarded by the central government as more or less independent of each other, and within the Siberian Prikaz the business of each of the *razriads* was dealt with separately" (G. Lantzeff, p. 39). In the second half of the 17th century several razriady were also established in the southern part of Muscovy for military and financial administration. From the military point of view those of Sevsk and Belgorod were the most important.

razrúb, or **rozrúb, -by** (=RAZMET). In Muscovy, the apportionment of taxes and various levies, including communal ones, among the separate households by special officials elected by the MIR and called *razrubnye tseloval'niki* (sworn appraisers or apportioners, see TSELOVAL'NIK).

razvód or **rozvód, -dy.** 1. In modern Russian, divorce. 2. In the northern regions of Muscovy, the assessment of tax quotas to be paid by each VOLOST' of the UEZD; this assessment was made by the elected officials of the uezd and communicated to the volost' officials who then apportioned the required amount among the separate households according to their economic strength. 3. In Muscovy also, the demarcation of neighboring landholdings.

razvódnaia, -nye (grámota or **zápis').** Document describing the boundaries fixed by the RAZVOD (demarcation) of neighboring landholdings.

rech', réchi. Speech, word, language; negotiations, discourse, dispute; subject, question, point; testimony in court. In West Russian also: thing, object; property.

réchi lezháchie: immovable property.

réchi rukhómye: movable property.

rech pospolítaia (Pol. *rzecz pospolita,* trans. from the Latin *res publica*). Commonwealth, the state of the Grand Duchy of Lithuania. After 1569 the Commonwealth of Poland and Lithuania.

réchnik, -ki (W. R.). Orator; advocate representing a litigant in court.

regáliia, -lii (Latin *regalia*). In general, the rights and prerogatives of a king (*rex*) or emperor. 1. Emblems, symbols, or insignia of royalty. The regalii of the Russian emperor were the crown, the scepter, the DERZHAVA (a globe adorned by jewels with the cross above), the state banner, the state sword and shield, and the state seal. 2. The economic and financial regalii were the state monopolies on the exploitation of certain natural resources and the sale of certain commodities; mining and coinage were recognized regalii. In Muscovy and under Peter the Great the government applied the state monopoly system widely to the sale of goods; most profitable for the treasury was the liquor monopoly. At times this was changed to the system of farming out exclusive sales licenses (see OTKUP); in the 1860s otkupa were replaced by the excise system, but in the 1890s the state monopoly on selling liquor (mainly vodka) was reestablished. A law of 1719 gave mining privileges to private persons if they paid 10 percent of the revenues to the treasury. Other treasury monopolies (including salt and tobacco) appeared and disappeared over the course of time. At the beginning of the 20th century four branches of the state revenues were termed regalii—revenues from mining (*gornyi dokhod*), from coinage (*monetnyi dokhod*), from the post and telegraph services, and, the most important, from the sale of liquor. In 1913 the revenues from the regalii netted the treasury 1,025 million rubles (30 percent of the state revenues); of this amount 900 million rubles (26.3 percent of the total state revenues) were from the liquor monopoly.

registrátor, -ry. Registrar. *Kollezhskii registrator* was the lowest (the 14th) rank of civil official in the Table of Ranks. (See TABEL'.)

regláment, -ty. A statute regulating various government institutions established under Peter the Great. The *General'nyi Reglament ili Ustav Kollegiiam* was issued on February 28, 1720, in order "to provide for orderly direction of state affairs." Separate KOLLEGII received their own reglamenty.

dukhóvnyi regláment: among the reglamenty given to various kollegii, the historically most interesting is the church statute, *Reglament ili Ustav Dukhovnoi Kollegii,* issued on January 25, 1721, and compiled by Archbishop Theophanes (Feofan) Prokopovich. The document emphasized the advantages of the newly established collegial administration by the Holy Synod over the earlier personal administration by the patriarch.

reitár, -ry. Cavalry. In the 17th century the Moscow government found it necessary to strengthen the Muscovite armed forces by the formation of regiments (*soldaty, reitary,* and *draguny*) organized and trained on western European models (see POLK). The reitary formed cavalry regiments; they were young Russians trained by foreign officers then in Muscovite service. Before Peter the Great's military reforms soldaty and reitary were not a regular standing army. Their regiments were formed only in wartime and disbanded when military operations ceased. Only certain foreign officer cadres remained permanently in Muscovite service.

reketméister, -ry. An office established by Peter the Great's decree of May 13, 1720; the NAKAZ (instruction) to the reketmeister was issued on February 5, 1722; his duty was to oversee the administering of justice, to accept complaints about unjust decisions of the KOLLEGII, to present them to the Senate, and to demand necessary redress.

rékrut, -ty. Recruit. The practice of recruiting for the standing army began in 1699, but the term rekruty was not used until 1705. Peter's government directed the landlords and communities in each locality to deliver a specified number of young men, according to population. The nobility, officialdom, and clergy were free from this obligation, but other military or civil service was obligatory for the nobles until the liberation manifesto of Peter III in 1762. Merchants could avoid being recruited by paying a rather large sum of money to the state treasury. Recruiting levies (*rekrutskie nabory*) were ordered by the tsar's manifesto as needed. Only after 1831 were they made every year. The term of service, initially unlimited, was reduced to 25 years in 1793 and to 15 years in 1859. The rekrutskie nabory ceased in 1874 when universal military service (VSEOBSHCHAIA VOINSKAIA POVINNOST') was introduced.

réktor, -ry. Head administrator of a Russian university, according to the university statutes of 1804, 1835, 1863, and 1884. He directed all university activities, presided over the general assembly of the professors (SOVET UNIVERSITETA), and chaired the executive board (PRAVLENIE UNIVERSITETA) consisting of the deans (DEKANY) of the faculties. Early in the 19th century the university rektor supervised even the high schools (GIMNAZII) in a given region (UCHEBNYI OKRUG). By the university statutes of 1804, 1835, and 1863, and the temporary regulations of August 27, 1905, the rektor was elected (for a four-year term) by the general assembly of professors. By the decree of October 11, 1849, and the university statutes of 1884, the rektor was selected from the university professors by the minister of public education. In both cases the choice had to be confirmed by the emperor (see UNIVERSITET). The title of rektor was assumed also by the heads of church academies and schools (*dukhovnye akademii* and *seminarii*).

revíziia, -zii. Review. Censuses of population by the government began in 1718–19 when Peter the Great introduced the poll tax (see PODAT' PODUSHNAIA). They met with many difficulties and delays and were usually subjected to review and correction. Because of this the term reviziia assumed the connotation of census. There were ten revizii between 1719 and 1858: the first in 1719–21, with corrections until 1727; the second in 1743–47; the third in 1761–67; the fourth in 1781–82 (with corrections until 1787); the fifth in 1794–95; the sixth in 1811 (not completed because of the Napoleonic wars); the seventh in 1815–17; the eighth in 1833–35; the ninth in 1850–51; the tenth in 1857–58. The revizii included only the rural and urban PODATNYE SOSLOVIIA (tax-paying classes); they did not count the nobility, the officialdom, the clergy, and the army and there were certain geographic and ethnic exemptions. (Information on those not in the podatnye sosloviia could be obtained from the police registers and from the church METRIKI, parish registers of births and deaths.) The

first general census of the entire population took place in 1897.

revíziia senátorskaia, -zii skie. An inspection of GUBERNIIA administrative institutions by a senator appointed by the emperor's special order; such revizii were undertaken when the central government received reports of deficiencies or disorders in provincial administration.

rez, rézy. In old Russian, interest on borrowed money; profit, usury.

rézana, -ny. A small monetary unit in the Kievan period, a fraction of the GRIVNA KUN. In the 10th and 11th centuries 50 rezany were equal to one grivna kun.

rezoimánie or **rezoímstvo.** Usury.

riád, riadý. Row, line, order; rank, category, degree; contract, agreement, treaty; testament; administration; instructions, rules, regulations; sentence, legal decision in general.

riad. A settlement, a row of houses or shops. In Novgorod the Great, a part of the ULITSA (street) that consisted of several rows; each was the smallest unit of municipal self-government.
torgóvye riadý (pl.): market rows.

riádets, riádtsy. Witnesses present at the concluding of a treaty or legal document (RIAD or RIADNAIA GRAMOTA).

riádnitsa, -tsy. Written agreement. In the Pskov charter, acknowledgment of a loan; promissory note.

riadók, riadkí. Settlement inhabited by tradesmen and craftsmen.

riadóvich, -chi. In the Kievan period, a laborer hired by contract; "the *riadovichi* are believed to have been laborers who had made a contract (*riad*) with the proprietor to work for him a specified term" (J. Blum, p. 54). For various interpretations of the term riadovich, see *Pravda Russkaia II*, ed. by B. D. Grekov, pp. 166–70, 313–16.

riadovói, -výe. A private in the imperial army.

robá (or **rabá), -bý.** Female slave.

robíchich, -chi. Son of a female slave.

rod, ródy. Origin; family, klan, kin, relatives; generation; descendants; tribe, people.

rodoslóvets gosudárev. "The official Genealogical Directory prepared for the tsar" (G. Vernadsky, *Mongols*, p. 369). It included lists of the princely and boyar families called *rodoslovnye* (old aristocratic) from which the tsar selected high military commanders and civil officials according to their place on the aristocratic ladder (see MEST-NICHESTVO).

rogózina, -ny. A measure for salt in Muscovy, equal to about 18 PUDS.

rok, róki (W.R.). Year; definite period of time; a fixed term.

rok zavítyi: in the legal language of the Grand Duchy of Lithuania, the definite and final term for appearance of a litigant before the court lest he lose the case because of absence (Statute of 1529, section 8, article 3; Statute of 1566, section 9, article 2).

ról'ia. Plowland.

roskazánie, -niia, roskazánie gospodárskoe (W.R.). Order, command (of the grand duke).

roskól. See RASKOL.

róspash', -shi. Plowland.

róspis', -si. List, register, account.

róspis' gosudárstvennykh dokhódov i raskhódov: state budget. The financial reform of 1862–63 established a unified treasury, consolidating all financial resources in the hands of the Ministry of Finance; state finance ceased to be a state secret; from 1863 on, this budget of income and expenditures was published yearly as public information. After 1906 the rospis' had to be submitted to the State Duma for consideration and approval.

rospráva. See RASPRÁVA.

róspust, -ty. Divorce.

rossíiskii. See IMPERIIA VSEROSSIISKAIA.

rossúdok, -ki (W.R.). Court decision, sentence.

rost, -ty. Interest on borrowed capital; usury.

rostovshchík, -kí. Usurer.

rotá. Oath as a part of court procedure.

róta, róty. A company of soldiers. In the imperial army at the end of the 19th century an infantry regiment consisted of 4 battalions or of 16 roty; each rota numbered about 100 soldiers in peacetime, and about 200 after wartime mobilization.

rótmistr, -ry. Commander of a ROTA. In the Russian imperial army a rotmistr was a cavalry officer, commander of a squadron, while the rota commander normally had the rank of KAPITAN; the two were equal on the TABEL' O RANGAKH (they were in the 8th class). The rank of rotmistr was also used in the KORPUS ZHANDARMOV.

rótnik, -ki. Person taking an oath; allies bound by oath; conspirator; perjurer.

roz"iézd. See RAZ"IEZD.

rozmët, -ty. See RAZMET.

rozmír'e and **rozráť'e.** See RAZMIR'E and RAZRAT'E.

rozriád. See RAZRIAD.

rozrúb. See RAZRUB.

rubézh, -zhí. Border, especially state borders; border regions; obstacle, hindrance; customs duties collected on the border.

rubl', rublí. Ruble, basic monetary unit in Russia since the 14th century. In the wealthiest of the old Russian cities, Novgorod the Great, the rubl', replacing the old GRIVNA SEREBRA, appeared in the form of a long silver bar weighing about half a pound. In Muscovy the rubl' became a basic monetary unit in the 15th century, but it was not actually minted, being only an accounting unit equal to 200 Muscovite or 100 Novgorodian DENGAS (from the middle of the 16th century called KOPEIKI); the rubl' in Muscovy was also counted equal to 2 POLTINAS and to 10 GRIVNAS. In Muscovy in the 17th century the need for larger silver coins was handled in part by using foreign silver talers called EFIMKI. The coinage of the big silver coins called rubl' started in 1704 under Peter the Great. At first, 14 coins of one ruble each were minted from one FUNT of silver mixed with an alloy (*ligatura*). At the end of the 18th century 20 silver rubles were minted from one funt of metal that was 83.3 percent pure silver; the weight of pure silver in one rubl' was fixed at 4 ZOLOTNIKI and 21 *doli*, or 18 grams (about 0.6 ounce). Increasing state expense forced the government in 1768–69 to begin the circulation of paper rubles called ASSIGNATSII. The excessive issuance of assignatsii led to their depreciation. Under Nicholas I the government (in 1839) fixed the value of one silver ruble as equal to 3.6 rubles in assignatsii. By a manifesto of July 1, 1839, the silver ruble was recognized as the basic monetary unit of the state and the assignatsii as a "subsidiary medium of exchange." In the 1840s the government issued a new kind of paper money called KREDITNYE BILETY that could be exchanged for silver rubles at par, but during the Crimean War (1853–56) the exchange of paper rubles for silver was stopped. Under Alexander II, Finance Minister Reitern tried to raise the value of the paper ruble, but the Russo-Turkish War of 1877–78, with the resultant new issues of paper money, brought further depreciation. In the 1890s the government succeeded in assembling a gold reserve of over 500 million rubles, which enabled Finance Minister Witte to introduce the gold standard in 1896–97. By this financial reform the new ruble was declared equal to two thirds of the old silver ruble, and the new ruble banknotes became freely exchangeable for gold. The law of 1897 on the gold

backing of banknotes provided that the first 600 million rubles were to be backed by a gold reserve of 300 million rubles, and additional issues were to be supported on a ruble-for-ruble basis. The new *gosudarstvennye kreditnye bilety* were in fact freely exchanged for gold and enjoyed widespread public confidence. The value of "Witte's" ruble on the international market was equal to about 50 U.S. cents. World War I, of course, badly shattered the Russian financial system; the coinage of silver rubles and gold coins was stopped in 1915; gold and silver coins disappeared from circulation, and the value of the tsarist paper rubles sank rapidly to zero after the October Revolution.

For a general survey of the Russian monetary system, including the story of the ruble, see I. G. Spasskii, *Russkaia monetnaia sistema*. V. O. Kliuchevskii tried to determine the real value of the old ruble as compared with the modern one (on the basis of available information about grain prices) in his work, *Russkii rubl' XVI–XVIII vv. v ego otnoshenii k nyneshnemu*, in *Sochineniia*, vol. VII, pp. 170–236. In the work of S. G. Strumilin, *Ocherki ekonomicheskoi istorii Rossii*, Moscow, 1960, see table on p. 52, "Evolutsiia serebrenogo rublia v Rossii" (14th century until 1914).

rubl' litóvskii. In the Grand Duchy of Lithuania, one RUBL' was equal to 100 GROSHI or to one and two-thirds of the KOPA GROSHEI (which consisted of 60 groshi).

rúga (Greek *roga*). Emolument or salary (in money and grain) given to clerics.

ruká, rúki. Hand or arm. 1. Protection, care, guardianship, guidance; power, authority; guarantee; writing; signature. 2. In Muscovite military terminology, the flank of an army in the field.

býti pod rukói: to be under somebody's power or protection.

rúku dáti: to guarantee, to pledge, to vouch.

lévaia ruká: left flank.

právaia ruká: right detachment or flank.

rúkhlo or **rúkhliad'** (W.R.). Belongings, goods, movable property in general.

rukoémstvo and **rukodánie** (= PORÚKA). Guaranty, warrant, voucher.

rukopisánie, -niia. Manuscript, letter; esp. written testament.

rushénie pospolítoe (Pol., *ruszenie pospolite*). General mobilization in the Grand Duchy of Lithuania.

rúzhnik, -ki (usually pl.). Churchmen (priests, deacons, sextons, monks) who received RUGA.

rýnda, -dy. A court office in Muscovy; ryndy were bodyguards of the tsar, young men selected from aristocratic families and employed chiefly in the tsar's palace at receptions of foreign ambassadors and similar ceremonies.

rýtserstvo. Knighthood; the Lithuanian-Russian nobles of middle standing who were obligated to perform military service.

S

samodérzhets. One of the titles of the Russian monarch. "In the late 12th and early 13th century the Byzantine imperial title 'autocrat' (*autocrator,* in Slavic translation *samoderzhets*), was applied by the chroniclers to Prince Vsevolod III of Suzdalia and Prince Roman of Galicia, but there is no evidence that either of them assumed it officially" (G. Vernadsky, *Kievan Russia,* p. 175). Ivan III formally assumed samoderzhets as a title after Moscow's emancipation from the suzerainty of the Tatar khans. At that time, around 1500, samoderzhets meant a ruler independent of any foreign power. Ivan the Terrible interpreted it as unlimited (and arbitrary) power of the monarch over his subjects. In any case, in 1547 the title of the Moscow ruler became *tsar' i velikii kniaz' vseia Rusi(i) samoderzhets.* In 1654–55 (during the Russo-Polish War of 1654–67), when Russia occupied several Ukrainian and Belorussian provinces, the Moscow tsar assumed the title *vseia Velikiia i Malyia i Belyia Russii* (or *Rossii*) *samoderzhets,* and kept it after the peace treaty of 1667, although the Belorussian provinces were returned to the Polish-Lithuanian state. After Russia was proclaimed an empire in 1721, the title of the Russian monarch became *Imperator i samoderzhets vserossiiskii,* followed by a list of the Russian possessions (see IMPERATOR).

samosúd. In modern language, usually, lynching. In the old legal language, samosud had a broader meaning, in general, taking the law into one's own hands, settling with the criminal in a private way. For example letting an apprehended thief go without bringing him to court was samosud. The corresponding term in later Russian legislation was *samoupravstvo;* in West Russian, *samovol'stvo.*

sázhen', -ni. A measure of length equal to 3 ARSHINY or to 7 feet or to 2.133 meters; there were some local deviations from that standard.

sbor, -ry. A levy of various kinds.

obshchéstvennyi sbor: a communal levy for the needs of the peasant community.

pozemél'nyi sbor: a payment for the use of land.

sbor, -ry. Assembly.

sbor staníchnyi: see STANITSA.

sbórshchik, -ki podatéi. Tax collector, special communal official who was elected in some peasant communities (usually for a one-year term).

schádok (or **shchádok**), **-ki** (W.R.). Descendant.

Sech' (Ukr. *sich*) **Zaporózhskaia** (or **Zaporózh'e**). The stronghold of the Ukrainian Cossacks that was founded and grew rapidly during the second half of the 16th century on the islands of the Lower Dnieper (the main island was Khortitsa) situated below the Dnieper rapids (*porogi*, from which the word *zaporozh'e*). The Zaporozhskaia Sech' was intended to be a Polish border stronghold and a base of operations against the Tatars and the Turks, and indeed the cossacks did much harm to the Turks and Tatars by their bold raids on the Black Sea coast; but soon the cossack community grew into an independent and restive force. The community was organized along military lines, based on democratic and equalitarian principles. The general assembly of the host elected its commanders (ATAMANY and other officers) and decided all important questions. From the end of the 16th century on, the Zaporozhskaia Sech' began to assume a new role. The conditions of the Ukrainian peasantry after Poland annexed the Southern Ukraine from the Grand Duchy of Lithuania in 1569 provoked a mass emigration of the dissatisfied into the region of the Lower Dnieper, and the Zaporozhskaia Sech' soon became the leading force in anti-Polish uprisings which started in the 1590s and ended in the revolution of 1648–49 led by Bogdan Khmel'nitskii. In the second half of the 17th century the Ukrainian rulers bore the title *Hetman voiska zaporozhskogo*. According to the Russo-Polish peace treaties of 1667 and 1686, the territory of the Zaporozh'e and the cossacks themselves came under the protection of the Moscow tsar "along with all the ancient liberties and regions which they possess." In 1709 Peter the Great ordered the destruction of the Zaporozhskaia Sech' as a punishment for the Zaporo-zhian alliance with the Swedish King Charles XII with whom Peter was at war, but after Peter's death the Sech' was reestablished. During the 18th century the imperial government gradually limited Ukrainian autonomy. In 1775 a Russian army detachment occupied the Zaporozhian Sech', and Catherine's manifesto of August 3, 1775, abolished it. Some of the Zaporozhian Cossacks emigrated to Turkey; most of them were settled in the northern Caucasus (in the Kuban' River region), and in 1783 they formed the *Chernomorskoe kazach'e voisko* (Black Sea Cossack host), which in 1860 was renamed the *Kubanskoe kazach'e voisko*.

seim (soim) velíkii vál'nyi. The general diet in the Grand Duchy of Lithuania. It began to take definite shape at the end of the 15th century. Initially it was an assembly of the Lithuanian and Russian aristocracy, consisting of the council of lords (PANY-RADA), high government officials, and princes and lords (KNIA-ZHATA and PANY) specially invited by the grand duke. The rank and file nobility (SZLACHTA) did not have a formal representation but could attend sessions of the seim without the right to vote. Under Sigismund I (1506–48) the Lithuanian-Russian szlachta, influenced by the political and military situation (wars with Muscovy), and encouraged by the example of their Polish "brethren," endeavored to enhance their social and political power, and in the middle of the 16th century they achieved their goal. Beginning with the seim of 1512 the szlachta of each POVET normally elected two representatives (POSLY, envoys) to the general diet, which played an increasing role. It decided questions of war and peace, voted taxes for military needs, and discussed the draft of the code of laws (the future statute of 1529). The political rights and privileges of the szlachta and of the seim were formally recognized and confirmed by the Second Lithuanian Statute of 1566. The representatives of the szlachta, elected by the SEIMIKI (dietines) of the newly organized court districts (*sudovye povety,* see POVET), then constituted the second chamber (*kolo rytserskoe,* see KOLO) of the Lithuanian-Russian parliament, although the high aristocracy continued to play an important role in the political and social life of the state. By provisions of the Statute of 1566 the grand duke obligated himself to convoke the general diet whenever the needs of the state so required, upon advice of the pany-rada, or upon a request of the RYTSERSTVO (knighthood, or szlachta, sec. III, art. 6). A general mobilization could be declared and war taxes imposed only upon advice of the pany-rada and with consent of the general diet (except in the case of a sudden enemy attack, when the grand duke himself would call the rytserstvo to arms, sec. II, art. 2). New laws and amendments to existing laws could be issued only with the knowledge and advice of the RADA and with the consent of the general diet (sec. III, art. 12). Moreover, the Lithuanian (like the Polish) sovereigns in the second half of the 16th century recognized the right of the general diet to free election of the successor to a deceased sovereign.

seim, in the Kingdom of Poland, 1815–31. According to the constitutional charter of November 15, 1815, Poland (within the Russian empire) was to have a bicameral seim consisting of the Senate and the Chamber of Deputies or envoys (PALATA POSLOV). The Senate was composed of bishops, palatines (VOEVODY), castellans, and members appointed by the emperor. The Chamber of Deputies was composed of 77 envoys elected by the assemblies of nobles (seimiki) in 77 districts (povety), and of 51 deputies elected by local communities (GMINY). The seim was to convene for a regular session in Warsaw every second year. By the 1820s the voices of

opposition had already grown loud in the Polish seim, and during the uprising of 1830–31 the seim declared the independence of Poland and the dethronement of Nicholas I as the Polish king. After the uprising had been suppressed, the Polish constitution was abolished, and all the real power in Russian Poland was concentrated in the hands of the Russian vicegerent (NAMESTNIK).

seim, in Finland. The Finnish diet in the 19th century was organized on the principle of representation of the estates or legal classes (*soslovnoe predstavitel'stvo*), with a preponderance of the nobility; the Lutheran clergy, the cities, and the peasantry were also represented. Finnish autonomy, reduced at the end of the 19th century, was restored in 1905, and in 1906 the general franchise was introduced for elections to the Finnish seim. But very soon Finnish autonomy and the competence of the Finnish seim were again sharply curtailed by the law of June 17, 1910, which in fact made the seim hardly more than a consultative institution in the imperial legislative process.

séimik (sóimik) povétovyi, -ki -ye. District dietine in the Grand Duchy of Lithuania, or assembly of the Lithuanian-Russian nobility (SZLACHTA) in each POVET; at first the dietines took place irregularly, but during the 16th century they became a legally recognized institution with a definite sphere of competence. The Statute of 1566 provided that four weeks before the convening of the general diet (SEIM VELIKII VAL'NYI) the szlachta in every court district (*sudovyi povet,* see POVET) should convene so that the seimik povetovyi could discuss the affairs and needs of the land, as communicated by the grand duke, as well as the needs of their povet, elect two deputies to the general diet, and supply them with necessary instructions

(Statute of 1566, sec. III, art. 5). Aside from these political functions, the seimiki povetovye elected candidates for the offices of the ZEMSKII SUD (court)—the judge (SUD'IA), the assistant judge (PODSUDOK), and the clerk (PISAR')—four worthy men for each office, from whom the grand duke would choose and appoint three court officials (sec. IV, art. 1).

sekretár', -rí. In the imperial period, head of a KANTSELIARIIA (chancery, bureau) for one of the important offices, either administrative or judicial. In the KOLLEGII established by Peter the Great, this official had the title of *kollezhskii sekretar'*. When the kollegii were abolished, kollezhskii sekretar' remained as a rank of the tenth class in the Table of Ranks. (See TABEL'.)

gosudárstvennyi sekretár': the head of the state chancery (*gosudarstvennaia kantseliariia*), the chancery of the State Council (GOSUDARSTVENNYI SOVET). A *stats-sekretar'* (*gosudarstvennogo soveta*) headed each of the divisions (OTDELENIIA) of the state chancery. An *ober-sekretar'* headed the chancery in each of the Senate departments.

gubérnskii sekretár': in the 19th century, a rank of the 12th class, not a definite position in the service.

stats-sekretár' Egó Velíchestva: an honorary title granted to high-ranking civilian officials by the emperor at his discretion.

sel'chánin or **seliánin, -áne.** Rural inhabitant, peasant.

selénie, -niia. Rural settlement.

kazënnye seléniia (pl.): villages inhabited by state peasants.

poméshchichie seléniia: villages inhabited by serfs.

selíshche, -shcha. Village; empty village; arable land (W.R.).

seló, sëla. Village. In old Russia, a princely or boyar landed estate with a manorial homestead and farm managed by an appointed steward (*sel'skii starosta kniazhii* in the RUSSKAIA PRAVDA; later, POSEL'SKII). In the Muscovite and imperial periods, a relatively large rural settlement, usually with a parish church, a seat of peasant administration.

chërnye sëla (pl.): in Muscovy, state villages.

dvoróvoe or *dvortsóvoe seló:* in the 16th–18th centuries, a crown village, attached to the tsar's palace (DVORETS) by payments and work obligations (after 1797, *udel'nye sëla*).

sel'tsó. Village (=SELO) or hamlet.

semináriia, -rii. See UCHILISHCHE.

Senát. When going to war against Turkey, Peter the Great established (by the decree of February 22, 1711) the *Pravitel'stvuiushchii Senat* (ruling senate), a committee of nine members, as a temporary government during the tsar's absence. After returning from his unfortunate expedition Peter preserved the Senate as the highest administrative and judicial institution. When he had established the KOLLEGII Peter at first ordered that the president of each kollegiia should ex officio be a member of the Senate, but in 1722 he revoked this measure since the kollegii were held accountable to the Senate as their supervisory body. The Senate itself (in 1722) was put under the supervision of the GENERAL-PROKUROR, "the tsar's eye" in the Senate. The powers of the Senate under Peter the Great were very broad. It was a supreme court, a supervisory organ over the kollegii, and, in general, the highest institution in civil, military, and financial administration. During the post-Petrine years, 1726–41, the Senate's power was considerably reduced by the newly established Supreme Privy Council (VERKHOVNYI TAINYI SOVET, 1726–30) and the *Kabinet Ministrov* (1730–41), both of which gave orders to the Senate. Under

Empress Elizabeth (1741–61) the Senate played a most important role as the supreme organ for administration, for dispensing justice, and even for legislation. The Senate not only interpreted but also issued laws. Catherine II divided the Senate into six DEPARTAMENTY (judicial and administrative) and put it under the strict supervision of the general-prokuror. In the 19th century the Senate played the role of a supreme court and high administrative supervisory agency. The ministers were formally accountable to the Senate, but insofar as they had the right to report directly to the emperor they could settle matters without the Senate's intervention or protest. The judicial reform of 1864 preserved the Senate's position as a supreme court but only as a court of cassation, i.e., the Senate could not change or repeal a sentence of a lower court unless the rules of judicial procedure had been violated. On that basis two judicial departamenty of the Senate were newly organized, one for civil and one for criminal affairs. By the end of the 19th century there were four more departamenty for different branches of the state administration. In some cases joint sessions of the Senate departamenty took place. Special duties of the Senate were to publish new laws and to interpret existing laws. Besides regularly supervising the provincial administration and deciding questions brought into the Senate by provincial administrative organs, the Senate occasionally (upon the order of the emperor) sent one of its members to make a thorough inspection of a guberniia administration, as a *revizuiushchii senator*.

senát, in Finland. The supreme administrative and judicial institution, divided into two departments—*khoziaistvennyi* (economic) and *sudebnyi* (judicial), which in some cases met in joint session. The Senate's members were appointed by the emperor for three-year terms from among native Finns.

senozhát', -ti. Hay field.

serébren(n)ik, -ki. 1. Silversmith. 2. "Peasant debtor of a landlord in the 14th–16th centuries. . . . The freedom of the debtor began to be curbed by princely charters which prohibited the departure of *serebrenniki* save during the St. George's period [two weeks in November] and then only if they had paid their debts to the seignior" (J. Blum, p. 116). Serebrenniki were numerous on the lands belonging to monasteries since the monasteries usually possessed more SEREBRO for granting loans than private landowners. In the *Sudebnik* of 1550 (art. 78) the term serebrenik is applied also to the *kabal'nyi kholop* (see KHOLOP).

serebró. Silver; in the 13th–16th centuries, money in general; borrowed money; revenues; taxes; payments in general.

siábrenoe serebró: money belonging to a company of SIABRY.

serebshchína or **serebshchízna.** In the Grand Duchy of Lithuania, silver collection, an extraordinary general war tax voted by the diet. In Polotsk and Vitebsk provinces, also a regular tax.

sevooborót. Crop cycle.

prinudítel'nyi sevooborót: compulsory crop rotation, based on the three-field system, an essential feature of communal peasant landholding (typical for the 18th and 19th centuries).

s"ezd, -dy. Congress or conference in general. In the second half of the 19th century there were several official institutions known as s"ezdy.

s"ezd mirovýkh posrédnikov: conference of peace arbitrators (see POSREDNIKI MIROVYE), established in 1861 as the next echelon above the arbitrator in the district (UEZD) peasant administration. It was chaired by the district marshal of the nobility, and included also several local government officials. The office of the mirovye posredniki was abolished in 1874.

s"ezd mirovýkh súdei: the judicial reform of 1864 introduced the office of the MIROVYE SUD'I (pl.), justices of the peace. The next higher echelon for the justice of the peace in each district was the s"ezd mirovykh sudei, composed of the ordinary justices and of honorary (*pochëtnyi*) justices of the peace (both categories were elected by the local ZEMSTVO assemblies). In 1889 the newly established ZEMSKIE NACHAL'NIKI were given judicial power over the peasantry, but in 1912 the institution of elected justices of the peace was re-established (initially in ten provinces) and the district s"ezd mirovykh sudei as well. The chairman of the conference was appointed by the government. In St. Petersburg, Moscow, and five other cities the conference of the mirovye sud'i elected its own chairman from among its members.

uézdnyi s"ezd: when the institution of the ZEMSKIE NACHAL'NIKI was established in 1889, the uezdnyi s"ezd constituted the next higher echelon. The uezdnyi s"ezd had two bureaus (PRISUTSTVIIA), administrative and judicial. The administrative prisutstvie was composed of all the zemskie nachal'niki of the UEZD (usually five or six), the police captain (ISPRAVNIK), and the chairman of the uezd zemstvo executive board (*predsedatel' uezdnoi zemskoi upravy*). The judicial bureau included the zemskie nachal'niki, the uezd member of the circuit court (*uezdnyi chlen okruzhnogo suda*), the municipal judge (GORODSKOI SUD'IA), and the honorary justices of the peace (if they were elected by the uezd zemstvo). Both prisutstviia worked separately under the chairmanship of the uezd marshal of the nobility (*uezdnyi predvoditel' dvorianstva*).

shabr, -ry (=SIABR). "A co-owner, member of a cooperative land association" (G. Vernadsky, *Russia at the Dawn*, pp. 203, 329).

Shápka Monomákha (Monomach's crown). One of the REGALII of the Moscow grand princes and tsars, a masterpiece of jewelry art (gold filigree). It was mentioned for the first time in Grand Prince Ivan I's testament (1327) as the *shapka zolotaia* (golden cap). Early in the 16th century certain learned Russian monks created the legend that this royal cap (or crown) had been sent to Prince Vladimir Monomakh of Kiev (d. 1125) by the Byzantine Emperor Constantine Monomakh (Monomach). The crown is called *Shapka Monomakhovskaia* in the testament of Tsar Ivan IV of 1572. It is now kept in the Kremlin in the Armory (*Oruzheinaia Palata*). There is a picture of it in *Gosudarstvennaia oruzheinaia palata moskovskogo kremlia* (Moscow, 1958), plate 86.

shatsúnok (W.R.; Pol. *szacunek*, from the Ger. *schätzen*). Evaluation, estimation, appraisal; price; value.

shchádok, -ki (W.R.). Descendant.

shert'. The Moslem oath of allegiance; relation based on an agreement confirmed by oath.

shéstnik, -ki. In old Russia, infantry soldier; court servitor (sergeant).

shíia. Neck (W.R.). In the legal language of the Grand Duchy of Lithuania, capital punishment: *karati shieiu,* to punish by death (through hanging).

shikh or **shikhovánie** (W.R.). Review of armed forces.

shinók, -nki (W.R.=KABAK in Muscovy). Tavern.

shkóda, -dy (W.R., in Pol. *szkoda*). Damage, loss.

shliákhta (W.R., in Pol., SZLACHTA). The middle nobility in the Grand Duchy of Lithuania, who held landed estates (IMENIIA ZEMSKIE) and were obligated to perform military service if needed. A series of charters (PRIVILEI) of the Lithuanian-Russian grand dukes in the 15th century granted or confirmed the shliakhta's liberties, i.e., rights and privileges concerning inviolability of their persons and property. In the 16th century the shliakhta also achieved an influential position in local government and in the political structure of the Grand Duchy, since their representatives (*posly*, envoys) formed, beginning in the 1560s, the second chamber of the general diet which in fact enjoyed more political power than the grand duke (see SEIM VELIKII VAL'NYI). The Statute of 1566 formally and firmly established the shliakhta's status as a privileged social class. "Even before 1566 the gentry became a privileged social class, and its 'liberties' were secured by the laws. . . . The nobleman was not subject to either capital or corporal punishment, or to imprisonment or confiscation of his property without due trial in the court. For any offense against a nobleman, the guilty party had to pay more than for the offense against a commoner. In court the nobleman was regarded as a more reliable witness than a commoner. . . . The Second Lithuanian Statute made the *szlachta* rights and privileges even more extensive and the protection of them more effective. . . . While the *szlachta* rights and privileges were growing, the noblemen attempted to secure the enjoyment of their status as the exclusive top group of the society, on the one hand by undermining the position of the lords, and on the other hand by establishing a barrier against the penetration of commoners into the *szlachta* corporation. The former objective was reached in 1564–66, the latter in the 1520's" (G. Vernadsky, *Russia at the Dawn*, p. 198). In the Statute of 1529 (sec. III, art. 10) and in the Statute of 1566 (sec. III, art. 15) the grand duke obligated himself not to elevate commoners over the shliakhta (*prostykh liudei nad shliakhtu ne povyshati*), and (in the Second Statute) not to appoint commoners to government offices, so that a SHLIAKHTICH could never be subordinate to a commoner. In the second half of the 16th century the Polish and Lithuanian commonwealth (*rzecz pospolita*) became, in fact, more a szlachta republic than a monarchy.

shliakhétstvo. Russian serving nobility (from the Pol. SZLACHTA) in the 18th century, when Peter the Great strove to systematize the heterogeneous mass of Moscow service men. "Indulging his weakness for foreign words Peter chose the name the Poles used for their nobility, russifying it into *shliachetstvo*. In the second half of the [18th] century, however, Peter's selection was replaced by an old Russian word, *dvorianstvo*" (J. Blum, p. 347).

shliákhtich, -chi (W.R.). Member of the SHLIAKHTA class.

shliub or **sliub** (W.R., in Pol. *slub*). Promise; obligation; agreement; engagement.

shtab, -by. Staff. In the imperial army in the 19th century there were the *glavnyi shtab*, a part of the war ministry managing the army administration, and the *general'nyi shtab* (including the *akademiia general'nogo shtaba*), that dealt with questions of military science.

shtab-ofitsér, -ry. Field grade officer; in the imperial army this included the ranks of MAIOR (abolished in 1884), PODPOLKOVNIK (lieutenant-colonel), and POLKOVNIK (colonel). (See also TABEL'.)

shtab-rotmístr, -ry. An officer rank in the cavalry equal to the rank of SHTABS-KAPITAN in the infantry (a rank of the 9th class in the TABEL' O RANGAKH).

shtabs-kapitán, -ny. Captain 2nd grade, an officer rank of the 9th class in the Table of Ranks. (See TABEL'.)

shtat, -ty. Staff; organization chart of a government institution regulating the number, position, and salary of its officials.

shtof, -fy (Ger. *Stof*) (= *kruzhka*). A liquid measure, one-tenth or one-eighth of a VEDRO. The smaller shtof was 1.23 liters or 1.3 quarts.

shtraf, -fy (from the Ger. *Strafe*). Fine, monetary penalty (in contemporary Russian not used for punishment in general).

shúrin, shur'iá. Wife's brother.

siabr, -ry (or **shábry**). Co-owner, member of a large peasant family or of an association of neighbors jointly possessing common property or sharing in it.

sidélets, -l'tsy. Literally, sitter. Salesman in a store, esp. in liquor stores operated for the treasury. In Muscovy, also the garrison of a besieged fortress.

tiurémnye sidél'tsy (in Muscovy): prisoners, convicts.

síla. 1. Strength. In Muscovy, also economic power, esp. taxpaying capability, as in *platiti po sile*. 2. Violence (*silu chiniti*).

sinklít (from the Greek *syngkletos*). Council, assembly. In Muscovy, sunklit or *tsarskii sinklit* (tsar's council) was one of terms for the boyar duma (see DUMA BOIARSKAIA).

Sinód, Sviatéishii Pravítel'stvuiushchii Sinód. The Holy Synod. The supreme organ of administration of the Russian Orthodox church established by Peter the Great; first called the DUKHOVNAIA KOLLEGIIA.

sirotá, síroty. Orphan; poor people. From the 14th century on, this term was used to designate peasants and the lower classes of the urban population. In Muscovy those people, when addressing the tsar, called themselves *tvoii gosudarevy siroty*.

skarb (W.R., in Pol. *skarb*). Treasury.

skarb gospodárskii (in the narrow sense): treasury of the grand duke and of his household, where his regalia (KLEINOTY) and jewels also were kept.

skarb zémskii (or *gospodárskii*, in the broad sense): the state treasury of the Grand Duchy of Lithuania managed by the PODSKARBII *zemskii*, who was assisted by the SKARBNYE.

skárbnik, -ki or **skárbnyi, -nye** (W.R.). Treasury officials in the Grand Duchy of Lithuania (headed by the PODSKARBII *zemskii*).

skazánie, -niia (W.R.). Decision, sentence.

skázka, -ki. In modern Russian, tale. In Muscovy, statement, witness, testimony, explanation; (written) opinion, declaration. Skazki was the term for the written opinions with which groups of members of the ZEMSKIE SOBORY answered questions put to them by the government.

dushévnaia skázka: testimony confirmed by oath.

revízskie skázki: declarations concerning the number of male souls (DUSHA), submitted to the government by landlords or local officials during the censuses (REVIZII) in the 18th and 19th centuries (up to 1858).

skhíma or **skíma.** The highest and strictest monastic vows and practices.

skhímnik, -ki. Monk who accepted the SKHIMA, and thereby was consecrated to the highest monastic grade.

skhod, -dy. Assembly.

mirskói skhod: general assembly of the peasant MIR; in Muscovy, also of the *posadskii mir* (see MIR).

sél'skii skhod: village assembly; concerning its competence as regulated by the statutes of April 30, 1838, and of February 19, 1861, see OBSHCHESTVO SEL'SKOE.

volostnói skhod: assembly of the peasant representatives in each VOLOST' (township); according to the statutes of 1838, the state peasants elected to the volostnoi skhod one representative from every 20 households (DVORY); according to the statutes of 1861, the peasants sent to it one representative from every 10 households. The volostnoi skhod (according to the POLOZHENIE of 1861) elected the volost' officials (headed by the *volostnoi starshina,* see STARSHINA) and members of the volost' court, and discussed and settled questions concerning economic, financial, legal, and other public affairs of the entire volost' as well as the volost' obligations toward the government. Between 1889 and 1906 the activities of the village and volost' assemblies were under the strict supervision of the ZEMSKIE NACHAL'NIKI.

skit, -tý. A small monastery (hermitage) or even one or two huts inhabited by monks, most often situated in the dense northern forests. Covert monastery of Old Believers.

skítnik, -ki. Monk living in a SKIT; hermit.

skládka. Voluntary association for an economic or financial purpose.

skládnik, -ki. Participant in a common economic undertaking. In the northern regions of Muscovy in the 15th–17th centuries skladniki were companies or associations of co-owners each of whom possessed his share of the property as his own and disposed freely of it.

skládstvo. An agreement; a company or association formed for some economic purpose.

skomorókh, -khi. Buffoon or, more poetically, "wandering minstrel" (H. W. Dewey in *Slavic Review,* XXIII, p. 657); one of the singers, musicians, and actors in old Russia, who wandered from village to village and performed their acts and amusing tricks to the enjoyment of the peasants and to the distress of the church hierarchy.

skot. 1. Cattle. 2. In the Kievan period (10th–12th centuries) the term was also used in the sense of money.

sled, -dý (W.R.). Peasant farmstead.

slédovatel' sudébnyi, -li -nye. Judicial investigator. An office created in 1860 in order to remove from police investigation criminal cases subject to the examination of the courts. According to the judicial statutes of November 20, 1864, each circuit court (*okruzhnyi sud,* see SUD) had several sudebnye sledovateli. The eldest among them was the *sledovatel' po osobo vazhnym delam,* who investigated the most important criminal cases.

sliub, -by (or **shliub,** W.R.). Agreement; obligation; promise.

slobodá, slóbody. Settlement or group of settlements exempt for a number of years or permanently from the ordinary taxes and work obligations to which TIAGLYE KREST'IANE and POSADSKIE LIUDI were subjected (*sloboda = svoboda,* freedom). V. Kliuchevskii (*Terminologiia,* pp. 247–49) distinguished three basic kinds of slobody in Muscovy: 1) *slobody* inhabited by the *sluzhilye liudi po priboru* (see under LIUDI); 2) settlements (mostly suburban) of traders and artisans which could be divided into three categories— a) *dvortsovye,* attached to the tsar's palace; b) *chërnye,* which were under state administration, and c) those belonging to church institutions or private landowners; and 3) *pashennye* (ploughing), agricultural settlements.

The slobody in the first group were usually situated around fortified cities; its inhabitants served as a permanent garrison. These included the *streletskaia sloboda* (see STREL'TSY), *pushkarskaia sloboda* (see PUSHKARI), *kazatskaia sloboda* (see KAZAKI), and *iamskaia sloboda* (see IAMSHCHIKI). The names of these settlements, inherited from Muscovy, were preserved throughout the imperial period.

The populace of the *dvortsovye slobody* was obliged to perform work for the extensive palace household or to supply provisions for the court and fodder for horses kept at the court. Each of the Moscow suburban *chërnye slobody* was settled by some special group of artisans working for the needs of the palace and of the tsar's servitors, *kuznetsy* (smiths), *bronniki* (producing armaments), *sadovniki* (gardeners), *barashi* (making tents and marquees), *khamovniki* (linen weavers), and others (the names of many Moscow streets reflect the occupations of former inhabitants). Each of these slobody was a community headed by an elected elder (STAROSTA). Before the middle of the 17th century many suburban slobody populated by traders and artisans and belonging to church hierarchs, monasteries, or private landowners came into being. They were not included in the communities of the posadskie liudi and were free from the POSAD TIAGLO (taxes and services). This provoked dissatisfaction among the posadskie liudi and they constantly complained to the government. The Ulozhenie of 1649 (chap. XIX, art. 1) answered these complaints with a decisive measure: all these suburban slobody were confiscated and encompassed by taxpaying urban communities; the founding of new suburban slobody by church institutions or private landowners was prohibited.

Pashennye slobody were founded by the government in remote regions (especially in Siberia) with undeveloped agriculture; the settlers were recruited from among the VOL'NYE GULIASHCHIE LIUDI (free men, not included in tiaglye peasant or posad communities) and were given large land allotments and a temporary exemption from taxes and services. After the expiration of the grace period they were obligated to deliver set quantities of provisions for the tsar's service men, or to work for a definite time in the tsar's fields. A special case were the slobody founded by the government in the 17th century in the southwestern regions of Muscovy. Thousands of Ukrainian peasants fleeing from wars and internal disturbances accepted the invitation of the Moscow government to settle in this area, attracted by large land allotments, tax exemptions, and local self-government.

The number of slobody thus founded gave the region (encompassing the future Khar'kov province, and parts of Kursk and Voronezh provinces) the name *slobodskaia Ukraina*. Several cossack regiments were formed from the new settlers to serve as border guards of the state.

The *nemetskaia sloboda* was a Moscow suburban settlement in the 17th century, inhabited by western Europeans in the service of Moscow. (In Muscovite terminology all western Europeans, not just Germans, were called NEMTSY.)

slobódchik, -ki. Administrative official in Siberian SLOBODY in the 17th century.

slobodchánin, -ane or **slobozhánin, -ane.** Inhabitant of a SLOBODA.

slobódich, -chi (W.R.). Peasant enjoying (temporary) freedom from taxes and work obligations.

slobódka, -ki. Diminutive from SLOBODA. In the northern regions of Muscovy, also a small rural district.

slovénin, slovéne. Slav.

slóvo, -vá. Word; speech; sermon, advice; answer; testimony; promise; literary work; order, command; law; teaching.

Slóvo Bózhie: Holy Scripture.

slúchai, -aii. Precedent (esp. in MESTNICHESTVO litigations).

slugá, slúgi. Servitor in general. In the 13th–15th centuries the slugi of the Vladimir and Moscow grand princes "consisted of two main groups: the free servitors (*slugi vol'nye*) and the service-bound servitors, who were under the authority of the major-domo of the grand ducal court (*slugi pod dvorskim*) and eventually became known as the *dvoriane*" (G. Vernadsky, *Mongols*, p. 371). Slugi vol'nye, standing on the social ladder next to boyars, lost their freedom of service in the 16th century (at the same time as the Muscovite BOIARE). *Slugi pod dvorskim* were freemen, some of whom had originally been bondmen of the grand prince. In the 14th–15th centuries these two groups of slugi made up the bulk of the Muscovite armed forces, and both possessed landed estates either as their full property (VOTCHINA) or as military fiefs (POMEST'E). In the Muscovy of the 16th century both became DVORIANE and DETI BOIARSKIE. In the 18th century they and the former boiare merged into the legal class (SOSLOVIE) of the DVORIANSTVO.

slúgi, in the Grand Duchy of Lithuania: various categories of people who occupied a social and economic status between the SHLIAKHTA and the peasantry. Not only the grand duke but also Lithuanian and Russian princes and lords (PANY) in the Grand Duchy had their own *slugi dvornye* (court servitors); therefore, both *slugi gospodarskie* and *slugi panskie* constituted the military retinues of their respective lords and performed service in civil administration.

slúgi and *slúzhki monastýrskie:* secular officials, servants, or workers of various kinds in or for the monasteries.

slúgi pútnye: state messengers for the grand duke and other officials in peacetime who served in the army in wartime.

slúzhashchii, -chie. White collar worker, a term from the 19th century, as opposed to *rabochii* (blue collar worker).

gosudárstvennye slúzhashchie: government officials.

zémskie slúzhashchie: employees in ZEMSTVO institutions—teachers, physicians, agronomists, statisticians, clerks, and so on.

slúzhba, in Muscovy. Service of all kinds; office; duty. Also (collect.), servitors, retinue.

beregováia slúzhba: military outpost service on the southern borders of the state. In the early Muscovite period the bank (*bereg*) of the Oka River formed the borderline, and the term survived when the borderline moved farther southward.

gosudáreva slúzhba: state service.

polkováia slúzhba: war service in the active army.

tserkóvnaia slúzhba: church service.

vérnaia slúzhba: financial service under oath (*na vere*) in Muscovy.

slúzhba boiárskaia, gospodárskaia, or **zémskaia,** in the Grand Duchy of Lithuania. Usually military service, as opposed to the *sluzhba tiaglaia,* peasant obligatory work for the grand duke or for private landlords. Sluzhba meant also a service unit and a peasant farmstead.

sluzhébnik, -ki. Servitor in general; layman worker in a monastery; sometimes the term was applied also to clergy.

sluzhébniki, in the Grand Duchy of Lithuania. Servitors of high officials (such as VOEVODY, NAMESTNIKI, STAROSTY), lords (*sluzhebniki panskie*), or bishops (*sluzhebniki biskupskie*).

sluzhébnik, -ki. Book or manual containing the ordinary church services, liturgy; matins, vespers.

sluzhílye or **sluzhívye (liúdi).** See LIUDI SLUZHILYE.

slúzhka, -ki. Layman serving in a monastery or at the bishop's see.

smerd, -dy. Peasant in old Russia (Kievan and Novgorodian). The term designated either the peasants living on the prince's (state) lands, or the peasantry in general, or even the lower classes both rural and urban. The peasantry of the Kievan period was treated by the law as personally free. They paid state taxes and performed military service during wartime, but had low social standing and gradually became dependent upon the big landowners (princes and boyars). Some of the smerdy became tenants or hired laborers on the landed estates of the big landlords.

smíl'noe. In old church statutes, adultery on the part of a husband or, perhaps, adultery in general. As a crime it fell within the jurisdiction of the church court.

smotrítel', -li. Overseer, steward, administrator (a term used mostly in the 19th century).

bol'níchnyi smotrítel' or *smotrítel' bol'nítsy:* hospital administrator.

stantsiónnyi smotrítel': post-station chief.

tiurémnyi smotrítel': prison warden, and so on.

smúta. Riot, disorder, disturbance. The term for the Time of Troubles in Muscovy (1605–13).

snokhá. Son's wife.

snos, -sy. In Moscow legal language, things taken away by a slave or servant leaving his master.

sóbina. Private property; separate possession.

sobór, -ry. 1. Council, meeting, or assembly (see esp. ZEMSKII SOBOR). 2. Cathedral; in medieval Pskov, also an ecclesiastical district.

osviashchénnyi sobór: consecrated council, an assembly of the Muscovite high church hierarchy, headed until 1589 by the metropolitan and then by the patriarch and consisting of the metropolitans (four after 1589), archbishops, bishops, and abbots of several important monasteries. The tsar invited its consultation on important questions and it was a normal component of the ZEMSKIE SOBORY.

tserkóvnyi sobór: church council. In Muscovy church councils took place frequently. Some deserve mention here. The councils of 1490, 1503, and 1504 were called to discuss (and to condemn) the rationalistic heresy of judaizers (*zhidovstvuiushchie*) that emerged in Novgorod the Great in the 1470s and spread to Muscovy. At the sobor of 1503 the NESTIAZHATELI, headed by Nil Sorskii, challenged the right of the monasteries to possess landed estates with their peasant population, but the majority, led by the abbot Joseph of Volokolamsk, voted for the property right of the monasteries and for the inviolability of the church landed estates. The councils of 1547 and 1549, convoked by Metropolitan Makarii, decided on the incorporation of various regional Russian saints into the general church calendar and on many new canonizations. The council of 1551 (called the *stoglavyi sobor*) was convoked by Tsar Ivan IV in order to take measures to improve religious life and morals. The results of the sobor's deliberations were summarized in a book of one hundred short chapters—hence the name STOGLAV.

In the 17th century the church councils of 1654 and 1666–67 were most important. The first of them approved the reforms of Patriarch Nikon, consisting of corrections of church service books and rituals in accordance with those of the Greek Orthodox church. The great council of 1666–67 was attended by Eastern hierarchs including the patriarchs of Alexandria and Antioch; it condemned, and then deposed, Patriarch Nikon for his bid for supreme political power and his disobedience of the tsar; but it approved Nikon's church reform, and condemned and anathematized its opponents as RASKOL'NIKI (schismatics) and heretics. In 1682 a church council to discuss the question of the RASKOL was once more convoked in Moscow. During the 18th and 19th centuries church councils were no longer convoked by a government that claimed to be competent to solve all ecclesiastical as well as secular questions. Only in 1917–18 did a church council convene again, when the Orthodox Russian church stood on the threshold of great tribulation.

Uspénskii sobór: in the Moscow Kremlin, the Cathedral of the Dormition or of the Assumption, the most venerated church in Russia before 1917, the national religious shrine and the place of coronation of tsars and emperors. Originally built in 1326 by Prince Ivan Kalita on the initiative of Metropolitan Peter, it was rebuilt by the Italian architect Aristotle Fioraventi in 1475–79 (under Ivan III).

zémskii sobór, -kie -ry: assembly of the land or national assembly. Zemskii sobor is a literary, as distinct from a legal or historically contemporaneous, term for those assemblies in Muscovy that were called in documents of the time either SOVET VSEIA ZEMLI (the council of the whole land) or, simply, sobor. The first assembly of this kind is supposed to have been convoked by Ivan IV in 1549–50, but information about it is vague. In 1566, during the Livonian war with Poland and Lithuania, Ivan consulted a second sobor, which voted for the continuation of the war. This sobor was composed of the OSVIASHCHENNYI SOBOR, the boyar DUMA, the office-holding military service men, and elected administrators of the Moscow POSADSKIE LIUDI. Because of its composition, Kliuchevskii called this sobor a conference of the central government with its own local agents.

The function of the sobor changed after the end of the Riurik dynasty and during the Time of Troubles (1605–13). When there was no recognized tsar on the throne, the zemskii sobor emerged as the highest authority in the country. After the death of the last tsar of the Riurik dynasty, Fedor Ivanovich (in 1598), Patriarch Job convoked a zemskii sobor which, following the patriarch's recommendation, elected the boyar, Boris Godunov, to the throne. The eloquent electoral charter cited among the reasons for this choice the unanimous will of the people, adding that "the voice of the people is the

voice of God." In 1610–13, when the Polish prince Wladyslaw was elected by a group of boyars only and never came to Moscow, the principle of the tsar's election by the people as the only lawful way to the throne was generally recognized. During the most critical time in 1611–12, when Moscow was occupied by a Polish garrison and the whole country was in anarchy, the cities of the central and northern regions formed their local elected councils as organs of military and civilian authority. They entered into lively relations with each other in order to form a common military force for the liberation of Moscow and in order to elect a tsar. When the Second National Host (OPOLCHENIE), led by Prince Pozharskii, came to Iaroslavl' in the spring and summer of 1612, the leaders of the opolchenie summoned a zemskii sobor to assume the functions of civil and military government in Russia. After Moscow had been retaken by the national forces, the elected representatives of 50 cities with their UEZDY (districts) came to Moscow and formed, together with the boyars, clergy, and Moscow citizens, an electoral convention and in February 1613 elected the young Mikhail Romanov. This sobor included not only the representatives of the service men and townspeople (SLUZHILYE and POSADSKIE LIUDI) but also those of the UEZDNYE LIUDI (state peasants of the northern regions) and of the cossacks.

During the first ten years of Mikhail's reign the sobor was in session nearly every year. It voted new taxes and helped mobilize new armed forces and restore order. Foreign affairs, especially wars with Poland, also impelled the government to seek the sobor's help and to convoke it in 1632 and 1634. Another important issue of foreign policy arose in 1642, when the Don Cossacks seized the key Turkish fortress of Azov at the mouth of the Don River and asked the tsar to take possession of it. This would have meant a dangerous war with Turkey and the Crimean Tatars. The tsar asked the sobor whether Russia was able to wage that war. The answers were evasive; some of them painted a very gloomy picture of the country's economic and administrative conditions, and the tsar sent an order to the cossacks to retreat from Azov.

Under the second tsar of the Romanov dynasty, Aleksei Mikhailovich, the sobor of 1648–49 (convoked in consequence of internal disorders and of requests for a sobor) participated actively in the working out of a new code of laws. Issued in 1649 and called the *Sobornoe Ulozhenie*, it was discussed, approved, and signed by the sobor's members. In 1651 and 1653 the government summoned the zemskii sobor to discuss requests of Ukrainian Hetman Bogdan Khmel'nitskii to take the Ukraine under the tsar's protection; this meant a difficult war with Poland and Lithuania, but the sobor of 1653 advised acceptance of Khmel'nitskii's offer, and the tsar followed this advice.

In summary, there were two categories of sobor: 1) electoral, and 2) consultative. The sobor of 1648–49 participated in legislation, but the last word belonged to the tsar. The electoral sobors of 1598 and 1613 were, in fact, temporary bearers of the supreme state power. As to the composition of the zemskii sobor (aside from the osviashchennyi sobor and the Boyar Duma), the elected members in the 17th century represented mainly the middle and lesser nobility and the middle townspeople; their interests were particularly secured by the *Sobornoe Ulozhenie*, which prohibited the further acquisition of landed estates by the church, confiscated (and included into the POSAD TIAGLO) suburban private SLOBODY, and formally established serfdom by the general prohibition of peasant departures from their landlords. In

the second half of the 17th century the authority of the zemskii sobor declined as the government gained stability and self-confidence.

sobránie, -iia. Assembly, meeting, or gathering.

> *dvoriánskoe sobránie:* see DVORIANE.

> *sobránie fakul'téta:* see UNIVERSITET.

> *gorodskíe izbirátel'nye sobrániia* (pl.): assemblies of qualified city constituents electing (after 1870) *glasnye gorodskoi dumy* (members of the city council) or (after 1905) VYBORSHCHIKI (electors) for the elections of members of the State Duma.

> *gubérnskoe izbirátel'noe sobránie:* the provincial electoral assembly that elected deputies to the State Duma; it was composed of the electors (VYBORSHCHIKI) elected by four groups of constituents: 1) landowners, 2) peasants, 3) city dwellers, 4) factory workers. According to the electoral laws of 1905–06 the majority (absolute or relative) in most of the provincial electoral assemblies belonged to the peasant electors; according to the law of June 3, 1907, to the landowners' electors.

> *zémskie sobrániia* (pl.), *gubérnskoe zémskoe sobránie* and *uézdnoe zémskoe sobránie:* see ZEMSTVO.

sobránie. The title of many important collections of historical sources published in the 19th and 20th centuries.

> *Pólnoe Sobránie Rússkikh Létopisei:* the complete collection of Russian chronicles, published by the Archeographical Commission in St. Petersburg (Petrograd); from 1841 to 1921, 24 volumes were issued. Since 1921 the Academy of Sciences of the USSR has published several more; volume 29 was published in 1965. Some volumes have had a second edition. The collection is the basic source for studies of pre-Petrine Russia.

> *Pólnoe Sobránie Zakónov Rossíiskoi Impérii:* the complete collection of the

laws of the Russian empire. In 1826 Nicholas I established the Second Section of His Majesty's Own Chancery (under Balugianskii) for the codification of the huge and diverse mass of Russian laws issued since the *Ulozhenie* of 1649, the last previous codification. The organizer and supervisor was M. Speranskii. In 1830 Speranskii and his assistants finished the compilation of the 45 enormous volumes. Of these the last 5 volumes included annexes (tables, graphs, organizational charts, tariff data) and indexes (alphabetical and chronological). The first 40 volumes brought together in chronological order over 30,000 laws, beginning with the *Ulozhenie* of 1649 and ending with enactments of December 1825. Later the second and the third complete collections of the laws appeared. The second, covering the period from December 1825 until March 1881, was in 55 volumes. The third collection, from March 1881 to the end of 1913, included 33 volumes. Each volume of the second and third collections normally included the legislative output of one year.

Sobránie traktátov i konvéntsii, zakliuchënnykh Rossíei s inostránnymi derzhávami—recueil des traités et conventions conclus par la Russie avec les puissances étrangères, F. Martens, ed., 15 vols., St. Petersburg, 1874–1909: collection of treaties and conventions concluded by Russia with foreign powers in the 18th and 19th centuries. The documents, in French and Russian parallel text, are supplemented by a substantial historical commentary. This is the basic collection for studies of Russian foreign relations in the imperial period.

Sobránie uzakonénii i rasporiazhénii pravítel'stva: the collection of laws and regulations of the government published (in the second half of the 19th and the beginning of the 20th century) by the publishing office of the Senate as a supplement to the *Senatskie vedomosti* (Senate records); it included the emperor's manifestoes and decrees, Senate decrees, laws approved by the State Duma (after 1905) and the State Council, regulations, statutes, orders, and various documents issued by the government. With the publication of these enactments in the Sobranie uzakonenii, they were considered legally valid. Those documents that had the character of laws were later included in the annual volumes of the POLNOE SOBRANIE ZAKONOV.

sóbstvennost' podvórnaia or **seméinaia.** Property belonging to the household or family, as contrasted with *lichnaia sobstvennost'* (personal property, the property of an individual); an important distinction esp. in 1907–10 during the debates over agrarian reform.

sóf'ian, -iáne. "Literally, St. Sophia's man, that is, one connected with the cathedral of St. Sophia in Novgorod; a squire in the service of the Archbishop of Novgorod" (G. Vernadsky, *Medieval Laws,* glossary, p. 94).

soim velíkii vál'nyi. See SEIM VELIKII VAL'NYI.

sóimik povétovyi. See SEIMIK POVETOVYI.

soiúz, -zy. In international relations, alliance. In internal affairs, union, league, or association of various kinds, which before 1904–05 were not legal. During the "political spring" in the fall of 1904 and the early months of 1905, a great number of soiuzy were founded without official permission; they were mostly associations of professional men—lawyers, physicians, professors (*akademicheskii soiuz*), primary-school teachers, writers, engineers and technicians, clerks, bookkeepers, railway employees, and so on. (For information about the soiuzy founded in 1904–05, see the supplementary volume to the *Entsiklopedicheskii Slovar'* of Brockhaus and Efron, pp. 669–75.) In the spring of 1905 a gathering of delegates sent by the newly formed soiuzy founded an alliance of these associations called the *soiuz soiuzov,* which accepted a political program demanding the convocation of a constituent assembly and a radical democratization of the country. When the revolutionary movement ebbed in early 1906, the government issued (on March 4th, 1906) temporary regulations concerning societies and unions (*vremennye pravila ob obshchestvakh i soiuzakh*) that put all these public organizations under the government's supervision. All the unions and public societies were obliged to register their rules or by-laws (USTAVY) and the names of the members of their executive boards with the provincial authorities; registration could be refused if rules were found to conflict with existing laws. The government could close any union or association if it violated regulations or if its activities were found to be detrimental to public order and safety. Some of the noteworthy (mostly illegal) soiuzy are identified below:

Soiúz Blagodénstviia: the Union of Welfare. A secret society founded in 1818 by several Guards officers in St. Petersburg, replacing the dissolved SIOUZ SPASENIIA. The society at first did not have a directly revolutionary character, and its by-laws called for activities in four fields: 1) philanthropy, 2) education, 3) justice, and 4) socially useful economic activities. But with growing resentment against the *Arakcheevshchina,* radical political tendencies grew among union members; the union was formally dissolved in January 1821, only to give way to the formation of the Northern and Southern Societies, which had a clearly expressed revolutionary character (see DEKABRIST).

Soiúz bor'bý za osvobozhdénie rabóchego klassa: the League of the Struggle for the Emancipation of the Working Class. An underground society founded in 1895–96 in St. Petersburg by a group of Russian Marxists (including Lenin) whose goal was socialism under the Marxist slogan: "Workers of all countries unite!" Members of the League carried on revolutionary propaganda among St. Petersburg's factory workers, and soon became active members of the Russian Social Democratic Workers' Party founded in 1898.

evréiskii soiúz, Óbshche-evréiskii rabóchii soiúz v Rossíi i Pól'she: see BUND.

krest'iánskii soiúz, Vserossíiskii Krest'iánskii Soiúz: the All-Russian (Nationwide) Peasant Union. A loose grouping, illegally founded in the summer of 1905, influenced by revolutionary populism; it demanded the calling of a constituent assembly elected on the basis of universal suffrage, the abolition of private landholdings, and the transfer of all land to the toiling people. This soiuz engaged in energetic agitation among the peasants and played an active role in the agrarian riots and disturbances in 1905–06, but by the end of 1906 was declining and soon disappeared from the political scene.

Soiúz Osvobozhdéniia: in 1902 P. B. Struve, a liberal and former Marxist, founded in Stuttgart a journal entitled *Osvobozhdenie* (Liberation), which proclaimed Russia's political freedom and democratization as the most immediate and urgent task. The journal was smuggled into Russia and found a warm response chiefly among professional groups. In the summer of 1903 the illegal Soiuz Osvobozhdeniia was founded. In October of 1905 the members of the Soiuz Osvobozhdeniia together with the zemstvo constitutionalists founded the KONSTITUTSIONNO-DEMOKRATICHESKAIA PARTIIA.

professionál'nyi soiúz, professionál'nyi rabóchii soiúz: trade union. Free trade unions in Russia had a very short history. After the abandonment of the attempt to organize legal workers' societies under the leadership of the chief of the Moscow political police, Zubatov (in 1901–03, see ZUBATOVSHCHINA), many free workers' trade unions were formed without official permission in 1904–05, and a central bureau of trade unions was founded in Moscow. The regulations on unions and societies issued on March 4, 1906, put all unions and societies under the supervision of the government. Unions of unions were prohibited. According to information received by the commission which prepared a conference of trade unions early in 1907, there were in Russia 652 trade unions with 246,000 members; of these, 46 unions with 48,000 members were in Moscow, and 44 unions with 52,000 members were in St. Petersburg. In 1908–10 the trade union movement greatly declined, and the majority of unions disappeared. On the one hand the government was too suspicious of the unions' activities; on the other hand the revolutionary parties (esp. the Bolsheviks) used the unions mainly to spread revolutionary propaganda among their members. The trade union movement revived somewhat in 1912–14; and after the February Revolution of 1917 they mushroomed throughout the country, but their freedom and independence were short-lived.

Soiúz Rússkogo Naróda: the Union of the Russian People. An extreme rightist organization founded in St. Petersburg in October 1905 by A. I. Dubrovin. The program of the Union held that the welfare of the homeland lay in the preservation of "Orthodoxy, unlimited Russian autocracy, and nationality"; the Russian nationality should be the dominant one in the country and in the State Duma. The Duma, "avoiding any efforts to limit the supreme power of the tsar," should help him in his legislative activity "by informing him truthfully of the real needs of the people and of the state." From late 1905 through 1906 the Union's activity was at its peak; it opened 100 local chapters throughout Russia and carried on vigorous propaganda in which it combined extreme nationalism with anti-semitism; its activities included anti-Jewish pogroms and individual terroristic acts.

Soiúz Semnádtsatogo Oktiabriá: the Union of the 17th of October, or Octobrist Party (OKTIABRISTY). The name of the party referred to the date of the tsar's famous manifesto granting legislative power to the State Duma and promising expansion of the franchise and civil liberties. The Union of the 17th of October was established in late October and November 1905. Its strength was based on the moderately liberal nobility and zemstvo men (including the future president of the State Duma, M. V. Rodzianko) and on commercial and industrial leaders, esp. those of the Moscow business world, such as G. A. Krestovnikov and the brothers A. and N. Guchkov. Alexander I. Guchkov was the principal leader of the Octobrists. The Octobrist program called for a constitutional monarchy based on universal suffrage and civil liberties. On the agrarian question the Octobrists favored a number of measures for the improvement of the peasants' situation, but accepted the confiscation of landlords' land only when other means had failed, and then only with just compensation. The Octobrists demanded "the preservation of the Russian state one and undivided" but were willing to make allowances for the linguistic and cultural needs of various nationalities. After the electoral law was revised in 1907 to favor the wealthier classes, the Octobrists were able to send almost 150 deputies to the Third Duma (1907–12), and became the leading force in the chamber supporting the policies of Stolypin against opposition from the left and the right.

Soiúz Spaséniia: the Union of Salvation or of the True and Faithful Sons of the Fatherland. A secret political society formed in 1816 in St. Petersburg by a group of Guards officers, participants in the Napoleonic wars. Modeled after contemporary Masonic lodges, with elaborate initiation rites and three grades of membership, the society strove, according to the later testimony of its members, to introduce representative government in Russia and to abolish serfdom. In 1818 it was reorganized as the Union of Welfare (see SOIUZ BLAGODENSTVIIA).

Vserossíiskii Soiúz Gorodóv: the All-Russian (Nationwide) Union of Towns founded in August 1914; it was headed by the mayor of Moscow, M. V. Chelnokov. Its goals were similar to those of the VSEROSSIISKII ZEMSKII SOIUZ though the scope of its activities was considerably smaller.

zémskii soiúz, Vserossíiskii Zémskii Soiúz: the All-Russian (Nationwide) Union of ZEMSTVOS founded in August 1914 "for the relief of sick and wounded soldiers." The Union's central committee was headed by its elected president, Prince G. E. L'vov. A network of local committees was set up. Because the government gave this union strong financial support, its activities expanded rapidly. At first it helped the military authorities and the Red Cross establish and maintain military hospitals and hospital trains; it also operated its own hospitals and trains. Later the zemstvo committees set up dining and tea rooms, canteens, baths, storehouses, and workshops of various kinds near the front lines. They helped supply the army with food, clothing, and footwear. In 1915–16 the zemstvo union also assisted the millions of voluntary and involuntary refugees evacuated from the theater of military operations. In 1916 the annual budget of the zemstvo union increased to the huge amount of 600 million rubles, and hundreds of thousands of men and women were employed directly and indirectly in its service. But relations between the union and the government became strained shortly before 1917, when the general discontent with the government was reflected in the union and in the individual zemstvos.

Soiúz zémskikh (or *zémtsev) konstitutsionalístov:* a liberal group of zemstvo men in 1903–05, which, together with the SOIUZ OSVOBOZHDENIIA, formed the core of the *Konstitutsionno-Demokraticheskaia partiia* (see PARTIIA) in October 1905.

sok (W.R.). Accuser, prosecutor, plaintiff, claimant.

sokhá, sókhi. 1. A simple wooden plow with one or two iron plowshares. 2. A measure of arable land serving as a unit of taxation. In Muscovy the sokha, until the middle of the 17th century, was the basic unit of taxation. "Sokha was a territorial unit comprising either a specified area of farm land or a definite number of households. The size of the *sokha* varied greatly according to what was presumed to be the productivity of the land and the taxpaying capacity of the inhabitants" (M. Florinsky, *I,* p. 274). The dimensions of the Muscovite normal (or great) sokha differed according to the quality of the land and the categories of landowners. Lands belonging to the state (*chërnye* ZEMLI) were taxed more heavily than the lands of private landlords (who imposed their own levies on their peasants); therefore the dimensions of the taxable units on state lands were smaller than those on the lands of other categories. In the 16th and the first half of the 17th centuries the normal Muscovite sokha on state land measured 500 CHETVERTS of good land, 600 chetverts of medium land, and 700 chetverts of poor land; on the lands of the private landlords (POMESHCHIKI and VOTCHINNIKI), respectively, 800, 1,000, and 1,200 chetverts; on monastic properties, respectively, 600, 700–750, and 800–900 chetverts. All these measures were indicated in one field; therefore, under the dominant three-field system, they have to be multiplied by three to get the full size of the sokha; one chetvert' was equal to ½ DESIATINA (2.7 acres), therefore a chetvert' in the three fields was equal to 1½ desiatinas (4 acres). In the cities the sokha was composed of various numbers of households (DVORY) according to their economic status; normally, it was 40 of the best (LUTCHIE), 80 medium (SEREDNIE), and 160 MOLODCHIE (younger, therefore poorer) dvory. But the number varied from one town to another and from one time to another. According to S. Veselovskii (*I*, p. 291), the normal dimensions of the POSAD sokha at the beginning of the 17th century were 40 best households, 50–60 medium, and 70–100 (or more) poor or poorest dvory.

málaia sokhá or *sóshka:* a little sokha, a taxable unit in use in the 15th–16th centuries in the northern regions. It was normally equated to three OBZHI, or 30 chetverts in one field, i.e., 90 chetverts or 45 desiatinas in all three fields (122 acres).

sokól'nichii, -chie. A court official in charge of the princely, or tsarist, falconry.

sokól'nik, -ki. Falconer.

sol, sly (= POSOL). Envoy, in the Kievan period.

soldát, -ty. The term soldaty came to Muscovy in the 17th century when the Moscow government found it necessary to form *polki inozemnogo stroia,* among them *soldatskie polki* (see POLK), regiments of soldiers trained on the western European model. Recruited from young Russians, they were trained by foreign officers in Muscovite service. Once the immediate need was past, they were disbanded. When Peter the Great formed a standing army, he accepted the term soldat for all military service men. According to the Peter's military statute (*ustav voinskii*) of 1716, "the term *soldat* includes all the people who are in the army from the highest general to the last musketeer." Later the term soldaty was applied to enlisted men; the terms soldaty or *nizhnie chiny* (lower ranks, an official term, including privates, corporals, and sergeants) were used in contradistinction to the term OFITSERY (commissioned officers).

pákhatnye soldáty (pl.): farming soldiers. In the 18th century there were in the southern border regions of the empire several quasi-military units of military settlers. Under Alexander I the government undertook a misguided attempt to combine the occupations of regular soldier and peasant in military settlements (*voennye poseleniia;* see POSELENETS). After the revolt in the military settlements of Novgorod province in the summer of 1831, "in October 1831 Tsar Nicholas put the military colonists of Novgorod into a new class called 'farming soldiers' (*pakhatnye soldaty*). Despite the name these people were no longer part of the military. All their special army duties and the military control of their lives were ended, and the only difference between them and state peasants was that they had to pay a much larger obrok to the state. . . . In 1836 the colonists in Mogilev and Vitebsk were made 'farming soldiers' " (J. Blum, pp. 502–03). In 1857, with the abolition of all the remaining military colonies, the farming soldiers were transferred to the state peasantry.

sóshka or **málaia sokhá.** See SOKHA.

soslóvie, -iia. Estate, a social class with a special legal status. Old Russia did not know the sosloviia in such a definite, sharply outlined form as, for example, the German *Stände: Adel, Bürger,* and *Bauer.* In Kievan Russia "there were no such high barriers between single social groups and classes as existed in feudal Europe of the same period" (G. Vernadsky, *Kievan Russia,* p. 136). Nor did the early Muscovite period witness such barriers between the numerous and fluid groups of service men, POSAD people, peasants, and VOL'NYE GULIA-SHCHIE LIUDI. The *Ulozhenie* of 1649 moved toward more closed social groups, but the formal and legal class structure or *soslovnyi stroi* was established only in the 18th century. Peter the Great endeavored to bring order to the heterogeneous categories of Muscovite service men and, at the same time, to get some hold on the elusive vol'nye guliashchie liudi by forcing them to enter either the posad or peasant communities or military or private service. He tried also to give more definite form to the organization of posad society.

Under Catherine II the nobility became an entirely definite social and legal group with special rights, liberties, and privileges and with its corporate organization. But even in the imperial period the Russian nobility never became an entirely closed soslovie. Access to the nobility was open for persons of other classes through state service. By this means many individuals who had ability (and luck!) entered the hereditary (*potomstvennoe*) as well as the personal (*lichnoe*) DVORIANSTVO. (The children of *lichnye dvoriane* did not belong to the nobility.) The merchants formed in the 18th century a separate soslovie organized in GIL'DII. In 1832 Nicholas I created a new soslovie of POCHËTNYE GRAZHDANE (distinguished citizens). It was composed of the top merchants and industrialists, lower categories of state officials, non-noble persons with university education, and children of lichnye dvoriane.

The clergy (DUKHOVENSTVO) also was a separate soslovie; it was divided into the *beloe dukhovenstvo* (white clergy, the parish clergy) and the *chërnoe dukhovenstvo* (black clergy, the regular clergy, the monks). The city dwellers were divided by the charter of cities of 1785 into several groups, besides the KUPECHESTVO (merchant class); the most numerous were the MESHCHANE, who also formed a separate soslovie. The huge mass of the peasantry consisted of several groups (see KREST'IA-NE). There were also some sociolegal groups that stood outside the main soslovie ladder, such as the ODNO-DVORTSY, who stood between the nobility and the peasantry (in the 1860s they were transferred to the state peasantry); the KAZAKI; and the INORODTSY, native tribes and peoples, mostly inhabitants of Siberia and Central Asia. The lower classes of the population, the peasantry and the lower classes of the city dwellers, bore in the official language of the imperial period the label of *podatnye sosloviia* or *podatnye sostoianiia,* since they were obliged to pay the PODUSHNAIA PODAT' (the poll tax introduced by Peter the Great) and to deliver recruits for the army, while the higher sosloviia were free from the poll tax and recruitment, as well as corporal punishment.

In the second half of the 19th century, after the peasant emancipation and other great reforms, the soslovnyi stroi to a large extent disintegrated: the judicial reform of 1864 equalized legal procedures for members of all sosloviia; universal military service, introduced in 1874, deprived the high sosloviia of their nonrecruitment privilege; the poll tax was abolished in the 1880s; imposition of corporal punishments by peasant courts was abolished in 1904. Although the period of reaction under Alexander III saw some attempts to restore the soslovnyi stroi, the revolution and reforms of 1905–06 brought still further dissolution. However, old terms and the formal division of the population into sosloviia survived until 1917. The percentages of the different soslovnye groups, according to official statistics around 1900, were as follows: peasants, 77.1 percent; meshchane, 10.7; inorodtsy, 6.6; cossacks, 2.3; nobility and officialdom, 1.5; clergy, 0.5; merchants and pochetnye grazhdane, 0.5; others, 0.8.

soslóviia podatnýe (pl.). See SOSLOVIE.

sostoiánie and **podatnýe sostoiániia.** Sostoianie was used in the official language of the imperial period in the same sense as SOSLOVIE.

sótnia, -ni. One hundred, either as a military unit of 100 (*sto*) men or as a territorial administrative unit or some public organization. In Novgorod the Great each borough (KONETS) was divided into two sotni. In the Grand Duchy of Lithuania the sotnia was a subdivision of the VOLOST'. In Moscow the wealthiest group of merchants was called GOSTI, next in line were the *gostinaia sotnia* and the *sukonnaia sotnia* (clothiers); these groups within the Moscow merchant class were not self-organized but were formed by the government; its agents periodically recruited in provincial cities and transferred to Moscow the wealthier and more reliable local merchants for such services as GOLOVY (directors) or TSELOVAL'NIKI (sworn assistants) in collecting government revenues and in managing the tsar's (the state's) trading operations.

chërnye sótni (pl.): in Moscow, settlements of the lower categories of city dwellers—small traders, artisans, hired workers, and the like; each sotnia formed a local corporation which elected its head (SOTSKII or SOTNIK). During the revolution of 1905 the term chërnaia sotnia (black hundred) acquired a derogatory connotation, being applied to extreme rightist groups.

sótnik, -ki. 1. Hundreder, centurion, commander of a military unit of 100 men. In Muscovy there were *sotniki streletskie* (see STREL'TSY), *pushkarskie* (see PUSHKARI), and *kazatskie* or *kazachii* (see KAZAKI). Sotniki were also commanders of 100-man units in the *voisko zaporozhskoe*, as the Ukrainian army was called in the 17th century. In the Russian imperial army the rank of sotnik in cossack regiments corresponded to the PORUCHIK rank in the regular army (a rank of the 10th class according to the TABEL' O RANGAKH). 2. The head of a territorial administrative unit in the Grand Duchy of Lithuania and in Muscovy. But in Muscovy, particularly in the imperial period, the term SOTSKII was more common in civil administration.

sotsiál-demokrát. See ROSSIISKAIA SOTSIAL-DEMOKRATICHESKAIA RABOCHAIA PARTIIA.

sotsialíst revolutsionér. see PARTIIA SOTSIALISTOV REVOLUTSIONEROV.

sótskii, -kie. Civil official elected by the population of 100 (more or less) households. Sotskie (mentioned in the Primary Chronicle) existed in Kiev as early as the 10th century. Sotskie also headed the SOTNI in Novgorod the Great. The Moscow CHËRNYE SOTNI were headed by elected sotskie, who represented their settlements in dealing with the government. In the northern regions of Muscovy, sotskie, often mentioned in contemporary documents along with STAROSTY, were administrators and even judges in rural districts; sometimes their service positions and spheres of competence were equal, sometimes several sotskie were subordinate to one starosta. The chief duty of the sotskie was police service, and as police officials they were subordinate to the VOEVODY and the GUBNYE STAROSTY. In the imperial period the office of the sotskie, as lower police agents, was preserved. According to the statutes on *zemskaia politsiia* (rural police) issued in 1837, the peasants were obliged to elect sotskie (and DESIATSKIE), who were subordinate to the local STANOVOI PRISTAV. These elections were not a privilege but an onerous duty for the peasant communities.

soveshchánie, -niia. Conference, council, commission, or committee.

osóboe soveshchánie pri minístre vnútrennikh del: a special commission of the Ministry of Internal Affairs, established by the "regulations (POLO-ZHENIE) on measures for the protection of the state order and of public security" issued on August 14, 1881. This commission, composed of two officials of the Ministry of Internal Affairs and two from the Ministry of Justice, was to decide cases of political crimes when there was insufficient evidence for a trial in court. The soveshchanie could put persons regarded as dangerous to state security under police surveillance or could sentence them to a maximum of five years of administrative deportation to remote areas.

osóboe soveshchánie o núzhdakh seľskokhoziáistvennoi promýshlennosti: special conference on the needs of agriculture, established in January 1902 (under the chairmanship of the finance minister, S. Iu. Witte) to discuss measures for improving the economic condition of the peasantry. In provinces and districts of European Russia, local committees to discuss the question were established under the chairmanship of the marshals of the nobility. The committees consisted of persons invited by the chairman: leaders of local administration, the zemstvos, and experienced persons from various walks of life. The committees assembled and published a wealth of information on legal and economic conditions in the countryside. In 1905

the chief conference and the local committees were terminated.

osóbye soveshchániia (pl.) *po oboróne, po perevózkam, po tóplivu* and *po prodovóľstviiu:* various other special councils. Heavy setbacks on the front during the summer of 1915 induced the government to coordinate its defense efforts with those of various public organizations. A Special Council for National Defense was set up in June 1915 for this purpose. Presided over by the war minister, the Council included the president and nine members of the Duma, the president and nine members of the State Council, seven ministers, the heads of various departments in the Ministry of War, and representatives of industry, of the unions of zemstvos and of towns, and of the newly formed Central War Industry Committee. Shortly thereafter three more special councils were formed: for transportation, presided over by the minister of transportation; for fuel, presided over by the minister of commerce and industry; and for food supply, presided over by the minister of agriculture. Their membership included representatives of the government, the legislative chambers, and public organizations, as above. Government statutes concerning the four special councils were issued on August 17, 1915, but the work of these complex and cumbersome organizations hardly justified the hopes placed in them.

sovét, -ty. Advice, counsel; agreement; assembly, council, conference. Some important sovety follow.

sovét gospód: council of lords in Novgorod the Great (literary term). Chaired usually by the archbishop of Novgorod, the council consisted of senior city officials (incumbent and former POSADNIKI, TYSIATSKIE, STA-ROSTY, SOTSKIE) and some boyars. The council discussed questions and prepared drafts of decisions before issues were presented to the Novgorodian VECHE.

Gosudárstvennyi Sovét: State Council, Council of State. At the beginning of his reign (in March 1801) Alexander I issued a decree establishing a permanent council of 12 members to review all important affairs of state. This council did not play a significant role until it was transformed into an authoritative high-level state institution, according to Speranskii's plan, by the manifesto of January 1, 1810. This provided that all drafts of laws, statutes, and regulations were to be proposed to and examined by the Council of State, after which they were to be submitted to the emperor. The Council consisted of high dignitaries appointed by the emperor, and the ministers, who were members *ex officio*. The emperor himself, or the presiding member of the council appointed for one year, chaired the meetings. The Council was divided into four departments: 1) laws; 2) military affairs; 3) civil and ecclesiastical affairs; 4) state economy. (According to the regulations of March 30, 1901, the Council was divided as follows: 1) the deparment of laws; 2) the department of civil and ecclesiastical affairs; 3) the department of the state economy; 4) the department of industry, science, and commerce.) A general meeting of the Council was called whenever necessary. It was a consultative body. When the Council's opinions on a question were divided, both the opinion of the majority and that of the minority were presented to the emperor, who could confirm either of them.

The establishment of the new legislative system in 1905–06 brought substantial change in the composition and competence of the State Council. By the laws of February 20, 1906, and the Fundamental Laws (OSNOVNYE ZAKONY) of April 23, 1906, the State Council became an upper legislative chamber, half to be elected by privileged groups and half to be appointed by the emperor. The law stated that the total number of Council members selected annually by the emperor from the entire group of appointed Council members to serve on the acting Council assembly must not exceed the total number of the elected Council members. The chairman and the vice-chairman of the Council were appointed annually by the emperor. The elected members of the Council were to represent the church (6), the universities and the Academy of Sciences (6), the provincial ZEMSTVO assemblies (34), the provincial societies of the nobility (18), commercial and industrial associations (12), and the assemblies of landlords in provinces without zemstvos (22), or 98 in all. This chamber, clearly designed to give weight to the high-level and conservative groups in society, was to have the same rights as the State Duma, and its approval was required if a new law were to be valid.

Sovét Minístrov: the Council of Ministers, established in 1861 as a consultative assembly of all ministers to discuss questions concerning more than one ministry. Such a collective discussion was ordered occasionally by the emperor. In fact, the activities of this sovet and of its president (PREDSEDATEL') were weak and of little importance. By decree of October 19, 1905, the old Sovet Ministrov was replaced by a new one that was to represent the united government under the chairmanship of the *predsedatel' soveta ministrov,* who then acquired the character of a prime minister; all important measures and drafts of laws were to be discussed and approved by this Sovet Ministrov before being presented to the State Duma or to the emperor (if the decision fell to him personally).

Sovét Ob"edinënnogo Dvoriánstva: the Council of the United Nobility, a body created by the congress of representatives of the landowning nobility that took place in St. Petersburg in the summer of 1906. This organization vigorously protested against plans for the confiscation of privately owned landed estates, and in general tried to exert a conservative influence on government policy.

Sovét Rabóchikh Deputátov: the Council of Workers' Deputies, formed in St. Petersburg in the middle of October 1905 to head the revolutionary movement against the government. In the second half of November it consisted of 562 members representing 147 factories and mills, 34 workshops, and 16 trade unions. The Sovet published its *Izvestiia,* which called on the St. Petersburg proletariat to plan an armed uprising for the overthrow of the government, since the October 17 manifesto did not in the least satisfy the leaders of the revolutionary proletariat. When the second call for a general strike (in November 1905) attracted little response from St. Petersburg workers, the leaders of the Sovet tried to bring about bankruptcy of the government. On November 26, the chairman of the Sovet, Khrustalev-Nosar', was arrested; the next day, the Sovet elected Trotskii in his place and stated that it was "continuing to prepare for an armed uprising." Meanwhile, on December 2, the St. Petersburg Sovet (together with other revolutionary organizations) issued a financial manifesto calling on the people to refuse to pay taxes, to withdraw their savings from the banks, and to demand that wages be paid only in gold. On December 3, the leaders and most of the members of the Sovet were arrested. A substitute Sovet was elected immediately, but it did not enjoy the authority and influence of its predecessor, and its call for a new general strike, issued on December 6, was ineffective in St. Petersburg. Moscow and other industrial centers had formed their own sovety rabochikh deputatov in the fall

of 1905, but after the suppression of the Moscow armed uprising (in December 1905) the sovety soon disappeared from the political scene. In the fall of 1906, 29 leaders of the St. Petersburg Sovet were brought to trial for conspiracy to overthrow the government. Twelve were acquitted; several, including Trotskii, were sentenced to deportation to Siberia (from where Trotskii soon easily escaped abroad).

sovét universitéta: the assembly of the *ordinarnye* and *ekstraordinarnye* university professors, chaired by the REKTOR. Concerning its competence, see UNIVERSITET.

Verkhóvnyi Táinyi Sovét: Supreme Privy Council, established by decree of February 8, 1726 (under Catherine I) as the supreme government organ. Its size varied between 6 and 9 members. Under Catherine I (1725–27) the dominant position in the Sovet (and in the government) was occupied by Peter the Great's favorite, Menshikov, but after Catherine's death (in 1727) Menshikov lost his influence and was exiled to Siberia, while members of two old princely families—the Dolgorukiis and the Golitsyns—became the actual rulers of the state under the boy-emperor Peter II (1727–30). When Peter died (in January 1730), the members of the Verkhovnyi Tainyi Sovet decided to call to the throne the duchess of Kurland, Anna Ivanovna (daughter of Ivan, Peter the Great's brother and nominal co-ruler, who died in 1696). Striving to retain the power in their hands, the VERKHOVNIKI composed and sent to Anna at Mittau a set of KONDITSII, that gave all power in the state to the Verkhovnyi Tainyi Sovet. Anna, eager to exchange Mittau for St. Petersburg, signed the konditsii, but upon arriving in Moscow (in February 1730) she learned that most of the rank and file nobility did not sympathize with the oligarchic plans of the verkhovniki. She then tore up the conditions she had signed and by the manifesto of February 28, 1730, declared that "in accordance with the unanimous request of our subjects," she had restored the autocracy. The manifesto of March 4, 1730, announced the abolition of the Verkhovnyi Tainyi Sovet, and the authors of the konditsii were soon subjected to severe punishments.

vseuézdnyi zémskii sovét: in some northern Muscovite provinces in the 16th and 17th centuries, a council in the district (UEZD) center composed of representatives of the uezd center and of the rural VOLOSTI. Such a *vseuezdnaia* or uezd-wide organization was in addition to the assemblies in the villages and POSADY. It was headed by an elected *vseuezdnyi zemskii starosta* (see STAROSTA).

zémskii sovét or *sovét vseiá zemlí:* the land or national assembly, term used in documents of the 17th century for the ZEMSKII SOBOR.

sovétnik, -ki. Adviser or companion of a prince; later, councillor. When Peter the Great established the KOLLEGII in 1718 and then issued the Table of Ranks in 1722, the councillors of the kollegii had the rank of *kollezhskii sovetnik;* the members of the *nadvornye sudy* (see SUD) were *nadvornye sovetniki;* the presidents of the kollegii and the Senate's members were *tainye sovetniki;* thus, in Peter's Table of Ranks, the rank of an official corresponded to his service position. In the 19th century, after the kollegii had been abolished and the government institutions changed, this correspondence was lost, but the old ranks remained. The Table of Ranks was somewhat revised in the 19th century, and at its end the sovetniki were ranked as follows: *tituliarnyi sovetnik* (9th class), *nadvornyi sovetnik* (7th class), *kollezhskii sovetnik* (6th class), *statskii sovetnik* (5th class), *deistvitel'nyi* (actual) *statskii sovetnik* (4th class), *tainyi sovetnik*

(3rd class), *deistvitel'nyi tainyi sovetnik* (2nd class). For the full list of ranks see TABEL' O RANGAKH. Some offices using the term sovetnik remained in the 19th century, like *sovetnik gubernskogo pravleniia.*

kommértsii sovétnik and *manufaktúr-sovétnik:* honorary titles established by the government in 1800—for outstanding merchants, kommertsii sovetnik, and for outstanding industrialists, manufaktur-sovetnik.

spádok, -dki (W.R.). Inherited property, esp. a landed estate.

spádok gospodárskii: escheat, landed estate that, in the absence of legitimate heirs, came into the possession of the Grand Duke of Lithuania.

spál'nik, -ki. Courtier of the tsar's bedchamber; one of the young men recruited from aristocratic families for the group headed by the POSTEL'NICHII; several of them took turns spending the night in the tsar's palace and helping him with his dressing.

spísok, -ski. Written record, transcript, duplicate copy, list. In Muscovy there were such spiski as the following.

dokládnyi spísok: record of court proceedings presented by a lower judge to the next higher court for reexamination of the case (*k dokladu*).

dokhódnyi spísok: record of income.

moskóvskii spísok: list of service men (*dvoriane moskovskie*) who had their POMEST'IA in the Moscow UEZD (i.e., near the capital).

nakáznyi spísok: transcript of written instructions given by the central government to local authorities.

obysknói spísok: record of an investigation or interrogation (see OBYSK).

okládnyi spísok: tax register.

smétnyi spísok: record of revenues, expenses, and arrears from the previous fiscal year.

statéinyi spísok: list recording cases or articles (STAT'I), such as were compiled in Moscow *prikazy* concerning enactments issued between the *Sudebnik* of 1550 and the *Ulozhenie* of 1649. Stateinye spiski also meant reports of Moscow ambassadors on their travels and negotiations abroad.

    súdnyi spísok: record of court proceedings.

správa, -vy. In the legal language of the Grand Duchy of Lithuania, a court case, a trial. In Muscovy, the words *sprava pod'iachego,* along with his signature, indicated which clerk had written a given document.

správka pomést'ia. In Muscovy, registration in the POMESTNYI PRIKAZ of a POMEST'E granted to a service man.

srébrenik, -ki. Silver coin minted in Kiev in the 10th–11th centuries (under Vladimir and Iaroslav, 980–1054).

srebró. See SEREBRO.

sróchnaia. See GRAMOTA SROCHNAIA.

sródnik, -ki. A relative.

srok, -ki. 1. Term, date. 2. Delay, postponement.

    ukáznyi srok: a fixed term, esp. a date for appearance in court.

ssúda, -dy. Loan.

    domoobzavódstvennye ssúdy: loans for the establishment of new households by settlers in the Asian provinces, granted by the government in the 1890s and later. According to the regulations of July 5, 1912, they allowed up to 400 rubles per household in the Trans-Baikal region and up to 250 rubles in other Asian territories.

ssýlka, -ki. 1. Temporary or permanent exile or banishment as a form of punishment. In the Muscovite period, according to Kotoshikhin, there were three kinds of banishment—to the remote regions (*v dal'nie gorody*) of European Russia (chiefly western border regions), to Siberia, or to monasteries for humility (*v smirenie*). In sentences of the first two, the government ordered local authorities to use the exiles for state service (chiefly military), according to their legal status and their abilities. In the imperial period the government considered the Siberian exile system from two points of view—as a kind of punishment and as a means of colonizing Siberia. By a decree of 1760 the landlords were granted the right to send to Siberia any of their serfs who were recalcitrant, and the government discounted the exiled serfs from the army recruiting quota of these landlords' villages. In the 19th century there were three ways of effecting banishment to Siberia for penal settlement. First, by court sentence: all those sentenced to KATORZHNYE RABOTY, after they had finished their term of penal hard labor, had to stay in Siberia as penal settlers (SSYL'NO-POSELENTSY); penal settlement without previous katorzhnye raboty was also a form of punishment imposed by the courts. The second way was exile by administrative order. The third was the banishment of vicious or harmful (POROCHNYE) members of peasant communities (as decided by not less than two thirds of a MIR's members). (The right of communities to banish undesirable members to Siberia was abolished in 1900.) According to information received by George Kennan from local officials there were, in 1885, over 10,000 exiles in Siberia, of whom about 4,400 had been sentenced by the courts; 2,100 were vagrants and exiles by administrative order, and 3,750 had been exiled by village communities. In addition there were about 5,500 relatives voluntarily accompanying the exiles (G. Kennan, *I,* p. 79). Politically unreliable or suspect persons were banished by sentences of the special commission in the Ministry of Internal Affairs (see OSOBOE SOVESHCHANIE) either to Siberia or to northern regions of European Russia. The number of persons banished in this way was considerable after the revolution of

1905: from the end of October 1905 to the end of April 1906, 6,825 persons were banished by administrative orders of the special commission.

2. In modern language, ssylka means a reference, as in a footnote. 3. In legal language, the summoning of third persons for verification of testimony. 4. In Muscovy, ssylka or ssylki meant also connections, negotiations, correspondence; conspiracy.

ssýl'nyi, -nye or **ssýl'no-poselénets, -ntsy.** Exile; see SSYLKA.

stáchka, -ki. In modern language, strike; in Muscovy, conspiracy, secret agreement.

stan, -ny. 1. Military camp. 2. Stand, place for the temporary quartering of princes or their agents while on official business. 3. Rural territorial-administrative unit corresponding, approximately, to the VOLOST'; in Muscovy, a subdivision of the UEZD; in the Grand Duchy of Lithuania, a subdivision of the POVET. In some northern regions of Muscovy stany were composed of several smaller volosti; in others, volosti were composed of stany; in still other regions, stany and volosti appear to have been identical types of administrative units. 4. According to the statutes on rural police issued in 1837, each uezd was divided into several police stany, each headed by a STANOVOI PRISTAV; each stan included several volosti. 5. In the legal language of the Grand Duchy of Lithuania, stany meant also estates, sociolegal groups (corresponding to the Russian SOSLOVIE). 6. In the *Ulozhenie* of 1649 stan meant also a shelter arranged by robbers and thieves for keeping stolen items.

chërnyi stan: in Muscovy, a taxpaying rural district on state lands.

gubnói stan: in Muscovy, a courthouse, a residence of the GUBNOI STAROSTA and his aides.

staníchnik, -ki. Inhabitant of a STANITSA; a cossack.

stanítsa, -tsy. 1. In the 17th century, a Don Cossack embassy sent to Moscow. 2. In the 18th–19th centuries, a cossack settlement composed of one large village or of several lesser villages (POSËLKI) and hamlets (KHUTORA). When the imperial government deprived the cossack hosts of their autonomy and began to appoint all the top cossack commanders and officials, the sphere of cossack self-government was limited to the stanitsa administration. In the Don Cossack region (*oblast' voiska donskogo*, see OBLAST') the *stanichnyi sbor* (assembly) elected the *stanichnoe pravlenie* (administration), headed by the *stanichnyi* ATAMAN, and the *stanichnyi sud* (court). Until 1891 all cossacks who were heads of a household took part in the stanichnyi sbor; according to the regulations of 1891, in large stanitsy the sbor included only one representative from each 10 households. 3. In the old church language, stanitsa was a term for the church choir.

stanóvshchik, -ki. In the 14th–15th centuries, an administrator of a STAN. In the 17th century this term was applied to people who gave shelter to robbers and thieves and kept stolen things (as in the *Ulozhenie* of 1649, chap. XXI, art. 63).

staréishina, -ny or **staréishie** (pl.). Outstanding citizens heading old urban communities.

staréishinstvo. Seniority, highest authority attributed to the grand prince in the Kievan period. After Iaroslav's death (1054) it was more an honorary title than one conveying any real authority over other princes.

stárets, stártsy. 1. Monk in general, or an elder monk who possessed outstanding spiritual authority. 2. In the Grand Duchy of Lithuania, a term for a village or VOLOST' elder (corresponding to the Russian terms STAROSTA or STARSHINA).

stártsy grádskie: in Kievan society in the 10th—11th centuries, either elected commanders of the people's militia, or, in general, local elders of the urban community. A literary term sometimes applied to them was *boiare zemskie.*

stártsy sobórnye: senior monks, members of the monastery council.

stártsy zavólzhskie: see NESTIA-ZHATELI.

stariná. Old custom, precedent, tradition. The Grand Dukes of Lithuania in their PRIVILEII and the Novgorodian princes in their treaties with Novgorod the Great usually promised not to violate *starinu* (acc.).

po stariné: in accordance with old customs and rights.

stáritsa, -itsy. Nun.

staroobriádtsy (pl.). Old Ritualists. According to a decree of April 17, 1905, on religious tolerance, the old official term for Orthodox dissenters—RASKOL'NIKI—was replaced by staroobriadtsy.

stárosta, -ty, in Kievan Russia. Elder, elected head of an urban or rural community. Such elders, according to the chronicles, existed in Kiev and Novgorod by the 10th and 11th centuries. Novgorod the Great especially, with its complex and stratified population, had many elected officials called starosty. Each of Novgorod's five KONTSY (boroughs) was headed by a *konchanskii starosta;* each street, ULITSA, had its *ulitskii* or *ulichanskii starosta.* The Novgorodian merchant class, in the time of Novgorodian independence, was organized around the Church of St. John (*Sviatogo Ivana*), and this merchant corporation was headed by the *starosty Ivanskie* or *starosty kupetskie* or *kupecheskie* (see KUPETS).

stárosta, in Muscovite Russia. The institution of the starosty elected by urban and rural communities was present everywhere in Muscovy. VOLOSTI, STANY, and urban communities (POSADY) as well as the suburban Moscow SLOBODY were headed and represented by their starosty. The *Sudebnik* of 1550 (art. 68) ordered the introduction of starosty and TSELOVAL'NIKI (sworn assistants) in all volosti that did not already have such elected officials. The *Sudebniks* of 1497 and 1550 ordered that the local government agents—NAMESTNIKI and VOLOSTELI—should not render justice without the presence in court of starosty and other representatives of local population.

In the 1550s the government of Ivan IV went farther in this direction. The offices of appointed namestniki and volosteli were abolished, and the local communities were permitted (according to their wishes) to elect *izliublennye starosty* (and SUD'I) as local administrators and judges; they were also obligated to collect government taxes for the Moscow PRIKAZY. In the 17th century the authority of the elected starosty, sud'i, and tseloval'niki was considerably limited when the appointed VOEVODY were entrusted with more power in the UEZDS, and the starosty and tseloval'niki became their subordinates in local administration and tax collecting. The elected starosty and sud'i retained more authority in some northern regions of Muscovy. There were in some uezdy *vseuezdnye zemskie starosty* who headed at the same time the posad and the rural volosti of the whole uezd, but they also were subordinate to the local voevoda. Some of the special categories of starosty in Muscovy also deserve explanation.

gubnói stárosta: elected elder with the duties of a district criminal judge. The growth of criminal offenses in the middle of the 16th century disturbed both the local communities and the central government; local government agents were unable to combat it effectively and this induced the government beginning in 1539 to introduce in several districts the office of the elected gubnoi starosta, assisted by the *gubnye tseloval'niki* (sworn assistants) and instructed by the RAZBOINYI PRIKAZ (central department for criminal affairs); he was to investigate criminal cases and punish offenders. In the 17th century the office of gubnoi starosta became a general institution in Muscovy. According to the *Ulozhenie* of 1649 (chap. XXI, art. 4), the gubnye starosty were to be elected by all classes of the local population, preferably from the local DVORIANE, reliable and prosperous men, who had been discharged from military service because of age or wounds and could read and write. The institution of the gubnye starosty was abolished by Peter I in 1702.

popóvskii stárosta: senior priest entrusted with supervisory duties over all the parishes in a given district (he corresponded to the modern BLAGOCHIN-NYI).

posádskii stárosta: elected head of an urban unit; see POSAD.

rúzhnyi stárosta: church treasurer in churches where clerics received an emolument called a RUGA.

sudétskii stárosta: a judge elected by the local population.

tserkóvnyi stárosta: elected manager of the financial and economic affairs of a parish.

starósta, in the Grand Duchy of Lithuania. Provincial administrator with judicial, civil, and military powers. He was appointed by the grand duke from the local nobility with its consent and approval. After the administrative reforms of the 1560s the starosty headed the *sudovye povety* (see POVET) and stood in the administrative hierarchy between the VOEVODY and the NAMEST-NIKI-DERZHAVTSY. The starosta of Zhomoit (Zhmud', Samogitia) occupied a service position equal to that of the voevody and was a member of the RADA GOSPODARSKAIA.

stárosta, in imperial Russia. A term broadly used, esp. in the peasant world.

According to the statutes on the administration of the state peasantry of April 30, 1838, a STARSHINA stood at the head of the village administration, and *sel'skie starosty* were his assistants. According to the *Polozhenie* of February 19, 1861, a sel'skii starosta, elected by the MIR, headed the village administration, while the starshina was head of the VOLOST'. Private VOTCHINY in the 17th–19th centuries (before 1861) usually also had starosty elected by the peasant mir, but they acted only as auxiliaries to the manorial administration appointed by the landlord or (in small votchiny) to the landlord himself. According to the city charter of 1785, elected starosty headed separate categories of the city population; the most numerous of them—MESHCHANE—was headed by the *meshchanskii starosta*. Elected starosty also headed voluntary workers' associations (ARTELI), as well as territorial associations (ZEMLIA-CHESTVA) of students in the universities.

starovéry. Old Believers. (See RASKOL.)

starozhíl, -ly or **starozhílets, -l'tsy.** Long-term resident of a settlement or long-time peasant tenant of the same landlord. Such peasants, over the years and even generations on the lands of the same landlord, were likely to contract indebtedness and other obligations, thereby losing their freedom of movement and thus becoming serfs. As early as the 15th century some landlords (predominantly ecclesiastical) received from the grand prince special charters forbidding the starozhil'tsy to leave their landlords. Enactments concerning the ZAPOVEDNYE GODY at the end of the 16th century, and finally the *Ulozhenie* of 1649, deprived all peasants living in VOTCHINY and POMEST'IA of their right to move. The term starozhil'tsy was used in the same sense in the Grand Duchy of Lithuania.

starshiná, starshíny. Elder, administrator elected by local communities. Starshina was the term for the village chief on state lands in the 18th century, and also according to the statutes on the administration of the state peasantry issued April 30, 1838. According to the *Polozhenie* of February 19, 1861, the elected village chief was called the *sel'skii starosta,* while the chief of the VOLOST' administration was called the *volostnoi starshina.* According to the charter of cities of 1785, the city craftsmen—*mastera*—were organized in a corporation called an UPRAVA; it was headed by an *upravnyi starshina.*

starshína (collect.). Officers in the Ukrainian Cossack army in the 17th century. The *general'naia starshina* was the supreme command of the whole host (VOISKO), including the HETMAN and the *voiskovoi* SUD'IA, PISAR', ESAUL, and OBOZNYI. The commanding personnel of the POLKI (regiments), which were military as well as territorial-administrative units, was called the *polkovaia starshina,* headed by the POLKOVNIK. The commanding personnel of the SOTNIA (hundred) was called the *sotennaia starshina* and was headed by the SOTNIK. In the 18th century this officer corps of the cossack army (called, in general, the *malorossiiskaia starshina*), with its descendants, formed the *malorossiiskoe* SHLIAKHETSTVO or DVORIANSTVO, which became a part of the privileged Russian nobility.

voiskovói starshiná: in the imperial army in the 19th century, an officer rank in the cossack regiments equal to the rank of MAIOR, and after 1884 to the rank of PODPOLKOVNIK (lieutenant-colonel) in the regular army.

stat'iá, -t'í. 1. Matter, point, item, article; separate enactment such as the enactments issued between the *Sudebnik* of 1550 and the *Ulozhenie* of 1649, included in books (STATEINYE KNIGI) compiled in Moscow PRIKAZY. 2. Category, rank. In the Muscovite official

language the service men (SLUZHILYE LIUDI) were sometimes classified as the men of *bol'shoi* (large), *serednei* (middle), and *men'shei* (lesser) *stat'i.*

kazënnye obróchnye stat'í: state lands, forests, fisheries, and other natural resources that were leased for use by private persons or peasant communities.

státok, státki. Property in general; inherited property.

státki domóvye or *rukhómye* (W.R.): household things, movable property.

státseia, -iia, -ii (W.R.). An obligation of the local population to deliver provisions (or a corresponding amount of money) to the grand duke or his agents when traveling on official business and to military detachments on the march.

stats-sekretár', -rí. In the 19th century, a chief secretary who headed a department of the state chancery (GOSUDAR-STVENNAIA KANTSELIARIIA, the chancery of the State Council).

Stats-sekretár' Egó Velíchestva: an honorary title granted by the emperor to high state officials.

Statút. The code of law in the Grand Duchy of Lithuania. The first Statut was issued in 1529, the second (confirming the old and establishing new political and social privileges of the SZLACHTA) in 1566, the third in 1588.

stávka, -ki. Rate; stake.

óchnaia stávka: in legal language, the confrontation of litigants, defendants, or witnesses.

stávka verkhóvnogo glavnokomán-duiushchego: the headquarters of the supreme commander of the fighting armed forces. During World War I, the stavka of Grand Duke Nikolai Nikolaevich (1914–15) was situated in Baranovichi (Minsk province), and the stavka of Nicholas II (from August 1915 until the February revolution) in Mogilëv (both in Belorussia).

148

stépen', -ni. In modern language, degree; earlier, also dignity, office.

stiág, -gi. Banner, standard, also a military detachment marching and fighting under one banner.

sto. Hundred. A military or administrative-territorial unit; a division of the urban population in old cities. See SOTNIA.

kupétskoe sto: merchant corporation in Novgorod the Great.

Stoglív. Literally, hundred chapters. A collection of the decisions of the church council of 1551 (headed by Metropolitan Makarii) in response to negligence, abuse, and irregularities in contemporary church life. (See TSERKOVNYI SOBOR.)

stol, -lý. Literally, desk, table. In old Russia (esp. in the Kievan period), the throne (like the modern *prestol;* hence *stol'nyi gorod* or *stolitsa,* capital); it meant also the bishop's see. In the imperial period a stol was a subdivision of large government offices; the MINISTERSTVA were divided into DEPARTAMENTY, departamenty into OTDELENIIA, and otdeleniia into stoly; each of the latter was managed by a STOLONACHAL'-NIK.

stoléts vdóvii (W.R.). Status of a widow and the share she received from the property of her husband.

stól'nik, -ki. Initially a court office; the stol'niki served the sovereign and his guests at the table, esp. at gala dinners, but in Muscovy their court service was not their chief occupation. The stol'niki were a rather high ranking and numerous group of the tsar's service men; in the hierarchical ladder they were placed immediately after the members of the Boyar DUMA. According to Kotoshikhin, they numbered about 500 men and served in the military, civil, and diplomatic services either as assistants to the BOIARE and OKOL'NICHIE or as heads of offices (for example, provincial VOEVODY) or military units.

stolonachál'nik, -ki. A clerk in the imperial bureaucracy managing a department or bureau subdivision called a STOL.

stolp, -pý. In Muscovite offices, a paper roll on which business records were written.

storoná, stórony. 1. A part of a city; in Novgorod the Great there were the *Sofiiskaia storona* on the left bank of the Volkhov River (with the Kremlin and the Cathedral of St. Sophia), and the *Torgovaia* (commercial) *storona* on the right bank. 2. Party in litigation. In the legal language of the Grand Duchy of Lithuania, *storona otpornaia* or *pozvanaia* meant the defendant.

storózha or **strázha.** Guard, watch, custody; a military or police detachment on guard duty.

stráva (W.R.). 1. Food; subsistence. 2. Damage, loss.

strázha = STORÓZHA.

strázhnik, -ki. Watchman, guard. *Politseiskie strazhniki* were rural policemen provided by a decree of May 5, 1903.

streléts, strel'tsý. Literally, shooter. Musketeers, the first permanent regular regiments of the armed forces in Muscovy. Although their chief weapons were muskets, they were armed also with swords, pikes, and battle-axes. Some of them were mounted, but the great majority (about 90 percent) were infantrymen. The strel'tsy regiments (called PRIKAZY) were organized in the middle of the 16th century. During the time of Ivan IV there were about 5,000 strel'tsy in Moscow and 7,000 in frontier towns, accordingly designated as *strel'tsy moskovskie* and *strel'tsy gorodovye*. In the 16th century the strel'tsy were a relatively small auxiliary force added to the mounted army of the DVORIANE and DETI BOIARSKIE, but in the 17th century the number and military importance of the strel'tsy grew considerably. According to a special study (by Professor E. Stashevskii) the Muscovite armed forces in 1632 numbered 26,185 dvoriane and deti boiarskie and 33,775 strel'tsy. According to Kotoshikhin, in the middle of the 17th century in Moscow alone there were more than 20 prikazy of the strel'tsy, each of them numbering between 800 and 1,000 men. A prikaz was commanded by a STRELETSKII GOLOVA (later called POLKOVNIK). Under him came the POLUGOLOVA (the lieutenant-colonel), SOTNIKI (centurions), PIATIDE-SIATNIKI (commanders of fifty men), and DESIATNIKI (comparable to corporals). "During the first half of the 17th century, the *strel'tsy* on foot were considered the best infantry men in Russia. In time of war, they took part in the field, and in the defense of towns. In time of peace, they acted as the town gatekeepers, policemen, watchmen, and firemen" (G. Lantzeff, p. 66). The service of the strel'tsy, initially by contract, became lifelong and hereditary. They served as long as physically able, and their sons also entered the service. They lived with their families in suburban settlements (a *streletskaia sloboda*). They received from the government, in addition to homes, small plots of land and a salary in money and grain, as well as armaments and uniforms. They were also allowed to keep small shops and to carry on trade and handicrafts on a small scale without paying taxes; and they were permitted to make alcoholic beverages (for their own use only). At the end of the 17th century many Old Believers (STAROVERY) appeared among the Moscow strel'tsy, and this religious dissent, combined with political troubles and internal struggles, provoked riots among the strel'tsy in 1682, 1689, and 1698; the last of them (in the summer of 1698) was more an act of disobedience than an uprising, but the angry Peter I punished more than 1,000 actual or suspected rebels by death and disbanded the strel'tsy regiments.

striápchii, -chie. The term is derived from *striapat'*—to work, to serve—and had many meanings. In Moscow judicial documents striapchie in the courts were aides, seconds, or representatives of litigant parties. In the imperial period (before 1864) private solicitors in the courts were also called striapchie. At the court of the Moscow sovereign the striapchie were "courtiers attending to food, clothing and other household matters" (G. Lantzeff, p. 6). They also accompanied the tsar during his public appearances and travels. But for the majority of the striapchie court service was only an occasional occupation. In the 17th century they formed a group and a rank of service men numbering, according to Kotoshikhin, about 800; they were active in military and civil service, and on the Moscow hierarchical ladder they followed the rank of the STOL'NIKI.

According to the statutes of 1775 on GUBERNIIA administration, the office of striapchie was added to each high judicial and administrative guberniia institution; the striapchie were aides to the *gubernskii prokuror* (see PROKUROR). There were two positions, the *gubernskii striapchii ugolovnykh del* (a kind of state attorney or public prosecutor), and the *gubernskii striapchii kazënnykh del* who took care of state properties and revenues. In each UEZD capital one *uezdnyi striapchii* was appointed to represent the government's legal and financial interests in local affairs. The office of the striapchie was abolished by the general judicial reform of 1864.

strigól'niki (pl.). A rationalistic sect that emerged in the second half of the 14th century in Novgorod the Great and Pskov.

stroénie. Structure; arrangement. In a specific sense, the inclusion of the suburbs (SLOBODY) owned by private persons or ecclesiastical institutions in the taxpaying (*tiaglye*) urban communities, as carried out in 1649–52 in accordance with a provision of the *Ulozhenie* of 1649 (chap. XIX), and recorded in the *stroel'nye knigi.*

stroi soslóvnyi. Class structure. See SOSLOVIE.

stroítel'. Literally, builder. The superior in a monastery that did not have an ARCHIMANDRIT or an IGUMEN.

strýi. Uncle, brother of the father.

sud, -dý. Court; judicial power or jurisdiction; law or statute on court procedures; trial; litigation; court sentence; court procedures and records of them.

sud i raspráva or *sud i upráva:* trial and rendering of justice (in criminal cases—trial and punishment of a crime).

sud, in the Kievan and Novgorodian period. The rendering of justice was normally a prerogative of the prince (*sud kniazhii*) who judged his subjects himself or through his empowered agents (POSADNIKI or TIUNY). The secular court was sometimes called *sud gradskii* in church sources. Along with this secular court there was the church court (*sud tserkovnyi*); it was empowered to investigate and try cases concerning religion, morals, and family relations; the clergy and other persons legally and socially dependent on the church were under church jurisdiction in criminal and civil cases as well. The church courts were called *sud sviatitel'skii* (SVIATITEL', church hierarch), or *sud mitropolichii*, or *sud episkopl'*, according to the rank of the prelate. In Novgorod the Great the prince was obliged to administer justice together with the elected POSADNIK of Novgorod. Moreover, there was a special commercial court (*sud torgovyi*) headed by the TYSIATSKII to judge cases and controversies that arose in the Novgorodian commercial world.

sud, in Muscovy. Administrative and judicial spheres were not clearly delimited. In the 15th and 16th centuries the government's provincial agents, NAMESTNIKI and VOLOSTELI, served as both administrators and judges; but the law prescribed that representatives of the local population should be present as observers of court procedures or as court assistants. The namestniki *s sudom boiarskim* (abl.) had relatively broad jurisdiction in criminal cases and in legal cases involving bondmen (KHOLOPY). Beginning in the 1550s, the authority of the namestniki and volosteli was eliminated in many northern and central regions, and the elected ZEMSKIE SUD'I were entrusted with the rendering of justice. In the 17th century the provincial VOEVODY appointed by the government once again assumed both administrative and judicial power, although in many northern provinces the zemskie sud'i survived until the 18th century. In serious criminal cases justice was rendered by elected GUBNYE STAROSTY assisted by TSELOVAL'NIKI.

sud sméstnyi or *sud (v)ópchii* or *óbchii:* terms for a mixed trial in those cases when the litigants belonged to two different jurisdictions; in these cases justice was to be administered jointly by both judges, and the court fees shared equally.

tretéiskii sud: court of arbitration.

sud, in the Grand Duchy of Lithuania. The administration of justice was divided among the grand duke (GOSPODAR') and his officials, church dignitaries and secular magnates, municipal offices and peasant communities. Therefore the following terms are found in the documents:

sud gospodárskii: court of the grand duke.

sud dukhóvnyi or *právo dukhóvnoe:* the church court, in general.

sud komissárskii: courts of KOMIS-

SARY, when entrusted by the grand duke to render justice.

kópnyi sud (see KOPA): the court of the peasant community (usually with the participation of the government's or landlord's agent).

sud marshálkovskii: see MARSHALOK.

sud méstskii: the municipal court, esp. in cities governed on the basis of the Magdeburg Law.

sud naméstnika or *naméstnichii:* court of a NAMESTNIK.

sud pánskii: a trial by a single PAN, or a sentence of the council of the lords, PANY-RADA.

sud starósty or *staróstinskii:* court of a STAROSTA.

sud tivúnskii: see TIUN or TIVUN.

sud voevódy or *voevódskii:* court of a VOEVODA.

From the middle of the 16th century on, the court system in the Grand Duchy of Lithuania was basically composed of the following three kinds of courts:

sud (k)gródskii (from GROD, castle): court for criminal cases; there the chief judges were high provincial administrators, VOEVODY or *starosty sudovye* (or their deputies).

sud podkomórskii (or *sud podkomórigo,* gen.): court to handle cases concerning property lines on the SHLIAKHTA's landed estates. Several members of the local shliakhta were elected to be present at trials when the litigants or defendants belonged to the shliakhta class.

sud zémskii: land court or provincial court, established for judging civil litigations among the members of the nobility. The shliakhta of each *sudovyi povet* (see POVET) elected four candidates for each of three offices, SUD'IA (judge), PODSUDOK (assistant judge), and PISAR' (secretary), and from them the grand duke appointed the members of the court.

sud, in imperial Russia. Peter the Great attempted to establish a court system as a separate branch of government. In his energetic but precipitate reforming activity Peter created and soon abolished a series of judicial offices, such as those of the LANDRIKHTERY and *oberlandrikhtery, sudebnye komissary, komendanty,* and *ober-komendanty.* The courts known as *nadvornye sudy,* established in 1719 in 10 major cities, were abolished in 1727, and the judicial power returned to the provincial VOEVODY. The statutes of 1775 on GUBERNIIA administration introduced a regular system of court institutions. They established, as the high courts for each province, the *palata ugolovnogo suda* (criminal court) and the *palata grazhdanskogo suda* (civil court), with personnel appointed by the government (see SUDEBNAIA PALATA). For the three basic classes of the free population—the nobility, the townspeople, and the state peasantry—three parallel court institutions were created in each guberniia and each UEZD: for the nobility, the *verkhnii zemskii sud* and the *uezdnyi sud;* for the townspeople, the *gubernskii magistrat* and the *gorodovoi magistrat* (see MAGISTRAT); for the state peasantry, the *verkhniaia rasprava* and the *nizhniaia rasprava* (see RASPRAVA). The presidents of these class courts were appointed by the government; the members (ZASEDATELI) were elected by each of the three classes. In addition to this basic court system the law of 1775 established the *sovestnyi sud* (court of conscience), a court of arbitration or mediation set up if both contestants asked for it; and the *slovesnyi sud* (verbal court), instituted for settlement of small civil suits, especially those concerning commerce. The law of 1775 established also in each uezd the *nizhnii zemskii sud,* a police office headed by the *zemskii ispravnik* or KAPITAN-ISPRAVNIK elected by the local nobility.

The general judicial reform of November 20, 1864, established a fair and well-ordered court system. The highest court institution was the Ruling Senate (SENAT); it included the civil and the criminal Departments of Cassation; they could reverse the verdicts of the lower courts only if these verdicts violated the judicial procedure established by law. The Senate's decisions in the settlement of special cases served to guide the lower courts in their decisions on similar cases. The next lower echelon, under the law of 1864, was the SUDEBNAIA PALATA. The basic institution of the system was the *okruzhnyi sud* (circuit court), whose authority embraced several uezdy. The okruzhnyi sud was divided into criminal and civil departments (*ugolovnoe* and *grazhdanskoe otdelenie*); in criminal cases a jury of twelve (called PRISIAZHNYE ZASEDATELI) decided questions of "guilty," "not guilty," or "guilty but with extenuating circumstances," and then the three crown judges determined the court sentence on the basis of this verdict. Civil litigation was decided by the crown judges without a jury, on the basis of pertinent documents and of oral and written testimony of witnesses and invited experts. The president and members of the courts were appointed by the government, but they could not be dismissed without their own request, nor suspended except by the verdict of a criminal court. The competence of the new courts encompassed persons of all classes equally; the trial procedures were open and public, with the active participation of a newly created class of attorneys (PRISIAZHNYE POVERENNYE). For less important criminal and civil cases the law of 1864 established the office of the justice of the peace (MIROVOI SUD'IA). Each peasant community in the 19th century had its own court (see RASPRAVA), with elected members, to settle local affairs and small criminal offenses; according to the regulations on the administration of the state peasantry, of April 30, 1838, it was the VOLOSTNAIA RASPRAVA (the township court), and according to the general statutes (POLOZHENIE) of February 19, 1861, the *volostnoi sud* (see VOLOST'). The law of July 12, 1889, deprived all the elected peasant administrative and judicial organs of their autonomy and put them under the strict supervision of the ZEMSKII NACHAL'NIK. But the power of the latter was curtailed by the decree of October 5, 1906, and by the law of June 15, 1912, the judicial authority of the zemskie nachal'niki was abolished (initially the reform was introduced in only ten provinces), and the mirovye sud'i, elected by the district zemstvos, were reestablished. According to a law of 1912 the court of appeals for the volostnoi sud was the *verkhnii sel'skii sud* (the higher rural court); its president was the justice of the peace, and its members were chairmen of the local volostnye sudy.

Verkhóvnyi Ugolóvnyi Sud: the Supreme Criminal Court, in the imperial period, established only in exceptional cases, each time by a special order of the emperor. It was composed of several members of the Senate and other especially appointed high officials; it was organized, for example, to try the participants in the Pugachev rebellion and the Decembrist uprising. According to the judicial statutes of 1864, the Verkhovnyi Ugolovnyi Sud was to be established, by a special order of the emperor, to try the gravest political crimes and crimes committed by high officials in violation of their duties. According to the regulations of April 22, 1906, the Verkhovnyi Ugolovnyi Sud was to be instituted annually, under the chairmanship of a member of the State Council, and to be composed of the presidents of three of the Senate departments and of five senators, all appointed by the emperor.

voénno-polevói sud: field court martial. In the summer of 1906, when revolutionary terroristic activities were in full swing and attempts on the life of government agents—from the highest officials down to policemen on the beat —became everyday events, the government decree of August 19, 1906, established courts martial (consisting of military officers) to examine and to punish terroristic acts immediately. They issued 683 death sentences. The field courts martial were discontinued on April 20, 1907, the day the Second State Duma convened. Courts martial as a normal institution were called *voenno-okruzhnye sudy;* they were a part of the military administration in each VOENNYI OKRUG.

Sudébnik, -ki. Code of Law in Muscovy. The first Sudebnik was issued in 1497; its text was discovered and edited in the 19th century; the editors divided the text into 68 articles; it was essentially a collection of procedural rules. The second Sudebnik (1550), consisting of 100 articles, contained more elaborate and improved rules prescribing the participation of locally elected STAROSTY (elders), TSELOVAL'NIKI (sworn assistants), and ZEMSKIE D'IAKI (public clerks) in the courts of NAMESTNIKI and VOLOSTELI appointed by the government. Both sudebniki contained regulations concerning the right of the peasant tenants to depart from their landowners (around St. George's day, the 26th of November). The so-called third Sudebnik (1589) was, in fact, not a Code of Law confirmed and issued by the government, but only a private draft code, compiled for practical purposes, and probably applied in the judicial practice of the northern provinces.

sudébnitsa (a term found in the Pskov charter). Courtroom.

sudéika, sudéiki zémskie. Another term for SUD'IA, SUD'I ZEMSKIE.

sudéistvo. Office of the SUD'IA.

sud'iá, súd'i. Judge, justice. In Muscovy, the term also meant the head of a PRIKAZ. In the Ukraine in the 17th century (and part of the 18th), sud'ia was the term for an elected judicial official of the cossack host. The *voiskovoi sud'ia* was the chief justice. The *polkovoi sud'ia* was the justice for a POLK (regiment), which was a military and also a territorial administrative unit. The *sotennyi sud'ia* was the judge for a SOTNIA (hundred), a subdivision of the polk.

gorodskói sud'iá: municipal judge. When the statute of July 12, 1889, abolished the office of the MIROVYE SUD'I elected by the zemstvos, the judicial power in the rural districts was given to the ZEMSKIE NACHAL'NIKI, while in the towns (except the two capitals and several larger cities) it passed to the gorodskie sud'i, who were appointed by the government.

mirovói sud'iá: justice of the peace. An office established by the general judicial reform of November 20, 1864. Each UEZD was divided into several parts (UCHASTKI), and for each of them the district ZEMSTVO assembly (*uezdnoe zemskoe sobranie*) was to elect an *uchastkovyi mirovoi sud'ia.* The zemstvo assembly could also elect one or more honorary justices of the peace (*pochëtnye mirovye sud'i*). The justices of the peace elected by the zemstvo assemblies were likewise established in cities and towns; in St. Petersburg and Moscow they were elected by the city council (GORODSKAIA DUMA). The conference of justices of the peace (S"EZD MIROVYKH SUDEI) was the court of appeals for the mirovoi sud'ia. The jurisdiction of the justice of the peace extended to misdemeanors, insults, and various transgressions, not subject to judgment by the *okruzhnyi sud* (see SUD); in civil litigation the justices of the peace were competent to decide cases where the litigants' claims did not exceed 500 rubles. With the introduction of the ZEMSKIE NACHAL'NIKI in 1889, the office of justice of the peace was abolished except in several large cities; the judicial power in the rural districts was given to the zemskie nachal'niki, and in most cities and towns to the GORODSKIE SUD'I. The law of June 15, 1912, reestablished the justice of the peace elected by the zemstvos; in 1913 this institution was introduced in ten provinces; World War I stopped the further extension of the reform.

poliubóvnyi sud'iá (W.R.): an arbitrator elected by consent of litigant parties.

zémskii sud'iá: 1) in Muscovy, land or local judge elected by the local community. In the 1550s the government (on request of the local population) abolished in many northern and central regions the offices of appointed NAMESTNIKI and VOLOSTELI, and granted the local communities the right to elect their zemskie sud'i instead. In the 17th century the VOEVODY appointed by the government became the chief organs of administrative and judicial power in the provinces, but in many northern regions the office and activities of the elected zemskie sud'i survived through the 17th century. 2) Zemskii sud'ia in Moscow in the 17th century designated the chief of the city police, the head of the ZEMSKII PRIKAZ.

súdnitsa. 1. Courtroom. 2. A written court decision (in the Pskov charter).

sumézhniki (pl. W.R.). Holders of adjacent landed estates.

surnachéi, -éii. Court musician in Muscovy.

sutiázhii or **sutiázhnik, -ki.** Litigant.

sváda, -dy. Quarrel.

svédetstvo, svédotstvo; svédome, svédomo (W.R.). Testimony, evidence.

svédok, svédki or **svétki** (W.R.). Witness.

svétki gódnye: reliable witnesses.

svëkor. Father-in-law, father of the husband.

svekróv'. Mother-in-law, mother of the husband.

sviaschénnik, -ki. Priest.

sviashchénstvo. Priesthood; clergy.

sviatítel', -li. Church hierarch (patriarch, metropolitan, archbishop, or bishop).

sviáto, -ta (W.R.). Holiday.

sviatotátets, -átsy. Sacrileger.

sviatotátstvo. Sacrilege.

svobóda, in the sense of settlement. See SLOBODA.

svod. In the old legal language, the procedure of identifying a thief by confrontation with those persons through whose hands the stolen object had successively passed.

Svod Zakónov Rossíiskoi Impérii. Code of Laws of the Russian Empire, compiled under Speranskii's direction in 1831–32, promulgated by Nicholas I's manifesto of January 31, 1833, and proclaimed effective January 1st, 1835. The *Svod,* based on the POLNOE SOBRANIE ZAKONOV, included only operative laws systematically grouped by subjects. The text of the laws was divided into short numbered articles, without any commentary. The collection filled 15 large volumes. The second edition of the *Svod* was published in 1842, the third in 1857. In 1864, when the statutes on the newly created court institutions and the regulations on civil and criminal procedures in the courts were published, they formed the sixteenth volume of the *Svod Zakonov.* Thereafter several single volumes of the *Svod* were republished in which new laws were included and those superseded or abrogated were excluded. In 1906 the first volume of the *Svod* was republished, including the new version of the basic laws (OSNOVNYE ZAKONY) and the laws on the newly established legislative institutions, the State Duma and the (reformed) State Council.

svoezémets, -mtsy. Petty landowner, "a numerous class of small-scale landowners in the Novgorod [the Great] region" (G. Vernadsky, *Kievan Russia*, p. 167).

svoiáchenitsa, -tsy. Sister-in-law (wife's sister).

svoiák, -kí. Brother-in-law (wife's brother or husband of wife's sister).

svoistvó. Relationship by marriage.

syn boiárskii. See DETI BOIARSKIE.

sýnovets, -vtsy. Nephew, brother's son.

sýshchik, -ki. In Muscovy, special investigator in criminal cases; later, detective.

sysk. Conduct of an investigation.

sýtnik, -ki. In Muscovy, court servitor who managed the operations of the SYTNYI DVOR, which prepared beverages for the tsar's household.

szláchta. The Polish term for the nobility; see SHLIAKHTA and DVORIANE.

T

tabátchik, -ki. Keeper and seller of tobacco. In Muscovy the use of tobacco was strictly prohibited. The *Ulozhenie* of 1649 (chap. XXV, arts. 11–16) threatened the tabatchiki with severe punishments, from the *knut* to the death penalty and confiscation of property. The sale and use of tobacco was legalized by Peter I in 1697.

Tábel' o Rángakh. The Table of Ranks was issued by Peter the Great on January 24, 1722. "It drew for the first time a clear line of demarcation between the civilian and the army service. All offices and ranks in each of these two branches were rearranged in hierarchical order in fourteen classes, and every army officer or civil servant was to start his career in the lowest class, proceeding gradually from grade to grade up the official ladder" (M. Florinsky, *I*, p. 420). All ranks conferred upon the holder the status of either hereditary nobility (passed on to one's descendants) or personal nobility (could not be transmitted). At first, all fourteen military ranks and the first eight civil service ranks (through *kollezhskii assessor*, see ASSESSOR) conferred the dignity of hereditary nobility. Later, access to hereditary *dvorianstvo* was made more difficult (see DVORIANE). With the Table of Ranks, in

Platonov's words (p. 233), "the principle of individual merit now triumphed over aristocratic lineage." The Table of Ranks included 5 series of ranks for different service branches, the army, the guards, the navy, the civil service, and the court service. The Table was later revised, and several of the original ranks were abolished. At the end of the 19th century there were the following ranks in civil and military service (all are described more fully under individual entries). In the civil service: 1. kantsler. 2. deistvitel'nyi tainyi sovetnik. 3. tainyi sovetnik. 4. deistvitel'nyi statskii sovetnik. 5. statskii sovetnik. 6. kollezhskii sovetnik. 7. nadvornyi sovetnik. 8. kollezhskii assessor. 9. tituliarnyi sovetnik. 10. kollezhskii sekretar'. 12. gubernskii sekretar'. 14. kollezhskii registrator. In the army (in parentheses are indicated cavalry and cossack ranks, if they differed): 1. general-fel'dmarshal. 2. general-ot-infanterii, general-ot-kavalerii, general-ot-artillerii. 3. general-leitenant. 4. general-maior. 6. polkovnik (colonel). 7. podpolkovnik (voiskovoi starshina). 8. kapitan (rotmistr, esaul). 9. shtabs-kapitan (shtabs-rotmistr, pod"esaul). 10. poruchik (sotnik). 12. podporuchik (kornet, khorunzhii). 13. praporshchik. In the navy: 1. general-admiral. 2. admiral. 3.

vitse-admiral. 4. kontr-admiral. 6. kapitan pervogo ranga. 7. kapitan vtorogo ranga. 9. leitenant. 10. michman.

tábor, -ry. Camp, esp. a military camp.

tal', táli. Hostage.

tamgá. "In both Mongol and Turkish the term 'tamga' meant 'emblem,' specifically a clan emblem, and hence 'brand' to designate horses and other kinds of property as belonging to the clan. As an emblem of administration, *tamga* denoted the design on a seal or a stamp, and then the stamp itself, especially the stamp on goods taxed" (G. Vernadsky, *Mongols,* p. 222). Initially the tamga, introduced by the Tatars in Russia in the 13th century, was the basic city tax paid by merchants and artisans; later it took the form of a tax on the turnover of transported goods and was collected as a customs duty.

tamózhnia, -ni. Customs house.

tamózhnik, or **tamózhennik, -ki.** First, a collector of the city tax; later, a collector of customs duties (see TAMGA).

tarkhán, or **torkhán, -ny** (Mongol). A person free of taxation. In Muscovy, (1) a document granting exemption from taxes or putting the grantee under the direct jurisdiction of the grand duke (later the tsar) (see TARKHANNAIA GRAMOTA); or (2) a privileged landlord, clerical or secular, who possessed a tarkhan charter.

tarkhánshchik, -ki. See TARKHAN(2).

tastáment (W.R.). See TESTAMENT.

tat', táti. In old Russia, a thief or a robber.

golovnýe táti: probably kidnappers of slaves or serfs; perhaps also those who committed an act of robbery aggravated with murder.

konëvyi tat': horse thief.

tserkóvnyi tat': sacrileger. Theft in a church in Muscovy (according to the *Sudebniki* of 1497 and 1550 and the *Ulozhenie* of 1649) was punishable by death.

tatárshchina. One of the terms for tribute paid to the Tatars.

tát'ba, -by. In Muscovy, theft or robbery. A decree of 1781 introduced the term VOROVSTVO-KRAZHA into the legal language, to replace tat'ba. Also, stolen objects and their value.

tát'ba s políchnym: thievery with material evidence, red-handed.

tát'ba golovnáia, tát'ba tserkóvnaia: see TAT'.

témnik, -ki. The Russian term for the Mongol-Tatar commander of a military unit (T'MA, Mongol *tümen*) that numbered 10,000 soldiers.

testamént or **tastáment, -ty** (W.R.). Last will, testament. A legally valid testament was called a *pravyi,* or *riadnyi, slushnyi,* or *spravedlivyi* testament.

tiagléts, -tsý. Members of the peasant MIR or of POSAD communities that were obligated to bear TIAGLO.

tiagló, tiágla or **tiágly.** Burden, a term which came into use during the era of Mongol-Tatar domination. In Muscovy, the term tiaglo designated the sum total of fiscal obligations and labor and service duties imposed by the government on the listed members of a rural or urban community. The term tiaglo designated also the capacity of the taxpayers to meet their obligations, based on their labor force and taxable objects, such as lands and businesses. On the landed estates of the 18th and 19th centuries, tiaglo meant the peasant labor unit usually consisting of an adult, able-bodied couple of male and female serfs, who received from the landlord a certain allotment of land and were obligated to perform in return certain work assignments or to pay a certain amount of OBROK.

tiázha, -zhi or **tiázhba, -by.** Court proceedings, court case, litigation; contest, strife.

tiún, tivún, -ny. The agents of princes, grand dukes, secular magnates and church hierarchs; agents who performed various economic, administrative, and judicial functions, a term very broadly used in the Kievan period, in Muscovy, and in the Grand Duchy of Lithuania. Initially tiuny were housekeepers or stewards selected from lord's bondmen and entrusted with the management of certain economic and financial affairs; later they became also administrators and judges. In Muscovy tiuny also were stewards, bailiffs, and judges; they were also assistants and deputies of the provincial administrators (NAMESTNIKI and VOLOSTELI). The church hierarchs and the rich monasteries which owned landed estates had their own tiuny with various administrative functions. The Russian Law referred to several kinds of *tiuny kniazheskie* or *kniazhii* (prince's *tiuny*) and *tiuny boiarskie,* as follows:

tiun dvórskii: prince's majordomo, manager of affairs in the princely household (in Muscovy the corresponding official was called for short DVORSKII, later DVORETSKII).

tiun koniúshii: master of stables.

tiun ogníshchnyi: another term for the steward of the prince's household (see OGNISHCHE).

tiun sél'skii: administrator of a SELO, a prince's or boyar's landed estate, a village with its inhabitants.

tiun ratáinyi: an overseer of farm work in the field of a lord.

tiún, in the Grand Duchy of Lithuania. One of various officials, including those below.

tivúny gospodárskie: in the 14th–15th centuries, officials of the grand duke; they administered landed estates and collected taxes from and rendered justice for the local peasantry. Beginning with the 16th century such officials were called DERZHAVTSY, and only in the provinces of Zhomoit, Vilna, and

Troki was the old name tivuny preserved into the 16th century.

tivúny pánskie: stewards on the landed estates of the Lithuanian and Russian magnates, appointed by the lords from their bondmen or dependent peasants.

tiúnstvo or **tivúnstvo.** Office of the TIUN or TIVUN.

tivúnshchina. In the Grand Duchy of Lithuania, revenue received by the TIVUNY from the local population as payment for their official activities.

t'ma, t'my. The Russian word for the Mongol *tümen* meaning a military unit of 10,000 soldiers; or a taxation district in Mongol administration.

tolkóvnik, -ki. Translator and interpreter (mainly of written works).

tolmách, -chí. Interpreter (oral).

tolóka. Group labor by a peasant community, either by order of a landlord in his fields, or as voluntary assistance given by the community to needy neighbors.

torg, -gí. Commerce; business transactions, market; marketplace; time of market activities; goods offered for sale; payment for using the market place.

torgovíshche. Marketplace, city square.

torgóvlia tsárskaia. Government trade in Muscovy. The Moscow government, especially in the 17th century, maintained active commercial relations with foreign countries, exporting chiefly goods that the treasury had received as taxes in kind from the state peasantry and from Siberian natives. The port of Archangel was the main outlet for the export of Russian goods to Western Europe. A GOST' appointed by the government and his assistants (TSELOVAL'-NIKI) managed this operation under the general direction of the PRIKAZ BOL'-SHOGO PRIKHODA (the central financial organ of the state). The most profitable exports were Siberian furs, traded to Western Europe in exchange for various goods and particularly for badly needed EFIMKI; other items of government commerce were grain, hemp, hides, and products from the tsar's vast forests.

torgóvoe. A general tax imposed on merchants who used the marketplace for their trade.

torkhán and **torkhánshchik.** See TARKHAN and TARKHANSHCHIK.

torpósta or **torpóstai.** In the legal language of the Grand Duchy of Lithuania (the *Statut* of 1529), a kind of a guarantor, attorney, or aide of one of litigants (claimant, or SOK) in court.

tórzhishche. Market, marketplace.

továr, -ry. Stand, camp; movable property, goods, merchandise.

véschii továr: goods sold by weight.

továrishch, -chi. In general, comrade, companion, colleague. In the legal language of Muscovy and the imperial period, an assistant or associate to some higher official. The Moscow senior VOEVODY had usually one or more tovarishchi (the ordinary expression in contemporary documents was: *voevoda* so-and-so *s tovarishchi,* abl. plur.). In the 19th and early 20th century, its usage extended to *tovarishch ministra, tovarishch prokurora,* and so on, and, finally *tovarishch Predsedatelia Gosudarstvennoi Dumy.*

továrishchestvo, -va. Association, company, society, esp. in commerce, industry, or agriculture.

kredítnye továrishchestva: credit associations. The rapid growth of credit cooperatives among the Russian peasantry in the early years of the 20th century was an important feature of rural life. In 1897 there were only 619 credit associations with 222,200 members; in 1914 there were 9,536 kreditnye tovarishchestva with 6,209,900 members, mostly peasant householders. The kreditnye tovarishchestva were organized with the financial support of the treasury or the ZEMSTVOS.

ssúdo-sberegátel'nye továrishchestva: savings and loan associations. As of 1914, there were 3,479 with 2,044,700 members; they were based on shares (PAI) paid by their members and were organized along with the credit associations.

tréba, -by. Religious ministrations.

trébnik, -ki. Church service book containing such special services as weddings, baptisms, funerals, and various *molebny* (petitionary or thanksgiving prayers).

trëkhpól'e. Three-field system of agriculture with a three-year crop cycle that rotated the winter crop, the spring crop, and the fallow, the traditional system dominant from the 16th century on.

tret', -ti. Literally, one third, a territorial-administrative division in Muscovy. According to the testament of Ivan Kalita (d. 1341), the city of Moscow was bequeathed in common possession to his three sons, and each of them appointed an administrator in his tret'; this divided administration continued in the 14th and part of the 15th century. In several northern provinces of Muscovy a tret' was a rural district, a subdivision of a STAN or VOLOST'.

trétchik or **trétnik, -ki.** 1. Administrator of a TRET'. 2. Tenant peasant (similar to a POLOVNIK) who had to pay one third of the harvest to the landlord for using his land.

trétii, -tie or **tretéi, -tii.** Arbitrator chosen by the litigants (*Ulozhenie* of 1649, chap. XV, art. 5: *O treteiskom sude*).

trúbnik, -ki. Trumpeter, court and military musician in Muscovy.

trudovikí (pl.) or **trudováia grúppa.** Labor group, a parliamentary faction in the State Duma. Its main goal was the satisfaction of the peasants' need for land by distribution of all arable lands among the peasant communities, according to the program of the Russian populists. In the first and second Dumas, the trudovaia gruppa had about 100 members. After the sharp reduction of peasant representation by the electoral law of June 3, 1907, the number of trudoviki deputies was reduced to 14 and 9 in the third and fourth Dumas respectively.

tsar', tsarí. Sovereign, ruler, usually interpreted as the contraction of the Roman, and hence Byzantine, *caesar*. In old Russian the term was equivalent to suzerain. The Russians used this title for the Byzantine emperors and later for the Mongol-Tatar khans; then the Turkish sultan was called *tsar' turskii*. When the Golden Horde had disintegrated into several independent states, their sovereigns were still called tsars by the Russians, and so there appeared *tsar' Sibirskii, tsar' Kazanskii, tsar' Astrakhanskii,* and *tsar' Krymskii,* or *Perekopskii*. When the grand prince of Vladimir and Moscow (*velikii kniaz' Vladimirskii i Moskovskii*), Ivan III, had become independent of the Tatar khans, he and his son and successor, Vasilii III, were addressed (initially by clergymen) as tsar, and this title was occasionally used in contemporary writings and even in official documents. Finally, in 1547, the young Ivan IV was solemnly crowned in the Uspenskii cathedral as the "tsar of all the Russias" (*vseia Rossii* or *Russii*), and thus officially assumed the title that had been occasionally used by his predecessors. After the union of the Ukraine with Russia (1654) and the occupation of Belorussia in the subsequent war with Poland, the Moscow tsar assumed the title: *velikii gosudar' tsar' i velikii kniaz' NN* (so-and-so) *vseia Velikiia i Malyia i Belyia Rossii* (or *Russii*) *samoderzhets* (autocrat). On October 22, 1721, Peter the Great assumed the title, Emperor of all the Russias (*Imperator i samoderzhets vserossiiskii*), followed by a list enumerating the pos-sessions of the Russian crown. But in spoken and written Russian the term tsar remained widely used while the use of the title IMPERATOR was limited to official language.

tsarévich, -chi. Son of the tsar, either of the tsar of Muscovy or of a Tatar khan. Many of the Tatar tsars (khans) and tsarevichi—both Moslem and baptized—were in Moscow service in the 16th and 17th centuries. In the matter of honor (*chest'*), they took precedence over Moscow princes and boyars. Kotoshikhin mentioned in his work the *tsarevichi tatarskie, tsarevichi sibirskie* and *kasimovskie*. Many of those who had been baptized married Russian girls of aristocratic families. In the wars of the 16th century the Tatar tsars and tsarevichi (with their retinues) took a prominent part as military commanders. By the middle of the 17th century (by which time most of them had become Christians) their services had lost importance, but they still had places of honor at court celebrations and in solemn processions.

tsarévna, -ny. Tsar's daughter.

tsarítsa, -tsy. Tsar's wife.

tsárstvo, -va or **tsárstvie, -iia.** Tsardom, realm; also reign, dignity of a tsar. *Rossiiskoe tsarstvie:* the Muscovite realm; the Tatar realms were called *tsarstvo Kazanskoe, tsarstvo Astrakhanskoe, tsarstvo Sibirskoe.*

tsárstvo Pól'skoe: the official term for the part of Poland (previously divided between Austria and Prussia, later organized by Napoleon as the Grand Duchy of Warsaw) that was annexed to the Russian empire and granted a constitution by Alexander I in 1815. After the uprising of 1830–31 the Polish constitution was revoked by Nicholas I. After the uprising of 1863–64, *Privislianskii krai* (the Vistula territory) became the official name for the ten Polish provinces, but the old term was also used and the Russian emperor preserved the title of *tsar' Pol'skii*.

tsáta, -ty. In old Russia, a small coin or metallic adornment.

tsekh, tsékhi (from the Pol. *cech,* old Ger. *Zech*). Mandatory artisans' guild or trade corporation in West Russian cities administered on the basis of the Magdeburg Law. Peter the Great intended to introduce the artisan guild organization in all Russian cities; the regulations (REGLAMENT) issued on January 16th, 1721, for the GLAVNYI MAGISTRAT provided that all branches of urban handicrafts have their tsekhi, headed by elders (*aldermany* or STARSHINY). The decree of April 27, 1722, provided for a voluntary organization of the tsekhi, which the artisans could join on a permanent or temporary basis. The tsekhi were given a more official and rather compulsory character by the *remeslennoe polozhenie* (artisans' statute) in the city charter of Catherine II, issued in 1785. The character of the tsekhi was made still more formal by a statute of November 19, 1799. In spite of government efforts, the Russian artisan guilds or corporations failed to create such viable and self-governing organizations as those of the earlier trade corporations in West European cities, and not nearly all Russian artisans joined the tsekhi.

tsekhmístr, -ry. Guildmaster in the West Russian cities administered on the basis of the Magdeburg Law.

tsekhovói, -výe. In the 18th and 19th centuries, artisan who was a member of a TSEKH.

tselkóvyi, -vye. Silver ruble, or ruble in general (a vernacular expression).

tselovál'nik, -ki. In Muscovy, literally one who kissed [the cross], a sworn man, an official elected by peasant and POSAD communities; when taking the oath of office he kissed the cross and the Bible, hence the name. They were elected usually for a one-year term, and most of them performed services not for their communities but for the government. The term tseloval'niki was first used officially in the *Sudebnik* of 1497, and during the 16th and 17th centuries numerous categories of tseloval'niki were active in judicial, administrative, and financial affairs. The *Sudebniki* of 1497 and 1550 prescribed that tseloval'niki elected by local communities should be present in the court of the NAMESTNIKI and VOLOSTELI to watch over the administering of justice. Beginning with the 1550s the government abolished in most provinces the administration of the appointed namestniki and volosteli and replaced it with the administration of the elected *izliublennye starosty* (see STAROSTA) and ZEMSKIE SUD'I, who were always assisted by several *zemskie tseloval'niki*. The assistants in the local courts were called *sudetskie* or *sudnye tseloval'niki*. Beginning in the middle of the 16th century, when the elected GUBNYE STAROSTY were entrusted with the investigation and punishment of criminal offenses, the *gubnye tseloval'niki* were required as their assistants. As prison warders there were the *tiuremnye tseloval'niki*. The tseloval'niki were also active in tax collecting. The government imposed taxes on the communities rather than on the individuals, and the elected local authorities had to apportion and to collect the taxes. The *razrubnye tseloval'niki* apportioned taxes among the separate households according to their taxpaying ability. The tseloval'niki who collected taxes (SBORY, in general) were called *sbornye tseloval'niki* or *dannye tseloval'niki* (from DAN'); the OBROK was collected by the *obrochnye tseloval'niki*. The Moscow government mobilized a great many tseloval'niki for collecting customs duties imposed on goods transported from city to city or from one region to another. Working under the authority of the TAMOZHENNYI GOLOVA, the *tamozhennye tseloval'niki* examined and appraised transported goods and exacted customs duties according to the regulations. When and where the government managed the sale of liquor, the *kabatskie* GOLOVY and their assistants, the *kabatskie tseloval'niki,* built and maintained the KABAKI or *kruzhechnye dvory* and managed the production and sale of liquor. The general name for *tamozhennye* and *kabatskie tseloval'niki* was *vernye tseloval'niki,* sworn men (VERA, oath), and their service was called VERNAIA SLUZHBA. The treasury was further engaged in trading the goods collected from the population as taxes in kind; perhaps the most important were furs collected as tax from the Siberian natives. The *kazënnye tseloval'niki* "accepted, appraised and sorted furs and other goods of the Siberian *Prikaz,* and disposed of them in various ways. They kept the records and performed all the work within the sable treasury. Only at the end of the 17th century did there appear among them the regular employees of the *Prikaz*—the *pod'iacheis"* (G. Lantzeff, p. 11). The election of the numerous tseloval'niki for all these state services was a heavy burden on the local communities; this burden was borne chiefly by the POSAD communities. The tseloval'niki were elected with the guarantee of the community for their honesty and efficiency. "Representatives of the population served not the community but the state, and were chosen from the wealthiest inhabitants because it fell upon them to make up any deficiency in local government revenues. . . . No one was anxious to fill such an office, which, although honorable, was burdensome and involved too many responsibilities. Hence, men qualified for the office would take turns in holding it" (G. Lantzeff, p. 117). On large private estates (votchiny) in the 17th–18th centuries, the term tseloval'niki also designated those elected by the MIR to perform auxiliary duties in the manorial administration.

tselovánie kréstnoe. Literally, cross kissing, therefore oath.

tsená, -ny. Price.

ukáznaia tsená: In Muscovy, the price for provisions and fodder bought by military service men, which was fixed by the tsar's decree and by regulations issued by the VOEVODAS; it was lower than the *vol'naia* or *torgovaia tsena,* the free or market price (*Ulozhenie* of 1649, chap. VII, arts. 21 and 25).

tsenzúra. Censorship. The newly-established DUKHOVNAIA KOLLEGIIA (Holy Synod) was entrusted in 1721 with the censorship of theological works and of all religious books generally. This *dukhovnaia tsenzura* remained the responsibility of the censors appointed by the Holy Synod until the Revolution of 1917. The secular literature and journalism that developed under Catherine II (1762–96) were relatively free from government intervention until the empress became frightened because of the political results of literary activity after the French Revolution. By a decree of September 16, 1796, private printing houses were closed, and censorship offices were established in St. Petersburg, Moscow, Riga, Odessa, and the border town of Radzivilov, the location of the only customshouse through which the importation of foreign books and periodicals was permitted. Under Paul I (in 1800) the importation of foreign books was prohibited. Immediately after Alexander I's accession to the throne (1801) private printing houses and foreign books were permitted again. According to regulations of 1804, censorship committees had to be composed of university professors; they were to prohibit literary works offensive to religion, government, morals, or the personal honor of individuals. In 1810 the Ministry of Police and in 1819 the Ministry of Internal Affairs were charged with censorship functions. The *Ustav o tsenzure* of April 22, 1828, prescribed that censorship should ban works of literature, science, and art if they were offensive to the Orthodox church, to the supreme autocratic power or existing laws, to morals and decency, or to the honor of any person. Censorship was put under the Ministry of Public Education; the minister of public education headed the Chief Censorship Administration (*Glavnoe upravlenie tsenzury*). Local censorship committees were established in seven larger cities; they were composed of university professors and chaired by the POPECHITEL' UCHEBNOGO OKRUGA (superintendent of the educational district). Under Nicholas I the security police also watched over literature and the periodical press; the secret committee on censorship (under Count D. P. Buturlin) established in April 1848 and dissolved in December 1855 was notorious for both severe and foolish actions. However, neither Nicholas' gendarmes nor censorship succeeded in silencing Russian literature or making it servile.

In 1863 the censorship of the press was transferred from the Ministry of Public Education to the Ministry of Internal Affairs. Censorship under Alexander II was relaxed considerably. After the temporary regulations of May 12, 1862, the decree of April 6, 1865, granted the press "certain facilities and conveniences" (*nekotorye oblegcheniia i udobstva):* it freed from preliminary censorship periodical publications issued in St. Petersburg and Moscow, original books in Russian of more than 160 pages, translated works of more than 320 pages, and all the publications of academies, universities, and learned societies and institutions. For the management of the press, a new institution,

the *Glavnoe upravlenie po delam pechati,* was established within the Ministry of Internal Affairs. The Minister was accorded the right to issue warnings (*predosterezheniia*) to periodical publications in cases of reprehensible articles, and, after the third warning, to suspend the publication for a period of time not exceeding six months. Publication could be prohibited entirely by Senate decision. Censorship became more strict under Alexander III, and the security regulations issued on August 14, 1881, granted local administrators more power in curbing pernicious tendencies in the periodical press. During the Revolution of 1905 the temporary regulations of November 24, 1905, repealed preliminary censorship of all books and periodicals published in cities and towns, and permitted only the courts to punish the crimes and transgressions of the press. The decrees of March 18 and April 26, 1906, contained detailed regulations for the publication of periodicals and books. In practice during the period 1906–14 the periodical press experienced much harassment from the authorities, but the great majority of periodicals, though in opposition to the government, were permitted to continue publishing. Even the Bolshevik *Pravda* was published in St. Petersburg in 1912–14, and, when suppressed by a court sentence, it appeared the next day with a slight change in the title. Book publication was, in fact, free, including works of Russian and foreign socialists, Communists, and anarchists.

tsérkov' liádskaia (W.R.). In the 14th–16th centuries, the Roman Catholic church.

tsérkov' rússkaia (W.R.). In the 14th–16th centuries, the Russian Orthodox church.

tserkóvnik, -ki. Member of the clergy.

tsésar' (caesar) or **tsésar' rímskii.** The Russian term for the emperor of the Holy

Roman Empire, the Austrian emperor.

tsésartsy (pl.). The Russian term for the Austrians (until the 19th century).

tsesarévich. The emperor's son, or brother, who had been proclaimed the heir to the throne.

tsesarévna. Wife of the TSESAREVICH.

tsinsh or **tsynsh** or **chinsh** (Pol. *czynsz,* Ger. *Zins*). The West Russian term for quitrent (corresponding to Russian OBROK).

tslo, -la (W.R., Pol. *clo*). Customs duties (corresponding to Russian POSHLINY).

tsren, -ny. A large iron pan used for evaporation in salt works in northern provinces; an object of taxation in Novgorod the Great and in Muscovy.

tubýlets, -l'tsy (W.R.). Permanent longtime resident of the locality.

tümen. See T'MA.

tvérdost', -ti or **lísty-tvérdosti** (W.R.). 1. Document, a term corresponding to the Muscovite KREPOST', esp. one confirming a right to property. 2. Validity of a document.

týsiacha, -chi. Thousand. In the Kievan period the large cities with their adjoining territories constituted, for military and police purposes, a tysiacha subdivided into SOTNI (hundreds). Tysiacha was also the term for the citizens' land militia mobilized in wartime.

týsiatskii, -kie. Literally, thousandman, chiliarch, commander of a TYSIACHA.

"In the Kievan period there was a tysiatsky in each major city, that is, in each capital of a principality. While the office was originally an elective one, eventually the prince assumed the prerogative of nominating the candidate for it, except in Novgorod. . . . Even though the chiliarch became the prince's appointee, he always was considered the commander of the city militia (thousand) as contrasted to the prince's retinue. . . . Although chosen by the prince from among the leading boyars, he was considered the people's mouthpiece" (G. Vernadsky, *Kievan Russia*, p. 188). In Novgorod the Great the tysiatskii was the second highest official in the city administration (following the POSADNIK). Initially appointed by the prince, he had become by the 12th century an official elected (and dismissed) by the VECHE. In wartime the tysiatskii, together with the posadnik, commanded the Novgorodian militia; in peacetime his responsibilities were mainly in Novgorod's commercial administration, and he was also the chief justice for commercial litigation. The incumbent tysiatskii was called the *tysiatskii stepennyi;* the former ones were *starye tysiatskie.* Together with the posadniki, the tysiatskie were members of the Novgorodian SOVET GOSPOD (council of lords). In Moscow the last tysiatskii (Vasilii Veliaminov) died in 1374, and Grand Prince Dimitrii did not make a new appointment.

U

ubóets or **ubóitsa, -tsy.** Murderer, assassin.

gosudárskii ubóitsa: murderer of his master; according to some scholars, it could also mean insurgent, conspirator against his sovereign.

ubrús, -sy. Towel.

novozhénnyi ubrús: literally, newwedding towel, a fee paid in the 14th–17th centuries by a newly mar-

ried couple to the local administrator or to the landlord.

uchástok, -tki. Part, share; plot of land.

kazënnye uchástki: government landholdings.

otrubnýe uchástki: in the period of agrarian reform started in 1906, consolidated plots apportioned from communal holdings (see OTRUB).

podvórnye uchástki: plots belonging to the peasant household (DVOR).

usádebnye uchástki: house-and-garden plots.

uchástok, -tki, in the imperial period. A district, an administrative or judicial subdivision of an UEZD or city.

mirovói uchástok: a judicial borough, a district under the jurisdiction of the MIROVOI SUD'IA in 1864–89 and in 1912–17.

politséiskii uchástok: in cities, police precinct.

zémskii uchástok or *uchástok zémskogo nacháĺnika:* a district under a ZEMSKII NACHAL'NIK, 1889–1917.

uchílishche, -shcha. The most common official term for a school on the primary and secondary level. The first attempt to establish a network of secondary and primary schools for general education was made under Catherine II. According to the statute on public schools (*narodnye uchilishcha*) issued on August 5, 1786 (drawn up by the educator Iankovich-de-Mirievo), two kinds of public schools were to be established, namely, the *glavnye* (upper) *uchilishcha* in the GUBERNIIA capitals, and the *malye* (lower) *uchilishcha* in the UEZD centers. The glavnye uchilishcha were to consist of four grades or classes with a rather broad curriculum; the malye had two grades, corresponding in program to the first and the second grade of the glavnye uchilishcha. According to the regulations and statutes of 1803 and 1804, the glavnye uchilishcha were transformed and renamed *gubernskie gimnazii,* see GIMNAZIIA; the malye uchilishcha were called *uezdnye uchilishcha* (district schools). The statutes of 1803–04 provided also for primary schools in rural settlements, called *prikhodskie uchilishcha* (parish schools), but before the peasant emancipation of 1861 and the

establishment of zemstvo institutions in 1864, primary education made only moderate progress among the state peasants (chiefly from 1838 on, under P. D. Kiselev's administration) and was practically absent in privately owned villages. The uezdnye uchilishcha in the middle of the 19th century numbered about 400. Most of them had three grades, the education in each grade lasting two years. Beginning in 1872 they were transformed and renamed *gorodskie uchilishcha* (municipal schools). In 1912 they became *vysshie nachaĺnye uchilishcha* with four grades for children between the ages of 10 and 13 who had previous schooling of not less than one year. In 1915, schools of this type numbered 1,547.

The majority of the primary schools (*nachaĺnye narodnye uchilishcha*) in the countryside in the second half of the 19th century, supported by the ZEMSTVOS, were under the authority of the Ministry of Public Education; a considerable minority were parish schools (*prikhodskie* or *tserkovno-prikhodskie shkoly* or *uchilishcha),* under the authority of the Holy Synod. According to regulations of 1864 and 1874, the intermediate bodies which administered primary education were the *uchilishchnye sovety,* either *uezdnye* (in districts) or *gubernskie* (provincial); they were composed of local government officials and of representatives of the zemstvo and of the clergy. Those responsible for the immediate supervision of primary education in the uezdy were the *inspektory narodnykh uchilishch,* headed by the *direktor narodnykh uchilishch* in the chief city of each guberniia. According to data quoted by Miliukov (*Ocherki II,* p. 382), in 1899 there were 29,900 regular primary schools with 2,074,100 pupils under the authority of the Ministry of Public Education, and 18,300 schools with 882,100 pupils under the authority of the Holy Synod. In 1915 in Russia (excluding Finland and Poland) there were 116,200 elementary schools with 8,040,000 pupils, including 80,800 schools with 5,942,000 pupils under the authority of the Ministry of Public Education (N. Hans, p. 233). Most of the primary schools had a three-year program.

In secondary education an important role was played by the *real'nye uchilishcha* established according to the statutes of May 15, 1872. The classical languages (the main subject in the *klassicheskaia gimnaziia*) were excluded from their program which, instead, stressed mathematics and natural and technical sciences; modern languages were also taught. The course of education took 6 or 7 years, with one preparatory class. In 1914, along with 453 GIMNAZII for boys (with 152,100 students), there were 291 real'nye uchilishcha with 80,800 students (N. Haus, p. 235). Specialized schools important in secondary education follow:

dukhóvnye uchílishcha: a special system of schools for ecclesiastical education (*dukhovnoe obrazovanie*). At the end of the 19th century there were 185 (with about 30,000 pupils) where sons of Orthodox clergymen were prepared for the *dukhovnye seminarii* (in 1913 numbering 57 schools with about 22,000 students). These were the standard educational institutions for future Orthodox priests. Special secondary schools called *eparkhial'nye uchilishcha* (diocesan schools) existed for the daughters of the clergy; in 1913–14 there were 73 such schools with about 23,000 students.

kommércheskie uchílishcha: established by the statutes of April 15, 1896, and rapidly growing at the beginning of the 20th century. They were under the authority of the Ministry of Finance (headed at that time by S. Iu. Witte); they had a seven-year curriculum and gave a combined general and commercial education. In 1913, there were 217 kommercheskie uchilishcha with 51,600 students.

uchílishche pravovédeniia in St. Petersburg: a law school with a seven-year course combining general and professional education, it occupied a special place among various trade and professional schools. It was founded in 1835 and, according to the original statute, admitted only sons of noblemen; after graduation the former students were obliged to serve not less than six years in the Ministry of Justice.

promýshlennye uchílishcha: there were many junior technical, commercial, and industrial schools with short courses (of two, three, or four years). Promyshlennye uchilishcha were divided into *tekhnicheskie uchilishcha* and *remeslennye uchilishcha* (handicraft schools). Special schools— *zheleznodorozhnye uchilishcha*— trained future railroad employees. There were also several uchilishcha in the various fields of art.

voénnye uchílishcha and *iúnkerskie uchílishcha:* two kinds of military schools for the training of future army officers. The latter were established in 1864–65 when the military OKRUGA were organized. At the end of the 19th century there were 6 voennye uchilishcha and 14 iunkerskie uchilishcha; both had two-year courses of training. To the voennye uchilishcha boys were regularly admitted who had completed the *kadetskii korpus;* to the iunkerskie uchilishcha, noncommissioned officers (with some additional training) and boys who had completed a sixth-grade education in a secondary school.

zemledél'cheskie uchílishcha and *zemlemérnye uchílishcha:* schools for instruction in agriculture and surveying.

uchrezhdénie, -niia. Institution. *Uchrezhdéniia* (pl.) *Imperatrítsy Maríi* were educational and charitable institutions —schools, orphanages, hospitals— established or patronized by Empress Maria Fedorovna (wife of Paul I), who died in 1828. Later these institutions were expanded and formed a separate branch of administration called the *Vedomstvo Uchrezhdenii Imperatritsy Marii*. In the imperial period, uchrezhdenie was also a term for statutes and regulations of various kinds, from the *Uchrezhdenie ob imperatorskoi familii* issued by Paul I in 1797, or the *Uchrezhdenie sudebnykh ustanovlenii* (statutes on court institutions) of 1864, down to regulations and instructions issued by landlords for the administration of their estates before 1861.

udél, -ly. That portion of an ancestor's property inherited by one person as a result of the division (*del,* or *razdel*) of the property among the ancestor's various heirs. This term was applied specifically to princely holdings (appanages) in the 13th–16th centuries, and was already a common term for princely possessions in the 14th century. The successive division of princely possessions among male heirs turned some udely into relatively small districts in which the prince combined the functions of a political ruler with those of a private landlord. "The individual *udel* was more the private manor of its possessor than a political unit, so that the *udel* prince was more seignior than sovereign" (J. Blum, p. 66). In the 15th and 16th centuries the grand princes of Vladimir and Moscow gradually eliminated the appanage regime (*udel'nyi poriadok*), although its remnants lingered until the end of the 16th century.

udély (pl.). The term for landed properties and for revenues set aside for the maintenance and remuneration of all persons of imperial blood, according to the statutes of the imperial family issued by Paul I in 1797 (earlier these lands were called DVORTSOVYE, from DVORETS, palace). For the administration of the udely a special *departament udelov* was established in 1797; in 1826 the Ministry of the Imperial Court and of the Appanages (*Ministerstvo Imperatorskogo Dvora i Udelov*) was established by Nicholas I. Before the peasant reforms of the 1860s about one million male peasants lived under the udel administration; after they were freed, they received from it about 4,800,000 DESIATINAS of land as their allotments. At the end of the 19th century the udely included 7,900,000 desiatinas of land (one desiatina = 2.7 acres), of which 5,720,000 desiatinas were in forests.

uézd, -dy. The first meaning of the term was a delimited landholding. In Muscovy it was a district or county, an administrative-judicial unit that centered about a city or town and included the rural districts (called VOLOSTI or STANY) adjacent to it. In the imperial period the uezd, according to the statutes on GUBERNIIA administration issued in 1775, was a subdivision of the guberniia. There could be up to 15 uezdy in each guberniia, depending on the number of inhabitants. The main town of the uezd, the *uezdnyi gorod* (see GOROD), was the seat of several administrative and judicial offices; where there was no town, a village was designated the uezdnyi gorod. In the 19th century each uezd was subdivided into stany and UCHASTKI. At the end of the 19th century the 50 guberniias of European Russia (not including Finland, Poland, and the Caucasus) contained 504 uezdy. Nine of them were in the region of the Don Cossacks (*oblast' voiska Donskogo*) where the uezd was called an OKRUG.

ufála zémskaia or **ukhvála zémskaia.** A decision or a decree of the general diet (SEIM VELIKII VAL'NYI) of the Grand Duchy of Lithuania.

ugóda, -dy (W.R.). Agreement.

ugódie or **ugód'e** (mostly used in the pl.),

ugódiia, ugód'ia. Lands and their productive resources; appurtenances to arable lands that could be utilized for profit, such as meadows, pastures, lakes and rivers with fisheries, and forests with hunting places.

ugovórshchik, -ki. Contractor who supplied drinks and provisions for the tsar's palace (Kotoshikhin).

úi or **vúi.** Uncle, mother's brother.

ukáz, -zy. Decree, order, ukase.

> *ukáz gosudárev* or *gosudárskii:* tsar's decree or order, in Muscovy.

> *imennói ukáz:* in the imperial period, a decree signed by the emperor.

> *senátskii ukáz:* Senate decree.

> *ukáz sviatítel'skii:* order of a church hierarch—patriarch, metropolitan, archbishop, or bishop.

ukhvála zémskaia, -ly -skie. See UFALA ZEMSKAIA.

ukráina, ukráiny. Borderland, in the original sense of the word. Therefore in Muscovite sources one finds the plural, *gosudarevy ukrainy,* meaning borderlands in general, and specifically *ukraina Riazanskaia, ukraina tatarskaia,* and so on. "The fringe belt all along the southern border of the Moscow state consisted of a chain of *ukrainy* (plural). One spoke of the Riazan *ukraina,* the Tula *ukraina,* the Putivl and the Severian *ukrainy.* . . . Further west the term ukraina was applied to the southern border lands of the Grand Duchy of Lithuania, annexed by Poland in 1569. Specifically, the region south of Kiev as well as Podolie were called Ukraina, and this became the nucleus of the Ukraine in a national and political sense" (G. Vernadsky, *Russia at the Dawn,* p. 249).

ukráinnik, -ki or **ukráiniane** (pl.). Inhabitants of borderlands, frontiersmen, for example, in the Hypatian Chronicle of 1268: *Liakhove* (Poles) *ukrainiane.*

ulán, -ny. A group of Tatar nobility (mentioned together with KNIAZI, princes, and MURZY). Later a special type of cavalry regiment (along with the *draguny, gusary,* and *kirasiry*), distinguished mainly by different uniforms.

úlitsa, -tsy. Street; in Novgorod the Great, the ulitsa was an administrative subdivision of a SOTNIA; its inhabitants formed an association headed by the elected *ulitskii* or *ulichanskii* STAROSTA, and enjoyed a degree of self-government.

ulozhénie. Statutes, regulations, code of laws. The code of laws issued in 1649 was usually called the *Sobornoe Ulozhenie,* since its draft was approved by the ZEMSKII SOBOR.

ulús, -sy. In a broad sense, realm or domain of a Tatar sovereign. In a narrow sense, a Tatar settlement, or settlement of natives (as in Siberia).

umóva, -vy (W.R.). Agreement, contract.

umýchka or **umykánie.** Abduction of women.

umýchnik, -ki. Kidnapper, abductor of a woman.

uniát, -ty. A member of the Uniate church. See UNIIA BRESTSKAIA.

úniia Bréstskaia. The agreement concluded at Brest in 1596 between the Roman Catholic church and the majority of the Orthodox prelates in the Polish-Lithuanian state; according to it the former Orthodox church had to recognize the Roman pope as its head and to accept Roman Catholic dogma, although Orthodox rituals and the Church-Slavonic language were to remain in use. Within the Russian empire this religious union was formally dissolved in 1839 by the decision of a SOBOR (council) of Uniate bishops (headed by Metropolitan Iosif Semashko of Lithuania) in Polotsk, and the Uniates were accepted in full and complete communion with the Orthodox church. At the time of the union, as well as after it was dissolved, both parties—Catholics and Orthodox—charged each other with coercion and trickery. After 1839 the Uniate church remained within the Austro-Hungarian monarchy.

úniia Liúblinskaia. The union agreed upon in Liublin in 1569, during the Livonian war against Muscovy, by the representatives of the Kingdom of Poland and of the Grand Duchy of Lithuania; under its terms both states were to form a single indivisible nation, a joint commonwealth (*rzeczpospolita*) with a commonly elected king and with one parliament (SEIM). In fact, the Grand Duchy of Lithuania retained its individuality, with its own separate laws (the new code of laws, the third STATUT of 1588, was issued without any Polish participation and without mention of the union), its own army, its privy council (PANY-RADA), and its governmental institutions. Only in the 17th and 18th centuries did Polish influence in the political, legal, and cultural life of the Grand Duchy become predominant.

universál, -ly. The term for a proclamation or decree of the Ukrainian HETMANS.

universitét, -ty. University. The first Russian university was founded in 1755, in Moscow, with almost all foreign teachers. Broader development of higher education started under Alexander I. In 1802 the old German university in Derpt (Iuriev) received the status of an Imperial university (with German as the language of instruction until the end of the 19th century), and in 1803 an old Polish Catholic academy in Vilna became a university. In 1804 the universities in Khar'kov and Kazan' were founded, and in 1819 the *glavnyi pedagogicheskii institut* in St. Petersburg was transformed into a university. After the Polish uprising of 1830–31, the university in Vilna, which had be-

come a center of Polish patriotic aspirations, was closed, and in 1834 the university in Kiev (called *universitet Sviatogo Vladimira* or St. Vladimir University) was established. In 1864–65 the *Novorossiiskii universitet* was established in Odessa. In 1869, a university was established in Warsaw (with Russian as the language of instruction; only courses in Polish language and literature could be given in Polish). In 1888 a university was established in Tomsk, and in 1909, in Saratov. During World War I, the Warsaw university was transferred to Rostov-on-Don; a new university was opened in Perm' in 1916. Each of the eleven universities was called an *imperatorskii universitet,* and all were supported by the state treasury. In 1914, the total enrolment in the Russian universities was about 40,000 students. Women students (normally educated at institutions of higher learning called VYSSHIE ZHENSKIE KURSY) were first admitted to the universities in 1905, excluded in 1908, and again admitted in 1915. The relatively low tuition and numerous scholarships in Russian universities made university education accessible to young men of various social classes. In 1914 the social origins of students in Russian universities were as follows: gentry and officials, 36.1 percent; clergy, 10.3 percent; merchants and town dwellers, 14.8 percent; workers and craftsmen, 24.3 percent; peasants, 14.5 percent (N. Hans, p. 239).

The statutes governing the universities were originally issued separately for each university in 1802–04. General university statutes (*obshchii ustav Rossiiskikh universitetov*) were issued on July 26, 1835, June 18, 1863, and August 23, 1884; the latter regulations were changed considerably by the temporary regulations of August 27, 1905. In educational structure the Russian universities were normally divided into four departments, which in 1804 were called OTDELENIIA, and after 1835, FAKUL'TETY. According to the statutes of 1804, there were the *otdelenie slovesnykh nauk* (including linguistics, literature, and history); the *otdelenie fizicheskikh i matematicheskikh nauk;* the *otdelenie nravstvennykh i politicheskikh nauk* (including law and philosophy), and the *otdelenie meditsinskikh nauk*. According to the statutes of 1835, the newly established *filosofskii fakul'tet* was divided into a first department (otdelenie) which included linguistics, literature, philosophy, and history, and a second department for natural and mathematical sciences; then there were the *iuridicheskii fakul'tet* (law school) and the *meditsinskii fakul'tet*. According to the statutes of 1863 and 1884, there were *istoriko-filogicheskii, fiziko-matematicheskii, iuridicheskii,* and *meditsinskii fakul'tety*. The University of St. Petersburg had a special *fakul'tet vostochnykh iazykov* (Oriental languages) and did not have a meditsinskii fakul'tet, since there was in St. Petersburg a special medical school (*voenno-meditsinskaia akademiia*). The normal course of university education lasted four years (eight semesters), except for the meditsinskii fakul'tet, which was five years.

The administrative structure of the Russian universities, as covered by the statutes, provided a more or less autonomous status for the professors' organization. According to the statutes of 1804, the chief university administrator or REKTOR was elected (for a one-year term) by the general assembly or council of professors, and then confirmed by the emperor. The deans (DEKANY) of the departments were elected by the council of professors and confirmed by the Minister of Public Education. The rektor and the dekany constituted the executive board (PRAVLENIE UNIVERSITETA); the general council elected new professors and decided educational

and administrative matters. These procedures were ordinarily followed except during the period of *arakcheevshchina,* when two superintendents of UCHEBNYE OKRUGA, Magnitskii and Runich, purged the universities of Kazan' and St. Petersburg of freethinking professors. Under Nicholas I the university statutes of 1835 preserved, in general, the old administrative structure of the universities; the council of professors elected the rektor (for a four-year term) and the new professors; the dekany were elected by the professors' assembly of each fakul'tet; then the rektor was confirmed in his office by the emperor, the dekany and the professors by the Minister of Public Education. But the minister was also granted the right to appoint professors from among outstanding scholars and scientists possessing proper degrees. For supervision over the students a special official (*inspektor*) was selected by the superintendent (POPECHITEL') of the uchebnyi okrug and confirmed by the minister. The universities were entrusted to the special supervision of the superintendents, not all of whom were well-qualified for the job. After the European revolutions of 1848–49, the government undertook a series of restrictive measures, which fortunately were repealed in 1855.

The university statutes of 1863 fully recognized university autonomy. The offices of the REKTOR, the DEKANY, the new professors, and the inspector for student affairs (called PROREKTOR when he was elected from among the professors) were all recognized as elective, subject to confirmation, as above. The statutes of 1884, however, brought restrictions. They emphasized again that the university was subject to the supervision of the superintendent (popechitel' uchebnogo okruga). The rektor was selected by the minister of public education from the university professors and appointed (for a four-year term) by the emperor's order. The dekany, selected by the superintendent, were confirmed in office (for the same term) by the minister of public education. The inspector was appointed by the minister after nomination by the superintendent. The minister was granted the right to appoint the new professors (from qualified persons), or to permit the faculty and the university councils to elect the candidates and to present them to the minister for approval. If he did not approve the elected candidate, he himself appointed another. In 1905 the regulations of August 27 reestablished university autonomy and again permitted the election of the rektor by the university council (SOVET UNIVERSITETA) and of the dekany by the faculty council (*sobranie fakul'teta*).

The student body of the Russian universities from the 1860s onward was in considerable part friendly toward radical political and social ideas, and student protests and disorders (*besporiadki*) became almost a tradition in university life. As early as 1861, the University of St. Petersburg was temporarily closed by the government because of disorders. In 1899–1905 the student movement, beginning with demands for reestablishment of university autonomy, ended with radical political demands in accordance with the programs of the Social Democrats and Socialist Revolutionaries. After the Revolution of 1905–06, university life became nearly quiet for several years, but the restrictive and tactless measures of two ministers of public education, A. N. Shvarts (1908–10) and L. A. Kasso (1910–14), both professors themselves, provoked new student strikes of protest; and violations of university autonomy by Kasso even provoked a strike of Moscow university professors in 1911, when about 100 members of the academic staff submitted their resignations in protest. Kasso's successor

was the liberal Count P. N. Ignat'ev. Despite the vacillations of government policy and many dark spots in the picture, the general development of the Russian universities had raised them, by the beginning of the 20th century, to a level equal to that of the best Western institutions of higher learning.

únter-ofitsér, -ry. Sergeant in the imperial army.

upráva (or **óprava**). In the old language SUD I UPRAVA (or RASPRAVA) meant a trial and the rendering of justice; uprava meant also execution of the court sentence, satisfaction for the victim of an injury.

upráva, in the imperial period. A term for various administrative boards.

   upráva blagochíniia: the collegiate police organ (see BLAGOCHINIE) in the cities established by the *ustav blagochiniia* of 1782 and abolished in the 1860s; it was headed by the POLITSII-MEISTER or the GORODNICHII, and included two police officers (PRISTAVY) and two elected RATMANY (aldermen).

   gorodskáia upráva: according to the municipal statutes (GORODOVOE POLOZHENIE) of June 16, 1870, this was the municipal executive board under the chairmanship of the mayor of the city (GORODSKOI GOLOVA).

   meshchánskaia upráva: established in 1785, see MESHCHANE.

   reméslennaia upráva: a craftsmen's organization, then the board that headed the city's craftsmen, as established by the city charter of 1785.

   zémskaia upráva, gubérnskaia zémskaia upráva, and *uézdnaia zémskaia upráva:* Provincial and district zemstvo executive boards established by the statutes of January 1, 1864 (see ZEMSTVO).

upravlénie, -niia. A term for various administrative bodies in the imperial period.

   glávnoe upravlénie: chief administration, in the 19th and early 20th century, a term for various branches of administration, either separate branches on the level of a ministry, or an important department within a ministry. By the organization of the MINISTERSTVA in 1810–11, there was established the *Glavnoe upravlenie putei soobshcheniia* (Chief Administration for Transportation), which in 1865 was renamed the *Ministerstvo putei soobshcheniia*. In 1905 the *Ministerstvo zemledeliia* was renamed the *Glavnoe upravlenie zemleustroistva i zemledeliia* (Chief Administration of Land Settlement and Agriculture). A separate administrative unit was the *Glavnoe upravlenie gosudarstvennogo konnozavodstva* (Chief Administration for Horsebreeding). Within the Ministry of Internal Affairs there were, at the end of the 19th century, the *Glavnoe upravlenie pocht i telegrafov* (Post and Telegraph Administration); *Glavnoe tiuremnoe upravlenie* (Chief Prison Administration); and *Glavnoe upravlenie po delam pechati* (for matters of the press). Within the Ministry of War and the Ministry of the Navy there were several *glavnye upravleniia* subordinate to the minister.

urekánie. An old term for offence by insulting words; contumely.

uriád, -dy. In old Russian, settlement, agreement, contract. In the Grand Duchy of Lithuania, office.

uriády (or *urády* or *vrády*) *dvórnye* (pl.): grand ducal court offices.

uriády zémskie: land, therefore, state offices.

uriádnik, -ki. An officeholder, in the Grand Duchy of Lithuania and in the Ukrainian Cossack army. In the imperial period, a sergeant in a cossack regiment, or a rural police officer subordinate to the STANOVOI PRISTAV. According to the regulations of May 5,

1903, there had to be one *politseiskii uriadnik* and several STRAZHNIKI in each VOLOST'.

uriazhénie. An old term for testament.

urók, -ki. In old Russian, rules or regulations; settlement, agreement, contract; fixed amount of payment, hence rents and taxes of all kinds; fines and fees, also wages and salaries; task or fixed period of work.

ushkúinik, -ki (from *ushkui,* boat). In Novgorod the Great, a member of a party of young adventurers assembled for the exploration and exploitation of vast northern and northeastern regions. Using waterways for their expeditions, they subjugated scattered Finnish tribes and then, by exacting tribute, by trade, and by plundering, they gathered a rich booty, mainly in furs which were the principal Novgorodian export. They also undertook such expeditions down the Volga River to the Caspian Sea, plundering not only settlements of the Tatars and of Finnish and Mongol tribes, but Russian cities and villages as well.

ustáv, -vy. 1. Order, settlement, instruction, charter, statute, set of special rules and regulations for public organizations or for various branches of government administration: *tserkovnyi* (church) *ustav; monastyrskii ustav; universitetskii ustav; sudebnye ustavy* (court statutes); *voinskii* (military) *ustav; torgovyi* (commercial) *ustav* and so on. 2. Establishment or institution, especially for charitable and medical purposes.

ustáva, -vy (W.R.). Settlement, decision, order, or regulations issued by the grand duke of Lithuania (*ustava gospodarskaia*) or by the general diet (*ustava zemskaia*).

útisk, -ki, or **vtisk** (W. R.). Oppression, offense, injury.

uvezánie, or **uviazánie,** or **uviazovánie.** In the legal language of the Grand Duchy of Lithuania, the act of putting someone in possession of property adjudicated to him by a court sentence or granted by the grand duke.

uviázchii, -chie (W.R.). An official who carried out the act of UVIAZANIE.

uvolóka, -ki. Land measure, in the Grand Duchy of Lithuania; see VOLOKA.

úzhik, -ki. An old term for a relative.

V

vatága, -gi. "Cooperative association for fishing, hunting or other purposes" (G. Vernadsky, *Russia at the Dawn,* p. 252; glossary, p. 330). In Siberia in the 17th century, a company of PROMYSHLENNIKI.

vatamán, -ny. Elected head of a VATAGA or ARTEL' or the chief of a vessel. In Western Russia, elected elder of a rural community (another term for the ATAMAN). In northern regions of Muscovy, also a rural official.

vázhnitsa, -tsy (from *vaga,* scales). In West Russian cities, a place for weighing goods offered for sale.

vázhnoe (W.R.). A weighing tax, or the fee exacted for weighing goods on the city scales.

vdach, -chi (a term from the RUSSKAIA PRAVDA). Men or women who "gave themselves into a lord's temporary service" (G. Vernadsky, *Kievan Russia,* p. 148); the loan or subsidy they had received from the master was considered to be a favor or gift (*dacha*) from him, but in recompense the debtor was obligated to work for his master for a fixed period of time.

véche, -cha (from *veshchati,* to speak). Town meeting or assembly. "The town meeting was a universal institution in old Russia, both in the cities and in the rural districts. In large cities the population of each of the district communes met to discuss their communal affairs and besides that there were also meetings of the whole city population. In this sense each old Russian city had its own *veche*. However, the assembly of the capital city of the land constituted the *veche* in the technical sense of the term, that of a full-fledged political institution" (G. Vernadsky, *Kievan Russia,* p. 185). All the city freemen who were heads of families were entitled to attend the city meeting. They normally gathered in the marketplace when called by the tolling of the city bell. All those present had an equal right to speak and to vote. Custom required that the decision be unanimous; the minority bowed voluntarily before the majority or was forced to do so.

In the 10th–12th centuries veche gatherings took place in all Russian cities, esp. in capitals of provinces or lands (ZEMLIA or KNIAZHENIE), but only in Novgorod the Great and in Pskov did the veche develop into a continuously functioning institution. In other cities the veche gathered usually for such special purposes as to decide on the invitation, recognition, or expulsion of a prince or to settle questions of war and peace. With the proliferation of the princely descendants of Riurik and with permanent rivalries among various princes, the populations of the capital cities could choose among them at will and "show the way" to a prince they did not like. In questions of war and peace the will of the veche was often decisive. The prince's own retinue (DRUZHINA) was not large enough to fight a strong enemy, and to mobilize the militia the prince had to have at least the tacit consent of the people. Under those conditions a prince had to take into account the needs and wishes of the population as expressed by the veche. Under a strong and popular ruler, the people tended not to intervene in state affairs, but in cases of the prince's failure or other difficult situations, the veche of the capital city often became a decisive organ of the people's will. Thus the political structure of the Kievan principalities, after Iaroslav the Wise's death in 1054, was characterized by an unstable balance between two elements of political power: the monarchical element represented by the prince, and the democratic element represented by the veche of the capital cities. During the period of Mongol-Tatar domination beginning in 1238, the institution of the veche rapidly declined. The Russian princes, now recognized, appointed, or expelled by the khans, did not have to seek popularity at home, but only to curry favor with the Mongol-Tatar overlords. "The authority of the veche was thus drastically curbed, and by the mid-14th century it had ceased to function normally in most East Russian cities and could be discounted as an element of government" (G. Vernadsky, *Mongols*, p. 345). During Tatar rule the term veche (except in Novgorod and Pskov) was used in the Russian chronicles in the sense of popular gatherings revolting against Tatar oppressors, like the veches in Rostov, Suzdal', Vladimir, Iaroslavl', and Pereiaslavl' in 1262, in Tver' in 1327, and in Moscow in 1382.

The full development of the *vechevoi stroi*, a political structure with the veche clearly predominant, took place in the ancient Russian cities of Novgorod the Great (the capital city for the vast northern territories) and Pskov, Novgorod's "younger brother." Those cities and their territories were not devastated by the Mongol-Tatar invasion in 1237–40, and later were not subjected directly to Mongol-Tatar rule. Already, at the end of the 11th century, the entire Novgorodian administration had become elective, and beginning in 1156 the veche elected even the candidate for the see of the archbishop of Novgorod (who was then consecrated by the metropolitan of Kiev). For almost four centuries (until Novgorod's annexation by Muscovy in 1478) the Novgorodian veche was the dominant political body in the state. It combined supreme executive, legislative, and judiciary powers; it approved the Novgorodian SUDNAIA GRAMOTA (the charter of legal procedures); it invited a new prince and concluded a treaty with him, and expelled the incumbent prince when it pleased; it elected, judged, and dismissed the principal officials of the government, the POSADNIK and the TYSIATSKII; it decided questions of peace or war, and sent envoys and concluded treaties with foreign states; it judged the gravest criminal and political offenses, and it was a supreme court of appeal for the ordinary courts; it granted Novgorodian state lands to officials, private persons, or ecclesiastical institutions. The secretaries of the veche (called *vechnye d'iaki*) prepared documents embodying the decisions of the veche and presented them to high officials for signing and sealing. These documents or charters (*vechnye gramoty*) were done in the name of the "Lord Novgorod the Great" (of the Novgorodian government and of all the classes of the Novgorodian free population). Novgorodian democracy had its negative aspects. There were internal disorders connected with the constant change of princes and the clashes of rival princely parties, and in the 14th and 15th centuries, when the social cleavages in Novgorodian society became deeper, the disorders frequently acquired the character of a struggle between the poor and the rich classes of the Novgorodian community; the Novgorodian chronicle of 1445 bitterly complained that "there was no law and justice in

Novgorod." The veche in Pskov, which became independent of Novgorod in the middle of the 14th century, had the same political power as that in Novgorod but was less numerous and more orderly than the unruly assembly of the Novgorodian people.

véchnik, -ki. 1. Member of a VECHE assembly. 2. The bell used to summon the veche.

véchnost'. In the West Russian legal language, full property right.

védomstvo. A branch of administration in the imperial period.

> *dukhóvnoe védomstvo:* ecclesiastical administration.

> *sudébnoe védomstvo:* judiciary administration.

> *voénnoe védomstvo:* military administration.

vedovstvó. Clairvoyance, knowledge of mysterious things, sorcery; in olden times considered legally a serious crime, punishable even by death.

vedró, vëdra. Literally, pail, a liquid measure equal to 10 SHTOFY or 12.3 litres or 3.25 gallons. A *vedro vodki* consisted of 20 *butylki* (bottles).

véksha, -shy, or **véveritsa.** Literally, squirrel, the lowest monetary unit in the KUNA system. Presumably (according to L. Cherepnin) it was equal to one fourth of a kuna.

velíchestvo. Majesty. *Vashe Velichestvo* was the normal form of personal address to the emperor.

Velíkden'. Easter holiday.

venchánie. Church wedding.

> *venchánie na tsárstvo:* coronation.

véno. In the Kievan period, either the payment from the bridegroom to the parents of the bride, or the dowry brought in by the bride (later called PRIDANOE). In the legal language of the Grand Duchy of Lithuania, veno was a certain part of the landed property of the husband which, after his death, was transferred to his widow as compensation for the dowry she had brought with her.

véra. 1. Faith, creed, religion, denomination. In West Russian the *vera Liadskaia* or Polish faith meant Roman Catholicism; *vera Russkaia,* Orthodoxy. In Muscovy, the corresponding terms were *vera Latynskaia* and *vera pravoslavnaia khristianskaia.* 2. Oath; *na vere,* upon oath.

verkh. In Muscovy: (1) the upper floor of the palace where the tsar was living; (2) the supreme state power in general.

verkhóvniki. Members of the Supreme Privy Council (colloq.), 1726–30. See VERKHOVNYI TAINYI SOVET.

vershénie. In Muscovy, *vershenie dela* meant decision of a case by the court or by another office; *vershiti* could mean either to decide a case or, specifically, to execute a court's death sentence.

vershók, -shkí. A measure of length equal to 1.75 inches (DIUIMY); one-sixteenth of an ARSHIN.

verstá, vërsty. 1. In Muscovy, equal age (*sverstnik* in modern Russian), or equal social or official position. 2. A measure of length, usually equal to 500 SAZHENI, or to 0.663 miles, or 1.067 kilometers. For surveying large areas in Muscovy a *versta mezhevaia* equal to 1,000 sazheni was also used. A *versta litovskaia* (according to L. Cherepnin, p. 84) was equal to 798 sazheni, or a little more than a mile.

verstánie. In Muscovy, enrollment of a service man in a service category according to his ability and social origin and the designation of his POMEST'E grant and monetary salary (*pomestnyi i denezhnyi oklad,* see OKLAD).

verv', -vi. In the Kievan period, a rural administrative-territorial unit; "an association of neighbors in a country district" (G. Vernadsky, *Medieval Laws,* glossary, p. 95); presumably it grew out of the ancient patriarchal community.

In some cases the verv' was bound by collective responsibility (for a summary of learned opinions concerning *verv'* see *Pravda Russkaia*, ed. by B. Grekov, *II*, pp. 261–74).

ves or **véschee.** A weighing tax, a fee paid for weighing goods on public scales.

ves', vési or **vsi.** In the ancient period, a small rural settlement, later called DEREVNIA.

véveritsa, -tsy. See VEKSHA.

vézen' or **viázen', -ni** (W.R.). Prisoner.

vezénie or **viazénie** (W.R.). Imprisonment.

viáshchie (liúdi). Socially outstanding people, the same as *luchshie* or *bol'shie liudi.* See LIUDI.

viázen' and **viazénie** (W.R.). See VEZEN' and VEZENIE.

vidók, -ki. Eyewitness, in old legal language.

viná, víny. 1. Guilt, crime, offence, e.g., *vina rozboinaia,* robbery, brigandage. 2. Penalty for an offence, especially monetary penalty, fine (W.R. *vina penezhnaia*).

vínnik, -ki. Culprit, guilty person.

víra, víry (véra, vírnoe). Bloodwite, monetary penalty or ransom paid by the guilty for murder (of a free person); according to the RUSSKAIA PRAVDA it was graduated in size in accordance with the social and official standing of the victim.

díkaia víra or *liudskáia víra:* a payment by the local community (VERV') if a slain man was found within its territory but the perpetrator was not discovered.

vírnik, -ki. A court agent who collected VIRY and performed other duties by court order.

vizh, vízhi. In the Grand Duchy of Lithuania, a court agent, bailiff, who investigated criminal or civil cases, reported on his findings, and summoned the litigants before the court.

vizh gospodárskii: bailiff of the grand duke.

vklad, -dy. 1. In old Russian, a gift or contribution, esp. a contribution to a monastery when the donor entered the monastery community as a member or contracted for the right to live in the monastery without taking monastic vows. 2. In the modern language, vklad may mean a deposit in a credit institution, or the purchase of a share in a business enterprise.

vkládchik, -ki. In the old language, donor; in the modern, depositor or shareholder.

vkládnaia. See VKLADNAIA GRAMOTA.

vladýchestvo. Bishop's see; the dignity of a church hierarch.

vladýka, -ki. A church prelate: metropolitan, archbishop, or bishop.

vlast'. Power.

verkhóvnaia vlast' in the imperial period: the supreme authority or the supreme power, the emperor.

vlastél', -li. In old Russian, superior, chief, official.

vlásti (collect.). In Muscovy, the higher church authorities.

vlástnost'. In the legal language of the Grand Duchy of Lithuania, ownership.

vlástnost' dédichnaia: hereditary ownership.

voevóda, -dy. An old Slavic term meaning military commander, leader of VOI (warriors). During the Kievan period this term was frequently used in the chronicles and with this meaning it was used in Muscovy, but there the voevoda was either a military commander, or (esp. in the 17th century) the governor of a province, an official holding both military and civil power. The voevody commanding Muscovite troops were called *ratnye* or *polkovye voevody,* or *voevody v polkekh,* since the Muscovite army in the field was divided into five units called POLKI. At the head of each polk stood a voevoda (either alone or *s tovarishchi*, with associates), and the senior voevoda of the main body (*bol'shoi polk*) was sometimes called *bol'shoi voevoda* (see POLK). During and after the Time of Troubles (1605–13) the Moscow government appointed voevody to administer provinces. They were called *gorodovye voevody* or *voevody v gorodekh;* they supervised and if necessary mobilized the local service men to maintain order in the province; gradually they concentrated in their hands the military and civil power and some of the judiciary power. Their office, called *s"ezzhaia* or *prikaznaia izba*, managed normally by a D'IAK, was the chief center of the provincial administration. (Criminal affairs, however, were handled normally by the GUBNYE STAROSTY.) The communal organs of local self-government (rural and urban) continued to exist in the 17th century, but were subordinated to the voevoda as auxiliary organs of administration. Under Peter the Great the rank of voevoda was abolished in the army (by then commanded by GENERALY) but preserved in civil administration. Peter divided Russia into several (from 8 to 11) large administrative units called GUBERNII, and each of them was subdivided into several PROVINTSII (about 50 in all). Beginning in 1718–20 each provintsiia was put under a voevoda, subordinate to the GUBERNATOR (governor). Peter tried to separate the administrative and judicial powers, and established in several larger cities provincial courts (*nadvornye sudy*, see SUD), but soon after his death the nadvornye sudy were abolished (in 1727), and the voevoda again combined in his hands all the administrative and judicial power in his province. (The office of the gubnye starosty had been abolished in 1702.) The voevoda's office, instead of *s"ezzhaia izba* (see IZBA), was now called the *voevodskaia*

kantseliariia. Appeals from the judgments of the governors and voevodas were sent to the College of Justice. The rank and office of voevoda were abolished by the statutes on guberniia administration issued on November 7, 1775.

voevóda, in the Grand Duchy of Lithuania. Governor of a province or ZEMLIA, such as those formerly headed by princes from the dynasties of Riurik or of Gedymin. The voevoda was appointed by the grand duke usually from the local nobility, with its overt or silent consent. Some of the grand ducal PRIVILEI (charters), like the charters granted to the Vitebsk and Polotsk lands, explicitly promised the *Vitebliane* and the *Polochane* that the grand duke would appoint voevody in accordance with their wishes, and would replace a voevoda if he were not liked (*ne liub*). Therefore the voevoda appointees of the grand duke, were, at the same time, representatives of local interests. They administered their provinces with the assistance of councils composed of members of the local nobility. They were military commanders over the militia of the whole VOEVODSTVO, and they were judges and administrative heads in those POVETY where the capital city of the voevodstvo was located; the *starosty povetovye* (see STAROSTA) had judicial and administrative powers in other povety, and the cities governed on the basis of the Magdeburg law were exempt from the powers of the voevody and starosty. The voevody were also members of the council of lords (PANYRADA) of the Grand Duchy of Lithuania.

voevódstvo, -va. The rank and office of a VOEVODA and the territorial unit under his administration. In the Grand Duchy of Lithuania, the first voevodstva—those of Vilna and of Troki—were established in 1413, following the Polish model. Then, by subdivision of these two large territories, by acquisition of new territories, and by transformation of old West Russian principalities into voevodstva with voevody appointed by the grand duke as his lieutenants, the number of voevodstva increased in the 1560s to 13. The majority of the voevodstva were subdivided into several POVETY, from 2 to 5 in each (two of the voevodstva and the STAROSTVO of Zhomoit had only one povet each); the total number of povety in the 1560s was 31. In 1569 Poland annexed from the Grand Duchy of Lithuania 4 voevodstva (those of Kiev, Volynia, Braslav or Podolia, and Podliashie), which included 10 povety.

vói (pl.) = *voisko* in modern Russian. An old term for warriors, soldiers; in the Kievan period it was not a professional army but a temporary militia mobilized in wartime from the urban and rural population.

voiná. 1. War, struggle. 2. A tax imposed during the Mongol-Tatar domination, a war tax or soldiers' tax, presumably "collected in the years when no recruits were drafted" (G. Vernadsky, *Mongols*, pp. 221–22).

voit, -ty (Ger. *Vogt*). The mayor of a city in the Grand Duchy of Lithuania. He was initially appointed by the grand duke, but later the cities governed on the basis of the Magdeburg law bought the right to make this office elective. The voit headed the city council (RADA), whose members were elected by agreement of the voit with the city community. Together with the RADTSY and the BURMISTRY, the voit administered the city and rendered justice. In several cities the government was divided into an administrative and a judicial department; while the rada managed police and economic affairs, the LAVA, headed by the voit, judged criminal affairs. Appeals from decisions of the voit and the LAVNIKI could be sent only to the grand duke.

Voit in the Grand Duchy of Lithuania was also a term for the magistrate who headed the peasant administration in rural districts or VOLOSTI. On state lands he was appointed by the NAMESTNIKI-DERZHAVTSY or STAROSTY with the consent of the peasants. In the 19th century, according to the regulations of February 19, 1864, abolishing the patrimonial jurisdiction of landlords in Russian Poland, the voit, elected by peasants and confirmed in office by the Russian administration, was made prefect of the GMINA.

vóitovstvo. Office of a VOIT.

vólia. Will or liberty.

Naródnaia vólia: the People's Will, the name of an underground revolutionary organization that emerged in the summer of 1879, when the party called Land and Liberty (ZEMLIA I VOLIA) split (at the congress in Lipetsk and Voronezh) into two parts: the minority forming a small party called the Black Partition (CHERNYI PEREDEL) and the majority forming the militant revolutionary and terroristic organization called Narodnaia volia. The new party aimed at immediate political revolution, the overthrow of the monarchy, and the convocation of a constituent assembly that would achieve radical political democratization, the ownership of the land by the people, and measures for transferring the factories to the workers. In its tactics the party placed faith in terrorism, esp. in the assassination of the emperor Alexander II. A series of attempts on his life followed, culminating in his assassination on March 1, 1881. After this, the party tried to continue its terroristic activities but government repressions and unfavorable public reaction diminished its following and its influence, and by the end of the 1880s it had practically disappeared from the political scene.

volkhv, -vý. 1. Heathen priest. 2. Magician, sorcerer.

volkhvovánie. Witchcraft, sorcery. In medieval Russia (as elsewhere at that time), a serious crime punished by the knout and exile or even by death.

vol'noopredeliáiushchiisia, -shchiesia. Army volunteer. The statutes of 1874 on universal military service granted a number of exemptions and privileges based on family status and education. Young men (over 17) who had completed a certain level of education could enter the army as vol'noopredeliaiu-shchiesia, without drawing lots (see POVINNOST'); the term of service in the active army for them was 3 months to 2 years, instead of the normal 6 years. By the end of the 19th century volunteers of the first category (*vol'noopredeliaiu-shchiesia pervogo razriada*) had to serve in the active army for one year, and those of the second category, for 2 years. According to the law of June 23, 1912 (which changed the statute on military service), the term of active service for all volunteers was fixed at 2 years instead of the then normal 3 years; that term was followed by reserve status of 16 years. Those volunteers who completed their active service and passed a certain examination were commissioned as officers and entered the reserve with the rank of *praporshchik zapasa* (see PRAPORSHCHIK).

vólok, -ki. Portage.

volóka or **uvolóka, -ki.** A land measure in the Grand Duchy of Lithuania ranging from 15 to 20 Russian DESIATINAS. The surveying (VOLOCHNAIA POMERA) of state lands in the 1550s fixed the normal size of the voloka at about 19.5 desiatinas (about 21 hectares or 53 acres). "The basic unit, called a *uvoloka,* consisted of 19½ desiatinas divided between plowland, meadow, house lot, and garden. This was considered a full holding. A small number of peasant families had a full holding, but most of them had from one quarter to three quarters of a *uvoloka"* (J. Blum, p. 461).

vólost', -ti (= *vlast'*). Power or government; then, by extension, a territory under a certain power, a district, region, or land. In the Kievan period the term volost' was used as a synonym for ZEMLIA or KNIAZHENIE. Volost' was also the term used for the vast Novgorodian territories in the north and northeast, and for rural districts in the Grand Duchy of Lithuania. In Muscovy volost' meant not only an administrative territorial division but also a peasant community that was composed of several rural settlements and formed a peasant MIR (called in the sources *starosta so krest'iany*). In the 15th century "the commune was usually called a volost. . . . Each commune was semi-autonomous, and was run by officers chosen by the commune members from among their fellows. The volost managed all those parts of its territory that were not held by individual peasants, such as forests, common pasture, streams and fisheries. It supervised the establishment of new homesteads within its boundaries, the distribution of unoccupied arable, and the resettling of vacated holdings. . . . The prince levied his imposts upon the commune as a unit. . . . The commune's own assessors had to apportion these royal taxes and obligations equitably among its members, gather the levies and turn them over to the prince's officials. Volost officials were also responsible for the maintenance of public order and security within the commune's boundaries" (J. Blum, p. 96). In the second half of the 16th century volosti of the state peasantry became autonomous and self-governing units with administrative and judicial functions which at first belonged to the appointed VOLOSTELI; but during the 17th century their autonomy was considerably reduced by the power of the VOEVODY. In

Muscovite sources we find the terms *volosti chërnye tiaglye,* which were inhabited by TIAGLO-bearing state peasants, and *volosti dvortsovye,* which served the needs of the grand prince's, later the tsar's, palace (DVORETS). On the private estates (VOTCHINY and POMEST'IA) the activities of the old peasant volosti, which were now dismembered and divided among the landowners, became impossible, and in such places the volost' as a self-governing unit ceased to exist. But in the northern and central regions where there were extensive state lands the volost' was still a living institution in the 17th and 18th centuries. The inner life and structure of the volost' were usually regulated by local custom, without intervention of the central government.

Only by the end of the 18th century did the government begin to regulate the size and organization of the peasant volost'. The regulations of 1797 tried to establish standards for the administrative organization of the state peasantry. The size of a volost' population was set at not more than 3,000 male peasants (REVIZSKIE DUSHI). In each volost' a volost' board (VOLOSTNOE PRAVLENIE) was to be established, headed by the VOLOSTNOI GOLOVA, elected by the peasants for a two-year term, and consisting of STAROSTY or VYBORNYE (selectmen) from the villages that constituted the volost', and of a volost' clerk (PISAR') also elected by the mir for two years. The volost' board was to take care of collecting taxes and maintaining good order in the volost', and the volostnoi golova was to administer justice and seek reconciliation in all minor disputes among the peasants. The Kiselev reform of the state peasant administration (1838) included detailed regulations on the volost'. Every volost' was to consist of several adjacent village communities with a total population of up to 6,000 male peasants. The volost' assembly (VOLOSTNOI SKHOD) was to consist of representatives elected by the village communities on the basis of one for every 20 peasant households; it was to meet every three years to elect the volost' board (volostnoe pravlenie) and the volost' court (RASPRAVA). The volost' board was headed by the volostnoi golova and consisted of two elected assessors (ZASEDATELI) and a clerk appointed by the OKRUZHNYI NACHAL'NIK (district administrator). The volost' board was responsible for the maintenance of order; it took care of communal forests, waters, and pastures; it also handled passports for the state peasants (granting of permission for temporary leave of absence from the volost'). The volost' court, chaired by the volostnoi golova, had two upright citizens (DOBROSOVESTNYE) as members; it was the court of appeals for the village court (SEL'SKAIA RASPRAVA). All the elected peasant officials had to be confirmed in their offices by the provincial administration of the state domains.

Following the emancipation of the serfs on February 19, 1861, the liberated peasants formed village communities (SEL'SKIE OBSHCHESTVA); several villages and hamlets were combined in a volost' with a total number not less than 300 and not more than 2,000 male peasants. The volost' assembly (volostnoi skhod) was composed of officials elected by the peasants and peasant representatives, elected one from every 10 households; it elected the volost' executive board (volostnoe pravlenie) and the peasant court (*volostnoi krest'ianskii sud*). The board was headed by the *volostnoi starshina* (see STARSHINA), assisted by several deputies and by the volostnoi pisar' (clerk). The starshina was responsible for the maintenance of general order, peace and tranquility in the volost', as well as for passports. He was subordinate to the government authorities of the district (UEZD), and in fact the volost' board increasingly became an executive bureaucratic office, leaving peasant self-government to find its real expression in the village mir (sel'skoe obshchestvo and sel'skii skhod). The volost' court consisted of 4 to 12 judges elected annually; sittings of the court had to consist of no less than 3 judges. They could decide disputes and litigations between peasants involving no more than 100 rubles and could punish minor offenses. The administrative organization of the state peasantry was, in the 1860s, equated to that of the emancipated serfs. The abortive reform of rural administration in 1889 put all the peasant institutions of the volost' and the village mir under the strict control of the ZEMSKIE NACHAL'NIKI, but their role in peasant life was considerably reduced first by the decree of October 5, 1906, which awarded the peasants equality with other social groups in matters of civil rights, and then by the law of June 15, 1912, concerning the reform of peasant courts. Until 1917 the volost', as a territorial-administrative subdivision of the uezd, remained an organization of the peasant class alone, and many plans to introduce the all-class (vsesoslovnaia) volost' were not realized. At the beginning of the 20th century there were, in the 50 guberniias of European Russia (excluding Finland, Poland, and the Caucasus), according to official statistics, 504 uezdy which included 10,669 volosti (among them several hundred cossack STANITSY). The average peasant population per volost' at that time greatly exceeded the norms set in 1861.

volostél', -li. Chief of a rural district called a VOLOST' in the 14th–16th centuries. The NAMESTNIKI in the cities and the volosteli in the rural districts of Muscovy were vicegerents of the grand prince as long as the KORMLENIE system was dominant in the Muscovite local administration.

volóstka, -ki. A small VOLOST'.

volóvshchina (from *vol*, ox). Cattle tax; the chief agricultural tax, esp. in Volynia (oxen were the main draft animals in the Ukraine).

vor, -ry. In Muscovy, villain, rogue, outlaw, brigand, mutineer, criminal in general. In the modern legal language, vor means thief only.

vorótnik, -ki. Gatekeeper in Muscovy. A category of service men in fortified cities who were *sluzhilye liudi po priboru* (see PRIBOR).

vorovstvó. In Muscovy, a crime or offense of various kinds. The term *vorovstvo-krazha* meaning theft or larceny appeared in the legal language in the 18th century.

vorozhéia, -zhéi (fem.). Fortune-teller, sorceress. A person very popular with the public, but a criminal in the eyes of the law in old Russia.

vosmníchee or **osmníchee.** An old customs duty on transported goods.

vótchich. See OTCHICH.

vótchina or **ótchina, -ny.** Any of various kinds of hereditary property, rights, or claims (see OTCHINA). The term votchina, frequently used in Muscovy, referred mostly to patrimonial or hereditary landed estates, and also to all the landed property that belonged to the holder in full ownership; the votchina was frequently opposed in documents to the POMEST'E, which originally was a landholding granted by the sovereign to his service men on the condition of military serice. Referring to estates according to the category of owner, Muscovite documents mention *votchiny boiarskie, dvorianskie, monastyrskie, patriarshie, domovye, vladychnye,* and *vlastelinskie* (the last two often designating the sees of metropolitans, archbishops or bishops). According to the ways of acquisition there were *votchiny rodovye, starye,* or *starinnye* (inherited from forefathers), *kuplenye* (bought), *pridanye* (received as dowry), *zhalovannye* (granted by the sovereign), and *vysluzhennye* (received as reward for service). Although initially votchiny were the unconditional property of their owners, the middle of the 16th century saw military service in Muscovy become obligatory for all private landholders whether their estates were of the votchina or pomest'e type. On the other hand, by the end of the 17th century the pomest'ia tended more and more to become hereditary holdings, and under Peter the Great the new term *nedvizhimoe imenie* (immovable property) referred to both types of landed estates. Finally a decree of March 17, 1731, formally and explicitly recognized both former types of landholding as hereditary immovable property: *nedvizhimoe imenie votchina.* In the 18th and 19th centuries the meaning of the term pomest'e became reversed, and was frequently used in the sense of the Muscovite votchina.

vótchinnik, -ki. In Muscovy, the usual term for the owner of a VOTCHINA.

> *obél'nye vótchinniki:* a small group of tax-free landowners in the northern regions in the 17th and 18th centuries.

vozh, -zhi. Leader, guide.

vóznyi, -nye (or **enerál vóznyi**). In the Grand Duchy of Lithuania, a court investigator and executive agent of the court (his duties are described in the Lithuanian Statute of 1566, sect. IV, art. 5).

vrad, vriad, -dy (W.R.). Office, see URIAD.

vrádnik, vriádnik, -ki (W.R.). See URIADNIK, -KI.

vrázhda (old and W.R.). Murder and crime in general; the penalty for it.

vserossíiskii. See IMPERIIA VSEROSSIISKAIA.

vskaz, -zy or **vskazánie, -niia** (W.R.). Order, decision, esp. court sentence.

> *vskaz gospodárskii:* grand duke's decision.

vstáva (W.R.). See USTAVA.

vtisk or **útisk, -ki** (W.R.). Oppression, offense, injury.

vúi. Same as UI.

výbliadok, -dki. In Muscovy, illegitimate child.

výbor, -ry. 1. Election. 2. In Muscovy also a certificate of election. *Vybor za rukami,* a signed certificate of election. 3. *Vybor* or *iz gorodov vybor:* in Muscovy this was the upper element of the provincial DVORIANE; see DVORIANE VYBORNYE.

výbornyi, -nye. Elected representative; see VYBORNYE LIUDI. In the 17th–19th centuries (before 1861) vybornye were officials elected by the peasants on the state lands and on the large private estates; they were, at the same time, peasant representatives and auxiliary agents of the local state and manorial administration.

výborshchik, -ki. Elector. After 1905, one of the members of the provincial electoral assemblies (GUBERNSKIE IZBIRATEL'NYE SOBRANIIA) who were elected (in several stages) to elect members of the State Duma; the electoral assemblies were composed of four categories of vyborshchiki: (a) from peasant communities, (b) from private landowners, (c) from city residents, and (d) from factory workers. In several big cities the vyborshchiki formed a separate GORODSKOE IZBIRATEL'NOE SOBRANIE, which elected the members of the State Duma from these cities.

výdel, -ly. Apportionment of an individual share from common property. Among peasants vydel meant the separation from communal allotment land of individually held plots by householders who wished to make their plots hereditary. The emancipation laws of February 19, 1861, permitted such a vydel on the condition that the peasant pay the full amount of redemption payments due for his share (see PLATEZH). In practice this permission was little used, and the law of December 14, 1893, forbade the vydel of individual peasants without consent of the MIR. The free vydel of individual shares of allotment lands was permitted during the Stolypin era by the decree of November 9, 1906, and by the law of June 14, 1910. During 1907–14 more than 2,500,000 peasant householders (about 28 percent of all the householder members of repartitional land communes) submitted applications for leaving the commune, and for about 2,000,000 of them the vydel was completed by January 1915.

výgon, -ny. Communal pasture in or around Russian villages and towns. According to the *Ulozhenie* of 1649 (chap. XIX, art. 6) the vygon around the city of Moscow had to measure 2,000 SAZHENI (about 2½ miles) on all sides. Chap. XIX, art. 10 of the *Ulozhenie* prohibited the acquisition by an individual of parts of those vygony that were the possession of cities or towns.

výkhod. Literally, exit. During the Tatar domination, the term for the tribute that the Russian princes, empowered by the Tatar khans, collected from the Russian population and delivered to the Tatar overlords. Even after the end of the Tatar domination in 1480, the Russian grand princes sent the vykhod to the Tatar khans of the Crimea, Kazan', and Astrakhan', though by then it was considered not a tribute, but a "gift."

výkhod krest'iánskii, in Muscovy: the right of peasants living on privately owned lands to leave their landlords and move elsewhere. This right, on the condition of the discharge of all peasant obligations and indebtedness to their former masters (which payment might also be referred to as vykhod), was recognized by the *Sudebniks* of 1497 (art. 57) and 1550 (art. 88). But the peasant's right to leave was subjected to legal limitations beginning in the 1580s and was completely revoked by the *Ulo-*

zhenie of 1649 (chap. XI, arts. 1–11) for both state peasants and peasants living on private lands.

výkup. Redemption, ransom.

výkup plénnykh: a special tax imposed on all classes of the population by the Moscow government for the ransom of war prisoners (*Ulozhenie* of 1649, chap. VIII).

výkup vótchin: in the case of a Muscovite landowner's selling his hereditary estate, the right of his relatives to redeem the VOTCHINA during the 40 years following the sale (for details see the *Sudebnik* of 1550, art. 85, and the *Ulozhenie* of 1649, chap. XVII, arts. 27–34).

výkup krest'iánskikh nadél'nykh zemél': redemption of the peasants' allotment lands received by them in the 1860s; see KREST'IANIN, NADEL, and PLATEZH.

výprava, -vy (W.R.). 1. Expedition, esp. military expedition. 2. Equipment. 3. Dowry.

výpusk zhivotínnyi. Pasture for common use (like VYGON), a term from the *Ulozhenie* of 1649, chap. XIX, art. 7.

výriad. Cancellation of an agreement (RIAD).

výrok, -ki. In the legal language of the Grand Duchy of Lithuania, decision, court sentence.

výsluga, -gi. In the Grand Duchy of Lithuania, a landed estate received from the sovereign as a reward for service performed, or on condition of service.

výstup, -py (W.R.). Crime, offense, transgression.

vyt', výti. 1. Part, share. 2. Plot of land of varying size. 3. Taxable unit of several DESIATINAS in the countryside or of several households in the cities. In Muscovy the vyt' as a taxable unit was in use on the state and palace (*dvortsovye*) lands in the northern regions. The normal size of the vyt' was 12

CHETI of good land, 14 cheti of middling land, and 16–20 cheti of poor land in one field, which in the three-field system made 36, 42 and 48–60 cheti or, respectively, 18, 21 and 24–30 desiatinas (65–81 acres). 4. In court proceedings involving many litigants or many defendants vyt' meant a share of the claims, or a share of the compensation for damages or of the fine imposed by the court on the guilty party.

výtchik, or **výtnik, -ki.** Participant, one who has a VYT'. In court proceedings involving many litigants or defendants, one who either paid or received part of the compensation for damages, or who had to pay a part of the fine imposed by the court.

vývod. Literally, leading away. 1. The treaties concluded by Novgorod the Great with its princes forbade the princes to cause the vyvod of people from the territory of the Novgorodian state, i.e., to take Novgorodians into private dependence. 2. Vyvod was the payment to the landlord for a peasant girl who went to be married outside his possessions. 3. In the legal language of the Grand Duchy of Lithuania, vyvod meant proof, evidence.

vyvolánie (z zemlí). In the legal language of the Grand Duchy of Lithuania, the declaration that a criminal at large has been outlawed forever from the country.

vývoz (kresť ián). In Muscovy, exportation of indebted peasants from one landlord to another. For the peasants who themselves could not use their right of VYKHOD "there was another and entirely legal way by which peasants could move from one place to another. . . . This was by having their exit fees, debts, and tax arrears paid for them by another lord on whose property they then settled and in whose debt they now were. This was known as *vyvoz,* or exportation" (J. Blum, p. 251). Both vykhod and vyvoz were prohibited by the *Ulozhenie* of 1649.

význanie, -niia. In the legal language of the Grand Duchy of Lithuania, declaration, statement, testimony.

vzvod, -dy. Platoon. By the end of the 19th century, the ROTA (company) in the infantry was divided into four vzvody, each commanded by an UNTER-OFITSER (sergeant).

Z

zabítie or **zabóistvo** (W.R.). Murder, killing.

zabóitsa, -tsy (W.R.). Murderer.

zadnítsa. An old term for inheritance or inherited property.

zádruga, -gi. Ancient greater family commune among the southern Slavs.

zaëm or **zaím, zaimý.** Loan.

beskabál'nyi zaëm, in Muscovy: a loan not secured by a written acknowledgment of debt.

zaémshchik or **zaímshchik, -ki.** Debtor.

zágovór, -ry. Conspiracy, agreement, esp. agreement with some ulterior aim. In Muscovy in the 15th–16th centuries,

zagovor also meant a group of assistants to the court agent or NEDEL'SHCHIK.

zagovórshchik, -ki. 1. Conspirator, participant in a secret agreement. 2. Member of the company of assistants to the NEDEL'SHCHIK (*Sudebnik* of 1550, art. 47).

zaiézd, zaézd, -dy. In Muscovy, a payment from the local population to a visiting church hierarch or his representative.

zaímka, -ki or **zaímishche, -shcha.** A formerly unused plot of land (esp. in forest regions) that was occupied and cultivated by an individual and became his by virtue of occupancy.

zaímshchik, -ki. Owner of newly occupied land (see ZAIMKA).

zaisán, -ny. Hereditary head of nomadic clans in Siberia and in the Volga-Ural region.

zakáz, -zy (W.R. also *zakázanie*). 1. Order, instruction. 2. Prohibition.

zakázchik or **zakáznik, -ki.** In Muscovy and in the Grand Duchy of Lithuania, executive agent of secular or of church authorities.

zakhrebétnik, -ki. In Muscovy, someone who was personally free but lacked his own household; such persons were not enrolled in the lists of TIAGLYE LIUDI, and lived *za khrebtom* (behind the spine) of some householder as his dependents, often as hired workers. Another term for such people was *podsusedniki.*

zaklád, -dy. Security, pledge (= *zalog*); in the modern language, pawn and pawned object. In Novgorod the Great, a fee paid to court officials. In the Grand Duchy of Lithuania, an amount of money fixed by the court, which had to be paid by the guilty person.

zakládnaia, -ye (grámota, -ty). Document of pledge or mortgage.

zakládnik or **zakládchik, -ki,** or **základen', -dni.** A person who pledged himself to dependence on private persons or church institutions while evading TIAGLO-bearing communities. From the Novgorodian treaties with princes in the 13th and 14th centuries to the *Ulozhenie* of 1649, the state tried to prevent this practice. (In the opinion of V. Sergeevich, *I*, p. 317, the zakladniki were debtors living and working in the households or on the landed estates of their creditors.)

záklich. Old term meaning an announcement in the marketplace.

zakliuchénie. In legal language: *tiuremnoe zakliuchenie,* imprisonment; *odinochnoe zakliuchenie,* solitary confinement.

zakón, -ny. 1. Law, statute, rule, regulation. 2. In the old language, religion, faith. *Zakon khristianskii,* christianity. In West Russian, *zakon grecheskii,* (Greek) Orthodoxy; *zakon Rimskii,* Roman Catholicism. 3. In West Russian, a monastic order. See also POLNOE SOBRANIE ZAKONOV and SVOD ZAKONOV ROSSIISKOI IMPERII.

osnovnýe gosudárstvennye zakóny: the fundamental state laws that constituted the first part of the first volume of the Code of Laws issued in 1833. The first section of this part (arts. 1–81) contained, chiefly, statements concerning the supreme autocratic (*samoderzhavnaia*) power embodied in the person of the emperor. The second section (arts. 82–179) contained the statutes (UCHREZHDENIE) on the imperial family. On April 23, 1906 (on the eve of the First State Duma), an entirely new version of the osnovnye zakony was issued. Chapter 1, "On the supreme autocratic power," preserved this old definition, but the word *neogranichennaia*—unlimited (power)—was omitted. Chapters 2–5 contained statements on the rights and duties of Russian subjects, on the process of legislation, and on the institutions of the State Council, the State Duma, and the ministries. In final form, as included in the SVOD ZAKONOV, vol. I, part 1, issued in 1906, the first section of the osnovnye zakony included three introductory articles (stating the unity of the Russian empire, including Finland, and acknowledging Russian as the state language) and 11 chapters (arts. 4–124). Chapters 1–6 included detailed regulations concerning the emperor's power. Chapter 7 was concerned with religion; Orthodoxy was recognized as the dominant faith (art. 62), but other religions and denominations were recognized as free in their creed and religious activities (arts. 66, 67). Chapter 8, concerning the rights and duties of Russian subjects, acknowledged their civil liberties and inviolability of person and property. Chapters 9–11 were concerned with the State Council, the State Duma, the Council of Ministers, and the process of legislation. The second section of the Fundamental Laws (arts. 125–223) included the regulations on the imperial family. The Fundamental Laws could be changed only on the initiative of the emperor.

zakónnik, -ki. 1. Code or collection of laws. 2. Expert in laws, jurist. 3. In West Russian, member of a monastic order.

zakós. Tax paid in place of an obligation to mow hay.

zákup, -py. In the Kievan period, an impoverished SMERD who became an indentured and half-free laborer for a landlord from whom he usually received a plot of land, agricultural equipment, and a modest monetary loan. "During the Kievan era the peons were known as *zakupy*. . . . The terms of *zakup* indenture were harsh. . . . The debtor had to perform whatever work his creditor (or lord, *gospodin,* as the creditor was called in the *Pravda*) ordered him to perform. If he tried to escape his obligation by fleeing, he became the permanent slave of his lord" (J. Blum, pp. 53–54); the lord had also the right to use corporal punishment for a zakup. In the opinion of V. Sergeevich, a zakup was a hired worker who had received his wages in advance. For a summary of learned opinions on the term zakup, see *Pravda Russkaia,* ed. by B. Grekov, *II,* pp. 439–81.

roléinyi zákup: a half-free agricultural worker in the Kievan era.

zákup, -py (masc.) and **zákupka, -ki** (fem.). In the Grand Duchy of Lithuania, a bondman and bondwoman bought by their master.

zákup, in Muscovy. A preliminary (conditional) purchase, usually with partial payment (in the modern language called *zaprodazha*).

zákupen', -pní. In the Pskovian state, a wandering purchasing agent.

zamiátnia or (W.R.) **zamiátok.** Troubles, disturbances, disorders.

zámok, zámki. Fortress, castle; in the Grand Duchy of Lithuania, the residences and offices of VOEVODY, KASHTELIANY and STAROSTY.

zámki ukráinnye: castles on the frontiers of the state.

zamordovánie (W.R.). Murder.

zamýt. In Muscovy, a customs duty imposed on goods brought for sale into cities.

zápa. In the old legal language, presumably meant suspicion.

zapás, -sy. Stock, supply, equipment.

zapás ármii: army reserve. See VOINSKAIA POVINNOST'.

zápis', -si or (W.R.) **zápis, -sy.** A written document of any kind, like GRAMOTA in Muscovy and LIST in the Grand Duchy of Lithuania.

dánnaia zápis': see DANNAIA GRAMOTA.

dogovórnaia zápis': contract, agreement.

kabál'naia zápis': see SLUZHILAIA KABALA.

mirováia zápis': act of peaceful settlement, agreement.

poriádnaia zápis': see PORIADNAIA (GRAMOTA).

porúchnaia zápis': written guarantee vouching for someone's integrity or innocence or for his reliability in discharging his obligations.

ssúdnaia zápis': written acknowledgement of debt, promissory note.

súdnaia zápis': record of court proceedings.

tseloвál'naia or *krestotseloвál'naia zápis':* written confirmation of an oath.

zariádnaia zápis': an obligation guaranteed by forfeit.

zhilétskaia or *zhitéiskaia zápis':* a deed of habitation, an obligation to live in the household of the master and to work for him according to his orders.

zapíska, -ki. Record or note of various kinds. In the imperial period, zapiska in the official language meant memorandum. Zapiski, papers or proceedings, was used in the titles of many periodical publications of universities and learned societies.

razriádnye zapíski, in Muscovy: official records of appointments of serving men of the higher categories.

zaporózh'e. See SECH' ZAPOROZHSKAIA.

zápoved', -di. 1. Commandment, precept, admonition. 2. Rule, regulation, order. 3. Interdiction, prohibition. 4. Fine for violation of regulations or orders.

zapovédnik, -ki. Reservation.

zaprós, -sy. Inquiry; demand. During the Tatar domination, zapros was a term for the Tatar tribute that the Russian princes, on demand of the khan, collected from the Russian population and delivered to him. In Muscovy, zaprosy (or *zaprosnye den'gi*) were extraordinary taxes imposed, chiefly, for the payment of war expenses.

In 1906–16, zaprosy were interpellations frequently (esp. in 1906–07) presented by the State Duma to the ministers when acts of certain officials —in the Duma's opinion—violated existing laws.

zariád, -dy. In Muscovy, forfeit (*neustoika* in modern Russian).

zarók. In the charter of Pskov, a fixed term for repayment of a loan.

zarubézh'e. Foreign countries (from RUBEZH, frontier).

zarúka, -ki (W.R.). Forfeit; an obligation, secured by a fixed amount of money, that the person concerned will abstain from any illegal action in pursuing his claims.

zasádchik, -ki. In Muscovy, an appraiser elected by a community to determine the taxpayers' ability to pay their respective shares of the taxes.

zasedátel', -li. Assessor, advisor, assistant. According to the statutes of 1775, the newly established provincial administrative and judicial offices for each guberniia had a chairman appointed by the government and members, called zasedateli, elected by each of the three legal groups (SOSLOVIIA), the nobility, the city residents, and the state peasants. The city and the district offices also had their zasedateli.

prisiázhnye zasedáteli: sworn assessors, the group of twelve jurors established by the court statutes of November 20, 1864 (see PRISIAZHNYE).

zaséka, -ki. In Muscovy, a frontier barrier formed by felled trees. In the second half of the 16th and in the first half of the 17th century, a large defensive line (called ZASECHNAIA CHERTA) was built to protect the southern and southeastern frontiers from Tatar invasions. It consisted partly of masses of large felled trees, partly of a chain of wooden and earthen fortifications and ramparts between the zaseki. It embraced the southern borders of the future guberniias of Tambov, Riazan', Tula, and Kaluga. In the 17th century the defensive line, by then used against Crimean Tatar invasions, was gradually moved far to the south.

zastáva, -vy, in Muscovy. 1. An army detachment for the defense of some point, or for watch over enemy movements. 2. Customs barrier or barrier at the entrance to a city. 3. Forfeit, security for the fulfillment of an obligation by a fixed amount of money.

zastáva, in the Grand Duchy of Lithuania. 1. The garrison of a castle and the duty of the local population to help defend it if necessary (*zastava zamkovaia*). 2. Mortgage, esp. a landed estate that was mortgaged and turned over to the use of the creditor until repayment of the debt.

zastávshchik, -ki. In the period of the Tatar domination, a collector of customs duties at a ZASTAVA.

zasténok, -nki. In Muscovy, torture chamber. In the Grand Duchy of Lithuania, one of the plots of state land not included in the general land surveying (VOLOCHNAIA POMERA) of the 1550s.

zastupovánie v súdu (W.R.). Representation in court, solicitation.

zástuptse or **-tsa, -tsy** (W.R.). Representative before a court, solicitor.

zatínshchik, -ki. In Muscovy, stockade guard or defender in fortified cities, a position included in the categories of the *sluzhilye liudi po priboru* (see PRIBOR).

zaváda, -dy. (W.R.). Damage, loss.

zaveshchánie dukhóvnoe, -niia -nye. Testament, last will.

zavód. In Muscovy and in the Grand Duchy of Lithuania, demarcation of a landholding; borders of it, and indication of the existing borders in case of litigation.

zavódnik, -ki. In Muscovy, a land surveyor or a witness who knows and shows the court the borders of a landholding in case of litigation.

zazhigál'nik or **zazhigál'shchik, -ki.** Arsonist; according to the charter of Pskov, the *Sudebniks* of 1497 and 1550, and the *Ulozhenie* of 1649, premeditated arson was punishable by death.

zazhítie. In the chronicles describing military operations, an invasion of enemy territory with the purpose of supplying one's own army with provisions and forage.

zbliudénie. Preservation; *dati na zbliudenie,* to give into somebody's charge.

zbórnoe. Church tax paid to the metropolitan from parish churches in Muscovy.

zbórshchik, -ki. Tax collector, see SBORSHCHIK.

zbózhe (W.R.). Grain.

zbróden', -dni (W.R.). Mob, vagabonds.

zbróia (W.R.). Arms, weapons.

zdél'e = IZDEL'E = BARSHCHINA.

z"ednánie (W.R.). Contract, agreement.

z"ékhanie (W.R. = S"EZD). Congress, meeting.

zél'e, zélie. In Muscovy, (1) gunpowder; (2) special herbs used for medical treatment, or for making poison, or for sorcery.

zeléinichestvo. In Muscovy, sorcery.

zémets, zémtsy. In the Novgorodian state and then in the northern regions of Muscovy, petty landowner; see SVOEZEMETS. In the modern language, a member of a ZEMSTVO organization.

Zemgór. Popular name for the committee, established jointly in the summer of 1915, by the All-Russian Union of Zemstvos (VSEROSSIISKII ZEMSKII SOIUZ) and the All-Russian Union of Towns (VSEROSSIISKII SOIUZ GORODOV), in order to coordinate their efforts in helping the Russian armed forces and the civilian evacuees with supplies and medical care.

zemiánin, -iáne. Native of the land, a term applied to the gentry class particularly in the southern and southwestern regions of the Grand Duchy of Lithuania.

zemiánka, -ki. Lady from the ZEMIANE class.

zemlemér, -ry. Land surveyor.

zemlepól'zovanie obshchínnoe. Communal land tenure; see OBSHCHINA.

zemleustróistvo. Pattern of land settlement or land organization. This attracted serious government attention only around the beginning of the 20th century. In 1905 the Ministry of Agriculture and State Domains was renamed the *Glavnoe Upravlenie Zemleustroistva i Zemledeliia,* the Chief Administration of Land Settlement and Agriculture, and by a decree of March 4, 1906, the government established provincial and district land settlement commissions—*gubernskie* and *uezdnye* ZEMLEUSTROITEL'NYE KOMISSII. During the Stolypin era, after the decree of November 9, 1906, their chief work consisted in apportioning and delimiting peasant plots transferred from communal to private ownership. By 1914, about 7,000 government land surveyors and their assistants were at work modernizing the backward and tangled pattern of peasant land tenure.

zemlevladélets, -l'tsy. Landowner.

zemlevladénie. Landownership in pre-Revolutionary Russia. According to the official census of 1905, all lands in European Russia (without Finland, Poland, and the Caucasus), which amounted to about 395 million DESIATINAS, were divided into three categories. The first was land owned by the state and public bodies, 155 million desiatinas, of which 138.1 mill. des. were state lands (*kazënnye* or *gosudarstvennye zemli*), 7.8 mill. des. belonged to the imperial family (*udel'nye zemli*), 2.6 mill. des. to churches and monasteries, 2.0 mill. des. to city communities, and 3.5 mill. des. to the cossack hosts of the Don, Orenburg, and Astrakhan'. The vast state lands situated in the northern and northeastern regions and covered by tundra and forest were unsuitable for agriculture, while almost all arable state lands had been allotted to the state peasantry during the reforms of the 1860s and before. The second category was allotment land (*nadel'nye zemli,* see NADELY), 138.7 million desiatinas, of which 124.1 mill. des. belonged to the peasants and 14.6 mill. des. to the cossacks. The third category was privately owned land (*chastnovladel'cheskie zemli*), 101.7 mill. des., of which the DVORIANE owned 53.2 mill. des. (on the eve of the Revolution of 1917, they owned only c. 40 mill. des.), the peasants (individually and in associations) c. 25 mill. des., merchants and distinguished citizens (POCHËTNYE GRAZHDANE)—individually and in companies—c. 16½ mill. des., MESCHANE c. 4 mill. des., and others c. 3 mill. des. (*Ezhegodnik Rossii 1906,* pp. XXV–LI).

zemliá, zémli. Country; state and various kinds of territorial political units; nation; region; landholding; field; earth. In the Kievan period, the term zemlia was frequently used to designate a region headed by a senior city and administered by a prince. In the *Book of Annals* zemlia is used not as a geographical term but in the sense of nation or state. "All three terms, *zemlia, volost'* and *kniazhenie,* were used not only in the abstract sense but also to denote a given state with its government. In this concrete sense the three are almost synonymous" (G. Vernadsky, *Kievan Russia,* p. 173). In Muscovy, the term zemlia had its broadest meaning in the expressions *Russkaia zemlia* or *vsia zemlia.* During the Time of Troubles and later, the term vsia zemlia meant also the assembly of the representatives of the whole country (see SOBOR). The assemblies of two national hosts in 1611–12 were also called vsia zemlia.

The term zemlia in the sense of landholding was followed by various adjectives to designate to whom it belonged, or how it was utilized, or what was its quality. Therefore in Muscovite documents we find *zemli chërnye* (black lands, i.e., belonging to the state), *zemli dvortsovye* (belonging to the tsar's palace, DVORETS), *zemli boiarskie, dvorianskie, monastyrskie,* and so on, also *zemli pomestnye* and *votchinnye* (see POMEST'E and VOTCHINA). *Zemli oramye* or *pashennye* were arable lands. *Zemli obrochnye,* leased lands. Usually Muscovite documents classified arable lands as *zemlia dobraia* (good), or *seredniaia* (middle), or *khudaia* (poor).

Zemliá i Vólia. Land and Liberty. The

revolutionary populist movement in the 1870s found its organizational expression in the underground group, Zemlia i Volia, which was founded in St. Petersburg in 1876 and assumed this name in 1878. It published an organ of that name in which the following goals were set forth: the confiscation of the landlords' land and its distribution among peasant communities; the expulsion or the complete annihilation (*pogolovnoe istreblenie*) of government officials, and the establishment of "cossack circles"—autonomous communes with elected, rotating executives of the people's choice. The party program provided also for the establishment of a "disorganizing group" to undermine the government apparatus. In the summer of 1879 Land and Liberty split into two organizations—the terrorist People's Will (NARODNAIA VOLIA) and the Black Partition (CHERNYI PEREDEL).

zemliáchestvo, -va. An association of compatriots (*zemliaki*), esp. of university students from the same province or city.

zémshchina. An administrative division of the country after Ivan IV's "reform" of 1565. "By creating the *oprichnina* Ivan split his realm into two parts: the so-called *zemshchina*, which continued to be administered in the old traditional way by the boyar duma and other organs and officers of the Muscovite administration, and the *oprichnina,* . . . the tsar's personal domain" (M. Florinsky, *I*, p. 201). The people of the zemshchina were often exposed to the violence and cruelties of the OPRICHNIKI. The OPRICHNINA was abolished and the oprichnina corps was dissolved in 1572, but the process of returning to the landowners (or their descendants) the lands confiscated from them and of merging the oprichnina and the zemshchina administrative departments continued to the end of the 1570s.

zémskii, -kie. In the period of the OPRICHNINA, the zemskie were the inhabitants of the ZEMSHCHINA as opposed to the OPRICHNIKI. In the 18th and 19th centuries in large VOTCHINY, a zemskii was a clerk in the manorial administration. After the office of the ZEMSKII NACHAL'-NIK was established in 1889, the peasants usually referred to him as a zemskii.

zémstvo, -va. In the official language, **zémskoe uchrezhdénie, -kie -iia.** An organ for self-government in rural areas, as established by the statutes of January 1, 1864. Zemstva were set up in 34 provinces of European Russia. (The 34th was the province of Bessarabia annexed by Russia in 1878; excluded were several western and southeastern provinces and the GUBERNIIA of Archangel.) The authority of a zemstvo was defined by its statutes as including: management of zemstvo property and funds; construction and maintenance of local roads; the supplying of food in case of emergency; charity and help in the construction of churches; insurance of property; development of local trade and industry; support of public education and public health; prevention of livestock epidemics (veterinary service); assistance to the military administration in such matters as transportation and billeting; participation in the maintenance of postal service in the countryside; taxation of the local properties, including the collection and the allocation of the zemstvo tax; presentation to the government of information and petitions concerning local public needs; and the conducting of elections for the executive organs of the zemstvo. The district and the provincial zemstva each had regular assemblies (*uezdnoe zemskoe sobranie* and *gubernskoe zemskoe sobranie*) that elected—for a three-year term—an executive board called the *uezdnaia zemskaia uprava* (consisting of a chairman, PREDSEDATEL', and 2 or more members), and the *gubernskaia zemskaia uprava* (consisting of a chairman and 6 members). The members of the district assembly (called *uezdnye zemskie glasnye*) elected deputies to the provincial assembly (called *gubernskie zemskie glasnye*). The district and the provincial assemblies were chaired by the district and the provincial marshals of the nobility, respectively. The chairmen of the district and of the provincial executive boards had to be confirmed in their offices by the governor of the province and by the minister of interior, respectively. Deputies to the district zemstvo assembly were elected by three categories of voters: (1) private landowners of a set amount of property; (2) peasant communities; and (3) qualified urban dwellers. In all the provinces with zemstvo institutions there were about 13,000 deputies to the district assemblies, of which the private landowners sent about 47.7 percent, the peasant communities about 40 percent, and the city dwellers about 12.3 percent. According to article 6 of the zemstvo statutes, "the zemstvo institutions act independently within the sphere of matters entrusted to them." However, article 9 stated that the governor of the province "has the right to suspend the execution of any decision of the zemstvo institutions which is contrary to the laws or the general interest of the state." In this case the zemstvo institutions had the right to appeal the decision of the governor to the Senate, and the Senate would render the final decision in the dispute. In practice, the work of the zemstva was devoted chiefly to primary education and medical care, though in the beginning of the 20th century they were giving increased attention to technical aid for improving agriculture.

Under Alexander III the government undertook a reform to strengthen the influence of the nobility within the zemstvo institutions and to strengthen government control over zemstvo activities. By the end of the 19th century, as a result of that reform (embodied in the statutes of June 12, 1890), of a total of 9,523 members of district zemstvo assemblies, 57.1 percent were elected by noble landowners, 13.3 percent by nonnoble landowners and qualified city residents, and 29.6 percent by peasant communities. According to the new regulations, not only the chairman but also the members of the zemstvo executive boards had to be confirmed in their offices by the provincial governor, who was also granted the right to suspend execution of the assemblies' decisions when he considered them to violate existing laws or to be contrary to the interests of the local population or of the state. For the control of the zemstvo activities a new body was established called the *gubernskoe po zemskim delam prisutstvie* (see PRISUTSTVIE) under the chairmanship of the governor. In case of conflict between the zemstvo and the guberniia administration the Senate was the court of appeals.

In 1911 zemstvo institutions were introduced in six western guberniias (Belorussian and West Ukrainian) and in 1912 in the guberniias of Astrakhan', Orenburg, and Stavropol', bringing the total to 43 guberniias. A general picture of zemstvo activities on the eve of World War I is given in the record of zemstvo expenditures in 1914. Total expenditures were 347.5 million rubles. Of that sum, 30.8 percent went to education, 23.8 percent to medical care, 1.5 percent to public welfare, 8.2 percent to agriculture and other economic activities, 3.0 percent to veterinary service, 5.0 percent to local roads, 6.7 percent to zemstvo administration, and 21.0 percent to other expenses including service on debts.

zern'. In Muscovy, dice used for gambling (which was illegal).

zérnshchik, -ki. Dice-player, gambler.

zertsálo. 1. Mirror. 2. The trihedral prism which, in the imperial period, had to stand on the desk in all court and administrative offices to remind judges and officials of their duties; on its three sides were printed three decrees of Peter the Great (of 1722 and 1724) demanding observance of civil rights and honest performance of service.

zgóda (W.R.). Agreement.

zgúba (W.R.). Damage, loss.

zhádanie (W.R. = Russian *proshenie*). Petition, request.

zhálobnik, -ki. In Muscovy, plaintiff, claimant.

zhálobnitsa, -tsy. Written complaint.

zhálovanie. Favor, grace, mercy; gift, donation, grant; reward for service, salary; also property (esp. landed estates) received from the sovereign. In Muscovy there were many kinds of zhalovanie: *zhalovanie pomestnoe* (see POMEST'E), *zhalovanie denezhnoe* (monetary), *zhalovanie khlebnoe* (salary in grain). *Gosudarevo zhalovanie* designated the subsidies in money and in kind sent by the Moscow government to the Don Cossacks. The term zhalovanie in the sense of an official's salary was preserved during the imperial period.

zhandárm, -my. Gendarme, a member of a corps of political police; see KORPUS ZHANDARMOV.

zheléznoe. A court fee in old court procedures when the ordeal by hot iron was used.

zhelézo, -za. Iron; arms; irons, fetters; ordeal by hot iron.

zhérebei (pl. **zhéreb'i**) or **zhrébii.** Originally, lot or chance. Since lots were frequently drawn to divide landed property in shares among the heirs of a former owner, or among the members of an association dissolving itself, the term zherebei acquired the meaning of a plot of land as well, and *krest'ianskie*

zhereb'i in Muscovy was a common term for peasant lots, or for parts of a rural settlement. Sometimes a prince's share in the possessions of his late father was also called his zherebei. Zhrebii or zherebei (lot) was used in the 15th-17th centuries in court procedures, when conflicting claims or testimonies were sometimes resolved by the drawing of lots.

zhidóvstvuiushchii, -ie. Judaizer. In the second half of the 15th century a rationalistic sect appeared in Novgorod the Great, called by the Orthodox hierarchs the Judaizers (zhidovstvuiushchie from *Zhid,* Jew); its origin was ascribed to a Jew, Zechariah or Skharia, who arrived in Novgorod in 1470. The Judaizers rejected the dogma, sacraments, rituals, and hierarchy of the Orthodox church. They attracted followers in Moscow as well, even among clergymen and people close to the grand ducal court; there were indications that even the Metropolitan of Moscow, Zosima (1490–94), sympathized with the heretics. Their chief opponents and accusers were the Archbishop of Novgorod, Gennadii, and the abbot of Volotsk monastery, Iosif. The church councils of 1488 and 1491, and, more resolutely, the council of 1504, condemned the heresy, and some of its leaders were burned at the stake.

zhiléts, zhil'tsý. 1. Inhabitant. 2. In Muscovy, a group of service men of lower rank on the hierarchical ladder than the STOL'NIKI, STRIAPCHIE, and DVORIANE MOSKOVSKIE, but higher than provincial DVORIANE and DETI BOIARSKIE. According to Kotoshikhin, they numbered about 2,000 men; several scores of them, in turn, were present (*zhili,* dwelled) in the tsar's palace to carry out his orders and to handle official errands.

zhílo or **zhilóe.** In Muscovy, an inhabited or cultivated place as opposed to a PUSTOSH' or *pusto,* an empty or abandoned place; this difference was decisive in matters of taxation.

zhitié sviatógo, zhitiiá sviatýkh. The Lives of Saints.

zhít'i (liúdi). Middle-class burghers in Novgorod the Great, see LIUDI.

zhíto. Grain in general; sometimes it meant barley; later it meant mostly rye.

zhívnost' (W.R.). Provisions, supply.

zhivót, -ty. 1. Life; *zhivota ne dati,* to punish by death. 2. In the plural, property, esp. movable property, belongings.

zhivúshchee. In Muscovy, inhabited households or cultivated plowland or both; in financial language, all taxable objects.

zholnér, -ry (in Pol. *zolnierz,* from the Ger. *Söldner*). In Poland and in the Grand Duchy of Lithuania, a mercenary, a hired professional soldier.

zhónka nevól'naia, -ki -nye (W.R.). Female slave.

zhrébii. See ZHEREBEI.

ziat', ziat'iá. Son or brother-in-law; husband of a daughter or of a sister.

zimóvie, -iia, zimóvishche, -shcha, or **zimóvnik, -ki.** Winter camp or winter quarters of nomadic peoples, of groups of cossacks, or of Siberian PROMYSHLENNIKI.

zlátnik. See ZOLOTNIK.

zlochín, -ny or **zlochínstvo, -va** (W.R.). Crime, offense.

zlochínets, -ntsy (W.R.). Criminal, offender.

zlodéi, -déii. Criminal in general; in West Russian legal language, thief.

zlodéistvo, -va. Crime; in West Russian, theft, larceny.

zlóty(i) litóvskii. In the 16th and 17th centuries, a large silver coin equal to 24 Lithuanian GROSHI or 20 Moscow KOPEIKI.

znákhar', -ri. Literally, a knowledgeable one, expert; witness in court; in Muscovite documents znakhari were often longtime local residents called on by the court to show the boundaries of a landholding in case of litigation. In modern popular language, chiefly in the countryside, znakhar' was a kind of sorcerer, a person to whom a mysterious power of healing, clairvoyance, or prevoyance was ascribed.

známenshchik, -ki. Colors-bearer in an army unit.

známia, -mëna. Sign, mark, symbol; banner, standard, colors.

   známia bortnóe: the old term for an apiculturist's mark on a tree with a beehive (*bort'*) in a forest.

   známia polkovóe: regimental colors.

   známia tsárskoe: tsar's banner in Muscovy.

známia, in Muscovy. A term for the fee paid for some church certificates, esp. for a certificate of marriage.

zóbnia, -ni. A small dry measure in Muscovy (esp. for oats).

zóbnitsa, -tsy. A dry measure in the Pskovian state (according to D. Prozorovskii, it was presumably equal to about 10 PUDS).

zolotník or **zlátnik, -ki.** 1. In the Kievan period, a gold coin. 2. Later, a small weight unit equal to $\frac{1}{96}$ of a FUNT (pound) or to 4.26 grams.

zolóvka, -ki. Sister-in-law, husband's sister.

zráda (W.R.). Treason.

zrádtsa, -tsy (W.R.). Traitor.

zrázhenie maiestátu gospodárskogo (*crimen laesae maiestatis*). Term for treason and desertion to the enemy used in the first Lithuanian Statute, of 1529 (sect. I, art. 2). In the Statute of 1566, sect. I, arts. 3–5, the corresponding term was OBRAZHENIE MAIESTATU GOSPODARSKOGO.

zubátovshchina. A term applied to an experiment in police socialism early in the 20th century. S. V. Zubatov, the chief of the Moscow security police (O-

KHRANNOE OTDELENIE), set up in 1901–02, with government permission and using secret police agents, labor organizations in the form of mutual aid associations to promote the economic and educational needs of their members. The object was to assist the workers in their economic struggle (including the use of strikes against the manufacturers), and by improving their economic conditions to withdraw them from the influence of revolutionary propaganda. Zubatov's undertaking achieved some success. (Similar workers' associations were established outside Moscow, as in Odessa and Minsk.) But soon the movement met with bitter opposition from both the revolutionary intelligentsia and the manufacturers, and in 1903 the government dropped the whole venture.

zváda, -dy (W.R.) or SVADA. Quarrel, skirmish.

zvánie. Literally, calling; in the official language of the imperial period, official rank and position, or social status, sometimes used in the sense of SO-SLOVIE.

zvod or **svod.** Confrontation of witnesses in legal procedures.

zvod shliakhétstva. In the legal language of the Grand Duchy of Lithuania, proof of belonging to the nobility (SHLIAKHTA).

APPENDIX: MEASURES AND WEIGHTS

Russian measures and weights in the 19th century, with metric and U.S. equivalents

LINEAR MEASURES

1 *versta* = 500 *sazheni* = 1.067 kilometers = 0.663 miles
1 *sazhen'* = 3 *arshiny* = 2.133 meters = 7 feet or *futy*
1 *arshin* = 4 *chetverti* = 16 *vershki* = 71.1 centimeters = 28 inches
1 *fut* (foot) = 12 *diuimy* (inches) = 0.305 meters
1 *vershok* = 4.44 centimeters = 1.75 inches
1 *diuim* (inch) = 10 *linii* = 2.54 centimeters

LAND MEASURES

1 *desiatina* = 2400 *kvadratnye* (square) *sazheni* = 1.0925 hectares = 2.7 acres
1 *kvadratnaia sazhen'* = 4.55 square meters = 49 square feet

WEIGHTS (COMMERCIAL)

1 *berkovets* = 10 *pudy* = 163.8 kilograms = 361.13 pounds
1 *pud* = 40 *funty* = 16.38 kilograms = 36.113 pounds
1 *funt* = 96 *zolotniki* = 409 grams = 0.903 pounds
1 *zolotnik* = 96 *doli* = 4.26 grams = 65.83 grains

LIQUID MEASURES

1 *bochka* = 40 *vedra* = 492 liters = 131.5 gallons
1 *vedro* = 10 (sometimes 8) *shtofy* = 20 (sometimes 16) *butylki* = 12.3 liters = 3.25 gallons
1 *butylka* = 0.615 liters = 1.3 (or 1.6) pints

DRY MEASURES

1 *chetvert'* = 2 *osminy* = 8 *chetveriki* = 210 liters = c. 6 bushels

REFERENCES CITED

Akty Litovskoi Metriki, ed. F. I. Leontovich, 2 vols. Warsaw, 1896–97.

Arkheograficheskaia Komissiia, ed., *Polnoe sobranie russkikh letopisei,* 29 vols. St. Petersburg, 1841–1965.

Arkheograficheskaia Komissiia, ed., *Russkaia istoricheskaia biblioteka,* 39 vols. St. Petersburg, 1872–1927.

Berezhkov, N. G., *Litovskaia Metrika kak istoricheskii istochnik,* Moscow, 1946.

Blum, Jerome, *Lord and Peasant in Russia from the Ninth to the Nineteenth Century,* Princeton, 1961.

Cherepnin, L. V., *Russkaia metrologiia,* Moscow, 1944.

Domostroi, in *Chteniia v Imp. Obshchestve Istorii i Drevnostei Rossiiskikh pri Moskovskom Universitete,* 1881, book 2.

Entsiklopedicheskii Slovar', 43 vols. St. Petersburg, F. Brockhaus and I. Efron, 1890–1906.

[*Statisticheskii*] *Ezhegodnik Rossii 1906 goda,* St. Petersburg, 1907. (Similar statistical yearbooks were issued for subsequent years.)

Florinsky, Michael T., *Russia. A History and an Interpretation,* 2 vols. New York, 1953–55.

Gorbachevskii, N., *Slovar' drevnego aktovogo iazyka Severo-Zapadnogo kraia i Tsarstva Pol'skogo,* Vilna (Vilnius), 1874.

Gosudarstvennaia oruzheinaia palata moskovskogo kremlia, Moscow, 1958.

Grekov, B. D., *Kievskaia Rus',* Moscow, 1949.

———, *Kratkii ocherk istorii russkogo krest'ianstva,* Moscow, 1958.

Hans, Nicholas, *History of Russian Educational Policy, 1701–1917,* London, 1931.

Ianin, V. L., *Denezhno-vesovye sistemy russkogo srednevekoviia: Domongol'skii period,* Moscow, 1956.

Kennan, George, *Siberia and the Exile System,* 2 vols. New York, 1891.

Kliuchevskii, V. O., *Kurs russkoi istorii,* in *Sochineniia,* vols. I–V, Moscow, 1956–58.

———, *Russkii rubl' XVI–XVIII vv. v ego otnoshenii k nyneshnemu,* in *Sochineniia,* vol. VII, Moscow, 1959.

———, *Terminologiia russkoi istorii,* in *Sochineniia,* vol. VI, Moscow, 1959.

Kotoshikhin, Grigorii, *O Rossii v tsarstvovanie Alekseia Mikhailovicha,* 3d ed. St. Petersburg, 1884 (4th ed. issued in 1906).

Lantzeff, George V., *Siberia in the 17th Century. A Study of the Colonial Administration,* Berkeley, California, 1943.

Litovskaia Metrika. See Arkheograficheskaia Komissiia, ed., *Russkaia istoricheskaia biblioteka,* vols. 20 (1903), 27 (1910), 30 (1914), and 33 (1915).

Liubavskii, M. K., *Ocherk istorii Litovsko-Russkogo gosudarstva do Liublinskoi unii vkliuchitel'no,* 2d ed. Moscow, 1915.

Miliukov, P. N., *Ocherki po istorii russkoi kul'tury,* vol. II, *Tserkov' i shkola,* 3d ed. St. Petersburg, 1902.

Pamiatniki russkogo prava, 8 vols. Moscow, 1952–61.

Platonov, S. F., *History of Russia,* tr. E. Aronsberg, ed. F. A. Golder, New York, 1925, reprinted 1929.

Polner, Tikhon J., *Russian Local Government during the War and the Union of Zemstvos,* New Haven, 1930.

Polnoe sobranie russkikh letopisei. See Arkheograficheskaia Komissiia.

Polnoe sobranie zakonov Rossiiskoi Imperii, 134 vols. St. Petersburg, 1830–1914.

Povest' vremennykh let, ed. V. P. Adrianova-Peretts and D. S. Likhachev, 2 vols. Moscow, 1950.

Pravda Russkaia, ed. B. D. Grekov, 2 vols. Moscow, 1940 and 1947.

Prozorovskii, D. I., *Moneta i ves v Rossii do kontsa XVIII stoletiia,* St. Petersburg, 1865.

Ptashitskii, S. L., *Opisanie knig i aktov Litovskoi Metriki,* St. Petersburg, 1887.

Riasanovsky, Nicholas V., *A History of Russia,* New York, 1963.

Robinson, Geroid T., *Rural Russia under the Old Regime,* New York, 1932 (3d ed. 1957).

Sergeevich, V. I., *Drevnosti russkogo prava,* vol. 1, *Territoriia i naselenie,* 3d ed. St. Petersburg, 1909; vol. 3, *Zemlevladenie. Tiaglo. Poriadok oblozheniia,* St. Petersburg, 1903.

Sobornoe Ulozhenie 1649 goda, ed. M. N. Tikhomirov and P. P. Epifanov, Moscow, 1961.

Sobranie traktatov i konventsii, zakliuchënnykh Rossieiu s inostrannymi derzhavami, ed. F. Martens, 15 vols. St. Petersburg, 1874–1909.

Sobranie uzakonenii i rasporiazhenii pravitel'stva, izdavaemoe pri Pravitel'stvuiushchem Senate, St. Petersburg, 1863–1917.

Spasskii, I. G., *Russkaia monetnaia sistema,* 3d ed. Leningrad, 1962.

Stashevskii, E. D., "Biudzhet i armiia [in Muscovy]," in *Russkaia istoriia v ocherkakh i stat'iakh,* ed. M. V. Dovnar-Zapol'skii, vol. 3, Kiev, 1912.

Statut velikogo kniazhestva Litovskogo 1529 goda, ed. K. I. Iablonskis, Minsk, 1960.

"Statut velikogo Kniaz'stva Litovskogo 1566 goda," in *Vremennik Imp.*

Moskovskogo Obshchestva Istorii i Drevnostei Rossiiskikh, vol. 23, Moscow, 1855.

Stoglav: Tsarskie voprosy i sobornye otvety o razlichnykh tserkovnykh chinakh, Moscow, 1890.

Strumilin, S. G., *Ocherki ekonomicheskoi istorii Rossii,* Moscow, 1960.

Sudebniki XV–XVI vekov, ed. B. D. Grekov, Moscow, 1952.

Svod zakonov Rossiiskoi Imperii, 3d ed. 16 vols. St. Petersburg, 1857– 1906.

Vernadsky, George, *Kievan Russia,* New Haven, 1948.

————, *Medieval Russian Laws,* New York, 1947.

————, *The Mongols and Russia,* New Haven, 1953.

————, *Political and Diplomatic History of Russia,* Boston, 1936.

————, *Russia at the Dawn of the Modern Age,* New Haven, 1959.

Veselovskii, S. B. *Soshnoe pis'mo. Issledovanie po istorii kadastra i pososhnogo oblozheniia Moskovskogo gosudarstva,* 2 vols. Moscow, 1915–16.

————, *Issledovaniia po istorii oprichniny,* Moscow, 1963.

Zimin, A. A., *Oprichnina Ivana Groznogo,* Moscow, 1964.